# Seven Days
# in
# January

# Seven Days in January
## With the 6th SS-Mountain Division in Operation *NORDWIND*

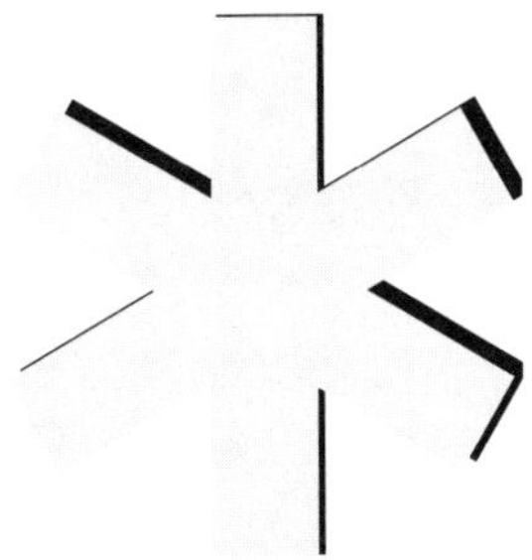

**Wolf T. Zoepf**

**Foreword by**
**Brigadier General Theodore C. Mataxis, US Army (Retired)**

THE ABERJONA PRESS
Bedford, Pennsylvania

*Developmental Editor:* Keith E. Bonn
*Production:* Patricia K. Bonn
*Technical Editors:* Keith E. Bonn and Hugh Foster
*Maps:* Aegis Consulting Group, Inc.

The Aberjona Press is an imprint of Aegis Consulting Group, Inc.,
Bedford, Pennsylvania 15522

Printed in the United States of America

ISBN: 0-9666389-5-6 (casebound)

# Contents

*To all of the men who fought the battle of Wingen, American and German*

# Foreword

This is an unusually fine and detailed account, at the tactical level, about a little-known, but crucial battle fought during the last months of World War II. It is also a book about an exceptional unit that has, for a variety of reasons, remained largely obscure to American students of the war.

As noted in the US Army's Center of Military History booklet about the Ardennes-Alsace campaign (published for the fiftieth anniversary of the event), the history of the "Alsace" part of this campaign has been "sparsely covered." Now taking its place beside campaign overviews such as Keith E. Bonn's *When the Odds Were Even* (Presidio, 1994) and Lise Pommois' *Winter Storm* (Turner, 1991), and the late Richard Engler's overview-plus-personal-account, *The Final Crisis* (Aegis/The Aberjona Press, 1999), Wolf Zoepf's book now adds the German perspective to the growing literature about this often-overlooked fighting.

The book captures, in vivid detail, the brutal reality of front-line infantry combat at battalion and company levels, for both Germans and Americans. As General Eisenhower pointed out in *Crusade in Europe,* in the especially cruel winter of 1944–45 (the coldest of the century to that point!), ". . . the infantry, which in all kinds of warfare habitually absorbs the bulk of the losses, was now taking practically all of them." This was as true for the Germans as it was for us, and this book nails that home as only a work by an infantry participant in the battle could.

It is military history at its finest, combining the facts gained from extensive archival research with the personal battlefield experiences of the author and those of other participants, from both sides. The account also allows clear insight into why the battle for Wingen-sur-Moder became the focal point for corps and field army commanders on both sides during Operation *NORDWIND,* the last German offensive in the West.

More than thirty years after the battle that is the main subject of this book, I met the author at a joint gathering of veterans of my own outfit, the US 70th Infantry Division, and his, the *6th SS-Mountain Division NORD*. Earlier observations of the phenomenon that occurs when former adversaries meet long after their war made lasting great impacts on me. At the age of twelve, as a Boy Scout marching in my hometown Armistice Day parade (1929), I witnessed Civil War veterans from both sides talking amicably about their experiences as they rode along in the touring cars which led the procession. In 1946, after my battalion had been inactivated, I was assigned to a military history detachment tasked with supervision of captured German generals who were writing their accounts of the war. Working closely with them, I was surprised to note how quickly the relationship changed from one of enmity and animosity to one of cooperation, in which professionals from both sides worked toward the common goal of documenting their collective and individual operational experiences.

At the first meeting between 70th Division and *SS-NORD* veterans, we were obviously initially somewhat uncomfortable with one another. Some of us were alone, others with their wives, but here we were, face to face with men who had tried their best to kill us during those the freezing days of early 1945 in the Vosges Mountains. Now, though, instead of fleeting images of ski-capped demons lurking in the houses of a small mountain village, or crumpled bodies sprawled on blood-stained snow, we Americans were seeing our former adversaries as real, live human beings and—to our surprise—our similarities were greater than our differences.

I later had opportunities to meet with former enemies from the Korean and Vietnamese wars and found that both of those events reinforced my feeling that while politicians may demonize and hate our foes, professional soldiers can neither afford that emotional luxury nor allow their judgment to become so impaired. The first Communist Chinese officer I met after retired from active duty was at a UN reception in 1982. When we discussed our military experiences, we discovered we had fought opposite each other in the Korean War. In the course of further conversation, he and several of his compatriots asked me if I hated them; when I said that I did not, that it was the professional soldier's job to fight, not to hate, they seemed at once pleased and surprised. This exchange resulted in an invitation to attend a conference in Beijing at their International Institute for Strategic Studies. After the conference, I was asked to review a People's Liberation Army infantry division; as I stood on the reviewing stand returning the commander of troops' salute, my mind was awhirl. In the spring of 1953, at Pork Chop and Old Baldy, I could not have imagined such an episode in my wildest dreams.

Still later, I was introduced to a Vietnamese Communist lieutenant general (at a conference at Texas Tech University), and although the atmosphere was restrained, by the end of the conference we were trading operational insights much more freely. As a result of these experiences, I feel strongly that veterans who have fought each other on the battlefield and "seen the elephant" are those who, after a war is over, can best lead their countries toward reconciliation. Further, even though I still firmly believe that *all* of the enemies against whom we fought were fighting for governments and many ideas that were and are hateful, I cannot bring myself to hate my former battlefield opponents.

As you will see when you read this book, Herr Zoepf's unit and mine had a lot in common, from a professional perspective.

As Wolf explains in the excellent background piece that he wisely included in this book, *SS-Division NORD* was incompletely prepared for its first combat in the summer of 1941. As a result, it sustained unusually heavy casualties, and its reputation suffered severely, not only in the minds of its superiors, but even among some of the German Army units alongside which it served on the Arctic Front. Thanks to the shortage of American infantry units corollary to the twin demands of the German Ardennes and Alsace offensives, the infantry regiments of the 70th Infantry Division (including my own 276th Infantry Regiment) were also thrown into battle prematurely, and suffered the highest casualties of any Seventh Army unit in the first two weeks of January 1945. This provoked heavy criticism from our own field army's commanding general, as well as some derisive comments from some of our more experienced comrades in arms in other outfits. Time, additional training, experience, valor demonstrated by our soldiers, and a great deal of bloodshed in our respective later battles changed those initial stigmas, but the lesson to be learned here is one that good commanders have known throughout modern times: sweat in training saves blood in battle.

There are other similarities as well. In the course of my Army service, I learned to admire well-disciplined and highly motivated units, and from the account you are about to read (as well as the first-hand testimony of my comrades in arms from my regiment's 1st and 3rd Battalions), the *Gebirgsjäger* of the *6th SS-Mountain Division NORD* were among the best in this regard, even at this late stage of the war. After almost three and a half years of combat near the Arctic Circle, the men of *SS-NORD* had attained numerous outstanding victories, yet practically speaking, their achievements and successes were obviated by the separate armistice concluded between the Finns and the Soviets in September of 1944. From my experience in Korea and Vietnam, I can unequivocably state that the most severe test of any unit's character and morale comes when valor, sacrifice, and great tactical proficiency go for naught in the face of greater strategic or geopolitical setbacks. The best soldiers and toughest fighters the 276th Infantry faced in WWII were the men of *SS-NORD*, yet they were also the only ones who had already been part of a failed operation in another theater of war. That's a sure mark of a professional outfit.

Aside from the shared organizational commonalities, Wolf Zoepf and I also shared several professional and personal similarities. We both enlisted as young men. During Operation *NORDWIND*, we both served as the senior staff officers and seconds-in-command of our respective battalions. By peacetime standards, we were very young to be entrusted with these responsibilities: Wolf was twenty-two and I was twenty-seven. (Such positions are normally held by men of thirty-four to thirty-seven years of age in armies that are not at war—or have not been at war for long.) Yet although we also both had young wives to whom we wanted dearly to return, we had both volunteered to serve as combat infantrymen with full knowledge of the associated risks. As we learned when we got to know each other long after the war, we both enjoyed traveling and experiencing other cultures, too. As a soldier, I was stationed at various times in Europe, the Middle East, and Asia, and as a civil engineer, Wolf had spent a great deal of time in Africa, Asia, and North America.

Perhaps the most important factor in the development of our veterans' attitude toward the author and his comrades was their unit's conduct toward the prisoners it took during the battle described in this book. According to the Germans who fought it, the fighting in and around Wingen was as fierce as any they had experienced on the Eastern Front. This can be confirmed by their casualties: *Combat Group Wingen* began the mission with 725 *Gebirgsjäger*, and returned with only 205. During the course of this vicious fighting, over 300 American soldiers from the 45th and 70th Infantry Division were captured by Wolf's outfit during the battle for Wingen-sur-Moder (in fact, he was personally in charge of accounting for and handling them during this action), but every one of the enlisted men were released unharmed at the end of the fight, and the eight officers whom the Germans were trying to evacuate to their rear escaped without even an attempt to forcibly halt them. Further, throughout the fiercest fighting in and around Wingen, the medics and doctors of *Combat Group Wingen* and their opposite numbers from the captured aid station of the 1st Battalion, 179th Infantry Regiment operated a joint aid station in which triage was supervised by the senior *SS* military doctor strictly on the basis of wounds sustained, without consideration for nationality. All of this is confirmed by American veterans with whom I served personally in our regiment, and stands as an amazing example of chivalry in a war otherwise often known for its pure ferocity and inhumanity.

Coming less than three weeks after another *Waffen-SS* unit brutally massacred unarmed American soldiers and Belgian civilians in and around Malmédy—and while the men of another *Waffen-SS* division and a *Luftwaffe* parachute regiment were shooting prisoners within a few dozen kilometers on either side of Wingen—this sets the author and his fellow mountain infantrymen apart even more.

Breaches of the rules of warfare are not uncommon in battle (by some of the soldiers of any army), but massacres are perpetrated by units suffering from poor morale, ineffective leadership, or bad training. I was the acting commanding general and assistant division commander of the Americal Division just after the massacre at My Lai 4, so I know more than I want to about this subject. However, just as good units don't massacre prisoners, it is the truly rare outfit that, in the heat of battle, actually cares for its prisoners as well as it cares for its own. This is exactly what the leaders of *Combat Group Wingen* did, and this fact is attested to by men in my personal acquaintance. Such comportment was apparently a division-wide trait; the latest scholarship of Lieutenant Colonel Hugh Foster (US Army, Retired) in his forthcoming book about the third battle of Reipertswiller documents similar treatment afforded by the men of Wolf's sister regiment in *SS-NORD* to the over 400 American prisoners captured by them a few weeks later.

Although clearly proud of his unit, Wolf has candidly and objectively listed the failures and shortcomings he noted, from the battalion level up—including the devastating mistake that deprived his unit of practically all communications throughout the course of the battle for Wingen. In fact, given its unique and comprehensive coverage of the first week of Operation *NORDWIND* from the German perspective, Wolf has effectively challenged some otherwise prevalent misunderstandings about the German armed forces at this stage of WWII. Just as Wolf's and his comrades' behavior reminds us to judge all military organizations on their individual merits, his book should inspire us to go beyond the accepted or conventional wisdom to study the lesser-known but important battles of every war.

Theodore C. Mataxis
Brigadier General, US Army (Retired)
Southern Pines, NC
February 2001

*During the the battle for Wingen, then-Major Mataxis served as Executive Officer, 2d Battalion, 276th Infantry Regiment of Task Force Herren. A few days later, he assumed command of the battalion and remained so assigned until the end of the war. Just after the action covered in this book ended, his battalion assaulted and seized the fortress town of Lichtenberg, and subsequently took part in the fierce fighting above Reipertswiller in the Bois de Lichtenberg. In the Korean War, he served as Executive Officer and then Commander of the 17th Infantry Regiment during bitter battles for the outposts on Pork Chop Hill and Old Baldy, and later commanded an airborne infantry battle group of the 8th Infantry Division in Germany. Subsequently, he served as Deputy Commander of the 1st Brigade of the 101st Airborne Division (separately deployed) in Vietnam; as Assistant Division Commander of the 82d Airborne Division at Fort Bragg, North Carolina; and as Acting Commanding General and Assistant Division Commander of the Americal Division in Vietnam. His final command assignment was as the commanding general of the US military equipment delivery team in Cambodia in 1972. He is currently a member of the faculty at American Military University.*

# Acknowledgments

The author and editor are grateful for the contributions to this endeavor made by the following individuals:

Frau Ruth Zoepf for providing the photos that appear in this book of her late husband during his WWII service.

Herr Sven Zoepf, for his gracious assistance with the publication of his father's manuscript.

Brigadier General Theodore C. Mataxis, US Army (Retired) for his thoughtful and highly insightful foreword to this volume. During the battle for Wingen, then-Major Mataxis served as Executive Officer, 2d Battalion, 276th Infantry Regiment.

Colonel Jim Hanson, US Army (Retired), Vice President of the 70th Infantry Division Association, coordinated the effort to identify the full names of many of the key Trailblazer Division soldiers identified in the text. A WWII member of the 274th Infantry Regiment, Colonel Hanson was assisted by the following Trailblazers: Paul Newman (Company D, 276th Infantry); Frank Lowry (Company A, 276th Infantry); Carl Settle (Company C, 276th Infantry); Steve Dixon (Webmaster of the excellent 70th Infantry Division Association website); Sergeant First Class Ed Lane, US Army (Retired), editor of the Association's quarterly magazine, *The Trailblazer*, as well as several others.

Captain Michael Gonzales, US Army, Retired, Director of the 45th Infantry Division Museum, Oklahoma City, OK, provided the author copies of primary source documents from Headquarters, 45th Infantry Division and the 179th and 180th Infantry Regiments. Captain Gonzales also provided full names of several of the key Thunderbird Division soldiers and officers identified in the text.

Dr. Jochen Seeliger of Essen, Nordrhein-Westfalen, Germany, a WWII veteran of service with the *6th SS-Mountain Division NORD* and current general counsel for the Division's *Traditionsverband*, for procuring permission to use several of the photos included in this book. Dr. Seeliger also coordinated the efforts of his comrades to identify the first names of numerous of the key *SS-NORD* soldiers named in this book.

Mr. Dave Giordano, Archivist, National Archives II, College Park, MD, cheerfully provided streamlined access to the operations and intelligence records of the US Army units which figured most prominently in this study, including those of the 179th, 180th, 274th, and 276th Infantry Regiments.

Mr. Mike Abernathy of Rapid Imaging Software, Albuquerque, NM, who provided patient and expert assistance in the use of his firm's software, which made possible the exceptionally detailed textured terrain images used in many of this book's maps.

Ms. Josie Sanchez of Land Info International, Ltd., Aurora, CO, who coordinated the aggressive and fruitful efforts of her firm to procure accurate terrain data for use in the Rapid Imaging program.

Herr Patrick Agte, president of Munin-Verlag, Osnabrück, Niedersachsen, Germany, for his very gracious permission to use several photos which have otherwise appeared in *Gebirgsjäger im Bild: 6. SS-Gebirgsdivision Nord 1940-1945* (Munin, 1976).

*Oberstleutnant* (then Major) Dr. Karl-Heinz Frieser of the German Federal Military History Research Bureau for providing many of the German documents on which this book is based, including the *Army Group G* planning map displayed on the cover of the Aberjona Press version of this book. Although he provided them in the course of the editor's own study of this campaign, they were later instrumental in confirming the author's research and facilitating work from the same documents by the author and the editor during the developmental and technical review of the manuscript.

Lieutenant Colonel Hugh Foster, US Army (Retired), for his expert copy editing and technical review of the manuscript.

Lieutenant Commander Ron Wolin, US Navy (Retired), for providing the *Waffen-SS* lieutenant's collar tabs used on the Aberjona Press version of the cover of this book. Commander Wolin's formidable and widely-recognized expertise on German WWII uniforms and insignia were instrumental in selecting other art for this book as well.

# Editor's Notes

This book was the result of many years of research and reflection by the author. He first contacted me in 1994, after a copy of my first book, *When the Odds Were Even* (Presidio, 1994) had been provided to him by Mr. Hyman Schorr of Queens, NY, a friend of his in the US 70th Infantry Division Association. Wolf was quite enthusiastic about the book, and appreciated that I had made exhaustive use of both German and American primary sources in its development. Quite simply, he applauded an American soldier's best effort to determine the truth and publish it, even though it challenged certain tenets of "conventional wisdom."

After I retired from active duty as an infantryman in the US Army, Wolf engaged me to help him complete and publish his history of the January 1945 battle for Wingen-sur-Moder, a subject about which he possessed a profound desire to discern and disseminate the truth. Through our correspondence and a single personal encounter in Berlin the year before, I had learned great respect for his formidable intellect; his straightforward and soldierly candor; his clear memory of details from the wartime era; and his insistence on thorough research and precise historical writing. During our collaboration on this project, in which I was privileged to serve as Wolf's technical and developmental editor, my estimates of these admirable qualities were only reinforced, and I am forever grateful for the opportunity to have known this fine soldier and considerate, thoroughly decent man.

I also learned a great deal. In addition to the opportunity to gain a much better understanding of details of German tactical and organizational procedures, working with Wolf taught me something about the supreme disappointment and frustration suffered by good soldiers who ultimately realize that they have been fighting in a deeply flawed cause. While extreme in the case of the German Armed Forces during the Third Reich, this dilemma is by no means unique to them during the twentieth century.

As with all Aberjona Press products, the facts, records, and even anecdotes on which Wolf based this book have been confirmed to the greatest extent possible. I have personally reviewed the author's *Rasse-und-Siedlungs Hauptamt* (*RuSHA*) file in the US National Archives, and have confirmed the author's identity by the photos and military records contained therein. We have confirmed the anecdotes recounted by Americans with many of the sources; checked the archival documents obtained at College Park and the Federal German Military Archives; and verified accounts with several of the surviving members of the *SS-NORD Traditionsverband* whose accounts appear in this book as well.

This is the work of an author who sincerely wanted "to get it right" about this important and overlooked battle and the units involved in fighting it. He not only affirmed every word of the text *after* all of the technical and developmental editing was done (Wolf's command of the English language was colloquially fluent), but he also personally rendered every battle diagram on contemporary WWII topographic maps, and even concerned himself with the design of the cover of this book. The inclusion of that portion of the *Army Group G* map used for planning NORDWIND on the cover of the Aberjona Press version of this book was his idea, as was the inclusion on the back cover of the insignia of both German and American units involved in the battle. We have gladly honored his desires.

A private man, Wolf specifically eschewed the opportunity to include in this book detailed *vitae* or even much information about his post-war life, but his lengthy and successful career as a civil engineer is reflected in his intense interest in the maps used in this book. Wolf envisioned a separate volume of fold-out maps, all printed in color, from which the reader could select those he or she needed for reference at any given moment while reading the text. Commercial realities prevented the realization of such a lavish product, but the textured terrain maps used in this book are a direct result of the author's insistence on the highest possible quality of visual aids to enhance readers' comprehension of the impact of terrain on this battle. Although he did not survive to see them, we are confident that Wolf would have been highly pleased with the "aerial" views made possible by Josie Sanchez and her cohorts at Land Info International and by Mr. Mike Abernathy of Rapid Imaging Software.

Although, as one would expect, he was thoroughly conversant with German WWII military graphics, the author chose to use standard NATO graphical symbols on most of the maps, as they are recognizable by the greatest part of the audience for this book. For those not already familiar with them, we have included a legend on page xiv. In a few cases, we have slightly modified them for the sake of simplicity and comprehensibility. On two maps, Wolf elected to retain certain German tactical symbols as he felt that they allowed portrayal of the action more precisely than their equally-obscure US Army WWII equivalents. In these cases, detailed legends have been placed immediately adjacent to each of the maps for the convenience of the reader.

Readers will note that there are very few photos in this book. Although both Wolf and Dr. Jochen Seeliger of the *Traditionsverband* of the *6th SS-Mountain Division NORD* conducted comprehensive searches for suitable photos in the German Military Archives and among their comrades, they came up with no photos of *Combat Group Wingen*, or even of any *SS-NORD* soldiers in action during January 1945. The tempo and tenor of operations during this period simply mitigated against photography. Rather than mislead or confuse readers with a selection of the many pictures that are available of *SS-NORD* operations and personalities during its three years of operations in northern Karelia, we have decided to include only the very few photos in the author's personal collection and one picture of a member of *SS-NORD* that is representative of how the men of *Combat Group Wingen* would have appeared in the battle. Even though this photo is actually of an officer after a long-range patrol in the Karelian taiga, Dr. Seeliger and others agree that it accurately represents the essentials of the uniform, equipment, and even the attitude of *NORD* soldiers in early January 1945.

The ravages of time are taking their final toll of the men who fought the Second World War. Wolf Zoepf passed away, completely unexpectedly, just after completing his review and approval of this book's final chapter. If his demise is a warning to us all of the importance of gathering the information we can in the time they have left, then this work is a reminder of the uniquely fine history that can result when soldiers from both sides cooperate to present the fullest possible account of battles of which they have intimate knowledge.

Keith E. Bonn, Ph.D.
Technical and Developmental Editor

# A Guide to Tactical Unit Symbols

## Types of Units

|  |  |
|---|---|
| ☒ | Infantry* |
| | Mountain Infantry |
| V | Volks-Grenadier (German only) |
| | Armored Infantry/ Panzer-Grenadier |
| | Armor/Tank/Panzer |
| | Mechanized Cavalry/ Armored Reconnaissance |
| | Mountain Pioneers (Combat Engineers) (German Only) |

## Sizes of Units

|  |  |
|---|---|
| • | Squad |
| •• | Section |
| ••• | Platoon |
| I | Company/Battery/Troop |
| II | Battalion/Squadron |
| III | Regiment |
| X | Brigade/Group/ Combat Command** |
| XX | Division |
| XXX | Corps |
| XXXX | Army |
| XXXXX | Army Group |

**Example**

**A** ☒ **276*****

Company A, 276th Infantry Regiment

US, Soviet, or Finnish Forces

German Forces

*Motorized infantry is simply indicated by "Mtz" with the unit designation

** Being larger than a regiment, but smaller than a division, Task Forces Herren and Linden were graphically portrayed as "brigades."

***Parent units are assumed to be of the same type as the unit portrayed, i.e. in this case, the "276" refers to the parent organization of the infantry company represented (in this case, "Company A"), namely the 276th Infantry Regiment. In situtations wherein this is not the case, such as the 19th Armored Infantry Battalion, which was a subordinate element of the 14th Armored Division, the type of the parent unit is specifically expressed. In US Army WWII terms, an armored division would be designated by the addition of a triangle after the number, e.g. "14▲."

Note 1. German corps and US divisions were the highest levels at which their respective armies assigned unit types, e.g. "Infantry" or "Armor/Panzer," and are so portrayed graphically. All organizations higher than these levels are portrayed without a type symbol, but rather simply with their numerical designation inside the unit "box."

Note 2. Generally, if a unit's parent unit is not portrayed, the unit designation appears to the left of the box. However, due to space constraints on some of the maps (particularly the *NORDWIND* Situation maps), the unit designation appears on the *right* of the box.

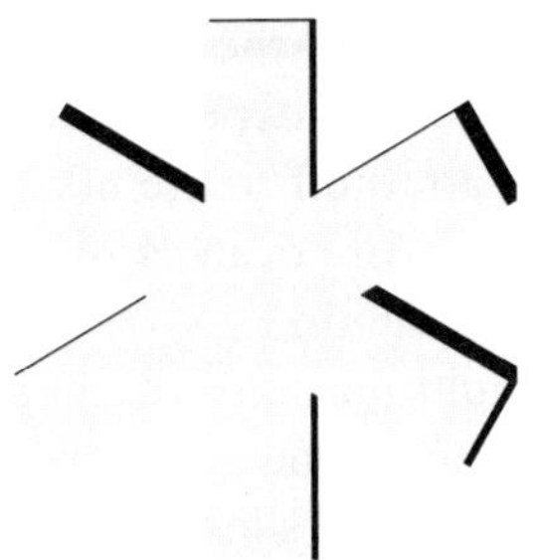

# Just Before Sunrise, 7 January 1945

The flickering light from the burning American tank behind me illuminated the otherwise seemingly pastoral scene to my front: the mixed conifer and deciduous trees of the forest stood fairly wide apart on the gentle incline leading to the top of the ridge, not 100 meters away. Continuing flurries added to the fresh snow already blanketing the ground, swallowing sounds and creating the illusion of peace. Beyond the light from the burning vehicle's flames, the woods lay shrouded in darkness, but it was the kind of twilight darkness from reflected moonlight that plays tricks on men's minds, at once concealing true danger while turning shadows into monstrous things.

It must be about 0700. Just a minute ago, we had knocked out the tank by tossing our last potato masher grenade through the open hatch. I was with the vanguard of our *3d Battalion, SS-Mountain Infantry Regiment 12*, breaking out from a tightening encirclement with the last men of the *11th Company*—which now consisted of the seven men who had made it out of Wingen-sur-Moder* last night. I selected this company to lead our exfiltration; the rest of the (now) 110-man strong battalion followed some 300 meters behind. Climbing up the forest road with the acting company commander, an *Oberscharführer*,† we had discerned the silhouette of the American tank only after rounding a bend. The Sherman appeared to us as a dark, looming hulk occupying the entire width of the road, but one that could only be fully recognized at the shortest distance. By the white, five-pointed star, there was no doubt that it was an American tank, facing away from us to the east.

Only ten meters in front of us, our six men had squeezed by the tank, either not cognizant of it out of pure exhaustion, or not caring for the same reason. Standing next to the vehicle, the *Oberscharführer* and I could hear voices from within, through the open hatch; the crew was aware that men were walking by their vehicle, passing from rear to front. We saw the bow machine gun move, taking aim at our mountain infantrymen who were slowly disappearing into the darkness.

*It should be noted that in this region of France, there are two villages with the name of Wingen. In this book, all references are to Wingen-sur-Moder.

†Equivalent to a US Technical Sergeant. For all subsequent rank references, see Appendix A.

After the grenade detonated inside the tank, I jumped over the roadside ditch into the forest, looking for a large tree as cover—I fully expected the tank to explode at any moment. My NCO must have darted off to the other side; I was now on my own. Worse, I had somehow lost my American carbine, which I had appropriated in Wingen to supplement my sidearm.

Besides the crackling of the fire from the tank (it could not have reached the ammunition boxes yet!), it was suspiciously quiet in the woods. In fact, it was just the lull before the fury, as a single rifle shot broke the silence and a .30-caliber bullet slammed into my right calf. This was the prelude to the hellish cacophony to come.

Aided by the light from the burning tank, I could make out the marksman who shot me, crouching in a foxhole some fifteen meters up the ridge. He was drawing a second bead on me. Unable to quickly reach my holstered pistol, I must have decided by some reflexive process to unsettle him by running straight at him. During this short stretch, he fired again but somehow missed me. Before he could shoot a third time, I was on him, and stunned him with a blow of my fist to his helmet.

Meanwhile, the American line had awakened to the threat from its rear. The staccato bursts of a machine gun joined the crescendo of rifle fire. I was definitely in need of cover now, so I pushed the GI deeper into the hole that I now shared with him. Stretching my wounded leg into the covered portion of the fighting position, I felt something soft which I first took to be a dog crouching in the dark warmth. But no, it was another GI, still in his sleeping bag! I pushed their rifles out of reach beyond the rim of the foxhole. Pulling my Walther P-38, I declared both GIs to be my prisoners of war.

After taking off my ski cap (which, with its Edelweiss, Death's Head and eagle, clearly did not resemble anything "GI"), I carefully craned my head up and ventured a glance around the area. I found what I had feared and expected—the next foxholes were not fifteen meters away, on both sides. However, cloaked in the darkness of the late mountain predawn, I was not recognized as one who did not belong on this line of American infantrymen.

Our battalion had assembled during the brief melee, and suddenly, my comrades attacked the American positions in which, by chance, I was now an occupant. During the assault, my own men came as near as fifteen to twenty meters, close enough that I feared getting a grenade into the hole at any moment. What an irony—being saved thirty minutes before by the shelter of an American foxhole, now only to be killed by my own men.

I retrieved my ski cap, and waved it frantically to the attackers, shouting, "*Hierher! Hierher!*"* But my yelling was in vain. The terrible roar from

*Over here! Over here!

machine guns, submachine guns, and rifles drowned out my puny entreaties, which were even further obliterated by the explosions of the American mortar rounds which began plummeting into the area.

I despaired when I could not immediately attract the attention of my men, for I knew that our attack must soon come to an end. Only two hours before, I had supervised the collection and equitable distribution of the ammunition remaining for the battalion—there were not more than ninety rounds for each machine gun, which was next to nothing for our new, fast-firing MG-42s!* As expected, my battalion's assault ran out of steam swiftly, and my comrades withdrew under a hail of everything the Americans could throw after them. In small groups, the remaining German force exfiltrated through the American lines, bypassing the strongpoints, to later successfully link up with our *Combat Group Schreiber* along the Rothbach Valley.

While our men slipped away and the last American mortar rounds dropped blindly into the forest, I was still stuck in an American foxhole with two GIs. We began a whispered conversation in English, which was difficult for me, since my basic school facility in this language was rusty from long neglect. There had been no use for it in the birch forests of northern Karelia,† where my unit had seen all but the last week of its combat! I thought I comprehended that my "underling," that is, the man on whose lap I was kneeling, was from Boston, while his buddy was from Texas. As far as I could tell, they didn't really belong to this unit, but were only attached from an antitank platoon that was in support.

There was finally time to apply a dressing to the wound in my leg. My prisoners ate their cold rations, which they shared with me. Afterwards, we smoked some American cigarettes, which I had liberated in Wingen. Then, carrying out perhaps my most important task, given my present situation, I took the map—the one with the positions to which we were withdrawing marked clearly—from my map case, tore off the pertinent section, and burned it.

I tried to conjure some feasible plan for getting out of this awkward situation and setting off into the evaporating darkness to rejoin my men. Blessed with a good sense of orientation, I had no doubt that I could find them. Nothing could be done for the moment, so I settled in and prayed for the return of the early winter night.

But darkness was still hours away, and when I next glimpsed over the rim of the hole, I found that in the broadening daylight, the first American GIs were warily climbing out of their positions to inspect the battlefield before—

*MG: machine gun.

†Karelia was in the east, where we had done all of our fighting; we had only been here on the western front for a week

or actually, behind—their line. They seemed to start collecting the wounded from this sector, their own first, then probably ours.

A small group led by a sergeant headed my way, crunching through the snow. At the last moment, I succeeded in yanking one of my prisoners' blankets over me. Under the blanket, I heard the sergeant come to the edge of the hole and ask the Boston fellow to join his group in the task of recovering the wounded. The other GI was still lying in the covered part of the foxhole, out of sight. Under the cover of the blanket, I pressed the muzzle of my Walther into his stomach, thereby suggesting that he'd better find a credible excuse for remaining in place, one that had better not give me away. Under the gentle prodding of my pistol, I heard him mumble an answer to the sergeant, something about "not feeling well"—which was certainly no lie. This made the sergeant grumble, but he evidently did not have the time or inclination to pursue the matter at the moment, and he moved on to try his luck at the next foxhole.

Any rejoicing on my part was definitely premature. Not fifteen minutes later, the same NCO returned with a group of his men, growling to my "underling," "If you're too lazy to come out, at least give me your damn blanket." Evidently needing it to carry wounded, he snatched it forcefully from the hole.

For some long moments, everyone stood stone-still and silent. I was staring up at the group standing around the foxhole, and they were staring down, in disbelief, at me. I broke the spell first by removing the magazine from my Walther and throwing it and the pistol into the woods. Only then did the group arouse from their stunned torpor and start yelling at me to get out of the hole.

Standing for the first time in hours, I asked the sergeant to be taken "to his officer." I was promptly escorted off in a southerly direction, even as my two former prisoners of war were being castigated as cowards by their comrades.

After more than a thousand combat days against the Red Army near the Arctic Circle, and three weeks of skirmishing with former comrades-in-arms, the Finns, during the long withdrawal through Finland, my active combat role against the US Army had come to an end after only seven days in January 1945.

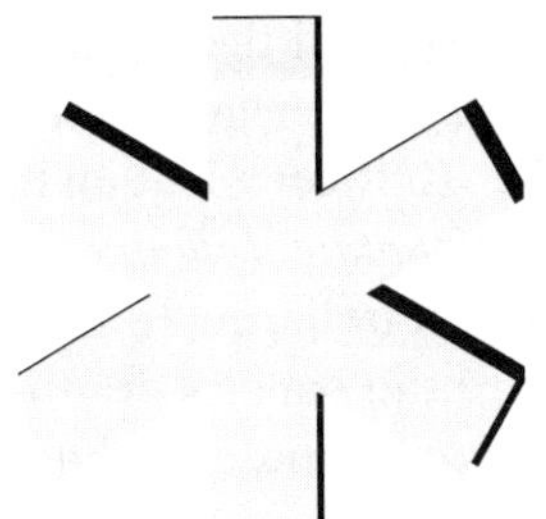

# Prelude to NORDWIND: The First Three Years of NORD in Action

## -I- Overview

The record of the *6th SS-Mountain Division NORD* (*6. SS-Gebirgs-Division NORD*) began on 24 February 1941, and ended on 3 April 1945.

During its life, its soldiers saw,

* 1,214 days of combat against the Soviet Army on the Finnish-Soviet Front, in the Salla-Kandalaksha* and Kiestinki-Louhi sectors of the German Northern Theater of Operations [1 July 1941 (Salla)–28 September 1944 (north of Kuusamo)];
* 23 (regrettable)† days of combat against the Finnish Army, from Kemi/Tornio to Rovaniemi to Muonio [7–29 October 1944]; and
* 92 days of combat against the United States Army, in the Low Vosges (Operation NORDWIND), the Saar-Moselle Triangle, Hunsrück, and Vogelsberg [2 January (Fuchsthal)–3 April 1945 (Büdinger Wald, east-northeast of Frankfurt-am-Main)].

*As a rule, the Finnish spelling of place names (toponyms) is used here, as these were used by German troops during the war. In a few instances, the Russian transliteration has been added to make orientation easier with late twentieth-century maps. The "Autonom Republic of Karelia," with an area of 172,400 square kilometers and a population of 795,000 (Capital: Petroskoi–Petrosavodsk), was originally settled by Finns. The indigenous populations, the Karelians, are ethnic Finns, speaking the Finnish language. Interestingly, one of the concessions to this folk made by Moscow was permission to use the customary Finnish place names first, in Latin letters, and the Russian equivalent, in Cyrillic, second.

†The reader is kindly asked to understand the qualification "regrettable" regarding combat against the Finns, with whom we had for so long fought side-by-side as brothers-in-arms against the common Soviet foe!

I participated in these battles from the summer of 1941 until the autumn of 1942 as an enlisted man in *Artillery Regiment 6 NORD*. After graduation from officer's training at the *SS-Junkerschule Bad Tölz* (Officer Candidate School) in 1943, I served with the *3d Battalion, SS-Mountain Infantry 12 "Michael Gaißmair."* During the withdrawal from northern Karelia, and until 7 January 1945, I served as the battalion's adjutant. Due to the paucity of officers in our battalion headquarters at the time, my duties amounted to those roughly equivalent of a US battalion executive officer.

# -II-
# Background

## *Origins*

*SS-Combat Group* (Kampfgruppe) NORD* was formed pursuant to a *Waffen-SS* Headquarters secret message dated Berlin, 24 February 1941.[1] This order may be considered the "birth certificate" not only of *SS-Combat Group NORD*, but also of the *6th SS-Mountain Division NORD*, its successor in 1942. It is the latter which participated in Operation *NORDWIND*, the last major German offensive in the west in World War II.

*SS-Combat Group NORD*, a motorized formation, was organized from *SS-Infantry Regiments 6* and *7*† and the *Combat Group Signal Battalion* already stationed in southern Norway at the time the orders were issued authorizing formation of the combat group.

The same order decreed the formation of further elements for incorporation into the new *Combat Group NORD*, to be activated on 15 March 1941. They included:

- ✱ Staff personnel for the Combat Group headquarters
- ✱ A cartographic section

*Doctrinally speaking, a *"Combat Group"* was an especially-tailored combined arms group formed for the accomplishment of a specific mission, which was dissolved upon mission accomplishment or change of situation. For a *"Combat Group"* of this definition, the term *"Combat Group"* is used in this book. However, *"Combat Group"* was sometimes used, as in this case, to define a nucleus around which a division was to be formed. We shall see the U.S. Army similarly apply the equivalent "Task Force" designation to several units in the Vosges campaign, such as Task Force Herren, which was the nucleus of the 70th Infantry Division.

†Formerly *SS-Totenkopfstandarte 6*, or *6th Death's Head Regiment*, from Prague, and *SS-Totenkopfstandarte 7*, from Brno in occupied Czechoslovakia.

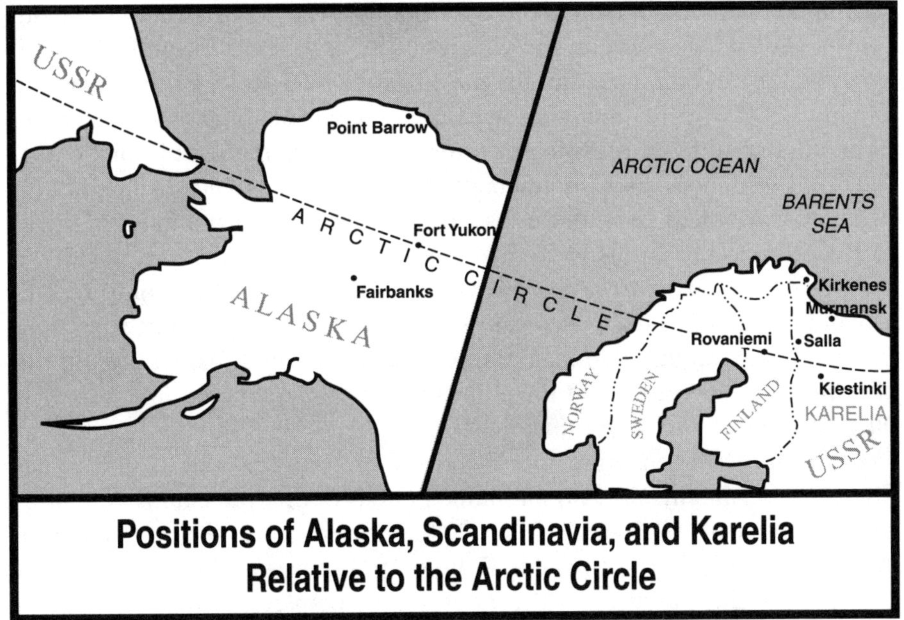


**Positions of Alaska, Scandinavia, and Karelia Relative to the Arctic Circle**

* Two companies of combat engineers
* A reconnaissance battalion
* A staff supply officer and other service elements

At a later date, *SS-Infantry Regiment 9,** stationed at Kirkenes on the Arctic Ocean coast, was temporarily added, as well as an antiaircraft battalion. All of these units were assembled in the Kirkenes region in northern Norway in April and May 1941.[†]

During this time, cooperation between Finland and Germany was being secretly negotiated at the General Staff level.[2] On 30 November 1939, the Soviets had attacked Finland, and the Finns stunned the world by holding off the Communist leviathan for 3fi months during the "Winter War" of 1939–40. Establishing a line of defenses known as the "Mannerheim Line" (after the Marshal of the Finnish Army, seventy-two-year-old Baron Carl Gustav Mannerheim), the Finns battled with extraordinary *élan* against hopeless odds. Despite violent League of Nations protests, including the expulsion of the Soviet Union from the League on 14 December, the predictable end came, however, and the Finns were forced to give in to Soviet demands. As part of the armistice negotiated in Moscow, after 12 March 1940, Finland ceded to the USSR the Karelian Isthmus, the large city of Viipuri (Vyborg)

*Formerly *SS-Totenkopfstandarte 9.*

†Kirkenes, Norway is located at 69 degrees 40 minutes N latitude. For comparison, Barrow, Alaska is at 71 degrees 17 minutes N latitude.

with its adjacent fertile lands, the naval base at Hangö at the mouth of the Gulf of Finland, and land in the vicinity of the towns of Salla and Alakurtti, north of the Arctic Circle. In all, the Soviet Union stole territory totaling roughly 42,000 square kilometers, with a population of about 450,000 people, all of whom had to be resettled in Finland. In the heroic, but losing, effort, the Finns lost about 20,000 soldiers dead and a further 10,000 maimed.[3]

A year and a half later, these losses were still fresh in the mind of every patriotic Finn. The Finns were ready for revenge, and Germany provided a willing and potent partner for the vengeance that would not only recoup Finland's national honor, but regain her lost territory and resources as well. Thus a strong, though informal, partnership was created that was called the "Brotherhood-at-Arms," and the Finnish Army was prepared to enter what they were to call the "Continuation War."

Under the Transit Agreement concluded between the German and Finnish governments on 22 September 1940 in Berlin, the extensive motorized columns of *SS-Combat Group NORD* commenced their march from northern Norway into Finland on 7 June 1941, crossing the new bridge at Nyrud over the Pasvik Elv, the river which demarcates the Norwegian-Finnish border in that region. Leading the Combat Group, *SS-Reconnaissance Battalion NORD*, with some eighty BMW 750 motorcycles, crossed the Pasvik Elv in bright nordic sunshine at 0500.[4] Upright on their motorcycles, MG-34s in evidence on many of the sidecars, the men of the *SS-Reconnaissance Battalion* led the truck-borne combat group along the Arctic Ocean Highway, which bore south for about 370 kilometers to Rovaniemi.*

After three days of motor march, the units of *SS-Combat Group NORD* bivouacked in the vicinity of Ranua, south of Finnish Lapland's administrative capital, Rovaniemi, hard by the Arctic Circle. The men had to adjust to the twenty-four-hour sunlight; the midnight sun season had begun.

On 18 June, *NORD* began the last 300-kilometer leg of the march. Traveling roughly northeast, the destination was Märkäjärvi, close to the

*The Finnish Arctic Ocean Highway was constructed in the 1920s to connect the railhead at Rovaniemi, the capital of the northernmost province of Lapi (Lapland) with the Finnish harbors of Petsamo (today the Russian city of Pechenga) and Liinahamari, both of which were ice-free, year-round, like the much larger Soviet port of Murmansk, 150 km to the east. This highway, in a way comparable to the Alaskan-Canadian Highway, facilitated the exchange of goods over its 533-kilometer length, and was kept trafficable throughout all seasons. Besides large truck combinations, it was traveled by buses as well. As a result of the Second World War, Finland lost both harbors to the USSR, its entire Arctic Ocean coast, and the rich nickel ore deposits at Kolosjoki (today the Russian city of Nikel). The highway (designated in the modern European road net as "E-76") now ends at the post-war border with the Russian Federation at the Finnish border village of Virtaniemi, 380 km north of Rovaniemi.

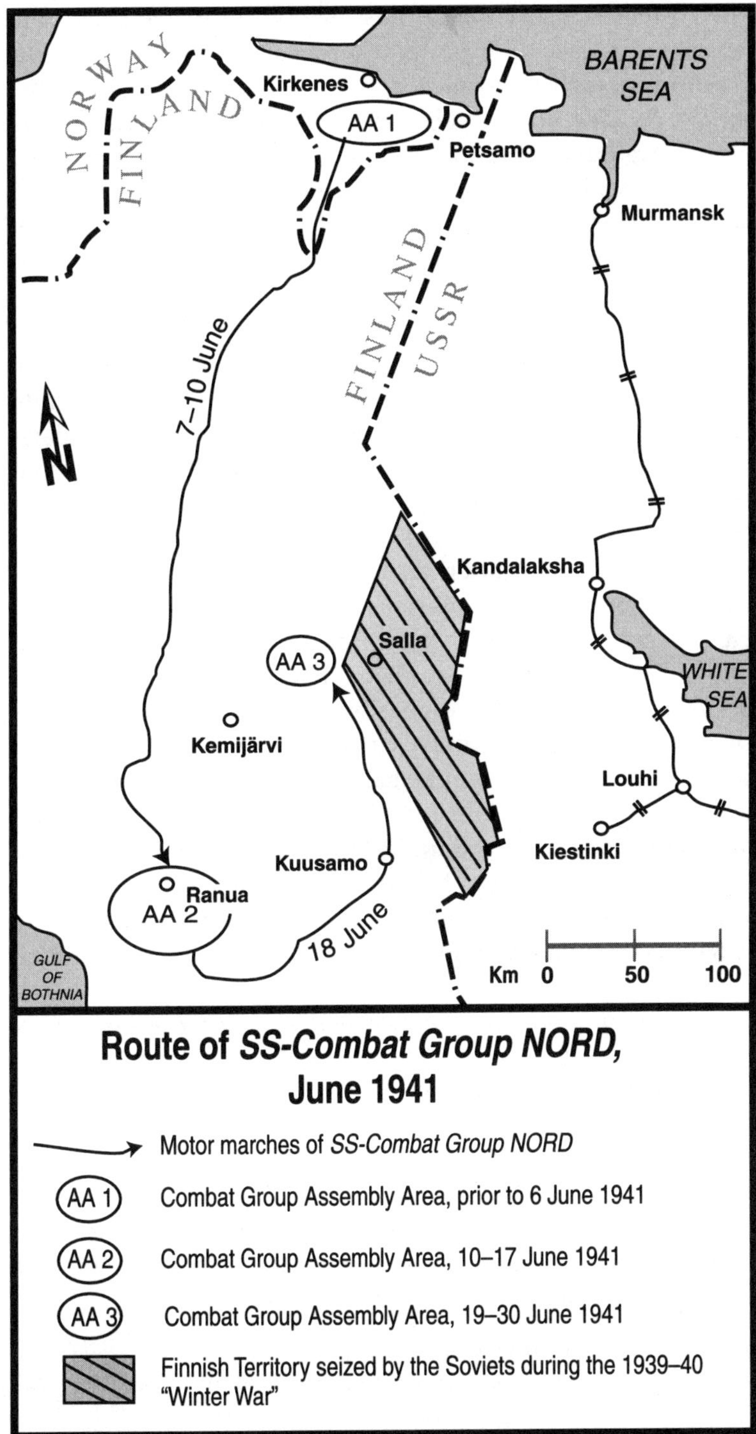


**Route of *SS-Combat Group NORD*, June 1941**

Motor marches of *SS-Combat Group NORD*

AA 1 Combat Group Assembly Area, prior to 6 June 1941

AA 2 Combat Group Assembly Area, 10–17 June 1941

AA 3 Combat Group Assembly Area, 19–30 June 1941

Finnish Territory seized by the Soviets during the 1939–40 "Winter War" recently-adjusted Finnish-Soviet border, just across the demarcation line from the fortress town of Salla.[5] One day previously, *SS-Combat Group NORD* had been officially upgraded to a full-fledged motorized infantry division, now designated *SS-Division NORD.*[6] The order from Berlin had reached the unit while it was still in Ranua, and was announced by the new commanding general, *Brigadeführer* Karl Maria Demelhuber. By order of *Reichsführer-SS* Heinrich Himmler, Demelhuber and an entirely new command staff replaced the old commander, *Brigadeführer* Richard Herrmann, and his combat group staff—*just days before commitment to combat!*

*SS-Division NORD* marched through Kuusamo, re-crossed the Arctic Circle (from the south this time) and bivouacked in its assembly area between Märkäjärvi [today called (New-) Salla], and Kelloselkä, the latter very close to the new border. In the meantime, the commanding general had conducted thorough inspections of his new command, and what he found had troubled him greatly. Although by no means the fault of the soldiers, the simple fact was that they had received no combat training!

On 23 June, just six days after arriving and assuming command, *Brigadeführer* Demelhuber expressed his assessment to the commanding general of the *XXXVI Corps*. In a formal letter, the commander of *NORD* informed *General der Kavallerie* Hans Feige that, due to the poor state of training, he, Demelhuber, could not take responsibility for committing his troops to combat. Demelhuber pledged however, that if given an opportunity to train his units for a short period, he would make up quickly for the neglect of the past.[7]

*Brigadeführer* Demelhuber received his answer from *General der Kavallerie* Feige a day later. Feige thanked him for his frank estimate of the division's training status, and assured Demelhuber of his confidence that the firm determination and good intentions of the soldiers would compensate for their training deficiencies.[8]

It was clear to everyone on the spot that neither *General der Kavallerie* Feige nor the commanding general of *AOK Norwegen,** *Generaloberst* Nikolaus von Falkenhorst, could spare *NORD* from the battle that was fast approaching. Just two days previously, on 22 June 1941, Operation BARBAROSSA, the invasion of the Soviet Union by Germany and many of her allies, had begun. *NORD* would go into combat untrained.

Yet Demelhuber did not give up. On 30 June, the division's first status report was submitted.[9] It showed—*inter alia*—the actual strength figures of *NORD* on the day before commitment to combat,

*"*AOK*" is the abbreviation for "*Armee Oberkommando*," or headquarters of a field army. *AOK Norwegen* was, therefore, the headquarters of the German field army titled "Norway."

* 306 officers
* 1,159 noncommissioned officers (NCOs)
* 8,040 enlisted men

Under the heading, "Commanding General's Assessment of Value," he bluntly listed all shortcomings, including the grave lack of combat training, both individual and collective. He added that this deficiency could not be held against the leadership and troops, since they had not been afforded the opportunity to conduct such training under proper coaching. Most commanders, he remarked, from company through regimental levels, had little (if any!) experience with modern warfare.

The division's artillery had fired just *once* and never in coordination with the infantry. Similarly, infantry leaders had never worked in concert with artillery. The antitank gunners had never fired their weapons, nor had the antiaircraft gunners. No combined arms training whatever had been accomplished. There was a marked shortage of support and service elements (there was a serious shortage of properly qualified officers), and the motorized transport consisted of a patchwork collection of many different makes and models, making support and maintenance a nightmare.

On the other hand, *Brigadeführer* Demelhuber rated the soldierly qualities of his soldiers as "good, and, in some cases, very good."

Reiterating his arguments of 23 June, Demelhuber said in closing that the division would be ready for combat following "two to three" months of formal training, the customary period for the raising of new formations of this size and type. This status report was distributed to *General* Feige's *XXXVI Corps* headquarters and to the *Waffen-SS Chief of Staff* in Berlin.

This, then, was the true situation of Division *NORD* on the eve of the war (contrary to what is held in the treatises by G. H. Stein and Bernd Wegner,[10] for example).

## An Inauspicious Beginning

Operation BARBAROSSA had started on the Eastern Front on 22 June, but it did not begin in the Northern Theater of Operations until 29 June. In Northern Finland, the plan, codenamed *SILBERFUCHS* (SILVERFOX), called for an attack with three corps to interdict the Murmansk Railway in multiple locations to prevent the possibility of the Soviets building a bypass around a single German interdiction. The Murmansk Railway was an absolutely key objective, being one of the main lifelines of supply to the Soviet Union from the rest of the world. The offensive to deprive the Soviets of this would be launched along four axes:

* Northernmost Corridor: The "Arctic Ocean Front," with Murmansk as the objective of Mountain Corps Norway (*Gebirgskorps Norwegen*), commanded by *Generalleutnant* Eduard Dietl, with the *2d* and *3d Mountain Divisions*, as well as *SS-Infantry Regiment 9*.
* Central Corridor: The "Salla-Alakurtti-Verman Front," with Kandalaksha as the objective of *XXXVI Corps*, commanded by General Feige, with the *169th Infantry Division* and *SS-Division NORD*, supported by the Finnish 6th Infantry Division.
* Two Southern Corridors:
  The "Kiestinki Front," with Louhi/Loukhi as the objective of the Finnish III Corps, commanded by *Keneraalimajuri* Hjalmar. F. Siilasvuo, with Finnish Group J.
  The "Uhtua Front," with Kem as the objective of Finnish Group F.

Overall command of these troops in northern Finland was vested in von Falkenhorst's *AOK Norwegen* at Rovaniemi. The Finns and Germans had agreed on a command and control boundary running west-east, from Oulu; *AOK Norwegen* operated north of this line, and the remainder of the Finnish Army, under the now-nearly seventy-five-year-old Marshal Mannerheim, operated to the south, controlled by his headquarters at Mikkeli.

Contrary to the practice in other theaters of war, there was no combined, multinational command of the German/Finnish forces in the Northern Theater of Operations. The two headquarters, that is, those of *AOK Norwegen* and Mannerheim's all-Finnish command, did maintain active liaison with one another, but never was there joint operational planning nor command and control.[11] This disadvantageous and unwieldy situation, stemming from the Finnish government's attempts to appear fully independent of Germany's influence, resulted in many dysfunctions.

At the outbreak of combat in the German-Soviet war on 22 June, the Finnish government took considerable pains to inform the world that Finland was a neutral state in the conflict, and intended to remain neutral as long as possible. She would, of course, be compelled to defend herself if the Soviet Union attacked, as she had in 1939. (There had been some misunderstandings due to Hitler's proclamation on 22 June, when he announced that the Finns stood side-by-side with the Germans and that they stood together to guard Finnish soil.)[12]

To safeguard her neutrality, the Finnish command had forbidden its commanders to cross the Finnish-Soviet border for any reason, even reconnaissance. The German command, *AOK Norwegen*, followed suit. However, Soviet Air Force aircraft began bombing Finnish towns on 22 June, and started carpet bombing on the morning of 25 June—without a declaration of war by either side. No fewer than fifteen communities were hit hard by

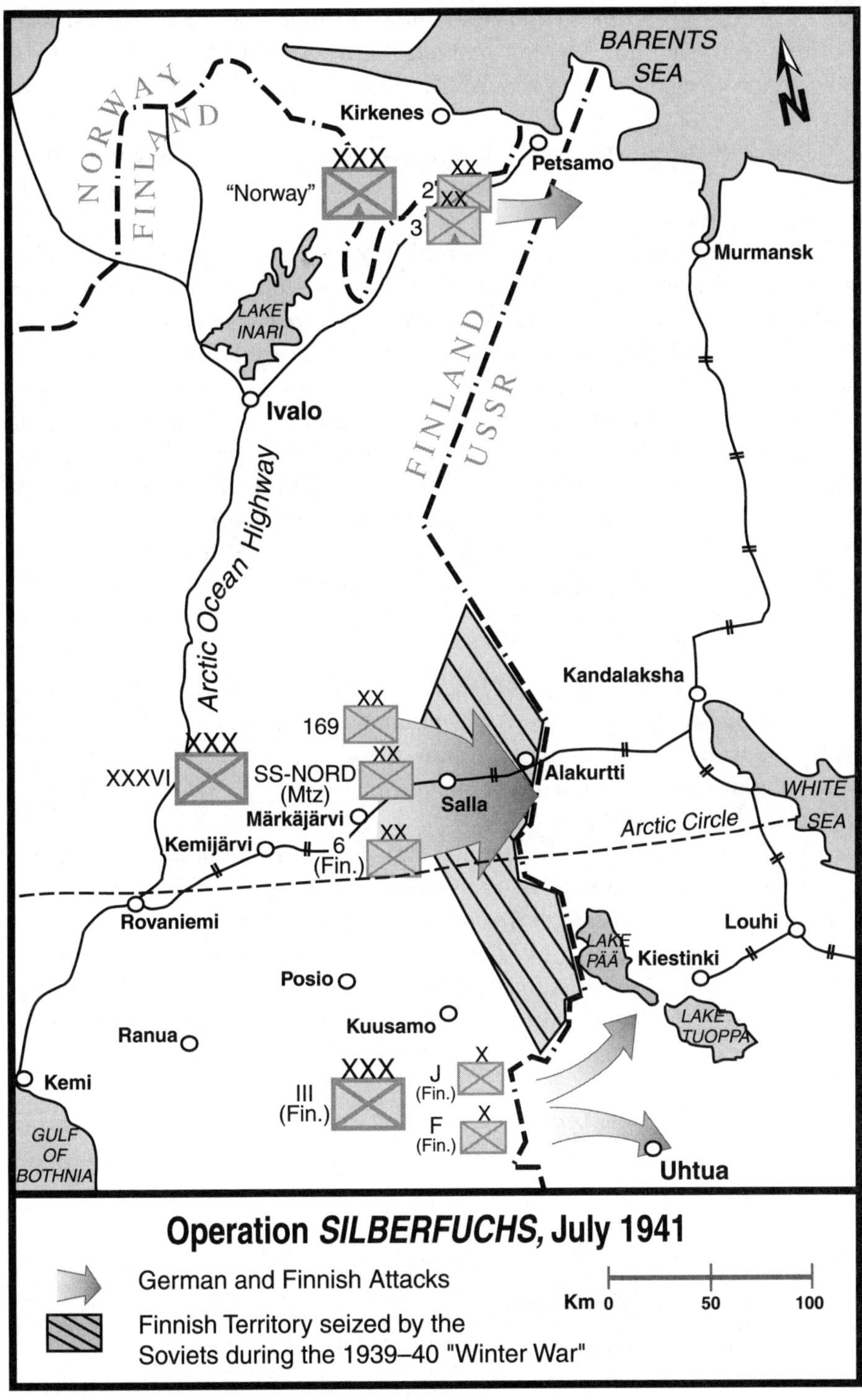
BARENTS SEA
NORWAY
FINLAND
Kirkenes
Petsamo
XXX
"Norway"
XX
2
XX
3
Murmansk
LAKE INARI
Ivalo
FINLAND
USSR
Arctic Ocean Highway
Kandalaksha
XX
169
XXX
XXXVI
XX
SS-NORD (Mtz)
Alakurtti
Salla
WHITE SEA
Märkäjärvi
Arctic Circle
Kemijärvi
XX
6 (Fin.)
Rovaniemi
Louhi
LAKE PÄÄ
Kiestinki
Posio
Kuusamo
LAKE TUOPPA
Ranua
X
J (Fin.)
XXX
III (Fin.)
X
F (Fin.)
Kemi
GULF OF BOTHNIA
Uhtua
Operation SILBERFUCHS, July 1941
German and Finnish Attacks
Finnish Territory seized by the Soviets during the 1939–40 "Winter War"
Km 0 50 100

Soviet bombs on 25 June alone, although Finnish fighters claimed twenty-six Soviet aircraft shot down within six hours of the first attack. Additionally, the Soviet Army began shelling Finnish towns in the border region on the same day.[13]

Despite these provocations, the commanders of the Finnish and German Army units facing the Soviets across the border did not respond, and maintained their strict inaction.

During a secret session of the Finnish parliament, Premier Johann Wilhelm Rangell came to the conclusion that having been attacked by the Soviet Union, a *de facto* state of war existed, and that Finland must defend herself by all feasible military means. The Parliament delivered a unanimous vote of confidence to the government.

On 28 June, Finnish Army headquarters rescinded the order forbidding reconnaissance of Soviet territory, and patrols were dispatched forthwith. On the all-Finnish southern front, belligerent operations finally began on 10 July. In the near-vacuum and confusion generated by the withdrawal of the best Soviet units for commitment elsewhere, the advance of the Finnish Army took on the character of a triumphal sweep forward. The Finns quickly reconquered the ancient Finnish territory lost in the Moscow Treaty of March 1940.

With the recovery of their lost lands and people, the Finns had essentially achieved the objectives of their "Continuation War." During the following thirty-eight months of war alongside their German co-combatants, the Finnish government took pains to avoid the appearance to the West of being a German "satellite."[14]

The situation north of the Finnish/*AOK Norwegen* boundary was significantly different. The assault by the German troops in the Northern Corridor commenced on 29 June, with *Generalleutnant* Dietl's two mountain divisions. The soldiers of Feige's *XXXVI Corps*, in the Central Corridor, followed suit on the afternoon of 1 July, surging forward with the arctic sun at their backs. In the midst of the "midnight sun" season, day and night had lost their meaning; it was bright daylight around the clock, as the sun simply moved around the sky in a huge circle!

On the same day, *Kenerаalimajuri* Hjalmar Siilasvuo's Finnish III Corps in the south crossed the border east of Kuusamo and Suomusalmi to attack Kiestinki (Kestenga) and Uhtua (now Kalevala).

Feige arrayed his units as follows:

* Left (northern) flank: *169th Infantry*
* Center: *SS-Division NORD*
* Right (southern) flank: Finnish 6th Infantry Division

The ill-trained *SS-Infantry Regiments 6* and 7 of *SS-Division NORD* experienced a baptism of fire that would have shaken soldiers of even the best-trained units. In a frontal attack against what came to be known as the "Jungle Fortress of Salla," these unprepared units hurled themselves against the Red Army's 42d Rifle Corps, consisting of the 104th and 122d Rifle Divisions, reinforced by about fifty tanks.[15] This and subsequent frontal attacks not only failed, but caused the combat novices of the SS infantry regiments to panic.

This disaster had numerous causes.[16] Lack of adequate reconnaissance, so crucial for success in any attack, effectively blinded leaders at all levels. Indirect preparatory fires, both from artillery and Stuka dive-bombers, began a massive conflagration in the thoroughly dried-out forest through which the assault troops had to advance; maintaining orientation would have been difficult for highly experienced leaders, and for the poorly-trained leaders of *SS-Infantry Regiments 6* and *7*, it was hopeless. Even the few veterans of the Polish and French campaigns had never experienced anything like the challenges of navigating in dense evergreen woods with thick secondary growth. Further, the thick smoke from the fires obscured Soviet defensive positions, and further blinded leaders already bereft of intelligence from reconnaissance.

Not all of the difficulties came from German gaffes or inexperience, however. In the fifteen months during which they had occupied the conquered territory, the Soviets had heavily fortified the border region. Fully cognizant of the criticality of the open-water port at Murmansk and the rail line connecting it to the rest of the Soviet Empire, they had turned the sector into a veritable fortress, defended by high-quality troops.

The terrain that the Soviets had fortified lent many advantages to such a usage. On the Soviet side of the border, the hills were 250–450 meters higher in relief than the undulating ground on the Finnish side, affording the defenders exceptional fields of fire and observation up to five kilometers deep in Finnish territory. Artfully camouflaged tanks, dug in up to their turrets, faced west across these same killing grounds. The Soviets had chosen well when they stole this terrain from the Finns in 1940!

Astonishingly, much of this misfortune for the German attackers was unnecessary. After their defeat in the Winter War of 1939–40, the Finnish Army had not rested; it industriously monitored Soviet military activity in occupied Finland—including preparation of a highly-detailed, nearly complete intelligence analysis of the Salla fortifications. As a sort of welcome present, the Finns turned the voluminous portfolios over to their new allies at the time of their arrival in June. The *Ic* (intelligence officer, equivalent to the US Army's G-2) of *AOK Norwegen*, a lieutenant colonel (name withheld)

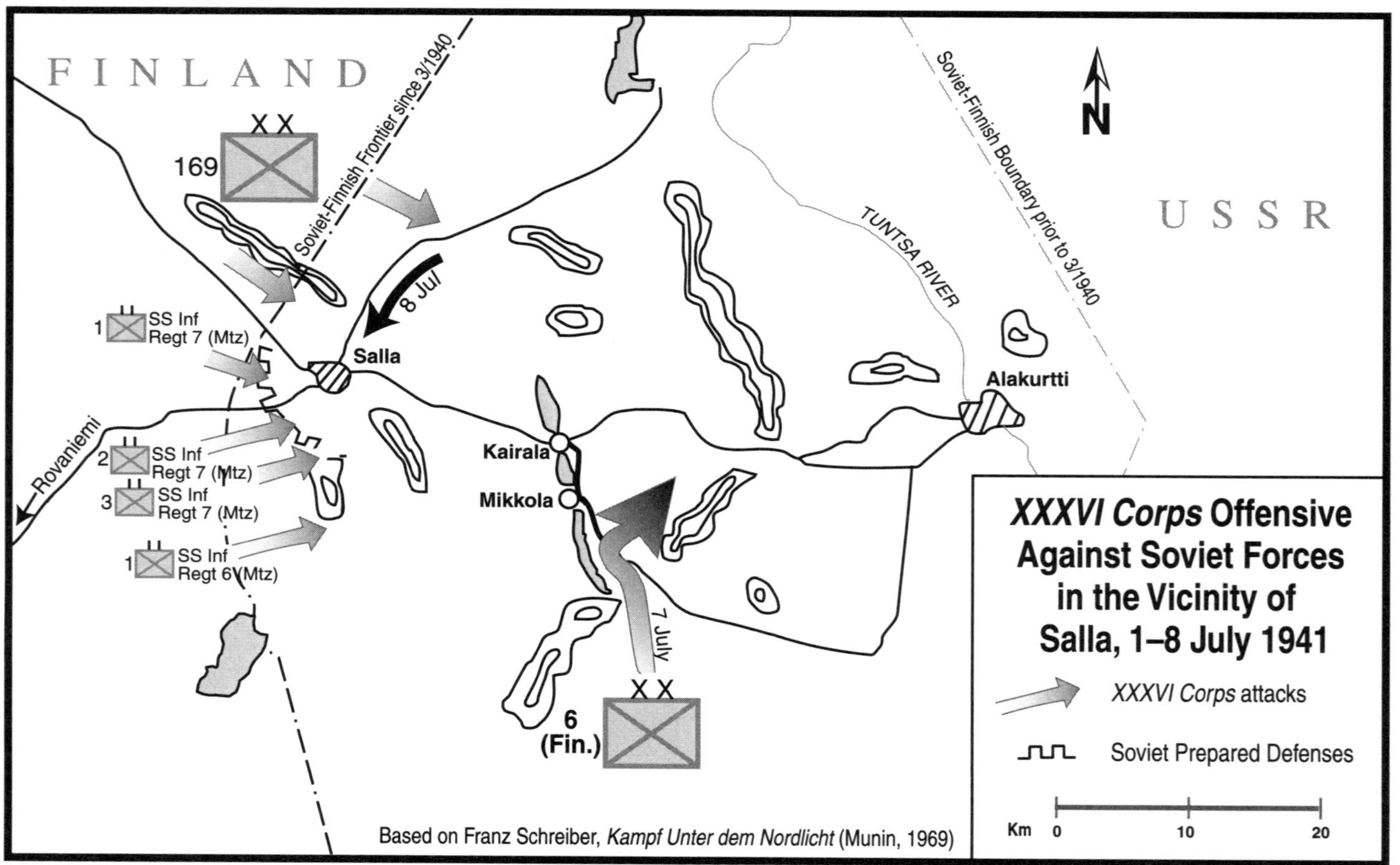


Based on Franz Schreiber, *Kampf Unter dem Nordlicht* (Munin, 1969)

received the files, briefly examined them, and put them away. In his arrogance, he never bothered to reexamine the priceless information, nor did he share it with the leaders of the units tasked with assaulting Salla.[17]

This almost unbelievable lapse of professionalism had predictably grave consequences. *SS-Division NORD* was ordered to conduct a frontal attack against a nearly impregnable objective and the resultant casualties were very heavy. The two committed infantry regiments lost 16 officers and 245 men killed or missing, with a further 307 wounded. The principal fighting echelons of *SS-Division NORD* had lost nearly twenty percent of their men in their first eleven days of combat![18] The severe impact of the losses on morale, confidence, and cohesion can only be imagined.

Added to these calamitous consequences was the damage done to the division's reputation. The nature of the first combat action of *SS-Division NORD* was a first-class *debâcle* that stigmatized the entire division within the German Armed Forces for about a year.[19] Eventually, after considerable reorganization and training, and weathering the hardening effects of sustained combat, the division would become "the best German infantry formation on the entire western front in early January 1945,"[20] but those who served under the *Hagalrune* still must endure the infamy of *NORD*'s first action.* There is only one chance to make a first impression, but just like many other ultimately fine fighting formations (such as the US 1st Infantry Division, mauled and embarrassed at Kasserine!), which evolved to excellence through steadfast leadership and tenacious soldiering, *NORD*'s initial failings are best viewed in the context of the unit's record of subsequent successes.

Salla finally fell on 8 July 1941. While *NORD* was still engaging the Soviet defenders frontally, *Combat Group Schack* of the *169th Infantry Division* succeeded in enveloping Salla from the north, while the Finnish 6th Division, hacking through the virgin forest country to the south, threatened to cut off Salla by pushing for the narrows of Lake Kairala. This so unnerved the Soviet corps commander that he withdrew his forces from Salla.

In the immediate aftermath of the Battle for Salla, *SS-Division NORD* was effectively dissolved for a time. *SS-Infantry Regiment 6* and *NORD*'s *Artillery Regiment* were attached to Finnish Group J, a brigade-sized infantry formation of the Finnish III Corps, attacking from Finnish Kuusamo toward the Sohjana Isthmus and Kiestinki. *SS-Infantry Regiment 7* was attached to the *169th Infantry Division* as reinforcements for its drive on Kairala and Alakurtti. *Reconnaissance Battalion NORD* was attached to the Finnish 6th Infantry Division to screen the division's right flank in the attack on Kairala.

**The Hagalrune*, or "Hail Rune," is the snowflake-shaped ancient Germanic symbol for life and death. It was adopted as the symbol of the Division, and displayed on vehicles, and so on.

All *NORD* elements that subsequently came temporarily under Finnish command profited greatly from their attachment to the Finnish units. During this time, some Finnish rifle platoons were, in turn, attached to German infantry companies. Enterprising commanders cross-organized even further, reinforcing German rifle platoons with Finnish squads for the conduct of patrols. Since most Finnish officers spoke German, communication problems rarely occurred. Novice German leaders and soldiers learned important lessons from these "old hand" Finns, who freely shared their knowledge and experiences gained in months of bitter combat against their now-common Communist foe.

After release from its security duties on the Arctic Ocean, *SS-Infantry Regiment 9*, undamaged but also totally inexperienced, joined *SS-Infantry Regiment 7* and *Reconnaissance Battalion NORD* in the *XXXVI Corps* push toward Kandalaksha on the Murmansk railway line. In concert with the *169th Infantry Division* and the Finns' 6th Division, they succeeded in seizing Alakurtti on 1 September, and advanced as far as the Voyta River and Lake Verman. In this region, about seventy kilometers due west of Kandalaksha, the German troops settled into defensive positions (the so-called "Verman Front"), which were defended successfully until the German withdrawal (Operation *BIRKE*) in September 1944, forced by the Finnish-Soviet separate armistice. Kandalaksha was not taken, nor were Murmansk or Louhi, nor was the railway ever permanently interdicted anywhere by German or Finnish ground forces. Of course, ultimately, the failure to seize this objective had highly significant, and quite possibly decisive, strategic consequences.

After dramatic initial successes, the combined German/Finnish forces of Finnish III Corps experienced similar frustration in their attempts to cut the Murmansk railway at Louhi/Loukhi. Using the Finns' "*Motti*" ("Envelopment") tactical techniques, elements of III Corps repeatedly infiltrated around the pockets of the toughest Red Army resistance, encircled them and destroyed them. Sometimes several "*mottis*" would be made simultaneously. These small-scale envelopments were rather effective in wooded regions, where the more sweeping type of encirclement favored by the German Army sometimes wove a net too porous to snag all escaping enemy forces.

By 19 July, this combined force had reached the isthmus at Sohjana/Sofyanga. Here, after rapid, slashing gains, *Major General* Siilasvuo and his men arrived before a truly formidable natural defensive barrier. The narrow neck between Lake Pää and the still larger Lake Tuoppa is also bisected by the Sohjana River, behind which the Soviets had deployed strong forces.

The main attack on the Sohjana isthmus defenses commenced on 30 July. As the assault echelons attacked the defenses, one battalion used small boats to simultaneously cross over the northwestern portion of Lake Tuoppa into the rear of the Soviet forces. After three days of heavy combat, the Soviet resistance was broken and elements of the Finnish III Corps seized the town of Kiestinki, on the northern shore of Lake Tuoppa.

The Red Army threw in what must have been their last reserves in the region at that time: 500 men from a forced labor battalion (from gulags along the Murmansk railway), 600 from the Soviet Fourteenth Army Headquarters security force, and a replacement battalion from the garrison at Murmansk.[21]

From Kiestinki, there was an improved gravel road that connected it to Louhi on the Murmansk railway, fifty-eight kilometers away. Parallel to the road, and eventually crossing it, was a railway branch line also that connected to the Murmansk main line at Louhi. The Finns of Division J advanced along the railway embankment of the Kiestinki branch line to a point only thirty-two kilometers from their objective at Louhi. Here, the Red Army again offered strong resistance. The fresh 88th Rifle Division had been rushed from Archangelsk on the White Sea to halt the Finnish/German advance at the last minute.

On 25 August, *Major General* Siilasvuo informed *Generaloberst* von Falkenhorst that his troops were exhausted, and that he did not consider the continuation of the thrust toward Louhi possible without reinforcement by a Finnish division experienced in forest warfare. Meeting with the *AOK Norwegen* commanding general and his chief of staff, *Oberst* Erich Buschenhagen, Siilasvuo pointed out that he had six Finnish and three *Waffen-SS* infantry battalions at his disposal, but that the combined strength of two of these *SS* battalions had been reduced to 280 men fit for combat.* Against these forces were arrayed at least thirteen battalions of Soviet infantry, mostly fresh and near full strength.[22] The Finnish commander also asserted his estimate that the enemy was capable of outflanking him to the north and cutting his lines of communication by striking southward to Kiestinki, behind him.

Von Falkenhorst's response was to request that the Finnish III Corps halt its advance, and defend in place. He promised Siilasvuo the remaining infantry from *SS-Division NORD* (two battalions of *SS-Infantry Regiment* 7), which then were detached from the *XXXVI Corps* in the Alakurtti sector.

*Actually, even the shocking strength figures do not adequately depict the direness of the situation. In a situation briefing on 4 September, the acting *Ia* (operations officer, equivalent of the US Army's G-3) of *SS-Division NORD* (an Army major) briefed his incoming *Waffen-SS* replacement that few of the actual locations of *NORD* subordinate units were known. In addition, many of the few remaining soldiers in these battalions were afflicted with dysentery and were literally fighting in their underpants. (Letter from Joachim Ruoff, the incoming *Ia*, to Erich Ehlert, 19 September 1994.)

These reinforcements arrived at Kuusamo on 2 September and assumed defensive positions between the railway and the Kiestinki-Louhi road.[23] At the start of September, *AOK Norwegen* ordered the return of all *NORD* elements to the command of the division headquarters (except, for the time being, the *Reconnaissance Battalion*, still committed east of Alakurtti in the *XXXVI Corps* sector). This reunited the division for the first time since the "Debacle of Salla."

At the end of August, the first large contingent of replacements, about 700 in all, reached *SS-Division NORD* from the Training Center at Wildflecken/ Rhön.* These men, none of whom had been members of the *Allgemeine-SS* (the political arm of the *SS*) but rather combat soldiers of the *Waffen-SS* from the outset, were assembled in a replacement battalion at Kokosalmi to receive advanced training in the peculiarities of forest warfare in the far north.

The last German offensive on the Kiestinki-Louhi Front took place in the first half of November 1941. During October, Red Army pressure on the Finnish III Corps sector lessened significantly. German aerial reconnaissance had revealed larger Soviet troop movements to destinations on other fronts. Both Siilasvuo and von Falkenhorst assessed the situation as promising for another attempt to permanently interdict the Murmansk Railway at Louhi.

Siilasvuo's plan had scheduled the Finnish Division J (formerly Group J, now upgraded to divisional status) to penetrate the Soviet positions north of the railway line. Simultaneously, *Division NORD* would sweep beyond the road and encircle the enemy.

The assault began on 1 November at 0630, after an artillery preparation on the Soviet bunker line. The ambient air temperature was -20 degrees Centigrade (-4 degrees Fahrenheit). On the second day, the Finnish/German forces reached the road at Kilometer 23.4, and blocked the road to the east to prevent the escape of the defenders as well as Soviet reinforcement.† Here, as before, the "*Motti*" encirclements were used, with multitudes of *mottis* conducted simultaneously.

*Wildflecken lies in the Rhön Mountains of northwestern Bavaria; interestingly, it became a heavily used tactical training area for the US Army in the years of the Occupation and beyond. Schreiber, 196; Roland Kaltenegger, *Die Gebirgstruppen der Waffen-SS, 1941–1945* (Podzun-Pallas, 1994), 11.

†"The road" here is the Kiestinki-Louhi road. As is customary in Eastern Europe, the distance to the next town is marked on 2.5 meter-high poles on the roadside, one kilometer apart. For the Kiestinki-Louhi road, the crossroad north of Kiestinki is at "Kilometer 0" and Louhi is at "Kilometer 58." For orientation of activities and localities during the actions in this area, this road's "kilometrage" is used.

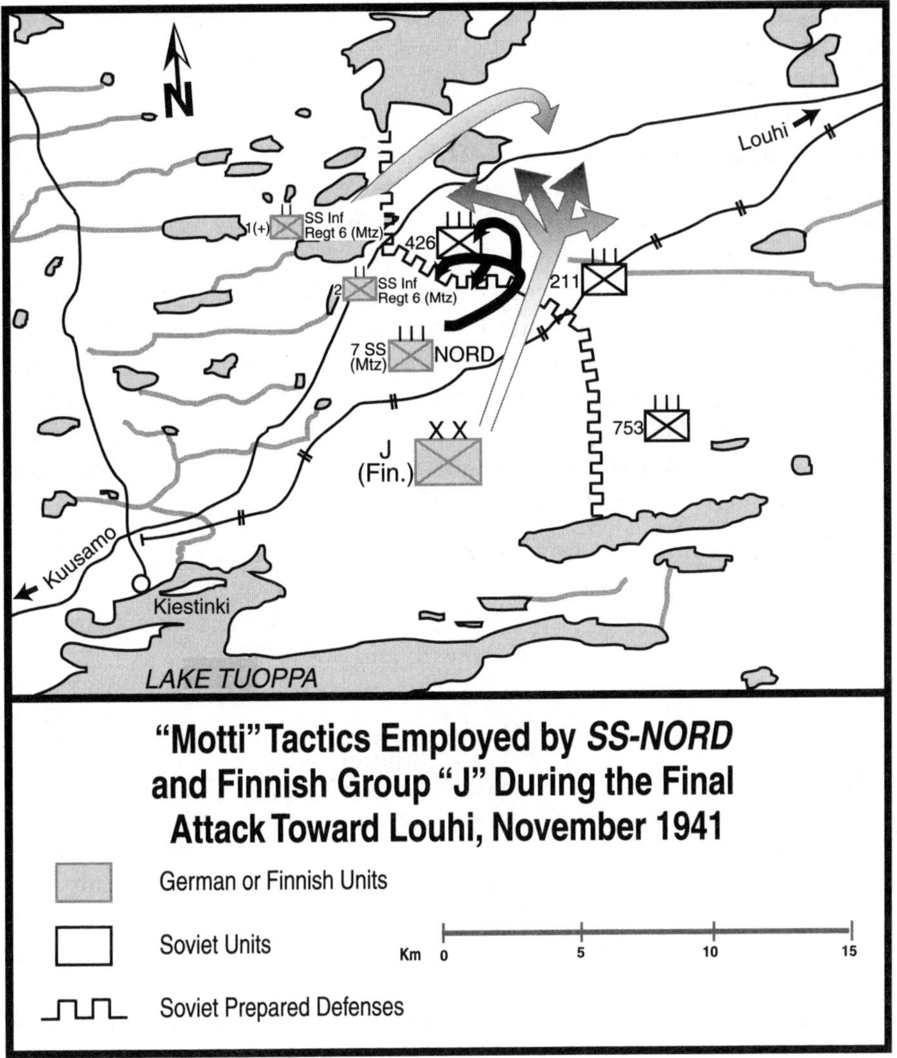


**"Motti" Tactics Employed by *SS-NORD* and Finnish Group "J" During the Final Attack Toward Louhi, November 1941**

A combat group commanded by *Sturmbannführer* Franz Schreiber* and consisting of the *1st Battalion, SS-Infantry Regiment 6*, reinforced by the Regiment's *11th Company*, reached the hills north of Kilometer 20.4, and blocked the sector between Kilometers 18 and 23 against sorties from the encircled Soviet troops across the road to the north. The noose had been tied, and

*As a *Standartenführer*, Schreiber would later command the *12th SS-Mountain Infantry Regiment* in the Battle for Wingen-sur-Moder.

pulling it tight would finish the destruction of the main Soviet resistance west of Louhi. The road to the Murmansk railway would be open.

Problems for the Germans and Finns, however, arose at various points where the Soviets had fortified themselves in strongholds made of clusters of blockhouses, tenaciously defending them in the face of repeated assaults. As many of our compatriots in other parts of the Soviet Union were also learning, unlike their counterparts in France and Belgium, the soldiers and leaders of the Red Army did not easily surrender, even when cut off and seemingly without hope. Their dogged defense and the casualties they continued to inflict took a toll beyond tactical implications, especially on the Finns.

During this Finnish/German offensive—the last attempt to reach Louhi for the rest of the war—the enemy lost some 1,400 killed in action (KIA) by *SS-Infantry Regiment 7* alone, as well as 542 prisoners, an indeterminate number of wounded in action (WIA) and large stocks of arms and equipment. German casualties were also high during the period 1 through 13 November:

| | |
|---|---|
| *SS-Infantry Regiment 6*(-)*: | 49 KIA, including 3 officers |
| | 171 WIA |
| | 369 Sick (ninety percent of them being frostbite casualties) |
| *Combat Group Schreiber*: | 19 KIA |
| | 76 WIA |
| | 115 Frostbitten |
| *SS-Infantry Regiment 7*: | 34 KIA, including 2 officers |
| | 135 WIA[24] |

The Finns of III Corps, mainly Division J, suffered exceptionally high casualties. In one week alone, they lost eighty-three officers, one-third of their total. This, of course, deeply upset Marshal Mannerheim. For a country of only 3.5 million people, which had been engaged in two wars within the last three years, such losses were impossible to replace, let alone continue to sustain.[25]

Thus, with winter at hand, the commanding general of Finnish III Corps ordered a halt to the offensive on 17 November. Defensive positions were prepared commencing on 24 November, roughly on a line from Kilometer 22 of the Kiestinki-Louhi branch railway to Kilometer 22 on the Kiestinki-Louhi road. On the German side, there was the impression that Siilasvuo had lost interest in continuing the offensive as early as 9 November, even after

*A unit is considered to be *minus* when at least one major subordinate unit has been detached. Symbolically, this is portrayed as "(-)." Similarly, a unit is considered to be *plus* when at least one major subordinate unit has been attached. This is portrayed as "(+)."

the greater part of the resistance by the encircled enemy had been broken. After 17 November, Siilasvuo encouraged *NORD* to go it alone, and to continue the attack as its leadership desired, promising that whatever success the division might have would be followed up by his Finns. By that time, however, the opportunities that had existed earlier in the month were lost, as the Soviets had moved in two rifle regiments of the 186th Division.* Thus, the successes of *Combat Group Schreiber* and the other German and Finnish forces during their drive on Louhi would be for naught.

This ended the last major attempt during the Second World War to seize Louhi and permanently cut the Murmansk railway. The effects were strategically disastrous for Germany, and extremely fortuitous for the Soviet enemy and the overall allied cause.

By the end of 1941, in six months of combat, *SS-Division NORD* had sustained very high casualties. These included 41 officers and 1,000 NCOs and junior enlisted men killed in action, and 95 officers and 2,300 NCOs and junior enlisted men wounded and sick.[26] Most of the sick cases were serious instances of frostbite, which is not surprising considering year-end temperatures as low as -40 to -50 degrees Centigrade (-40 to -60 degrees Fahrenheit). Nevertheless, the sheer volume of frostbite casualties is also indicative of the lack of logistical preparedness of the infantry regiments for combat. As with practically all the German units to the south in *Army Groups North* and *Center*, essentially no winter clothing or equipment had been brought to Finland. Hitler had not wanted to believe that the war against the Soviets could last into winter, and the General Staff in Berlin had not contradicted him by preparing for such an eventuality. Incredibly, even though combat in the far north had not begun until July, and the temperatures consistently plummeted well below freezing as early as October, with the exception of the *2d* and *3d Mountain Divisions*, the great majority of the German forces in *AOK Norwegen* were completely unequipped for combat in arctic conditions, and suffered casualties accordingly.

The huge casualty counts had several significant effects on the division. The overwhelming brunt of the casualties fell on the line and heavy weapons companies of *SS Infantry Regiments 6* and 7 (originally about 2,900 men), as well as the *Reconnaissance Battalion NORD* (originally about 650 men); these units suffered almost 100 percent personnel turnover due to casualties. Replacements, although slow in coming, were *bona fide Waffen-SS* soldiers,

*Long after the war, it became known that Siilasvuo's reluctance to continue the November offensive was not only a result of the brutal casualties his forces were sustaining, but were also heavily influenced by the Finnish government. On 27 October, they had received a stiff warning from the United States government not to attack the Murmansk railway and impede the transport of US supplies to the Soviet Union. (Ziemke, 182)

like the ones received earlier, in the fall of 1941. Some of these replacements, however, were not German citizens, but ethnic Germans (*Volksdeutsche*), mostly from Southeast Europe. Descendants of German settlers sent by monarchs of the old Austro-Hungarian Empire into their Danubian provinces, these men were not only ethnically German, but were German in culture and language as well. They assimilated well into the division's ranks. Intensely trained to be combat infantrymen at Wildflecken/Rhön, their phased arrival to replace the casualties amongst the *Allgemeine-SS* "originals" in the infantry regiments throughout 1942 signaled a sea-change in the character of the division. The militarily untrained policemen who suffered so fiercely at Salla were gone, either dead, maimed, or seasoned into effective soldiers. Their replacements/reinforcements were combat troops—young, fit, well-trained, and far better prepared for action. Even so, by 22 January 1942, the division's personnel situation was as follows:

| | Required | Actual | Shortage |
|---|---|---|---|
| Officers | 491 | 329 | 142 |
| NCOs | 2,081 | 1,338 | 743 |
| Junior enlisted | 10,144 | 8,225 | 1,919 |
| Total | 12,716 | 9,892 | 2,804 |

There was definitely room for more replacements!

## 1942—Changes in Character

The coming year, 1942, would be distinguished for the members of *SS-Division NORD* on the Kiestinki-Louhi Front by two major events,

* The final transition from an offensive to a defensive posture; and
* The reorganization of the division as *SS-Mountain Division "NORD" (SS-Gebirgs-Division "NORD").*

Other salient details of the activities of *SS-Division NORD* during 1942 were in large part corollary to an order (*Führerbefehl*) received from Armed Forces Headquarters in Berlin (*Oberkommando der Wehrmacht*, or *OKW*). The order of 10 October 1941* directed *Generaloberst* von Falkenhorst, commanding general of *AOK Norwegen*, to do the following:

* After destroying Soviet forces in the vicinity of the main objectives, desist in attempts to press on toward Murmansk.
* In priority, protect the nickel mines south of Petsamo, and prepare to attack to the east to seize the Fisher Peninsula and the Murmansk Railway in 1942.

**OKW/WFSt/Abt. L (1.Op) Nr. 441 696/41-gKdos Chefsache.*

* As an economy of force measure, defend during the winter months, construct winter quarters, and train for operations in winter conditions.
* Conduct reorganization of forces to facilitate detachment of Finnish III Corps and all Finnish subunits to the control of Finnish Supreme Headquarters.[27]

Construction of winter quarters proceeded despite the literally arctic conditions. Each infantry squad had a shelter immediately behind its defensive positions on the Main Line of Resistance (MLR). These sturdy dwellings were completely immune to artillery fire (shy of a direct hit by a howitzer of 152mm caliber or greater); the walls were built from double rows of heavy spruce and pine logs, sandwiching about sixty centimeters (roughly twenty-four inches) of stony dirt fill as insulation, covered by roofs of similar construction. Each hut was extremely well camouflaged with local vegetation, and this vegetation actually served two purposes: it obscured the positions from enemy aerial observation, and also effectively dispersed the smoke which rose from the woodburning steel stoves used to heat the huts in the winter months.

The division's defense in the Kiestinki-Louhi sector was peculiar for a twentieth-century defensive posture in that its flanks were open and subject to circumvention. Each of the four original "corridors"—namely the Mountain Corps Norway's Arctic Ocean Front, *XXXVI Corps*' Salla-Alakurtti-Verman Front, east of Kiestinki (ours), and the Finnish Group F Uhtua Front—now consisted of short lines of defensive works which feathered out into a few, single strongpoints verging on areas that were virtually "No Man's Lands." Although patrols were conducted to maintain contact with the enemy, each German unit's most distant outposts lay about 100 kilometers apart.

These huge gaps, consisting of mostly virgin woodland, were natural habitats for swarms of Soviet partisans, many of whom were familiar with the area. In the Kiestinki-Louhi sector, they would range around the countryside in groups of twenty to fifty men (and occasionally women!), concentrating mainly on raiding the only road, the life line of the German-Finnish front at Kiestinki, which ran almost 200 kilometers to Finland. Favorite targets for partisan raids included supply points and hospitals that had been established along the supply route to support the combat units. Convoys on the supply route were also lucrative targets for the partisans. With a mean speed of only thirty kilometers per hour, it took a convoy of supply trucks at least six to seven hours to cover the distance to the supply depots behind the MLR. Partisans would infiltrate through the vast gaps, ambush slow-moving convoys, and evaporate into the endless woods. More often than not, the partisans wore German uniforms and carried German small arms; this particular practice wreaked havoc among the troops charged with security of the rear areas, most of whom were older men. In response to the continued partisan activity, roadblocks and checkpoints of squad and even platoon strength were established at short intervals along the main supply route. Patrols were run along the route between these, but the partisan problem remained a thorn in our side, which constantly caused logistical and sometimes even operational uncertainty at the front.*

Ultimately, during the winter of 1941–1942, both the German/Finn forces and Soviets built formidable defenses on all four corridors. Pillboxes of heavy logs housed squad positions, machine guns, and antitank guns, which covered anti-personnel minefields and antitank obstacles. On both sides, the front remained static for the next thirty-three months. The impregnable nature of these fortifications deflected combat activity to the flanks. The northern end of the German line in this sector was anchored in the south on Lake Tuoppa. It was here that the Red Army concentrated their efforts.

While the units of *AOK Norwegen* were, in accordance with the *OKW* order of October, preparing to resume offensive activities in the spring, the Soviets were doing exactly the same thing on their side of the line. They began building roads in late winter, and established large supply depots along them, especially ammunition dumps. They envisioned an attack during the height of the spring thaw, when their logistical advantages would be the greatest. German supplies would have to come up along a muddy, deeply-rutted, 200-kilometer long road, subject to partisan attack every meter of the way, whereas the Soviet supply lines ran only two dozen or so kilometers from the Murmansk Railway, which was also capable of shifting masses of troops quickly. This advantage would tell in the coming Soviet spring offensive.

The winter of 1941–42 brought significant changes for the German command structure in the theater. On 28 December 1941, Hitler ordered *Generaloberst* von Falkenhorst to move *AOK Norwegen* out of its facility in the "Court of the North" Hotel (Finnish: *Pohjanhovi*) in Rovaniemi, and return to Oslo. On 15 January 1942, *AOK Norwegen* was replaced (in the same headquarters facility) by a new headquarters, namely *20th Army "Lapland"* (*AOK 20 "Lappland"* and, after 24 June 1942, *20. Gebirgs-AOK "Lappland"*),

*In early May of 1995, to mark the fiftieth anniversary of the war's end in Europe, the Finns invited veterans from all armies which had fought in northern Finland to a gathering in (New-) Salla, the Finnish border town north of the Arctic Circle. Second only to the many Finnish veterans, the largest contingent consisted of Germans (fifty in all), and the third, the Swedes who had served in this sector during the Winter War 1939/1940. The smallest contingent were the Russians, who numbered only eight. Of these, five had been partisans, including three women, who were all highly decorated. The Swedes, in particular, took great offense at their presence, maintaining that combat veterans had been invited, not "hit-and-run criminals."

commanded by General of Mountain Troops (*General der Gebirgstruppen*) Eduard Dietl, former commander of *Mountain Corps Norway* on the Arctic Ocean Front. Dietl, known as the Hero of Narvik, was an immensely popular and respected commander, and was promoted to *Generaloberst* later in 1942.[28]

Attempts by *20th Army* commanders to fulfill the *Führerbefehl* requirements to continue preparations for resumption of offensive activities were effectively nullified by the Soviet spring offensive, which began on 24 April and continued into late May. These attacks followed unsuccessful probes by the

**Soviet Offensive, 24 April–10 May 1942**

Soviet 758th Rifle Regiment against the German left flank, north of the Kiestinki-Louhi road, during the previous month.

The Red Army employed two infantry divisions against the German/Finnish fronts (at Kiestinki and Uhtua), while the 23d Guards Rifle Division and two independent brigades (including the 8th Ski Brigade) attacked the northern flank of the *NORD* Division and its Finnish neighbor, Division J. This attempt at a single envelopment against and behind the German/Finnish left flank was successful initially; the 8th Ski Brigade very nearly cut the only supply road west of the crossroads at Kiestinki! Only the timely and vigorous deployment of reserve forces arriving from Kuusamo prevented the planned Soviet envelopment.

Resolute counterattacks threw back the Soviet forces, destroying most of them with the decisive use of *mottis*. By 23 May, one month after the commencement of the Soviet offensive under the personal command of the commanding general of the Twenty-Sixth Soviet Army, the danger had been eliminated. The losses of the Soviet forces (counted and estimated)—among 40,000 men in the equivalent of four divisions—were a fearful 15,000 killed in action, and an indeterminate number wounded.[29] During the period from 1 April to 31 May 1942, *SS-Division NORD* lost 2 officers and 157 enlisted men killed in action; 21 officers and 769 enlisted men wounded; and 28 men missing in action.

But *NORD* was not destined to participate in any further operations as an infantry division. On 17 June, *SS-Division NORD* was officially reorganized as a reinforced mountain division, and renamed *SS-Mountain Division NORD* (*SS-Gebirgsdivision NORD*). This change in organization did not, by any means, result from the requirement to fight in alpine conditions—even the highest hills on the Kiestinki-Louhi Front could hardly be so termed—but rather by the logistical peculiarities of the zone.

The "road" from Kuusamo, the location of a large division supply depot, and the battalion trains* behind the MLR, covered 190 kilometers. After the harrowing six- or seven-hour trip along the rutted road through partisan-infested territory to the battalion trains, supplies were transferred to pack trains for transport to the units on the MLR. The table of organization and equipment of the mountain division covered this requirement perfectly, as it included trucks for the valley echelon (*Talstaffel*), and a mule pack train with associated equipment and personnel in the mountain echelon (*Bergstaffel*) of the Division service troops.

There were other logistical advantages of this conversion to a mountain division. The rucksacks issued to the combat troops made equipment much

*The term "battalion trains" refers to the trucks or other vehicles carrying ammunigtion, provisions, and other supplies. The unit aid station is also often part of the trains.

easier to carry than in the small assault packs issued to line infantrymen. Also, by October, two battalions of *Artillery Regiment NORD* received special mountain howitzers which broke down for easy transportation by pack animal through the most difficult of terrain, where trucks could not possibly haul the larger 105mm Model 18 howitzers with which the medium battalions of the *Artillery Regiment* had previously been equipped. Now, *Artillery Regiment NORD* possessed two battalions (twenty-four field pieces in all) of 75mm pack howitzers; a truck-drawn battalion (twelve pieces) of 105mm light howitzers; and a heavy battalion with two batteries (eight pieces in all) of 150mm Model 18 heavy howitzers and one battery of four 105mm cannons.

The reorganization ended almost all similarities with the original *SS-Division NORD*. Out of the "old" *SS-Infantry Regiments 6* and 7, three battalions were formed, including two mountain infantry (*Gebirgsjäger*) battalions and one motorized rifle battalion (*SS-Schützen-Bataillon NORD, motorisiert*). The *1st Battalion, SS-Infantry Regiment 6* became the *1st Battalion, SS-Mountain Infantry Regiment 6*; the *3d Battalion, SS-Infantry Regiment* 7 became the *3d Battailon, SS-Mountain Infantry Regiment 6*, and the *1st Battailon, SS-Infantry Regiment* 7 became the division's motorized rifle battalion (*SS-Schützen-Bataillon NORD, motorisiert*). The remainder of the two new mountain infantry regiments consisted of entirely new battalions, constructed from company-sized unit replacements, formed around battalion staff cadres consisting of *NORD* veteran NCOs and officers. In this way, *SS-Mountain-Division NORD* retained the combat experience of eighteen months' fighting, and replenished its strength strictly with young, fit combat soldiers.

These companies, which arrived starting in August 1942 and were comprised partly of the aforementioned ethnic Germans from southeast Europe, had been intensively trained in mountain warfare techniques at Wildflecken/Rhön, and transported by train to Danzig; then they traveled by ship across the Baltic to one of the Finnish ports on the Gulf of Bothnia. Another train ride, this time behind wood-fired Finnish locomotives, brought them to Oulu on the northern end of the Gulf.

At Oulu, *Brigadeführer* Mathias Kleinheisterkamp, who had replaced Karl Maria Demelhuber, had established a large depot for the training of fresh troops prior to their commitment to the front. An Army officer from *XVIII Mountain Corps*, *Oberstleutnant* Boysen, supervised the further training of all arriving *NORD* replacements in a six-week preparation for the conduct of forest warfare on the Karelian Front.[30] This individual and collective training finished the process of welding the companies into cohesive units, ready for the challenges of warfare in the far north against a tough and hardy foe.

General Dietl and the staff of his *20th Army "Lapland"* continued to pursue accomplishment of the 10 October 1941 *Führerbefehl* with the reassignment, in the summer of 1942, of Finnish III Corps to the Finnish Supreme Command of Marshal Mannerheim. Responsibility for command and control of the Kiestinki-Louhi front was taken over by the newly-committed *XVIII Mountain Corps* (*XVIII Gebirgs-AK*), commanded by General of Mountain Troops Franz Böhme, former Military Commander of Serbia. *XVIII Mountain Corps* thus controlled both *SS-Mountain Division NORD* and the recently-arrived Army *7th Mountain Division*. With Mannerheim's commitment of the Finnish III Corps in the Uhtua Corridor, a clear boundary line was finally established between German and Finnish zones of operation. The German zone extended from the Arctic Ocean in the north to the southern boundary of the Kiestinki-Louhi front in the south; the Finnish zone was to the south. Eventually, responsibility for even the Uhtua Corridor was taken over by *XVIII Mountain Corps*, as the Finns were hard pressed in what was, for them, the main theater of operations, namely southern Karelia.

While combat continued throughout the summer and autumn of 1942, against both partisans and regular troops, no great offensive activity was ever resumed by either side. This part of the *Führerbefehl* was simply never accomplished. The Murmansk Railway continued to carry the life's blood of the Soviet war effort from those ships of Allied convoys which survived the *U*-boat and *Luftwaffe* (German Air Force) attacks made against them in the north Atlantic and Arctic Oceans. In the winter of 1942–43, however, elements of *SS-Mountain Division NORD* began to make some progress in at least interrupting, if not exactly stanching, this flow.

With the conversion to a mountain division came the equipment (and the expectation of higher command that we would instantly be proficient with it!) that facilitated movement of the tactical elements of *SS-Mountain Division NORD* through deep snow by ski and snowshoes, pulling boat-like sleds for the transport of heavier weapons, wounded soldiers, and supplies. By wearing chest harnesses, men could pull these sleds across the deepest snow, and reach places that were otherwise impossible to get to in the depths of the long arctic winter. The "winter mobility" training was extensive; not only did we learn to ski, snowshoe, and pack and pull sleds, but we also learned—*inter alia*—how to judge the age of ski tracks, and the strength and loads of the wearers.

Usually, ski movement was carried out by platoon-sized formations, but full companies trained to move together in this fashion as well. It was a good thing, for there was no shortage of snow that winter. Between October 1942 and April 1943, the depth of snow was usually 1 to 1.5 meters.

With the advantages imparted by this new-found mobility, elements of *SS-Mountain Division NORD* conducted commando-like operations against sections of the Murmansk Railway. Platoon-sized patrols of infantrymen, accompanied by combat engineers, and, usually, a squad of Finnish infantry, conducted raids to demolish sections of the railroad track with explosives. Covering sixty kilometers in missions that often lasted a week or more, the raiders wore white coveralls and hoods, and carried white-painted weapons and equipment to maintain stealth to and from their objectives. Ski tracks were camouflaged by the last man in the patrol, who dragged a branch or even a small tree behind him to eliminate the evidence of the patrol's passing.

Some of the favorite objectives of the commanders of such missions were bridges along the railway line. With careful target selection—and luck—a blown bridge could hold up traffic for several days at a time. The Soviets, however, had built forced-labor camps at short intervals along the route, and had stockpiled huge depots with supplies for repairing any and all damage, including lumber for rebuilding destroyed trestles.

The harsh environment of such long-range missions behind enemy lines in winter dictated harsh rules for their conduct. If a member of a patrol took sick or was injured during the mission, he was left in a clandestine position along the route, with food and enough ammunition to defend himself, should he be detected. He could only count on getting picked up by a friendly patrol when it returned—days later—from actions at the objective. If he was not picked up, he was out of luck, because attempting to follow the trail was an extremely dangerous proposition; rather than camouflaging the return tracks, the patrol members would usually mine the tell-tale marks with special "ski mines," neatly buried directly in the track and artfully covered by an inch of snow.

## 1943—Stability and Seasoning

Most of 1943 proceeded in a nearly routine fashion. There was little or no movement frontally, but each side attempted to outflank the other to the north of the corridor. Defenses were strengthened and facilities such as battalion command posts and associated activities were improved. On more than one occasion, the planners at *OKW* desired to move the valuable *SS-Mountain Division NORD* from this "forgotten front" to more urgent focal points on the Eastern Front. The division had developed a *bona fide* reputation for reliability and combat proficiency that made the idea tempting to the planners in Berlin who were being pressed harder each day to come up with resources to match the growing requirements of warfare along the massive Eastern Front, to combat the burgeoning partisan problems in the Ukraine and in the Balkans, and to shore up our Italian allies and prevent a British breakthrough in North Africa. After all, the Kiestinki Front seemed stagnant, and static warfare appeared to be a wasteful use of a viable mountain division. Perhaps, the thinking went, if the front were to be withdrawn to the west bank of the Sohjana River, on the narrow isthmus between Lakes Pää and Tuoppa, the defensive line could be held with one division, releasing *NORD* for use where its organization and talents could be more tellingly employed.

On further consideration, though, all ideas of removing the division were rejected. Even if the front *could* be narrowed and held with a single division, this circumstance would only obtain in the summer; during much of the winter, these lakes froze over and became viable avenues of approach for even the heaviest of vehicles. Also, in the spring, annual Soviet attempts to outflank the positions on the Kiestinki-Louhi road required maneuver elements to secure the flanks, not just hold the front. As a result of these considerations, *NORD* remained in place in northern Karelia.

Overall, the outset of 1943 saw the division in a far better personnel posture than twelve months before:

| | Required | Actual | Shortage |
|---|---|---|---|
| Officers | 725 | 560 | 165 |
| NCOs and junior enlisted | 21,126 | 20,176 | 950[31] |

The officer situation, of course, was actually worse than it had been at the beginning of the previous year. This reflected the shortage of officers, particularly junior officers, being felt throughout the rapidly-expanding *Waffen-SS* in the period 1942–1944. Also, it reflected the inability of the *Waffen-SS* officer candidate schools (*SS-Junkerschulen*) to keep pace with the mounting number of casualties being sustained by units in combat.

In 1943, the division received its final redesignation. In August, all divisions of the *Waffen-SS* received numbers in accordance with their seniority. *SS-Mountain Division NORD* became *6th SS-Mountain Division NORD (6. SS-Gebirgs-Division NORD)*, and *SS-Mountain Infantry Regiments 6* and *7* were renumbered *11* and *12*, respectively. The *11th* also received a name, in keeping with a common *Waffen-SS* practice. In recognition of the original formation of *Death's Head Regiment 6* in Prague, the *11th* became the *"Reinhard Heydrich" Regiment* (*11. SS-Gebirgsjäger-Regiment, "Reinhard Heydrich"*), named after the former head of the *SS* counterintelligence service, who had been assassinated in Prague by British-trained Czech commandos in 1942. The division carried these designations with them to the end of the war, including the combat in Alsace.

Organizationally, 1943 brought an even more significant addition to the division's structure. Two Norwegian volunteer units joined the division in the course of the year. The *"SS-og Polit" Company*, a company of Norwegian

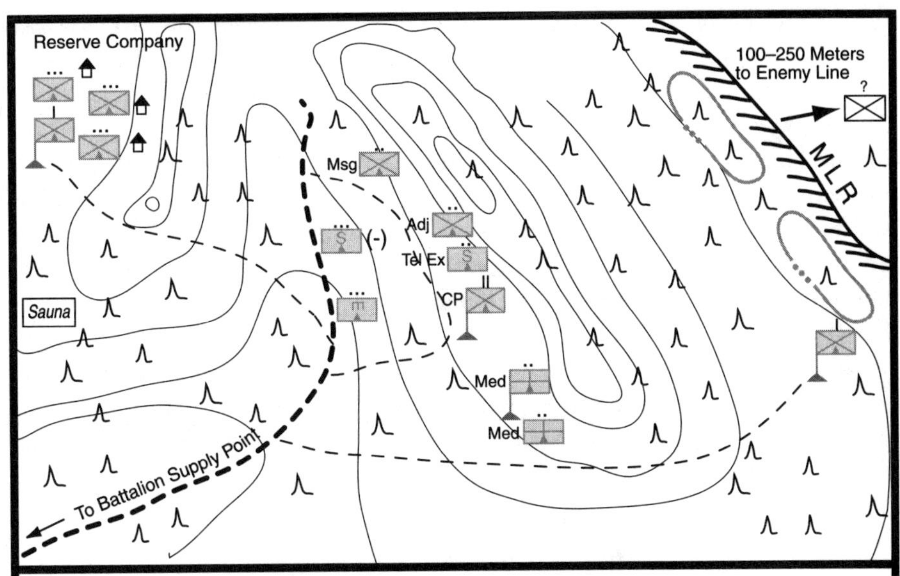
Reserve Company
100–250 Meters to Enemy Line
MLR
Msg
Adj
Tel Ex
CP
Med
Med
Sauna
To Battalion Supply Point

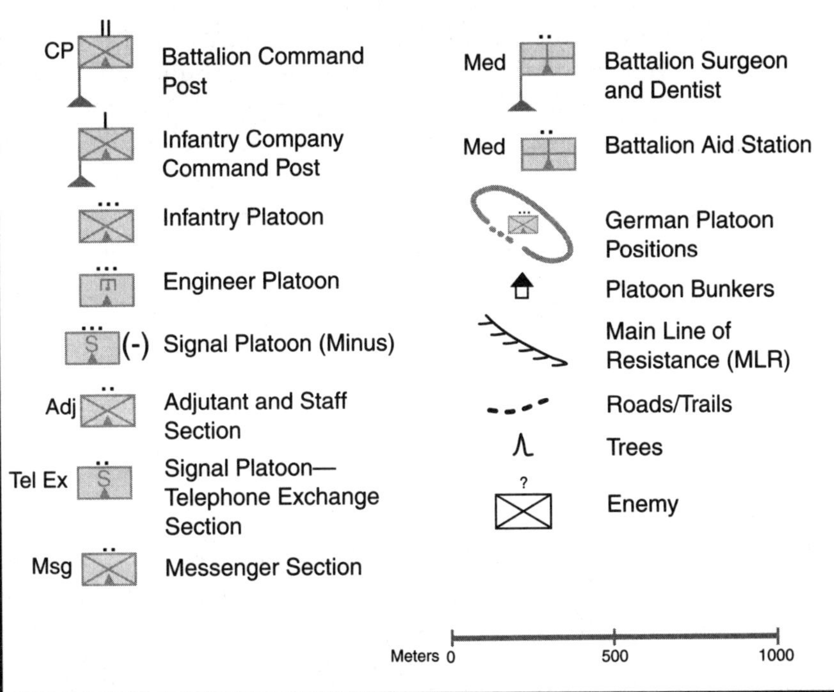
Battalion Command Post Diagram
3d Battalion, SS-Mountain Infantry Regiment 7,
Summer 1943
CP
Battalion Command Post
Infantry Company Command Post
Infantry Platoon
Engineer Platoon
Signal Platoon (Minus)
Adj
Adjutant and Staff Section
Tel Ex
Signal Platoon—Telephone Exchange Section
Msg
Messenger Section
Med
Battalion Surgeon and Dentist
Med
Battalion Aid Station
German Platoon Positions
Platoon Bunkers
Main Line of Resistance (MLR)
Roads/Trails
Trees
Enemy
Meters 0
500
1000

Police, arrived in late January, commanded by a Norwegian *SS* officer, *Obersturmführer* Jonassen. After appropriate adaptation training at the division training center at Oulu, this company was assigned to *Reconnaissance Battalion NORD*. The *SS-Ski Battalion "Norge"* (Norwegian for "Norway"), joined the division in September. Including in its ranks not only Norwegians, but also Danes and Swedes, it was committed with the understanding that its soldiers would not be required to fight against the Western Allies, but only against the Soviets (a primary motive for the enlistment of many of its members had been to fight Communism). It was committed to defensive positions on the left flank of the division.

With the addition of these units, *NORD* truly took on the characteristics of a reinforced mountain division, with two infantry battalions (the motorized battalion and *"Norge"*) more than a standard mountain division, as well as various extra support units.

## 1944—Profound Challenges

If 1943 had been marked largely by routine, 1944 was different! The division would need every ounce of additional combat power it could get.

This was the year in which the Soviets launched their great offensive against the Finnish main front in Ladoga-Karelia. This assault and its partial success against the worn-out Finnish Army were used by Moscow to bring pressure against Finland for a cease-fire and the conclusion of a Finnish-Soviet armistice. But the Soviets' first attempt in March did not succeed. However, Germany was warned of the impending dangers, and with the loss of Italy as an ally in late 1943, was fully aware of the perils of such a separate peace.

This was also the year when the Red Army made its strongest attempt, to that point, to outflank the German left, north of Kiestinki. The summer of 1944 brought the bloody battles for SennOzero (Russian for "Hay Lake") in which the *6th SS-Mountain Division NORD* would be engaged to the hilt.

The prelude to the Soviet offensive began on 7 March with an assault on a *NORD* defensive strong point near ShapkOzero (Russian for "Hat Lake"), far from the end of the continuous MLR. This strongpoint was defended by the *2d Company* of *SS-Ski Battalion "Norge,"* and one platoon of the *SS-Reconnaissance Battalion NORD*.

The Red assault began in the dark, at 0100. Due to the high snowdrifts, the attackers crossed the triple-belt minefield without losses and breached the outer defensive line. The Russians poured directly into the center of the stronghold and, using flamethrowers, torched several of the ten defensive bunkers. A *NORD* counterattack, however, restored the situation before daybreak.

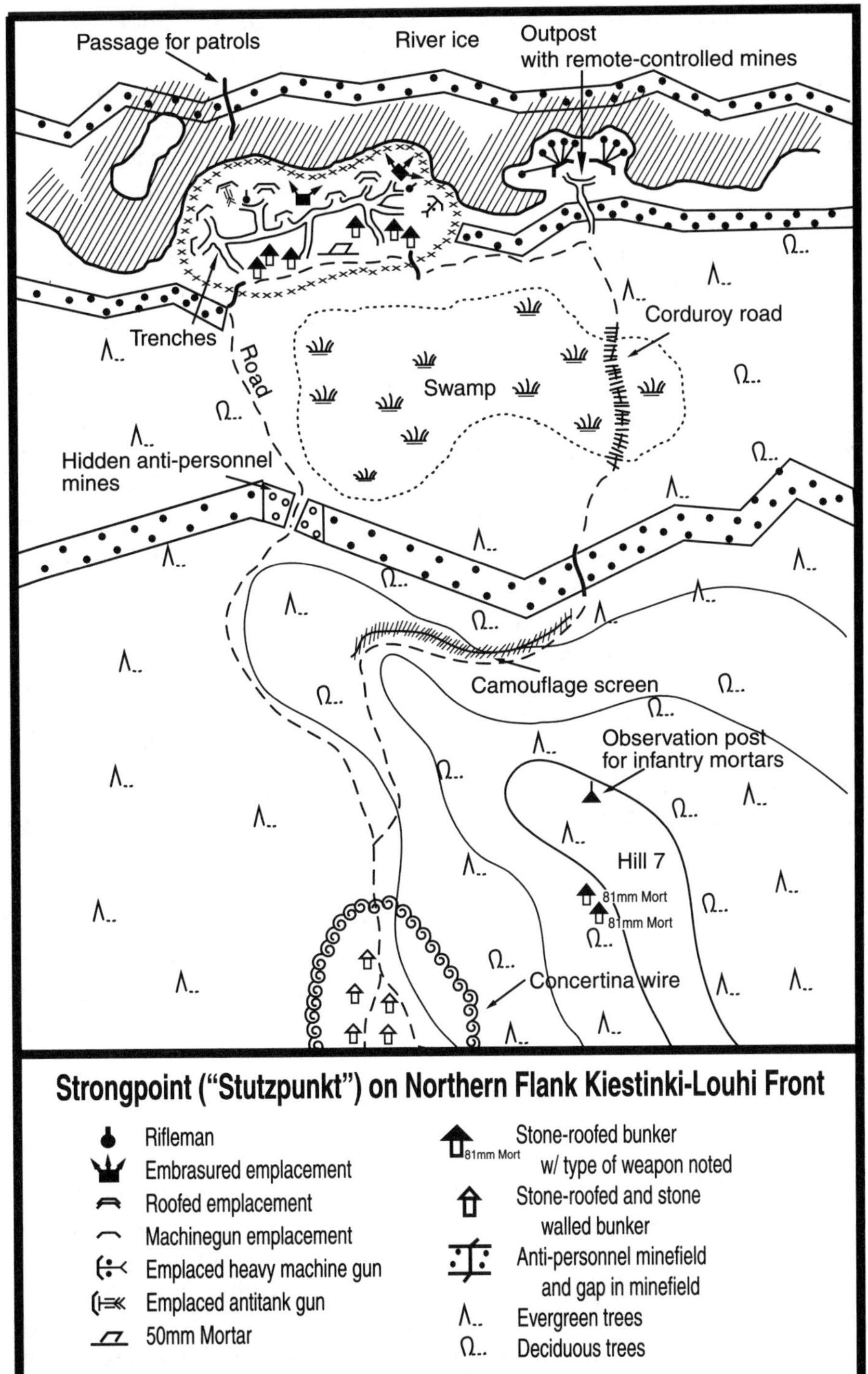


**Strongpoint ("Stutzpunkt") on Northern Flank Kiestinki-Louhi Front**

At daybreak, the Reds came again, with another 200 men, but these were pinned down and halted in the gathering light, this time by a cross-fire created by two heavy machine guns firing from a couple of the intact bunkers. A counterattack by a reserve platoon from the reconnaissance battalion at SennOzero (six kilometers to the south) broke the Soviet momentum. *NORD* elements took twenty-four Soviet prisoners, including the commander of the assaulting battalion. The attackers left ninety-one men KIA on the field, as well as many weapons including, interestingly, forty-two US-made submachine guns! *NORD* losses included only three KIA and five severely wounded; the latter were picked up by hydroplane and evacuated across the lake to the aid station.[32]

On 10 June, the Soviet Army started a new major offensive against the main Finnish front in southern Ladoga-Karelia, which caused a new political crisis in Finland. The political and military leaders in Berlin had to earnestly consider the possibility of losing Finland through the conclusion of a separate armistice with the USSR. Both *Generaloberst* Dietl of *20th Mountain Army "Lapland"* and General Eglseer, the commanding general of *XVIII Mountain Corps*, flew to Germany for conferences regarding this serious situation which might endanger the entire German military presence in Finland. After conclusion of the talks, their plane crashed on the return flight in the vicinity of Salzburg, and both generals lost their lives.[33] In the wake of this tragedy for German arms, *Generaloberst* Lothar Rendulic, former commander of the *Second Panzer Army* during counterpartisan operations in the Balkans, assumed command of the *20th Army* on 28 June in Rovaniemi; *XVIII Mountain Corps* was taken over by *Generalleutnant* Friedrich Hochbaum, the distinguished former commander of the *34th Infantry Division* in the Ukraine.

At the summer solstice on 21 June 1944, *SS-Mountain Infantry Regiment 12* received the title *"Michael Gaißmair,"* in recognition of the large number of ethnic Germans in the unit (Gaißmair was a sixteenth-century Germanic South Tyrolean folk leader). From this point on, all members of the regiment wore the name emblazoned in silver-gray thread on a 30mm-wide black strip of synthetic silk on the lower left sleeve.

Just a few days after the bestowal of this honorific, and in conjunction with the Soviet offensive in southern Finland, elements of *NORD* joined in the battle of SennOzero. An attack by the better part of three Soviet divisions (the entire 205th Rifle Division, and parts of the 83d and 367th Divisions) was spearheaded by three crack independent ski battalions (1st, 83d, and 364th).

These overwhelming enemy forces overran strongpoints of *SS-Reconnaissance Battalion NORD* and *SS-Ski Battalion "Norge"* on the extreme left flank of the division. It quickly became obvious that the attack on our positions at ShapkOzero in March had been a reconnaissance-in-force, testing the strength and extent of our defenses in this area. After overrunning and eliminating the German strongholds in the north, there did not seem to be anything to prevent the Soviets from reaching the only German supply route for the Kiestinki Front, and even the Finnish border region of Kuusamo. Aerial reconnaissance reported that the Soviets were constructing a new supply route from the Murmansk Railway through the dense forests, to the west, at a rate of almost one kilometer per day.

As a result of other aerial reconnaissance, both *NORD* and *XVIII Mountain Corps* had alerted their reserves in time. Division *NORD* quickly dispatched SS-*Motorized Rifle Battalion 6*, under the command of *Hauptsturmführer* Gottlieb Renz, and *Corps* sent its reserve, the *Ski Battalion 82* (an organic battalion of the *7th Mountain Division*, comprised mostly of Austrians), under *Hauptmann* K. W. Lapp. After many days of vicious fighting, including some that was literally hand-to-hand, these grossly outnumbered forces were able to clear up the difficult situation. Both battalion commanders won the Knights' Cross (*Ritterkreuz*) for their actions.

The *3d Battalion* of *SS-Mountain Infantry Regiment 12* at that time constituted the regimental reserve, and was located in a position some twenty kilometers south of SennOzero. The battalion was ordered to relieve the worn out *SS-Motorized Rifle Battalion* in place near SennOzero in mid-July, after the Soviet attacks had slackened somewhat. The men of the *3d Battalion* marched to the southern shore of SennOzero, opposite the former fishing village of the same name. Partly concealed by fog, they ferried across under Soviet heavy machine-gun fire in assault boats manned by brave crews from the division's combat engineer battalion.

The relief took place as intended, with the companies of the *3d Battalion* taking over the hotly contested emplacements and trenches of the defending motorized battalion. During the next three weeks, supplies came in only by air and parachute, as Soviet forces were still strong enough to effectively seal off all German units near SennOzero from supply by land.[34] Life was also made more difficult for the Germans in this battle by a simple, but highly effective Soviet organizational development. During the fighting near SennOzero, the Soviets began brigading their 82mm and 120mm mortars from their infantry units together to form independent mortar regiments. These units were devastatingly effective, as they could move and concentrate fires in the thickly-vegetated terrain much more quickly than field artillery.

During the first days of August, the *3d Battalion* was ordered to leave two of its line companies (*12th* and *13th*) in a defensive posture at SennOzero, and with the battalion-minus, consisting of the remaining line company, the

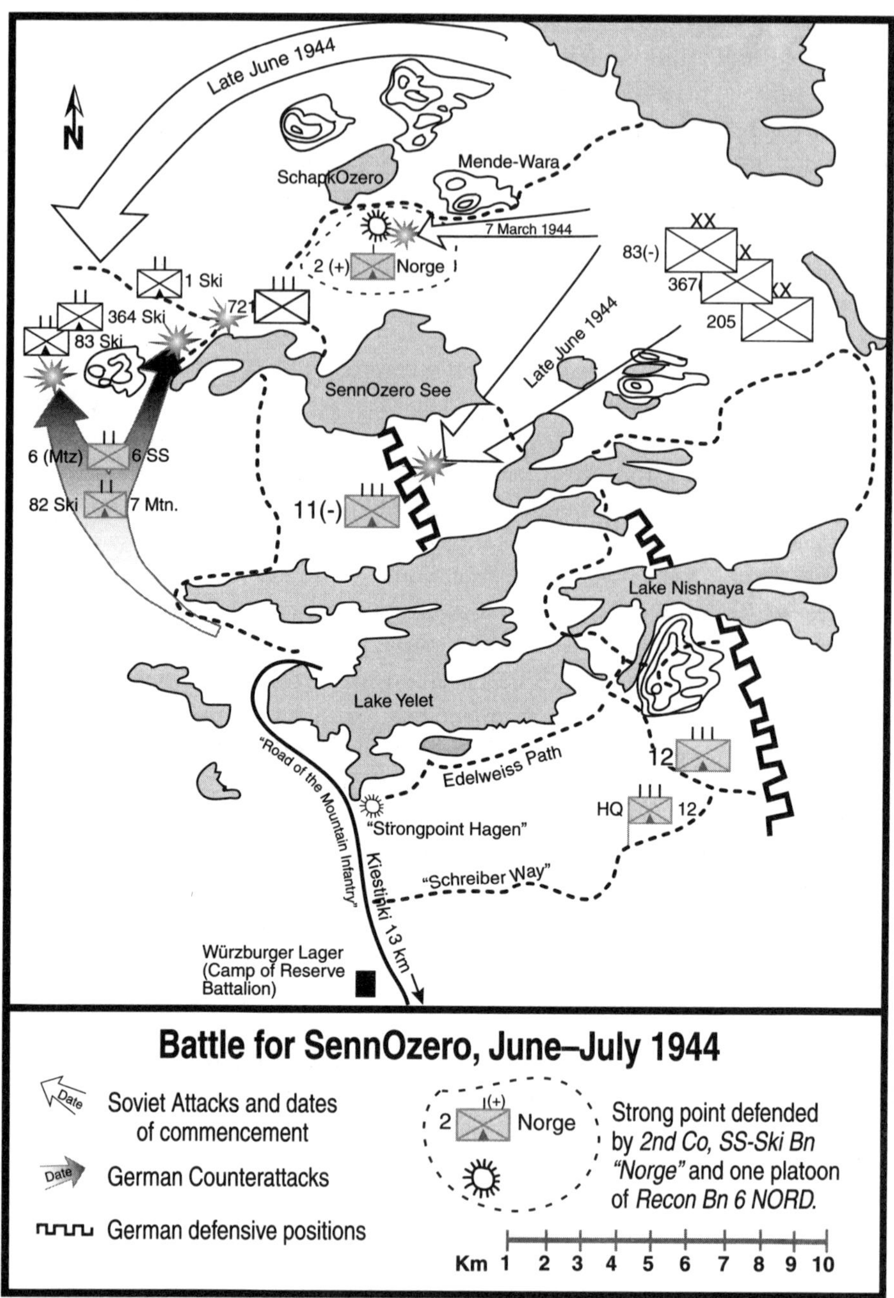


**Battle for SennOzero, June–July 1944**

heavy machine-gun company, the headquarters company, which included the heavy mortar, engineer and signal platoons, to take over the defense of "the most prestigious position" of all defensive works on this front, namely, the

Road Position. After a thirty-two-kilometer march all the way back to Kiestinki, and then an additional eighteen kilometers on the Kiestinki-Louhi road, the battalion arrived at the almost mystical place where the German/Finnish offensive had stalled in 1941. It was fortified against all conceivable attacks.* The battalion-minus retained responsibility for the defense of the Road Position for the next three weeks—until the commencement of Operation *BIRKE* (English: BIRCH) on 6 September.

Some sections of the Kiestinki-Louhi road that lay just behind the MLR were under enemy observation. To hide friendly traffic in these areas, long ranks of sawn-off trees were suspended along and across the road. To achieve a similar effect at the battalion command post (about 300 meters behind the MLR), continuous fires were set, using moist twigs and bushes; the resultant thick smoke obscured our activities from Soviet eyes.

A special war was fought by both sides in and around the Road Position—a propaganda war. Using powerful amplifiers and large loudspeakers, each side tried to convince the other that their cause was lost, and surrender was the best option. The German side employed skillful propaganda troops, former Soviet prisoners of war (often Ukrainians and other "Soviet peoples" oppressed by the Stalin regime) who volunteered to fight as part of the "Free Russian Army" of former Soviet General Vlasov. The Soviets did much the same thing, using German prisoners who had joined the "National Committee of a Free Germany" (*Nationalkomitee Freies Deutschland*, or *NFD*), a group of a few genuine German socialists and a lot of opportunistic turncoats. Ironically, some of the more prominent members of the *NFD* included *Field Marshal* Friedrich von Paulus, former Commander of the *6th Army*, destroyed at Stalingrad on 1943, and *AOK Norwegen*'s own Erich Buschenhagen, former chief of staff to *Generaloberst* von Falkenhorst!

Both sides' propaganda broadcasts were basically ineffective, but were useful for keeping sentries awake at night.

During the *3d Battalion's* defense of the Road Position, *Generaloberst* Rendulic appeared one day with his small entourage, as well as the corps and division commanders, to inspect the positions, familiarize himself, and receive situation briefings. His conduct of the familiarization tour—personal bearing, questions asked, comments made, and so on—indicated that he was competent and likable. Of course, he had huge shoes (or mountain boots!) to fill, replacing Eduard Dietl.

*On the day of departure from the SennOzero position, the commanding officer of the *3d Battalion, Hauptsturmführer* Walter Jensen, received some forty mortar shell fragment wounds in the rear portion of the body, and had to be evacuated. His adjutant, the author, was ordered to lead the battalion-minus to its new destination at the Road Position.

## *Operation BIRKE: Withdrawal Without Defeat*

A momentous event occurred on the morning of 7 September. A young officer from division headquarters presented himelf at the battalion command post (CP) with a large, fat, brown envelope, the receipt of which required a signature. Its contents were the detailed plans for the withdrawal of the entire division, with specific orders for the *3d Battalion, SS-Mountain Infantry Regiment 12*. Effective immediately—meaning that very night.

This was the start of Operation *BIRKE*. Its details had been worked out during the summer in anticipation of a possible Finnish-Soviet separate armistice.[35] The general plan called for a complete withdrawal of all German forces from the four front sections between Uhtua and the Arctic Ocean and, subsequently, from northern Finland to Norway. This plan had been assembled on the assumption that the position of the *20th Mountain Army "Lapland"* would be untenable should the Finns and Soviets conclude a separate armistice.

The plan's authors envisioned a phased withdrawal of the three German corps in the theater, beginning in the south with *XVIII Mountain Corps* from Uhtua to Kiestinki, followed by the divisions of the *XXXVI Corps* from the Verman sector, and, lastly, the troops of the *XIX Mountain Corps* from the Arctic Ocean sector.

For this major operation, only two narrow roads were available! The "border road" on the Finnish side of its border with Sweden, from Muonio to the Norwegian border at Kilpisjärvi, was earmarked for the use of *XVIII Mountain Corps*. The road reserved for the other two corps' use was the *Reichstraße* 50, the Norwegian coastal road that ran from Kirkenes in the east all along and parallel to the Arctic Ocean's coast, later in a southwesterly direction. This route was interrupted by many fjords, which could only be crossed by ferry. Eventually, it was joined by the Finnish-Swedish border road north of Kilpisjärvi, namely at Skibotn, on the southern tip of the Lyngen Fjord. A new branch road had been constructed from Ivalo (in Finland) via Karasjok to Lakselv (in Norway), where it met *Reichstraße* 50, in anticipation of its need during Operation *BIRKE*.

The leaders at *OKW* and *20th Mountain Army "Lapland"* headquarters were fully aware of the risks connected with Operation *BIRKE*. The risks only became greater as the year wore on, as neither road was "winterproof."

Operation *BIRKE* was, although a withdrawal when in contact with the enemy, a high-risk operation, even without enemy action. The German General Staff had to take into account the possibility that, upon commencement of the Finnish-Soviet ceasefire, all available Red Army units would converge on the northern Karelian/Lapland front to smash the only enemy left in the theater, namely the German *20th Mountain Army*! The staff had to

## Operation *BIRKE* (BIRCH)—The German Withdrawal Through Finland, September–October 1944

Finnish/Soviet Border before the Winter War and from July 1941–15 September 1944

Finnish/Soviet Border until 15 September 1944

Finnish/Soviet Border after 15 September 1944

Route of Withdrawal of *XXXVI Mountain Corps* (*163rd* and *169th Infantry Divisions and supporting units*)

Route of Withdrawal of *XVIII Mountain Corps* (*6th SS and 7th Mountain Divisions; Division Group Kräutler*, and supporting units)

Route of Withdrawal of *XIX Mountain Corps* (*3rd and 6th Mountain Divisions; 210th Infantry Division; Division Group van der Hoop;* and supporting units)

Major Finnish towns occupied by Soviets after withdrawal of German forces take into account the possibility that the Soviets might even violate the new Finnish neutrality, and thrust across the "waist" of Finland (between Suomussalmi and Tornio) to seize the Swedish iron ore fields at Kiruna-Gällivare, which still supplied the German war industry.

Lastly, the General Staff had to calculate how long our heretofore comrades-in-arms, the co-members of our *Waffenbruderschaft*, would remain on friendly terms with the withdrawing German forces. Would the Germans fight just one enemy on their way out, or two?

Unbeknownst to the *NORD Gebirgsjäger* at the time, the answer lay in the details and tone of the armistice agreement. It was concluded between the government of the Soviet Union, *et al.*, and the Finnish government in Moscow on 19 September 1944. It included two articles in particular which, in the near future, would govern Finnish behavior regarding the withdrawing German units.

Article 2 stipulated that Finland had to "disarm the German . . . forces which remained in Finland *after 15 September 1944*," and to "hand over their personnel to the Allied (Soviet) High Command as prisoners of war, *in which task the Soviet government will assist the Finnish Army*."* [Emphasis in this and the next two paragraphs by the author.] Of course, withdrawing the over 200,000 German soldiers in Finland between 6 and 15 September while at the same time fighting against the Soviets near the Finnish border between 6 and 15 September was impossible, and everyone knew it!

According to Article 22, an "Allied Control Commission" was to be established which would "undertake . . . the control of the execution of the present Agreement under . . . the Allied (Soviet) high Command, *acting on behalf of the Allied powers*."

An Annex to Article 22 stipulated that the "chief task of the Control Commission" was "to see to the punctual and accurate fulfillment by the Finnish Government of Article 2." Furthermore, in paragraph 5 of this Annex, it said that "Control Commission may through its officers make the *necessary investigations and the collection of information*."

Obviously, the Armistice Agreement was the tool of the Soviet Army to tie the hands of the Finnish government, and force the Finnish Army into a course it might otherwise not have taken. Over the next several weeks, events would take a turn unimaginable by the men of *NORD* before that grim September.

*It is interesting to note that Colonel General A. A. Zhdanov signed this agreement not only on behalf of the government of the USSR, but also for the United Kingdom. Furthermore, both governments were "acting on behalf of the United Nations at war with Finland."

The companies of the *3d Battalion, SS-Mountain Infantry Regiment 12* evacuated the famous Road Position in the dark of the earliest morning hours of 8 September 1944. All equipment that could not be carried had been evacuated to the rear three weeks before; nothing was left to fall into the hands of the Soviets. Further, entrances to most bunkers had been booby-trapped in anticipation of their arrival.

To mask the battalion's departure, normal radio traffic was maintained, and the lines thinned by a platoon at a time. The forward observers called for and adjusted routine artillery harassment and interdiction fires, fired by the *Artillery Regiment NORD.*

After the last rifle platoon had withdrawn in the early morning hours, the battalion's *Pioneer* (engineer) platoon remained behind to fire one last salvo before destroying the launchers for the formidable "Divebombers on Foot," short-range (1,000 meters!), super-heavy rockets of 280mm and 320mm caliber. Although the Reds didn't realize it, it was the battalion's Parthian shot to our Soviet enemies. The engineers then hurried to catch up with the battalion as it marched back to the crossroads at Kiestinki. There, the *12th* and *13th Companies*, which had remained at SennOzero, linked up with the battalion-minus to once again unite the *3d Battalion* under a unified command. After uneventfully occupying the first fallback positions during the daylight hours of 9 September, at 1900, the battalion continued its withdrawal. Oddly, there was no Soviet pursuit initially, nor harassment by partisans along the road.

During the night of 9–10 September, the battalion marched back to the west bank of the Sohjana River, where a major fallback bastion, the "*Bollwerk-Stellung,*" had been prepared for *XVIII Mountain Corps* units during the summer. With each flank anchored on huge lakes (Pää in the north and Tuoppa in the south), this position was immensely strong, relying as it did on the two natural barriers. It was already occupied by our sister regiment, *SS-Mountain Infantry Regiment 11.* They were tasked to be the rearguard for all *XVIII Mountain Corps* units on the rest of the way to the Finnish frontier, which still lay seventy kilometers to the west. In this capacity, the "*Reinhard Heydrich*" *Regiment* later (from 13 September) absorbed the impact of the pursuit of the Soviet Twenty-Sixth Army, and actually had to fight its way out of an encirclement near Suvanto, only fifteen kilometers from the Finnish frontier. Numerous casualties were sustained, including the deaths of some key leaders, such as *Sturmbannführer* Hans-Heinz Küchle, the Division *Ia* (operations officer, equivalent to the US Army's G-3).

The *3d Battalion, SS-Mountain Infantry Regiment 12* continued its march on the morning of 10 September, and crossed the Finnish frontier two days later, still unhampered by Soviet military activity. Here, at Kuusamo, it was met by parts of its service elements, which had supported operations from that Finnish border town during the combat echelons' action at the front. Here also, the officers received horses for riding during the upcoming long march back to Norway. They came in handy for checking the order in the column, but the officers generally marched with the men. Along with the rest of the *SS-Mountain Infantry Regiment 12*, the *3d Battalion* remained in and around Kuusamo for the next two weeks. The town was deserted, its civilian inhabitants having been evacuated to other locations in Finland prior to the arrival of the bulk of the withdrawing German units.

During this time, the battalion conducted reconnaissance patrols to the south to contact elements of the *7th Mountain Division*, which was withdrawing from the Uhtua sector. When not conducting patrols, the battalion's rifle companies occupied make-shift positions on both sides of the main road into Kuusamo from the south, about fifteen kilometers south of the town. Eventually, the *7th Mountain Division* linked up and passed through the *3d Battalion*'s positions, and on 26 September, the battalion moved out, leaving the town completely intact.* The *3d Battalion* was the tail unit of the last regiment of the rear division of the last/southernmost corps (*XVIII Mountain Corps*) during the withdrawal through Finland! The battalion would remain the corps rear guard for the next 430 kilometers, all the way to Muonio, which it reached on 29 October.

The *3d Battalion*'s first halt after leaving Kuusamo was the isthmus south of Lake Yli-Kitka, east of Posio. One rifle platoon had been left near Kuusamo to monitor the arrival of the Soviets, and after sighting their arrival on the afternoon of 27 September, it moved quickly to rejoin the battalion. Elements of the Red Army stayed in Kuusamo until November 1944, and completely burned down the town upon their departure. In this regard, Kuusamo shared the same fate as other Finnish border towns.[36]

A few days later, the battalion marched further westward toward Rovaniemi, the capital of Finnish Lapland. October had arrived, and with it, the first snows of winter. The battalion turned off the main road to Rovaniemi sixty kilometers shy of the town, and marched south for forty kilometers until

*Anticipating that the Soviets would occupy Kuusamo, the commander of *SS-Mountain Infantry Regiment 12*, *Standartenführer* Franz Schreiber, ordered his engineers to remove the bells from the steeple of the seventeenth-century Lutheran church, and bury them nearby. One of them, a bronze and silver monster weighing 525 kilos, was a gift of the Swedish King, in 1698; the other, smaller one was a gift to the parish dating from 1721. The engineers made a precise sketch of the location of the precious artifacts. In 1959, with the sketch in hand, Schreiber revisited Kuusamo with a group of *NORD* veterans, and directed local Finnish authorities to the burial site, near the church built to replace the one destroyed by the Soviets in 1944. The bells were undisturbed, and were soon mounted in the new steeple. (Schreiber, 435) it reached a region naturally favorable for the establishment of a security position to cover the withdrawal of *XXXVI Corps* coming from Salla.

With the 15 September pullout deadline long past, the officers and soldiers of the Finnish Army had ceased friendly relations with the departing German troops of *20th Mountain Army "Lapland."* Under the strict control of the Soviet officer watchdogs of the "Allied Control Commission," which had arrived at every Finnish division and regimental headquarters, the Finns had to prove their complete separation from the German Army. Without this distance, the Finns knew only too well that the Soviets would gladly use the codicil of the Armistice Agreement which authorized them to "assist the Finnish Government in their plight to intern all German troops that were still on Finnish soil" to justify a large-scale invasion of Finland. But mere separation and a cessation of cooperation were not to prove satisfactory to the Soviet "observers." The Soviets demanded much more *active* measures to demonstrate Finnish compliance with the Armistice requirements. We were soon to divine the reasons for the lack of Soviet pursuit or harassment during the withdrawal from Karelia!*

After *XXXVI Corps* passed through the town of Kemijärvi on their way to the Arctic Ocean Highway, the battalion resumed its march to Rovaniemi. Arriving in the eastern outskirts on 12 October, the men of the *3d Battalion* enjoyed a day's respite in a German camp, which had been established years earlier to accommodate soldiers on their way to or from the front.

The entire *3d Battalion* arrived in Rovaniemi in the early afternoon of 14 October. The town, which normally boasted 3,000 civilian inhabitants, had already been evacuated, and many of its wooden structures were ablaze when the battalion marched in. An ammunition train standing in the siding at the railroad station had exploded several hours before the battalion's arrival, whipping not only shrapnel from mortar and artillery ammunition throughout the town, but igniting large stores of pyrotechnic signals (flares and illumination rounds) as well. In a huge show of fireworks, the burning phosphorus munitions scattered throughout wooden buildings in Rovaniemi, and flames swiftly engulfed the town.*

*Contrary to the apprehensions of *Generaloberst* Rendulic and his staff—but in line with Finnish predictions and fears—Soviet units halted their advance upon reaching and occupying Finnish border towns. It has been suggested by historians, such as the prominent Finnish military historian Sampo Ahto, that Stalin himself crafted this plan: He desired that it be the *Finns* who chased the Germans from Finland, to forever sever the bonds of comradeship built during the previous three years as allies! Citing the Soviet source Karelski Front, *Manfred Menger* (op.cit., 229) stresses the fact that the "Supreme Headquarters" (meaning Stalin) quickly discarded the planning of the Soviets' Karelian Front Commander to use the combined Red 19th and Twenty-Sixth Armies in an assault against the exposed southern flank of the *20th Mountain Army*, for precisely this reason.

It was getting dark when a frantic colonel from *XVIII Mountain Corps* appeared at the battalion tactical command post. The concussion from the huge explosion had literally blown the demolition charges off the Kemijoki Bridge, five kilometers away. Combat engineers from the *7th Mountain Division* were hurriedly fastening new charges to the structure, but the first Finnish troops (infantrymen of Major Lounila's 5th Light Infantry Battalion, or *Jakeri Pattaljon* 5) were approaching rapidly from the south!

The colonel, *Oberst* Schuler, had been charged by *General* Hochbaum of *XVIII Mountain Corps* with the responsibility of destroying the bridge before the Finns could use it in their mounting pursuit. Unfortunately for him, Schuler had no security troops to fend off interference by the Finns; they had long since left Rovaniemi and were already well down the road north on the Arctic Ocean Highway.

*Oberst* Schuler asked that our *3d Battalion* provide two rifle companies for security on the south side of the bridge, and the *12th* and *13th Companies* were

*Sampo Ahto, *Aseveljet Vastakkain-Lapin Sota, 1944–1945* (*Brothers-in-Arms Fight Each Other–The Lappland War, 1944–1945*) (Helsinki: Kirjayhtymä, 1980), 250f. See also Ahto, lecture on the Lappland War for German veterans on 11 May 1995 in SallaTunturi, Finland (reprinted in *NORD Ruf* no. 62, March 1997, p.10); Lothar Rendulic, *Gekämpft, gesiegt, geschlagen* (Heidelberg: Wels, 1952), 306; Roland Kaltenegger, *Schicksalweg und Kampf der "Bergschuh-Division" (7. Gebirgs-Division)* (Stuttgart: Graz, 1995), 318; Schreiber, 303ff.

Other than the *debâcle* at Salla, there has only been one other stain on the honor of *NORD*. For many years following the Second World War, the division stood falsely accused of torching Rovaniemi. After all, it was the last unit to pass through Rovaniemi . . .who else could have done it? Soviet control commissioners leapt at the opportunity to show neutral nations' journalists an example of "German barbarity," and ensured them full access to the smoking ruins of Rovaniemi. In turn, the journalists themselves were equally quick to tell the world of another example of the criminality of the German Armed Forces—and not only German, but *Waffen-SS* at that! Although *NORD* members vehemently denied their complicity, three factors mitigated against widespread acceptance of their claims:

1. Undeniable instances of similar atrocities by *other Waffen-SS* units elsewhere;
2. The absence of Soviet Army units in the vicinity, and the ridiculousness of the idea that Finns would do such a thing to their own property; and
3. The nearly impossible requirement to prove a negative—that they did *not* do it.

Fortunately for the surviving members of *NORD* (and the memories of those who had passed on), vindicating evidence came to light more than fifty-two years after the tragedy at Rovaniemi. In the spate of veterans' publications in connection to the fiftieth anniversary of the war's end, Erkki Kerojärvi, a former Finnish Army sergeant, finally explained the genesis of the incident. In his memoirs, *Vedin Miekalla Paasikiven Linja* (*I Defended Paasikivi's Line With the Sword*) (Helsinki: Omakirja Oy, Hämeenlinna 1989), he explains that his commando unit infiltrated into Rovaniemi on 13 October 1944, and destroyed the German ammunition train on the siding at the station. In explicit detail, Kerojärvi conveys the full story of the destruction of train, and its unintended consequences for the buildings in Rovaniemi.

dispatched for this purpose. They took up positions on both sides of the bridge embankment, and before long, were engaged in a firefight to hold off the Finnish 5th Light Infantry Battalion.

For three hours, Germans and Finns exchanged shots, while the engineers finished re-rigging the Kemijoki bridge for demolition. Numerous small detachments from the *7th Mountain Division*, of squad and platoon size, streamed across the bridge in the meantime, mere meters ahead of the pursuing Finns. Shortly after 2100 hours, the *12th* and *13th Companies* were ordered to withdraw across the bridge. They stormed back across the 500-meter span, in a hail of small arms fire, with the Finns at their heels. The moment the last German soldier reported on the north bank, the order was given to the engineers to push the plunger on the firing device—the bridge blew up at 2132 hours![37] Miraculously, no Germans were lost in the action.

With the elimination of the bridge, the imminent danger of pursuit across the wide stream also disappeared. Nevertheless, as the corps rear guard, the *3d Battalion* took up positions on both sides of the road to Muonio during the night of 14–15 October. Sure enough, a Finnish reconnaissance patrol was detected and repulsed during the night, and the battalion continued its march on the afternoon of 15 October.

From this point, a few kilometers north of Rovaniemi, the battalion would be marching in regions north of the Arctic Circle. Only after the first week in December did the unit recross the Circle going south.

Somewhere along the line, we passed a deserted German supply depot. A hasty reconnaissance yielded the astonishing news that its stock included goods of unheard-of quality: French cognacs and other liquors; canned smoked hams; and chocolates—a truly fantastic sight! Every man could take what he wanted, with the understanding that he carried what he took. Smart ones took "Milkmaid," a high-fat sugar-sweetener cream for coffee. It provided much-needed calories for the demands of the march and the toll of the weather, and camouflaged the bitterness of the ersatz coffee in the bargain!

Someone posited that this bewildering collection of goodies must have been a *Luftwaffe* food distribution point. *Reichsmarschall* Hermann Göring, commander in chief of the *Luftwaffe*, was known to lavish luxuries on his pilots [although after mid-1944, he mainly lavished abuse on his *Jagdwaffe* (Fighter Arm) pilots], and these supplies may have been stockpiled for use by *Luftwaffe* crews who were attacking the Murmansk convoys.

As the corps rear guard, the *3d Battalion* had to adjust its rate of march in accordance with the progress of the myriad units in front of it. The village of Kittilä was reached on 20 October, and the weary marchers got another day's rest until the large number of German units there continued their movement on the next day.

After passing the abandoned town of Sirkka, formerly the home to a Finnish Army school for forest warfare techniques as well as commandos, the *3d Battalion* reached the isthmus between Lakes Jervisjärvi and Äkäsjärvi. This natural defensive boundary, 210 kilometers north of Rovaniemi, became the site of a *3d Battalion* security position for the next two days, oriented east and south toward the following Finns.

The now-hostile Finns had been following a little *too* closely. There had been a skirmish with an overly-curious Finnish patrol, and it was learned from interrogating a Finnish prisoner that the pursuing forces were from General Heiskanen's 11th Division. On the second day on the isthmus, 28 October, a Finnish patrol was sighted, but seemed to want nothing more than to maintain visual contact with the German rear guard. We left them undisturbed.

At noon on the same day, the *3d Battalion* began the last leg of its mission as the corps rear guard, a thirty-kilometer march to Muonio. Soon after assuming its customary march order, small arms fire could be heard ahead of the column. As we approached the road junction at Särkijärvi, where the road to Pallastunturi turns off to the northeast, we were met by our supply trains, which had been sent ahead. They had been ambushed by Finnish troops not three kilometers northwest of the junction, on their way to Muonio, and had sustained our regiment's first casualties in Finland. Among them was *Obersturmführer* von Hallasch, the commanding officer of the *2d Battalion*'s *6th Company*, which had been ambushed with our supply trains and cut off from its parent battalion. Clearly, our former allies had leapt ahead of our rear guard column, and could be expected to give further resistance later.

Darkness enveloped the battlefield, although it was only 1400 hours. The march was resumed, this time with the rifle companies leading. Less than an hour later, furious Finnish small arms fire stonewalled the advance. An estimate of the enemy situation revealed strong enemy forces (2d and 3d Battalions of the Finnish 50th Infantry Regiment of the 11th Infantry Division) in positions on a commanding wooded ridge that stood astride the Muonio road at right angles. In front of their position was a stretch of tundra, or open, frozen swamp.

The company commanders and battalion staff gathered for a conference behind a massive rock on the right side of the road, which provided cover and concealment.* This was the plan of action:

✱ Approach Phase:

—*13th Company* advances to the edge of the swamp on the right of the road.

*Since the battalion commander was temporarily incapacitated, the company commanders "appointed" the battalion adjutant (the author) to coordinate the combat.

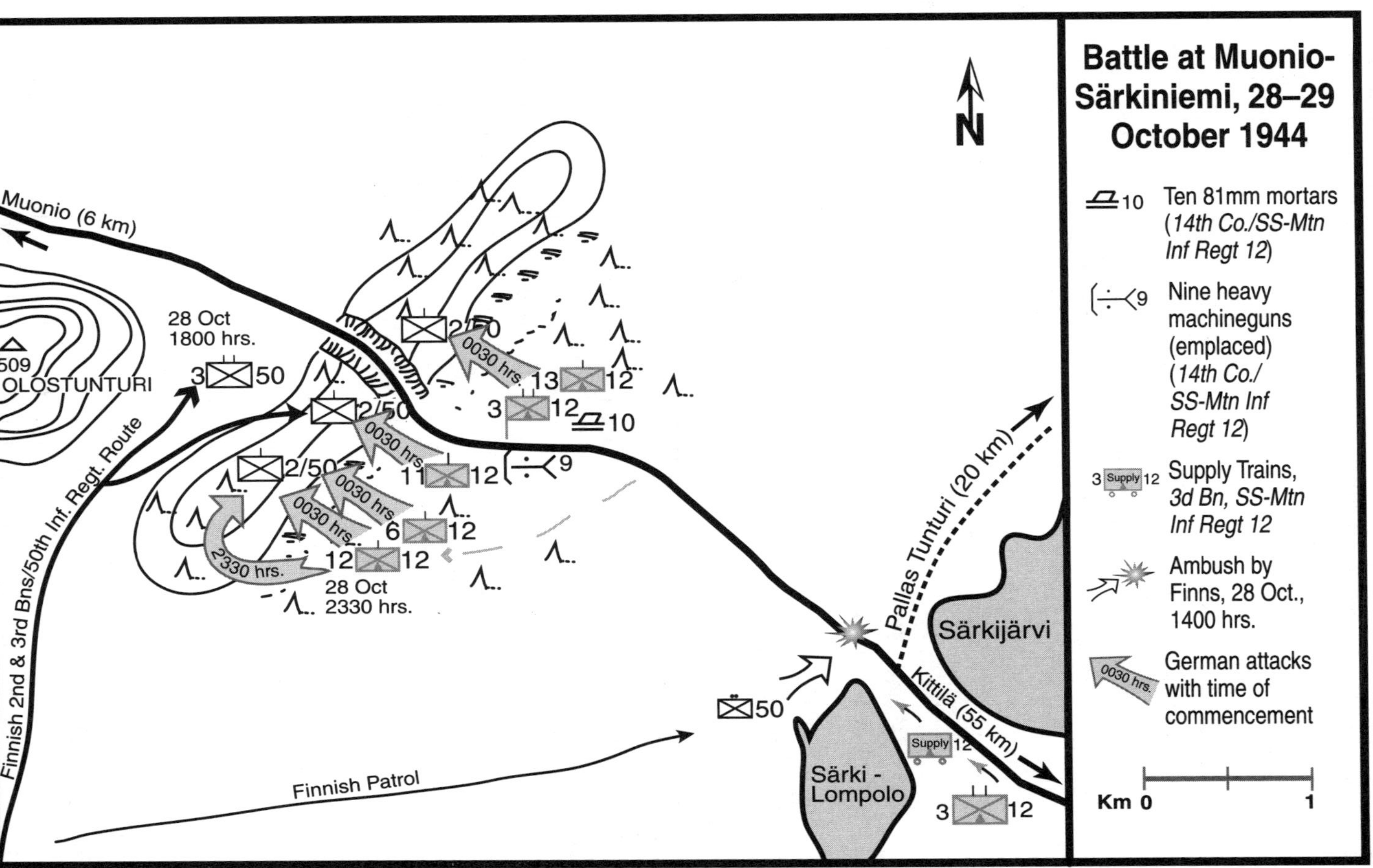
Battle at Muonio-Särkiniemi, 28–29 October 1944
Ten 81mm mortars (14th Co./SS-Mtn Inf Regt 12)
Nine heavy machineguns (emplaced) (14th Co./ SS-Mtn Inf Regt 12)
Supply Trains, 3d Bn, SS-Mtn Inf Regt 12
Ambush by Finns, 28 Oct., 1400 hrs.
German attacks with time of commencement
0030 hrs.
Km 0
1
N
Muonio (6 km)
509
OLOSTUNTURI
28 Oct 1800 hrs.
Finnish 2nd & 3rd Bns/50th Inf. Regt. Route
2330 hrs.
28 Oct 2330 hrs.
Pallas Tunturi (20 km)
Särkijärvi
Kittilä (55 km)
Särki - Lompolo
Supply
Finnish Patrol

*6th* and *11th Companies* advance to the edge of the swamp on the left.

*14th Company,* with its heavy machine guns and the battalion's ten 81mm mortars, takes up positions on the road itself, behind a bend to conceal their location.
*12th Company* stealthily swings wide to the left, orienting on approaching the enemy's right flank obliquely from its right.

* Supporting Attack Phase: On contact, *12th Company* opens fire, distracting the enemy from the main attack to come.

* Main Attack Phase:
Heavy weapons open fire to suppress the enemy with heavy machine-gun and mortar fire, and thereby support the line companies' assault.

*6th, 11th,* and *13th Companies* attack the distracted Finns on both sides of the road, driving them from the ridge.

The attack came off pretty much as planned. *12th Company* made contact around midnight, about 1,500 meters to the left of the road, and turned the Finnish flank, forcing them to focus on their right. The other three rifle companies then attacked the Finnish front, supported by the battalion's heavy machine guns and mortars, only 100 meters behind the battalion tactical command post.

The "Battle of Muonio" is well documented by the Finnish historian Sampo Ahto,

> It is impossible for an outsider to comprehend the fury of the combat on that October night at Särkiniemi, and what degree of tactical leadership was required. The result is known: The Finnish Battalion [2d Battalion, 50th Infantry Regiment], commanded by Major Manninen, who was wounded in the battle, had to fall back during the daring and bold attack of the Germans.[38]

In a three-hour fight in the arctic darkness, the reinforced *3d Battalion, SS-Mountain Infantry Regiment 12* attacked and routed two infantry battalions from an imposing blocking position. After witnessing the retreat of the 2d Battalion, the 3d Battalion of the Finnish 50th Infantry Regiment fell back as well, to the west. The 50th Regiment's 1st Battalion, the regimental reserve, did not participate in the battle.

At first light, patrols reported back that the Finnish positions were deserted. The road to Muonio was open.

There had been casualties on both sides. The official Finnish account claims their losses to be 27 KIA and 105 WIA. The wounded had to be manually carried a grueling thirty kilometers cross-country by their comrades—no small feat for even the freshest troops! German losses amounted to 12 KIA and 40 WIA. These were carried to a truck for transport to Muonio, now only six kilometers away. Among the wounded was the commanding officer of the *12th Company*, *Obersturmführer* Schindler, who had led the key supporting attack which unhinged the Finnish right flank and opened the front to the main blow. He has been shot through the scrotum.*

At daylight on 29 October, the weary men of the reinforced *3d Battalion* resumed their march to Muonio. On the way, *Stardartenführer* Schreiber, the regimental commander, stayed at the roadside to greet them. He wanted to personally congratulate and commend his *3d Battalion* soldiers who had so successfully broken through the Finnish encirclement. When the battalion commander rendered his report and salute, Schreiber took his Iron Cross 1st Class off his own tunic, and fastened it the tunic of the battalion commander, as a token of esteem for the entire battalion. In turn, we were immensely proud of our commander's commendation.

After a night's rest just north of Muonio, which was separated from neutral Sweden only by the Muonio River, the *3d Battalion* prepared to continue its march north for another 200 kilometers to the Finnish-Norwegian border. For the first time in thirty-four days, it was released from its responsibilities as rear guard of the *XVIII Mountain Corps*, a mission it had conducted without flaw. We were ready to move on to whatever the war might hold for us. But before the day's march began, there was a distressing incident which we later realized was a harbinger of the course of the war elsewhere.

The route we were to follow continued straight north, with the border river MuonionJoki always immediately on the left. In most places, the river was frozen over across its entire 400-meter breadth. In anticipation of the "temptations" this geographical situation might present, an order came down from Corps which leaders were required to read to every soldier before departing Muonio. In dire terms, it warned against attempts to desert to Sweden, and further, heaped injury upon insult with a threat of reprisals against the *families* of anyone who deserted. We were shocked and affronted by this needless and baffling intimidation: No one in the division would even seriously *consider* deserting his comrades! It was a sour and disheartening counterpoint to the pride we had felt just the day before.

The scenery became more classically arctic day by day. While the temperature had been below freezing for some weeks already, now the snows began.

*Although *Obersturmführer* Schindler survived the wound, he did not survive the war. Returning to resume command of his company on Christmas Day, he was killed by a direct hit on his fighting position by an American mortar round during the second day of combat against the Americans in the Vosges.

The vegetation also became sparser. While during the first few days, one could count on finding plenty of trees to provide long poles for the tents, soon the trees disappeared, replaced only be scrub bushes. One had to carry tent poles along the rest of the way.

The march proceeded without incident. The daily distance was thirty kilometers, more or less, with one day of rest allowed along the 200-kilometer route. During this break, we wrote up the award citations for men who had distinguished themselves in battle at Muonio, and passed them to the regimental commander for approval.

As Kaaresuvanto, a small Finnish village, we passed through the daunting "*Sturmbock Position*," a fallback position designed to protect the entry to *Reichstraße* 50 in Norway. Route 50 was not only the main road in this area, it was the *only* road for the withdrawal of the *XIX* and *XXXVI Corps*. This formidable defensive bastion was manned by members of the *7th Mountain Division*, our neighbors to the south at Kiestinki.

Our last night on Finnish soil was spent at a unique location. To the left of the road there was 100-meter cliff, falling away to Lake Kilpisjärvi. To the right, a widened road ditch lay at the base of a sheer rock face that was the base of the Saana, the holy mountain of the Lapps. The men of the *3d Battalion* had no choice but to pitch their tents in the drainage ditch on the right side of the road, single-file, for four to five kilometers. We felt especially good about our buddies in the *7th Mountain Division* in the *Sturmbock Position* behind us, as this was no posture to try to defend!

On that last night in Finland, many of us thought back to the 3fi years we had spent fighting shoulder-to-shoulder with our Finnish allies. They had been true and reliable comrades-in-arms. It took us many years to understand their awful plight, and to forgive what we felt at the time was nothing less than treachery, a terrible breach of faith. To soldiers whose concept of honor was built above all else on loyalty, the Finns' betrayal had seemed unconscionable.

The years of combat in the wilderness of Lapland and the endless forests of Karelia had definitely changed the character of the *Division NORD*. We had come very far from the sunny spring day in 1941 when *SS-Combat Group NORD* had boldly driven into Finland in trucks, Volkswagen jeeps, and motorcycles with sidecars. Unprepared for combat, many of the original members lay beneath wooden crosses and "Life Runes"* in cemeteries in

*Soldiers of the *Waffen-SS*, not specifying otherwise, were interred with their graves marked by the "Life Rune," a Nordic pagan symbol resembling a capital letter Y with an extended center stem. As mentioned previously, combining this with the "Death Rune," creates the "Hagel Rune," which was the division insignia.

the Soviet Union.* Rejuvenated with drafts of well-trained combat soldiers, *NORD* had evolved and been seasoned in the ensuing three-plus years of war. Perhaps the Finnish historian Sampo Ahto summs it up best,

> The *SS-Combat Group NORD* that appeared during the summer of 1941 in Lapland consisted of badly trained reservists whose performance was looked upon by the Finns with boisterous amusement, mixed with pity. The *SS-Mountain Division NORD* of the autumn of 1944 was an entirely different military formation. Unrelenting training, enforced with German thoroughness, and many years of experience in static warfare had created an adversary that was outstanding for everybody.[39]

## From Heiligskogen to the Hardt Mountains

The battalion crossed the Finnish-Norwegian border north of the Finnish hamlet of Kilpisjärvi during the night of 7–8 November 1944. Just a few hours before, we had lost a vehicle, a field kitchen drawn by two horses. Due to the extreme slipperiness of the ice-covered, narrow, gravel road, the wheels lost their hold and slid to the road's left side; there, it turned over and fell 100 meters before crashing into Lake Kilpisjärvi, which demarcated the border with Sweden. Fortunately, the driver leapt off just in time.

On 9 November, in Heiligskogen (Norwegian for "Holywood"), just south of the Lyngen Fjord, we held a battalion formation. There, men were decorated for gallantry at the Battle of Muonio, receiving Iron Crosses, 1st and 2d classes. At the same time, the battalion changed command. *Hauptsturmführer* Kurt Kreuzinger, a thirty-two-year old Sudetenlander, assumed command of the battalion.†

The battalion resumed its march the next day, reaching Skibotn, the northernmost point in the route through Norway.‡ While none of us realized it at the time, we were now turning south, and would continue so until we

*Cemeteries which, unfortunately, have been the sites of ghoulish desecration and mass grave robbing since the collapse of the Soviet Union in the early 1990s. One cemetery was even plowed up during the construction of an extension of the railway branch, and the bones dumped en masse into unmarked sites. Difficult and sensitive negotiations are underway at the time of this writing to try to relocate the remains of thousands of *NORD* and Army veterans to safer sites.

†Formerly the commanding officer of the *6th Company*, which had attacked with us at Muonio, *Hauptsturmführer* Kreuzinger ultimately commanded the *3d Battalion* during the battle for Wingen-sur-Moder.

‡Skibotn lies at 69 degrees, 24 minutes north latitude; for comparison, Point Hope, Alaska, is at 68 degrees, 21 minutes.

reached the southernmost point of our wartime odyssey—at Wingen-sur-Moder!

We still had to follow the orders for use of the *Reichstraße* 50, the narrow road which was reserved strictly for motorized traffic during the hours from 0600 to 1800. We marched in the dark between 1800 and 0600, and used the hours during which we could not march to pitch tents in the adjacent forest, rest, and prepare for the next day's trek. A typical night's march was thirty to thirty-five kilometers, so the rest was needed.

On the whole, the march through northern Norway was tiresome, but uneventful . . . except for one occasion.

The sun had just risen around 1100 hours on Sunday, 12 November, and the battalion had been off the road for about five hours. Suddenly, to our surprise, we could first hear, then see a large formation of Lancaster bombers heading north at high altitude. A while later, we heard the crack of flak batteries firing in the vicinity of Tromsö. As it turned out, the RAF bombers were on one of the most successful Allied anti-shipping missions of the war in Europe, namely, the attack on the German Navy's (*Kriegsmarine*'s) task group escorting the battleship *Tirpitz*. The *Tirpitz* task group's mission was to destroy Allied convoys in the Barents Sea before they could reach Murmansk and unload supplies and armaments for the Soviets. Destruction of the *Tirpitz* was, therefore, a high priority for the RAF, and they were quite successful on that day. The Lancasters surprised her, the last remaining German battleship that was in a position to threaten Allied shipping, in her harbor at the port of Tromsö, about fifty kilometers north of our position. The *Tirpitz* capsized, taking hundreds of her crew to their deaths. During the next few days of our march south, we often had to leave the road—despite the complete darkness—to make way for maintenance vehicles heading from southern Norway to Tromsö, rushing to deliver equipment to cut holes into *Tirpitz*' hull in attempts to rescue the crew trapped inside. Ultimately, about 1,000 German sailors could not be rescued and died in the capsized hull of the Tirpitz.[40]

During the next night, we passed the *Luftwaffe* airfield at Bardufoss. The only available officer there was the duty officer, since, by virtue of an order received just hours before from *Reichsmarschall* Göring, all *Luftwaffe* officers at the base were imprisoned awaiting trial by courts-martial. The officers of that airfield had been responsible for providing air cover for the *Tirpitz*, but had apparently been celebrating on the previous evening, and had been in no shape to stop the Lancasters, even though they had been warned in plenty of time.

Unexpectedly, the battalion enjoyed a long stopover at Setermoen. It took a week for the congested road ahead of us to clear of traffic. Ultimately, we were ordered to march to the harbor at Gratangen and to embark on one of the Danish railroad ferries there which had been transferred in a high risk move from Denmark to this point in the Arctic. Those ferries had been built for the calm waters between Danish coastal towns and were unfit for ocean-going sorties. All this had been accomplished to by-pass the bottleneck at Narvik.* After a sea voyage of about twenty hours, we disembarked at a small harbor north of Fauske, which turned out to be our next stopover. Here, as already in other places in Norway, we didn't experience anything like the resentment or hatred from the populace that we had expected. After all, Norway had been occupied for more than four years at this point. At worst, we perceived indifference. Many of the civilians were even friendly.

Our destination was Mo-i-Rana, 185 kilometers south of Fauske. In 1944, Mo was the northernmost terminus of the Norwegian railway.† To reach the end of our extended foot march, so long yearned for, we had to cross the Arctic Circle from the north in a windy, snow-blown, God-forsaken wilderness. The battalion reached Mo-i-Rana on 10 December. Since leaving the front between Kiestinki and Louhi on 8 September, we had negotiated a distance of some 1,600 kilometers, every inch of which had been on foot—and with some battles and skirmishes included.

After a short rest and obligatory visit to the delousing station, all units of the battalion were embarked on the train. To us, the railroad station looked like the Promised Land. A short day's stay-over at Trondheim was followed by a continuation of our rail journey to Oslo, the national capital. Most units of the battalion arrived there on 15 or 16 December, but some elements went straight on through to the harbor town of Moss, close to the southern end of the Oslo Fjord.

On 19 December, the battalion left Norway by embarking on freighters in Oslo and Moss, bound for Denmark. In a night passage, escorted by

*The author was ordered by *Hauptsturmführer* Kreuzinger to travel to Narvik and negotiate with the Chief Transport Officer to procure means by which our march south might be expedited. The commander equipped me with his command car and enlisted driver, but could not provide a signed trip ticket for the journey that far south. Now, the control of all movements, especially motorized, was extremely strictly enforced by the military police; anyone without a trip ticket was immediately arrested! But luck was with us. Turning onto *Reichstraße* 50, which led to Narvik, a larger command car passed just in front of us, evidently bound for the same destination. Carrying the pennant of an army corps, the corps commander was seated in the back seat. At each of the military police checkpoints we encountered along the way to Narvik, I pointed to the general's car just as the barrier was lifted, to imply that we were part of his entourage. It worked, and we were successful in our mission!

†Of course, there was the well-known "Ore-Railway" (*Erz-Bahn*), connecting the iron ore region of Swedish Kiruna with Narvik in Norway, which was the port for the export of Swedish ore. But this railway line was generally looked on as an extension of the Swedish railway network, the "Norland-Banen."

*Kriegsmarine* E-Boats and destroyers, the convoy steamed through the Skagerrak safely. We had expected attacks by Allied bombers and submarines, but none materialized.*

In the early morning hours of 20 December, we reached the harbor of Aarhus on the east coast of the Danish mainland. On the next morning, all officers attended a briefing in one of Aarhus' better hotels. Here it was disclosed that our division was to participate in Operation "*WACHT AM RHEIN*," the offensive in the Ardennes, commanded by *Generalfeldmarschall* Gerd von Rundstedt. (The Allies called it "the Battle of the Bulge," for the salient it created in their lines in the US First Army sector.) It was clear to all the attendees at the briefing that this operation had started five days previously, and that the combat units of the division were to be rushed to the front by battalion as soon as each appeared in Denmark. No leave was to be granted. All hopes for a short furlough home to recover from the 1,600-kilometer (1,000-mile) march had been in vain!

On the same afternoon, the battalion was entrained and transported to Kolding, halfway to the Danish-German frontier. In Kolding, a charming Danish town, and in some of the surrounding villages, the companies of the battalion already present were quartered for several days. Within the next forty-eight hours, everyone received a new issue of uniforms, underwear, socks, and boots—the events of the past three months had utterly worn out our old ones. We received these new items with enthusiasm.

We also exchanged our tried and reliable MG-34s for new MG-42s. The MG-42 had a much higher rate of fire than the MG-34, and this "improvement" was to prove crucial in the upcoming battle for Wingen, when we were cut off and ran out of ammunition much sooner than we would have with the weapons we were accustomed to using.†

Finally, the battalions of our regiment were significantly reorganized. An additional company was added to each battalion. The addition was to be the "heavy company," consisting of one platoon with two 75mm infantry howitzers, and one platoon of four 120mm mortars. Only one platoon of the heavy company later participated in the battle for Wingen, because the company was still forming when the *Jäger* (rifle) companies of our battalion joined the fray.

*The *6th SS-Mountain Division NORD* was in high demand indeed. On 22 November, *Generaloberst* Alfred Jodl, Chief of the *OKW* staff, ordered the German commanders-in-chief in Norway and Denmark, and the Navy, to afford highest priority for transportation to our Division. (*OKW WFSt Op (H) NORD Nr. 0013683/44 gKdos–Berlin, 22.11.44*)

†Practical rates of fire were 120 rounds per minute for the MG-34, but 250 rounds for the MG-42; cyclic rates were 900 and 1,400, respectively.

The addition of three companies to the regiment had significant consequences for the identification of all units. Because our companies had been consecutively numbered through the regiment, our three line (rifle) companies had been the *11th*, *12th*, and *13th*, the heavy machine-gun company had been the *14th*, and the headquarters company (with the signal, pioneer, and heavy mortar platoons) had been the *15th*. Now, with the addition of the three additional organic heavy companies, the line companies' and heavy machine-gun company designations jumped by two each (becoming the *13th*, *14th*, *15th*, and *16th Companies*); the new heavy company became the *17th*, and the battalion's headquarters company became the *18th*. This caused great havoc in our intra-unit communications and administration, and still does today when the veterans recall the war.

In this book, the more familiar, original company designations will be used, since the heavy company didn't participate in the raid on Wingen anyway.

For the exhausted and disappointed men of the *3d Battalion* of *SS-Mountain Regiment 12 "Michael Gaißmair,"* who could not go home for Christmas, at least the second-best option became reality. We spent Christmas Eve and part of Christmas Day in southern Jylland (or Jutland, the Danish mainland), around Kolding, before being committed to combat again. It was, at least, some compensation.

Here, the war seemed very far away, even unknown. Food was of a quantity and, more important, a quality, that had been unknown to us for years. Our supply people and company clerks went "above and beyond," making every effort to offer their men the very best of food and drink. And . . . some of the men found nice Danish girls to be quite sympathetic to their feelings.

Christmas Eve came and so did our order to entrain. The battalion, less the *14th* (heavy machine-gun) *Company*, which was still in southern Norway, was to depart Denmark on the afternoon of Christmas Day, embarking at the Kolding freight station on two separate trains. Thereafter, the trains would "convoy" to Germany. To ensure that this schedule was strictly adhered to, Berlin ordered the highest ranking transport officer in Denmark, an Army colonel, to rush from his Copenhagen headquarters to Kolding (on Christmas Day!) to personally witness the embarkation and report our departure to the *OKW*.

We left hospitable Kolding and crossed the Danish-German border in the late afternoon of 25 December 1944.

What followed was a nightmarish 750-kilometer tour of war-torn Germany, lasting four days, until the late night of 29 December. The contrast could scarcely have been more marked: we had left peaceful, serene, beautiful Denmark behind, and passed through a country that ached under RAF strikes by night and USAAF bombardment by day. Our trains by-passed many larger towns and cities, such as Hamburg and Frankfurt-am-Main, which could be seen burning in the distance.

In the early morning hours of 28 December, we crossed the Rhine south of Heidelberg. When we recognized that we were south of that historic university town, we knew we couldn't be headed for the Ardennes. Where we *were* going, none of us could guess.

Once on the left bank of the Rhine, the trains traveled only at night, for we were within the range of the Allied fighter-bombers—we were in "*Jabo*" Country!* The train crews would leave the passenger cars (and the occupants) wherever they were at daybreak, and would take the engines on alone to whatever shelter they could find to save them from the marauding *Jabo* pilots, who were searching for "targets of opportunity" for their bombs, rockets or even machine guns, and trains were among their *favorite* targets! On bright days, such as 28 December, nothing of military value that moved on the ground could be assumed safe from their depredations. So trains did not roll during daylight—period!

When darkness fell, our engines returned from their haven and pulled the trains on through the night for a very slow sixty-five kilometers. By then, a tunnel had been reached which was as good a place as any could be for protecting us during the coming day. Here again, the engine uncoupled and left our train in comparative safety.

Dawn on 29 December brought the dreaded *Jabos*. The inadequacy of our situation became immediately, terrifyingly apparent. Although one of the trains was indeed ensconced safely inside the tunnel, the second train, containing the *12th* and *13th Companies*, was largely exposed, due to the tunnel's insufficient length. To make things worse, the railway tracks here lay in a deep cut before the tunnel mouth, at the foot of steep slopes. There was nowhere to run to for the men of the *Jäger* companies in the exposed cars.

As the planes made a half-dozen passes at the cars, the terrified men of the *12th* and *13th Companies* desperately tried to climb up the steep slopes on either side of the cut, in an attempt to gain the safety of the forest adjacent to the upper rim. Nevertheless, fourteen men were killed, and about twice as many wounded. Losing this many men before we even had a chance to shoot back did not bode well for our coming combat.

On that dark and cold night that ended the day, the trains finally reached Pirmasens-Nord and Zweibrücken in the Palatinate (*Pfalz*). The station in Zweibrücken had been badly damaged by an airstrike just a few hours before

**Jabo* is short for *Jagdbomber*, the fighter-bombers of the Allied Air Forces. In our sector, they were mostly P-51 Mustangs and P-47 Thunderbolts of the USAAF.

our arrival. Also, the city's main post office had been hit. Trying to contact the responsible Army transport officer by telephone, one had to climb over the fresh rubble into a cellar, where a scared girl, huddled under blankets against the bitter cold, was trying to operate the remnants of the telephone exchange. After a while, she managed the right connection. Announcing the arrival of both trains by code number, we were apprised by the transport officer that our next destinations and quarters were to be the villages of Ludwigswinkel and Eppenbrunn, some thirty and twenty kilometers from Pirmasens, respectively. These were both small villages, nestled in the wooded slopes of the Hardt Mountains, which are called the Low Vosges, on the French side of the border. Once again, we would walk.

Both little towns were located just a few kilometers north of the German-French frontier, and to the east of Bitche, the historic French border town with its massive eighteenth-century Vauban citadel. A strongly fortified bastion of the Maginot Line, Bitche was still in our hands at that stage of the war, despite American attempts to take it in mid-December.

In November, with the approach of the American Seventh Army, the civilian population of Ludwigswinkel had been evacuated to the vicinity of Würzburg, in Bavaria. Ludwigswinkel, founded in 1783 by Landgraf Ludwig IX of Hesse-Darmstadt, was a charming little town that boasted a resort for nature-lovers, complete with hiking trails. We were quite familiar with nature by now, and would soon be taking a hike that none of the resort's guests had ever taken before.

The companies of the battalion arrived in both designated villages on the night of 30 December and during the following night. Thanks to the daylong overcast, there was no interference by *Jabos*.

Ludwigswinkel and Eppenbrunn were stuffed with all manner of German units, even before we arrived. Here, we met for the first time units with strange and unfamiliar designations, such as *Volks-Grenadier*, or "People's Infantry" divisions. We learned that the ones in our area had been formed from the shattered remnants of former infantry divisions after those units had been too badly mauled to reconstitute to their original form. These divisions had either two regiments of three battalions each, or three regiments of two battalions each, as opposed to their previous complement of three regiments of three battalions each. Even though the tables of organization called for an unusually large number of automatic rifles (the new MP-43 and MP-44 assault rifles, the forerunners of the postwar Soviet Kalashnikov line), submachine guns, and machine guns to compensate for the lost firepower of the three eliminated battalions, German tactical doctrine for infantry presupposed the old structure. As a result, operations were made stilted, and more difficult to conduct with the new units. These problems were only worsened by the personnel situations of *volks-grenadier* divisions. Although formed around combat-experienced officer cadres and some similarly experienced (but weary) NCOs, these units were manned by junior enlisted soldiers who largely came from the *Luftwaffe* or naval units which no longer had planes to fly or ships to sail. Hastily retrained in rudimentary infantry skills, these men had usually spent less than two months together before being flung into combat.

We also met some men of the *Magen-Bataillone* (literally, "Stomach Battalions"). These were men who had long been classified as ineligible for military service due to severe digestive ailments. Brigaded together in units to allow feeding of special rations, such as white bread that could be tolerated by their weak systems, these were the last reserves of the once mighty "One-Thousand-Year Reich."

Observing all this was a very alien and stark experience for the men of *NORD*, who had not been defeated in 3fi years of combat against the Soviets on the Arctic Front. If it had not dawned on the men before, here in Ludwigswinkel and Eppenbrunn, it crept—or even leapt—into their consciousness now: Could Germany still win this war? Could Germany even attain a fair peace? These were hardly comforting thoughts on the eve of battle.

Crowded as it was in the villages, our men succeeded in squeezing in, to get at least a fitful night's sleep, wondering when the fracas would start—it could not be long now.

New Year's Eve, the last day of the eventful year 1944, finally arrived. On the visit to Eppenbrunn, reporting to our regimental commander, *Standartenführer* Franz Schreiber, and congratulating him on the recent award of the Knight's Cross, Kreuzinger and I had been forewarned that march orders for the move across the border should be expected within twenty-four hours.

What would 1945 bring?

## Strategic and Operational Planning for Operation NORDWIND

Operation *NORDWIND* was conceived as an adjunct to Operation *WACHT AM RHEIN*, the German offensive in the Ardennes Forest in December 1944. Still known colloquially in Germany as the "*Rundstedt-Offensive*" after *Generalfeldmarschall* Gerd von Rundstedt, the Supreme Commander–West at the time, *WACHT AM RHEIN* was aimed at seizing the key port of Antwerp and splitting the Allied 12th from the 21st Army Group. In this way, Hitler hoped to achieve not only an operational victory over the US First Army, but also potentially a strategic victory in the West by causing a rupture in the

Anglo-American alliance. He imagined that the corollary benefits of such a success might lead to the conclusion of a separate armistice with the Western Allies—after all, such an arrangement had already happened to Germany's disadvantage with the Rumanians and the Finns.

Although *NORDWIND* was not conducted on a scale comparable to that of *WACHT AM RHEIN*, its strategic objective was nearly as grand; it was to split the major subordinate elements of the Sixth Army Group internally, along national lines. By separating the US Seventh Army from the French First Army, Hitler hoped to not only destroy thus isolated American units in the Low Vosges and on the Alsatian Plain, but to wreak decisive discord on the already strained relationship between Eisenhower and DeGaulle.[41]

*WACHT AM RHEIN* was steered from the *Führer* Headquarters above the village of Ziegenberg, west of Bad Nauheim in the Taunus Mountains. Known as the *Adlerhorst* ("Eagles' Nest"), this was where Hitler and his aides attempted to achieve their decisive victory in the West from 10 December 1944 until 15 January 1945; it was also where the *Führer* conceived *NORDWIND*.*

By the third day of *WACHT AM RHEIN*, General Dwight D. Eisenhower, the Supreme Commander, Allied Expeditionary Forces, realized that the Germans' Ardennes offensive was a major operation. From his headquarters at Fontainbleu, he directed the US Seventh Army—deployed between the Rhine River and the region southeast of Saarbrücken—to extend its left (western) boundary to St. Avold to free major elements of Third Army for action against the left shoulder of the Ardennes salient. This caused Lieutenant General Alexander Patch, commanding general of Seventh Army, to extend his sector from a frontage of 75 kilometers to one nearly twice as long, or 135 kilometers.[42]

On 21 December, General Jacob Devers, commanding the Sixth Army Group, ordered Patch to suspend offensive operations in the Maginot Line and the *Westwall* (the Allies called it the "Siegfried Line"), and assume a defensive posture. The order emphasized that Sixth Army Group would be prepared to yield ground rather than endanger the integrity of its forces.

*The *Adlerhorst* had been constructed as an underground headquarters for Hitler during the winter of 1939/40, in anticipation of the upcoming invasion of France. Its extensive facilities had been constructed at high cost, yet until December 1944, it had never been occupied; Hitler decided in 1940 that it was too far from the front: instead, he moved to his headquarters at Munstereifel (thirty kilometers southwest of Bonn) codenamed Felsennest ("Rocky Refuge"). During *NORDWIND*, Hitler's military staff was also either near the Adlerhorst or were quartered in a barracks at the southern exit of the Friedberg, fifteen kilometers to the southeast.

While this measure was aimed at preserving Franco-American battlefield unity, it caused an enormous political shock, as DeGaulle had no intentions of allowing recently liberated French territory to be returned to German possession without a fight.[43]

The result of this extreme extension of the Seventh Army Front was soon apparent to German intelligence, which noted that the Americans had abandoned their bridgeheads over the Saar River and had generally thinned out their lines. This weakening of the American defenses presented interesting opportunities for the German high command.

On the same night that the Americans in Seventh Army headquarters received their instructions to go over to the defensive, 21 December, *Generalfeldmarschall* von Rundstedt ordered the commanding general of *Army Group G* to exploit this situation by all means available. This exploitation was to include not only local limited-objective attacks, but even a surprise offensive to retake the Saverne Gap, the major pass which demarcates the High Vosges Mountains to the south from the Low Vosges to the north. Special security measures were to be enforced, and preparations were to be concealed and explained as preparations for moving the entire *Army Group* to another theater.[44]

On 22 December, Hitler ordered a feasibility study of an attack by two armored divisions and three infantry divisions from the vicinity of Bitche to the south. The objective of this attack was to thrust into the rear of the American forces deployed on the Alsatian Plain near Wissembourg. He further ordered a high level of activity along the entire *Army Group G* front to deceive and contain the enemy.

On the same day, von Rundstedt changed his orders to *Army Group G* accordingly. For the assault to the Saverne Gap, he now wanted to use four infantry divisions and three mobile (that is, *panzer* or *panzer grenadier*) divisions, with the operation to begin in the first week of January. *Army Group Oberrhein* (Upper Rhine), which was commanded by *Reichsführer-SS* Heinrich Himmler—answering only to *OKW*, not to von Rundstedt—was informed of these intentions, and asked to support them with an assault over the Rhine to create bridgeheads on the west bank, north and south of Strasbourg.

These orders were received at *Army Group G* by the newly-reappointed commanding general, *Generaloberst* Johannes Blaskowitz. One of the oldest generals (sixty-one years old) still on active duty in the German Army, Blaskowitz had commanded *Army Group G* during its painful withdrawal up the Rhône Valley before the advance of the Allies from the southern France beaches during the previous summer. Sacked at the end of September by Hitler and replaced by the highly-regarded *panzer* leader, *General der Panzertruppen* Hermann Balck, Blaskowitz now found himself reinstated with the mission to immediately prepare an attack to retrieve the situation in northern Alsace.

On 24 December, Blaskowitz and *Oberst* Horst Wilutzky, the *Army Group G Ia* (G-3), presented their concept for the attack to von Rundstedt. According to *Oberst* Wilutzky, when comparing the potential axes of advance for attacks by *Army Group G*, Blaskowitz's staff concluded that an attack west of the Low Vosges would "break down" in front of the Maginot Line, which was in American hands in this area. An attack east of the Low Vosges did not seem to promise much in the way of surprise, or to possess much potential for a quick breakthrough, as an advance down the Rhine Plain seemed too obvious. In the opinion of the *Army Group* staff, the only prospects for the early successes essential for victory in this effort came with an attack directly into the Low Vosges.[45]

In his briefing to von Rundstedt, Blaskowitz explained his vision of two separate thrusts, with the main attack originating from the region southeast of Bitche. This attack would be carried out by two corps (*XC* and *LXXXIX*), disposing four infantry divisions (*36th*, *256th*, *361st*, and *559th Volks-Grenadier*), one armored division (*21st Panzer*), and a rocket launcher brigade. The supporting attack, to be carried out by *XIII SS Corps* using the *257th Volks-Grenadier* and *17th SS Panzer-Grenadier* divisions, supported by a battalion of *Jagdtiger* ("Hunting Tiger") super-heavy tank destroyers, two companies of "Hetzer" self-propelled armored flamethrowers, and a field artillery "corps," was to fall east of the Blies River, to prevent US XV Corps from coming to the aid of the forces at location of the German main effort. The *25th Panzer-Grenadier Division* was held in *Army Group* reserve to exploit or reinforce the successes of either attack. In Phase I, both attacks were to penetrate the Americans' defenses and converge on Phalsbourg. From there, the unified forces were to press on to Saverne during Phase II. If successful, the attacking forces would then conduct Phase III, a thrust along the Rhine-Marne Canal in an easterly direction, supported by the attacks from *Army Group Upper Rhine*. These attacks would jointly converge to envelop American forces north of Strasbourg, and eventually reconnect with *19th Army* in the "Colmar Pocket."* Following the briefing, the Supreme Commander—West declared himself "in complete agreement with these plans," and submitted them to Hitler for approval. Shortly thereafter, Hitler ordered Blaskowitz, Wilutzky, and von Rundstedt to a meeting to discuss their proposed offensive operation. According to *Oberst* Wilutzky, Hitler was of the opinion that the

***19th Army* was also under the command of *Army Group Upper Rhine* at this point, after being cut off from *Army Group G* during the American penetration of the High Vosges in late November 1944.

troops deployed into the Low Vosges would not be able to stand the winter conditions there, and so dramatically altered the character of the proposed operation.[46]

He ordered that the supporting attack west of the Vosges by *XIII SS Corps* be upgraded to the status of a second "main attack," and to be weighted accordingly. The *21st Panzer Division* was to be held back from the initial attack, and kept with the *25th Panzer-Grenadier Division* to form a much more robust Army Group reserve. Hitler's intent was for this large armored reserve to then be committed as "an additional thrust" along either axis of attack, that is, immediately west of or across the Low Vosges.*

Although Hitler's inappropriate micromanagement and counterproductive meddling by this stage of the war is well known and extensively documented, there was perhaps some wisdom in these decisions. Even as he was announcing these decisions, large German armored formations were foundering on icy roads in the depths of the Ardennes. Within twenty-four hours, the skies over the Schnee Eifel would clear, and American fighter-bombers would be brought to bear on the stalled columns of German vehicles. Retention of the *21st Panzer* in a well-camouflaged assembly area less than an hour's drive from the potential objective areas not only preserved the precious and dwindling armored assets, but retained operational flexibility to commit both armored formations quickly to whichever attack achieved a breakthrough first.

Hitler's concerns about the durability of the infantry elements conducting the attack in the Low Vosges also had merit. As *Volks-Grenadier* units, all four were comprised essentially of men who were not seasoned infantrymen. While many of the leaders, from the company level up, were indeed highly-experienced soldiers, the rank and file *Landsers* (infantrymen) in most of the formations were recently reclassified *Luftwaffe* ground personnel and *Kriegsmarine* sailors. The *257th Volks-Grenadier Division* (*VGD*) had received about a month of collective training prior to its commitment to defensive combat near Bitche in December. The *256th* had about the same amount of training, and was recovering from costly combat against the British in the Netherlands during the autumn, and, more recently, the Americans on the Alsatian Plain. Since its equally brief unit training period during the summer, the *559th VGD* had been continuously engaged in defensive and retrograde action against the US Third Army in Lorraine and the Saar, while the *36th* had also seen plenty of recent defensive action against the same foe since its reorganization and training in August. The *361st* was at least fighting on

*German generals at this time were long since used to serving as *Befehlsempfänger* ("recipients of orders"), or as *Generalfeldmarschall* (*Luftwaffe*) Wolfgang Freiherr von Richthofen termed it, "highly-paid sergeants." (Schramm, volume 4, 39).

**Final Plan for Operation *NORDWIND*, 31 December 1944–1 January 1945**

familiar terrain, having withdrawn in December over the same ground on which it was about to attack; its personnel, however, had never conducted sustained offensive operations. Lack of collective training to harden and reorient the soldiers of these units, coupled with overwhelmingly defensive fighting experience, augured poorly for success in protracted offensive action in the open during the most bitter winter of the twentieth century to that point. No matter how highly motivated, inadequately conditioned and trained men cannot do the impossible.

The problems with these *VGD*s went beyond their training deficiencies, however. Their organizational design—the creation of *Oberst* Claus Graf (Count) Schenk von Stauffenberg, the would-be assassin of Adolf Hitler at Rastenburg in July 1944—was based on the assumption of mostly defensive fighting. Most of the infantry regiments in most *VGD*s had only two battalions; this meant that in offensive operations, unlike the traditional three-battalion regiments of earlier infantry units, both battalions would have to attack all the time. There would be little or no time spent in reserve. This structure, which could only facilitate short, "pulsed" attacks, could also have given Hitler pause in his appraisal of the utility of the *VGD*s for attacking through the Low Vosges in mid-winter.

Although Hitler's alterations to the original Blaskowitz plan had some merit, it nevertheless embraced confirmed German operational doctrine in an ambiguous manner. The designation of both attacks as "main attacks" clearly diluted the focus originally intended for a breakthrough in the Low Vosges. On the other hand, the retention of a powerful armored exploitation force seemed to provide Blaskowitz with exceptional flexibility for reinforcement of success, wherever it came.

This flexibility was somewhat illusory, however. Hitler at once deprived his *Army Group G* commander of full prerogatives regarding this force by insisting that the *21st Panzer* and *25th Panzer-Grenadier* divisions could not be employed before "gaining of the Wingen-Ingwiller road." He further placed many of the ninety assault guns and light or medium tank destroyers that might have reinforced the *panzerjäger* units of the *VGD*s in the Low Vosges directly under the control of the *17th SS Panzer-Grenadier Division*, making the thrust south along the western rim of the mountains. Along with the two companies of armored flamethrowers, the battalion of Hunting Tigers, and a company of Panthers from the *21st Panzer Division*, the *XIII SS Corps'* effort was as armor-heavy as that of the *XC* and *LXXXIX Corps* were armor-light. If an entire *panzer* division may have been too much to hurl into the Low Vosges, it was at least equal folly to commit practically none.

Hitler's changes to the originally-proposed plan did not end with these mixed blessings. Contrary to Blaskowitz's desires, he stipulated that any cooperation by *Army Group Upper Rhine* should not commence earlier than two days after the offensive—as of this day dubbed *NORDWIND*—commenced. This doubled the time available to the Americans to shift forces from the Rhine Plain to the threatened sectors to the west, although if the Americans did indeed transfer forces from the Rhine to the Vosges, it would concomitantly improve Himmler's units' chances of success.

On the basis of this Christmas Eve meeting and discussion, von Rundstedt issued his instructions to *Army Group G* on 26 December, incorporating all of Hitler's directives.

On Christmas Day, *Generaloberst* Blaskowitz and *Oberst* Wilutzky explained these changes to *General der Infanterie* Hans von Obstfelder, commanding general of the *1st Army*—the field army which was to exercise immediate control of *NORDWIND*. On the following day, *General* Gustav Höhne, commanding the *LXXXIX Corps* was also personally briefed. The *Army Group G* staff followed up these briefings with the delivery of a written order to their subordinate elements at 2000 hours on 28 December.

Ever since the first briefings, the continued maintenance of utmost secrecy played a major role in the planning and preparation for *NORDWIND*. To retain the element of surprise to the extent that had so assisted *WACHT AM RHEIN* in its initial phases, the following measures were enforced:

- Only corps commanders, division commanders and their immediately subordinate staff officers were to be informed about *NORDWIND*. Commanders below this level were to be apprised shortly before the commencement of the offensive.
- Reconnaissance missions forward of the existing MLR were to be conducted only by patrols of units already in place; the attack divisions were not afforded the opportunity, lest they be identified.
- No movements of units into the final assembly areas were allowed until the night of 29/30 December. Attack ("jump off") positions were to be occupied only two hours before commencement of the offensive. All movement limited to hours of darkness to prevent discovery by aerial reconnaissance.
- All attacking units were to observe radio silence. As a deception measure, units were to continue normal message traffic from their previous locations.
- Route reconnaissance was to be disguised as routine searches for "new supply lines." No markers or road signs were to be posted.
- No men were to be recalled from leave.
- The hour and date of the offensive (2300 on 31 December) were to provide further surprise, as was the total lack of artillery preparation.[47]

During the meeting on 24 December, Hitler ordered all corps and division commanders participating in *NORDWIND* to report to the *Adlerhorst* on 27 December. Blaskowitz ordered them to report first to his headquarters at Wachenheim (thirty-five kilometers east of Kaiserslautern) in the morning. At this gathering, each of them reported on the condition of his respective units. Every commander voiced his concern over the short preparation time for the looming offensive; there just wasn't enough time to rest the veterans, incorporate the masses of arriving replacements, and thoroughly prepare for the upcoming operation.[48]

From Wachenheim, the participants traveled to Ziegenberg to report to von Rundstedt, then moved on the *Adlerhorst*. Here, Hitler explained the reason for the failure of *WACHT AM RHEIN.* First, he blamed the "extraordinarily bad roads;" then the long times required to repair bridges blown by the retreating Americans. Furthermore, he cited the "gigantic ballast" of materiel and vehicles that the troops had to move along with them, and advised his audience, "In this regard, we should learn from the Russians!"[49]

Conceding that the Ardennes offensive had gotten stuck, Hitler proclaimed that the task of *Army Group B* had now changed; at least for the time being, its mission was no longer to seize Antwerp, but to contain enemy forces in the north. He then stressed the necessity of maintaining the initiative by attacking the Allied forces. It would have to be the aim of *NORDWIND* to exploit the weakened American front opposite the *1st Army*, and to deprive the Allies of the capability to resume their offensive operations. Since the threat of a Soviet winter offensive was imminent, there could be no talk about postponing the commencement of *NORDWIND.* The operation had to be executed as ordered, without regard to the condition of the troops.

Each division commander then reported on the status of his division and evaluated the feasibility of his mission. All generals repeated their reservations about the plan to Hitler. Of course, they failed to achieve any changes to Hitler's directives.

*****

As the *NORDWIND* division commanders vainly voiced their concerns to their superiors, their units' reinforcement and replenishment were already under way. Under the guise of preparation for transfer to another theater of war, men and materiel arrived at rates that sometimes astonished the commanders. Most of the ordnance requested by division commanders at the *Adlerhorst* conference on 27 December was received. Wherever feasible, front line troops were relieved for some rest and recovery in the rear, even if for the shortest periods.

*****

The commander and staff of *1st Army* reacted to their orders quickly. On the basis of the changed orders from *Army Group G*, *1st Army* planners issued the final operation order to all three corps commanders on 27 December, and called the chiefs of staff of the corps to a conference on the following day at the *Army* headquarters at Ramstein.[50]

In a conference presided over by the Chief of Staff of *1st Army* on 27 December, representatives from each corps were briefed on the requirements of *NORDWIND*, and details were explained as necessary. Specific guidelines for the course of the operation were issued. The *1st Army* Chief of Staff stressed the necessity of creating combined arms combat groups and employing them in a narrow zone of attack, echeloned in depth. These combat groups were to be instructed not to allow themselves to be decisively engaged by discrete enemy strongpoints, but rather to bypass them without regard for their neighbors' flanks. In this way, it was hoped that all directed objectives could be seized rapidly.[51]

*** * * * ***

The German picture of the American opposition in the zone of the *1st Army's* attack seems to have been not entirely accurate, although in some cases, German intelligence regarding the composition and location of enemy positions was positively superb.

At *1st Army* headquarters, the results of land and aerial reconnaissance seemed to indicate that along the entire *Army* front, from the confluence of the Saar and Moselle Rivers to east of Lauterbourg on the Rhine, American forces had been reduced drastically since 12 December. Between that date and the scheduled commencement of *NORDWIND*, the *1st Army Ic* (intelligence staff officer) believed that the US Third and Seventh Armies had been diminished in strength by six infantry and two armored divisions, for a remaining total of not more than eight infantry and three armored divisions opposite the *1st Army*. This was basically correct, but the Germans' understanding of the situation in the *NORDWIND* zone of attack was somewhat less accurate.

In fact, in the zone of the German offensive, the Americans disposed, from west to east, the XV Corps' 44th and 100th Infantry Divisions, and the VI Corps' Task Force Hudelson (an *ad hoc* mechanized cavalry/armored infantry task force of regimental strength) and 45th Infantry Division. The commanding general of XV Corps, Major General Wade Haislip, had one combat command of the French 2d Armored Division (*2éme Division Blindée*) in reserve, while Major General Edward H. Brooks, commanding VI Corps, possessed the 14th Armored Division as his reserve (minus the elements in Task Force Hudelson). Lieutenant General Patch retained the 12th Armored Division and the 36th Infantry Division in Seventh Army reserve.

The *1st Army* order stated that the enemy had weakened his positions between the Rhine and Saar Rivers, and listed only the 100th, 45th, and 79th Infantry Divisions as defending in that sector, with the 12th and 14th Armored Divisions in reserve. Nevertheless, the 1st Army staff remained of the opinion that, considering the condition of its own forces, the enemy was fully capable of adequate resistance. Also, the *Army Ic* deemed the enemy liable of rapid recovery and regrouping, using the superior road network behind his lines, by the fourth day at the latest.[52] *LXXXIX Corps* reiterated this estimate in its order, adding that the enemy was likely to possess reserves with which to counterattack, commencing on 2 January. Thus, the Germans underestimated the American infantry strength on the line by a full division, and misunderstood the situation of the American reserves as well; these, too, they underestimated by an infantry division.

In the case of the single German division that had the advantage of jumping off from its own MLR—and therefore had been allowed to reconnoiter its zone—the intelligence picture was much more accurate. The field order of the *361st VGD* read:

> Before us is an enemy reconnaissance battalion [that is, parts of Task Force Hudelson] arrayed on a wide front. Up front, there are only security outposts, with wide gaps between them. There are mines along the roads and paths. There are strongpoints in depth, especially in the towns of Bannstein, Philippsbourg, Baerenthal, and Mouterhouse. Expect the appearance of armored vehicles and tanks. Deployment of stronger forces in depth is unknown. Their posture along the front proves that the enemy does not expect an attack in the mountains.[53]

Unlike the situation of the *361st*, however, the *257th VGD* was new to the zone of its attack, and was therefore dependent on the intelligence it received from the German unit previously deployed along the MLR.[54] Furthermore, there was neither time for the *257th* to conduct its own reconnaissance, nor was it permitted for reasons of operational security. As a result, all the men of the *257th VGD* knew of the enemy was that he seemed to have recently moved troops out of the area to the Ardennes, and that there seemed to be parts of a reconnaissance battalion with "weakly occupied front lines" before them. The exact line of enemy defense was unknown, and it was also uncertain whether the enemy forward positions were only outposts, or part of their MLR. The leaders of the *559th* and *256th VGD*s were no better off than this, as well.

*****

The concomitant confusion over the unclear and in some cases, inaccurate, intelligence picture was only compounded by the extremely short planning time afforded to commanders at the regimental levels and below. According to statements written by key German officers after the war, regimental commanders were briefed on their units' responsibilities in the imminent offensive during the morning hours of *31 December*. As a result, battalion commanders were briefed in the afternoon, not more than eight to ten hours before they launched a major attack with their units, most of which had never attacked before in actual combat.

Even for highly-experienced, superior commanders and staffs—which were generally lacking in the *VGD*s, especially at the battalion and regimental levels—this was far, far too little time to conduct the detailed planning and other preparations necessary for committing soldiers to an attack. In exchange for the retention of the element of surprise, the German high command had sacrificed the benefits of solid intelligence and prudent preparation.

The events of the next seven days would test the wisdom of their decision.

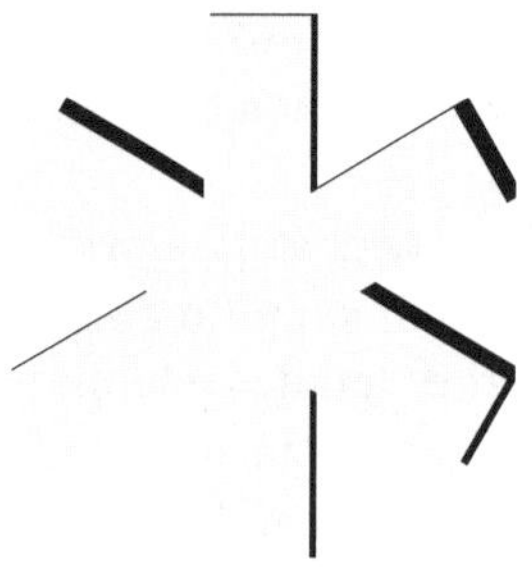

# The First Day: NORDWIND Commences

## -I-
## The *3d Battalion* Moves Up

My battalion clerk and I were attending to the prosaic task of writing the Operations Journal entry around midnight when a regimental runner knocked on the door of the house in Ludwigswinkel in which our CP was located. Hans Fritsche, the press secretary of Joseph Goebbels and his Propaganda Ministry had just spoken on the radio on the advent of 1945—the New Year had arrived.

The runner presented me an ominous sealed envelope, which contained the march order for our *3d Battalion*, issued by *Standartenführer* Schreiber. During our visit to the Regimental CP on the day before, we had been forewarned that such an order was forthcoming.

We were quartered in a second floor apartment of one of the buildings constructed in Ludwigswinkel to house the families of the customs officials who guarded the nearby German-French frontier. Its rightful inhabitants—the women and children, anyway—had been evacuated weeks before during the advance of the US Seventh Army toward this region.* The officers of the Customs Service had probably been called into military service, so they, too, were gone. Miraculously, however, when we entered the apartment on New Year's Eve, we found a little Christmas tree standing on the living room table, complete with candles.

The radio in the living room—a *Volksempfänger* which was a standard appliance in most German apartments at the time—emitted the sounds of Beethoven's Ninth Symphony. It was after midnight, so we were already

*Elements of the US 45th Infantry Division's 157th Infantry Regiment had reached Bundenthal, not twelve kilometers from Ludwigswinkel, on 19 December 1944.

writing "1 January 1945" on all correspondence. The air outside was crisp and cold, the stars were twinkling, and we could hear the rumble of artillery somewhere to the south.

A short while later, I had written the march orders for our companies and informed my battalion commander, *Hauptsturmführer* Kurt Kreuzinger, who then signed the orders. My clerk had already summoned the runners, one for each company. The companies were to assemble in Ludwigswinkel at 0900, next to the mill pond.

*****

When the companies arrived in the assembly area, there was new snow on the ground, and despite the sunshine, the air temperature was still below freezing.

Upon their arrival, the company commanders reported their unit personnel strengths. We knew that our battalion would enter the fray with only part of its total complement: present with us here, close to the French border on this first day of the new year, were only the three *Jäger* (mountain infantry) companies, but not our heavy machine-gun company, which was still in southern Norway or in Denmark, at best. Also, our headquarters company would not participate in these operations at full strength, since the heavy mortar platoon had to stay behind for conversion to an infantry howitzer platoon. They would then be assigned to the new *"Heavy Company"* which each of our three battalions were to receive as a sixth organic company.

A few of our communications platoon men would also be left behind: they were now assigned to the *Heavy Company* as well.

Overall, our *3d Battalion, SS-Mountain Infantry Regiment 12* started this morning with a combat strength of 73 NCOs, and 433 junior enlisted men, or about sixty-two percent of our authorized combat strength. Our most significant weakness was in officers; years of combat against the Soviets had taken their toll, and there were only five officers left in the battalion. One *Jäger* company, the *11th*, was without an officer, and was commanded by its seniormost NCO. Its former commanding officer was in the process of organizing the *Heavy Company*. Also, for some reason, both our battalion surgeon and his junior medical officer were not present. We would have to do without them for the next few days, wherever we were to be deployed.

In view of the terrain we would have to negotiate, we were limited in what we could take with us. Our *Jäger* companies would have to do without their 81mm mortars, and there would be no tripod mounts for the heavy machine guns—they would be used as light pieces. By relinquishing this weight, we could instead carry as much ammunition as possible for the upcoming missions.

Besides our battalion's combat complement, for this mission we were to be accompanied initially by our *Bergstaffel*, the mountain echelon of our supply unit, with their pack horses; this would allow us to traverse much more restrictive terrain than we would otherwise have been able to with wheeled vehicles.

* * * * *

Before departing from the Ludwigswinkel assembly area, our companies were issued *panzerfausts*, simple antitank grenade launchers with a short-range, but powerful punch. This issue was followed by an ultra-short demonstration of this weapon, which none of us had seen before—an example of the rushed and disorganized nature of our introduction to this campaign!

It must have been around 1000 hours when we left Ludwigswinkel on our march to the south, toward the German-French frontier. The sun was shining brightly, so we feared the appearance of American *Jabos* at any time. Surprisingly, our column was not threatened from the air during the entire day.

Only five kilometers beyond the border, we crossed the Schnepfenbach Valley south of Sturzelbronn, and continued southwest across the Mühlenberg and Abtsberg on a mountain path. The mountain countryside was beautiful, and deep in the snow-frosted woods, it was not terribly different from the terrain to which we were accustomed from our years of combat in northern Karelia. (Although the flora included more deciduous trees here than anywhere near the Arctic Circle!) In the afternoon, we crossed the pre-1940 French fortifications line, named after André Maginot, the Alsatian-born French War Minister from 1929–1932. Luckily for us, the Maginot Line in this sector was still in German hands; only a few kilometers to the east and west, it had been behind American lines since the middle of December. The large, steel-reinforced concrete casemates—with their formidable embrasures facing toward us—inertly stood guard on both sides of the path we were negotiating.

Again on the gravel road, we passed the tiny village of Schweizerländel (the French call it la Petite Suisse). After having to work with Russian, Finnish, or Norwegian toponyms during the last four years, most of which meant nothing to us, we sort of enjoyed the German names of localities and watercourses which we now encountered. They were a result of the German cultural heritage of Alsace and parts of Lorraine, originating in the Middle Ages. This area had been a part of the Holy Roman Empire of the German Nation for centuries, and had been an integral part of Germany for more than fifty-one of the last seventy-four years.

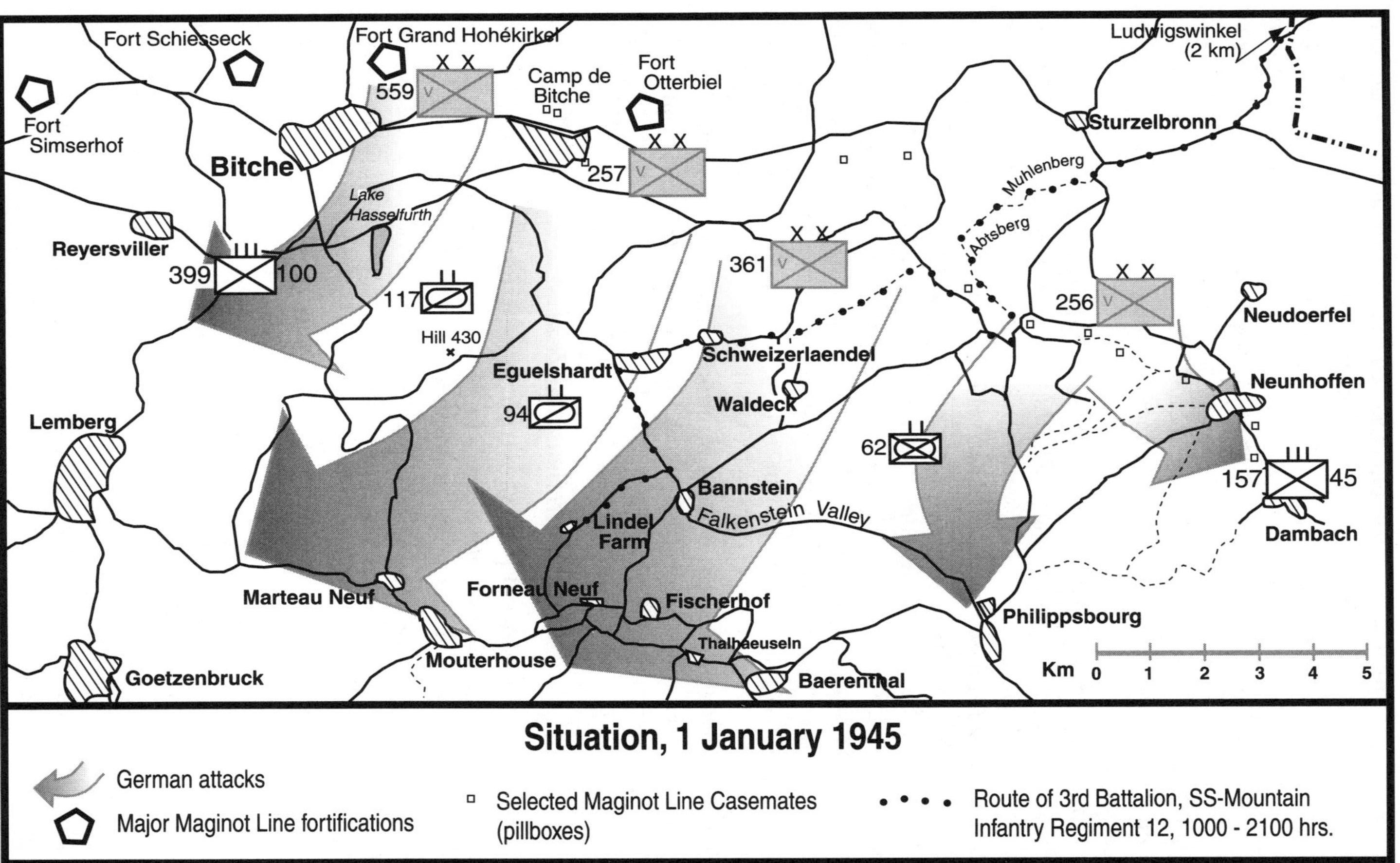


Situation, 1 January 1945

German attacks
Major Maginot Line fortifications
Selected Maginot Line Casemates (pillboxes)
Route of 3rd Battalion, SS-Mountain Infantry Regiment 12, 1000 - 2100 hrs.

The lead company of our battalion reached Eguelshardt and the road junction beyond the church there just as the early winter mountain dusk settled in. During the day, we had only heard the hammering and whooshing of artillery at a distance—our own and the strange-sounding American artillery as well. Now, however, we started receiving harassing and interdictory fires of American heavy-caliber guns. It was unobserved, but meant to hit the road junction and its vicinity. The low frequency of the fire (a very punctual one round per minute) afforded our men enough time to safely traverse the danger area.

Marching now in the dark in a southeasterly direction, after two more kilometers, we came to houses on the northern edge of the roadside hamlet of Bannstein. Here, it smelled of war; on both sides of the road were knocked-out American armored reconnaissance vehicles, as well as a few tanks. Some were still burning. It was our first sight of American equipment.

A little further along, we came to a turn-off to the right in the direction of Mouterhouse. Kreuzinger and I were marching with the lead company. At the turn-off, an Army messenger was obviously awaiting our arrival. He reported to Kreuzinger, identifying himself as a guide from the *361st Volks-Grenadier Division* whose mission was to lead us to his division's advanced command post. Kreuzinger gave orders to the CO of the lead company to see to it that the entire battalion was led down this turn-off road for the next two kilometers. After that, the men were to take a break while Kreuzinger and I were briefed at the command post of the *361st VGD*.

## Optimism and Zeal

The makeshift command post was in a farmhouse to the right of this road. Upon entering the *Ferme Lindel* (Lindel Farm), we were greeted by the *361st VGD Ia, Major i.G.* Ehlers. The atmosphere in the low-ceilinged, badly-lit main room was rather hectic. Signalers were in one corner with a few telephone sets on the dining table in front of *Major* Ehlers, while messengers from the subordinate regiments came and went. *Major* Ehlers was happy to see us, and said that just an hour before, *Standartenführer* Schreiber had informed *Generalmajor* Alfred Philippi, the commander of the *361st VGD*, of our impending arrival. *Major* Ehlers briefed us regarding the developments during the last twenty-one hours, or since 2300 on New Year's Eve, when *NORDWIND* had been launched.

*"*i.G.*" stands for "*im Generalstab*," meaning that the officer so designated has graduated from an approved general staff officer course, preparing him for higher-level operational staff and command assignments.

Like its neighbors on both sides, the *361st VGD* had started the assault one hour before midnight from its assembly areas near Eguelshardt and to the east, on both sides of Waldeck. To achieve maximum surprise, *Generaloberst* Johannes Blaskowitz, the commanding general of *Army Group G*, had forbidden any prior reconnaissance, and had ordered all assault divisions to dispense with artillery preparations prior to H-Hour.

The *361st VGD* was one of the few German elements participating in this operation whose leaders and men were familiar with the terrain on this front; its regiments had traversed it just the month before, during the retreat before the then-advancing soldiers of the US Seventh Army. This advantage turned out to be quite beneficial for the men of *Grenadier Regiment (GR) 952*, whose leading platoons sneaked through the American lines without even firing a shot. They succeeded in crossing not only the Falkenstein Valley and the road to Philippsbourg, but also in gaining the wooded hills over Fischerhof and Baerenthal—all in the dark of night.[55] During the daylight hours of this New Year's Day, the *952d* had taken Fischerhof (at 1400) and Thalhaeuseln (at 1600), and was now preparing to take Baerenthal after it had received the division's nine self-propelled assault guns to support its attack.

*Major* Ehlers was not so satisfied with the progress of *GR 953*, on the division's right; after a good start before midnight, the leading battalion had carelessly bungled the attempt to take Bannstein by surprise. The men of the *953d* only captured this hamlet in the Falkenstein Valley around dawn, with artillery support. Beyond Bannstein, the advance of this regiment met with stubborn resistance. Forneau Neuf could only be taken with the support of the assault guns during the late afternoon (around 1500) and the important junction giving access to the road to Reipertswiller to the south only fell by dusk (around 1700). During this latter operation, about 200 Americans were captured along with 20 light armored cars.

Nevertheless, all in all, *Major* Ehlers seemed to be satisfied with his division's achievements during this first day of *NORDWIND*. For him it was important that Baerenthal, in the Zintsel Valley, was in the hands of the soldiers of the *361st VGD*, and with the seizure of the road junction south of Forneau Neuf, the road to Reipertswiller was open.

Both roads led south through the Low Vosges range, and were essentially passes that eventually reached the open country of the wide Upper Rhine Valley. Ehlers explained that keeping the pass roads open was a precondition for employing armor, as stipulated by Hitler; the *21st Panzer Division* and *25th Panzer-Grenadier Division* would be kept in reserve until those basic requirements were met.

Returning to brief us on the current situation after numerous interruptions by incoming messengers, *Major* Ehlers reported that his unit's neighbor to the right (west), *XC Corps' 257th VGD,* had taken Mouterhouse just an hour ago, and was thus on about the same line of advance. Also, he said, the *257th* had taken a large number of American prisoners, and captured many weapons and armored cars that the enemy had left behind during his hurried, head-over-heels departure from his prepared positions.

The neighbor to his left (east), the *256th VGD,* had not enjoyed similar good fortune. Its regiments, attacking immediately after a tiresome foot march, had not even come close to accomplishing their first day's missions. Neither Dambach nor Philippsbourg had been taken. The spearhead battalion of *GR 481*, on the *256th*'s left, ran into an enemy fully prepared for defense in some of the Maginot Line casemates northeast of Dambach. Floodlights suddenly switched on by the defending Americans illuminated the entire battlefield and surprised the men of the *481st,* many of whom subsequently fell to well-aimed small arms fire.

If the *256th VGD* continued to lag behind over the next day or two, the advance of the *361st VGD* would be impeded, and *Major* Ehlers feared the danger of an unprotected left flank.

During our visit to our regimental command post on the day before, *Standartenführer* Schreiber had informed us that we would be part of a combat group that included our sister battalion, the *1st,* commanded by *Hauptsturmführer* Alois Burgstaller. A forward observer from the *3d Battalion, SS-Mountain Artillery Regiment 6* would also accompany us; some of its batteries of 105mm howitzers had already reached the theater of operations, as part of the advance elements of *NORD.**

After seeing to several necessary staff coordination activities, *Major* Ehlers explained that our mission was to seize the town of Wingen-sur-Moder and

*The advance elements of the *6th SS-Mountain Division NORD* that had arrived in the Pirmasens-Ludwigswinkel-Eppenbrunn assembly area before 1 January consisted of the following: *1st and 3rd Battalions, SS-Mountain Infantry Regiment 12*; *SS-Panzer-Grenadier Battalion 506*; *3d Battalion, SS-Mountain Artillery Regiment 6*; one company of *Panzerjägers*; one company of *Signal Battalion 6 NORD*; one platoon of combat engineers; and one medical platoon.

This advance team was commanded by *Standartenführer* Franz Schreiber, Commanding Officer of *SS-Mountain Infantry Regiment 12, "Michael Gaißmair."* For this reason, it is usually designated "Combat Group Schreiber" (*Combat Group Schreiber*). *Combat Group Wingen* was thus a *part* of *Combat Group* Schreiber, but was *not* the *Combat Group per se.*

The remainder of NORD, including the Commanding General, *SS-Gruppenführer* and *Generalleutnant der Waffen-SS* Karl Brenner, arrived in the operational area during the second week of January. Brenner emplaced his divisional CP at Schweizerländel (la Petite Suisse) on 9 January. *NORD* accepted front-line responsibility on 10 January, taking over the main line of resistance from the *361st VGD.*

block the road through the Moder Valley against likely American counterattack. Our first task *en route* to Wingen would be to seize Melch, a hamlet high in the rugged Vosges hills (366 meters above sea level), not later than sunrise the next day (roughly 0825 hours). In the absence of aerial reconnaissance, and with only limited success with other intelligence-gathering techniques (prisoner interrogations, signals intercepts, recon patrols, and so on), the area around Melch was *terra incognita* for the *361st,* and neither *Major* Ehlers nor anyone else could tell us what to expect there. In the vicinity of our ultimate objective, Wingen, our briefer told us to expect "the command post of a large unit, perhaps a division," but he was vague even on that score. With this last remark, we were dismissed. It was 2200 hours.

We soon found our battalion resting on either side of the road leading to Petit-Marteau. Our mission to arrive at Melch at daybreak so the next day would require a march of not more than three hours. That meant we still had some five hours to spare. I suggested that the battalion assemble for the remaining hours in a draw to the right of the road, where the rising slopes of this spur valley were steep and offered more shelter against artillery fire than our position on the open road.

That done, our supply people served hot soup and bread, the first meal on this long day. It was greeted by everyone with relish, despite the leaden fatigue.

Thus ended Day One for our *3d Battalion.*

## -II-
## The Other Side of the Hill

The US troops holding the zone in which we were to advance were part of Task Force Hudelson. This organization was an *ad hoc* creation built around Combat Command R (CCR) of the 14th Armored Division, but included some separate VI Corps units not normally assigned to the 14th. TF Hudelson was under the direct control of VI Corps, and took up its positions on 21 December. From west to east (left to right), it consisted of the following combat elements, arrayed in this fashion:

- 117th Cavalry Reconnaissance Squadron (a separate VI Corps unit commanded by Lieutenant Colonel Hodge) from Lake Hasselfurth in the west 2.5 kilometers to Hill 430.
- 94th Cavalry Reconnaissance Squadron (Lieutenant Colonel McCullum) from Hill 430 3.5 kilometers to the Bannstein-Forneau Neuf Road.

- 62d Armored Infantry Battalion (Lieutenant Colonel Robert Meyers) from Bannstein ten kilometers to Neunhoffen.
- Company B, 645th Tank Destroyer Battalion (another separate VI Corps unit) in support.
- Company B, 83d Chemical Mortar Battalion (VI Corps) in support.
- Company A, 125th Armored Engineer Battalion in support.
- Detachment, 540th Engineer Combat Regiment (VI Corps) in support.
- 500th Armored Field Artillery Battalion (Self-propelled 105mm Howitzer) in support.

This task force, on the left flank of the VI Corps, had been given the mission to screen the sixteen-kilometer sector from just east of Bitche, where it tied in with the XV Corps' 100th Infantry Division, to Neunhoffen, where it connected to the 45th Infantry Division. This deeply-compartmented, mountainous, and thickly-forested, area was considered the least passable terrain for an enemy attack, and so Major General Brooks, commanding general of VI Corps, had accepted risk there, screening this unlikely area of enemy attack with an *ad hoc* force ill-suited to defense against a major effort. Brooks intended to use the newly-arrived elements of the 275th Infantry Regiment of Task Force Herren (the three infantry regiments of the 70th Infantry Division, that is, the 274th, 275th, and 276th Infantry Regiments), attached to the 45th Infantry Division, to relieve Task Force Hudelson commencing 1 January.

The first part of the American line to collapse was held by Hodge's 117th Cavalry Squadron. According to the After Action Report of the 117th Cavalry Reconnaissance Squadron (Mechanized), and according to the memoirs of its staff officers, the elements of this squadron were taken by surprise by the German attack on New Year's Eve.

This is surprising in itself!

As early as 24 December, the very capable intelligence staff (G-2) of the US Seventh Army, headed by Colonel (later Lieutenant General) Bill Quinn, advised that an enemy attack was imminent. Specifically, they had warned that the Germans would strike southwards of Bitche with five to eight divisions!

On 29 December, Seventh Army G-2 issued "Estimate of the Enemy Situation No. 6," which outlined four possible German courses of action for the coming days. According to Colonel Quinn, the most likely was a series of limited objective attacks all across the Low Vosges, intended to keep the combat echelons of the Seventh Army in position, to "prevent dispatch of troops to the EIFEL area," to reinforce US First and Third Army efforts in reducing the Ardennes salient.[56] This alone should have caused American commanders to be alert to German offensive activity.

The next most likely German course of action was, "to attack south from the BITCHE-SARREGUEMINES area with five to eight divisions with [the] initial objective of seizing [the] SAVERNE and INGWILLER Passes."[57] In other words, Colonel Quinn and his section had divined precisely what the first *NORDWIND* action would be, and warned of it over forty-eight hours in advance!

As further reinforcement of the likelihood of this German course of action, on 30 December, Headquarters, Sixth Army Group warned the Commander, US Seventh Army of the possibility of "a hostile attack against your flank west of Bitche."[58] Subsequently, the commanding general of the US Seventh Army, Lieutenant General Alexander Patch, went to the XV Corps command post at Fénétrange on New Year's Eve. Here, he told the commanders of VI and XV Corps to cancel all holiday celebrations, and to expect a German attack that night. [59]

It must be assumed that Major General Brooks, commanding general of the VI Corps, ordered his staff officers to pass this message to all the major units under his command, including Task Force Hudelson.

Yet, to the surprise of the executive officer and the adjutant of the 275th Infantry Regiment, Colonel Daniel Hudelson gave no indication that he was expecting a hostile attack. During a liaison visit to his headquarters in Baerenthal, Hudelson briefed the 275th's officers on the quiet that reigned in his sector, and expressed no awareness of an impending attack on his unit. On the contrary, he was proud to state that his troops had kept the Germans ignorant of his Task Force's disposition![60]

Colonel Hudelson must have withheld from his visitors the sad (and embarrassing) information that on the night of 29 December, a German patrol had captured Lieutenant Stephen A. Middlebrook at his own command post, where he had been sleeping undressed.[61] Middlebrook had been in command of the 3d Platoon of the 117th's Troop B, in position along the northern tip of Lake Hasselfurth, only 100 meters from the German lines.

The two mechanized cavalry squadrons of Task Force Hudelson were the main victims of the New Year's Eve attack spearheading Operation *NORDWIND* in its eastern sector. They received the full brunt of the German onslaught, primarily from the *559th*, *257th*, and *361st Volks-Grenadier Divisions*. By equipment and training, mechanized cavalry units were entirely unsuited for defensive operations in such a rugged region, and at best could hope to screen, that is, report enemy actions and delay their progress. The squadron commanders were confident that their lines in the deeply-etched woods would not be heavily attacked.

Only six hours before the opening shots of the German offensive in this area, on the afternoon of 31 December, the executive officer of the 117th Cavalry, Major Harold Samsel, accompanied by Lieutenant Colonel Meyers of the 62d Armored Infantry Battalion, inspected the dug-in positions of Troop B of the 117th. When subsequently reporting back to Lieutenant Colonel Hodge, Samsel proudly stated that "in all [his] combat experience in Italy and France, [he] had never seen a better defense combining maximum fields of fire, mutual support, and all-round defense, employing every weapon of every platoon."[62] To further bolster the strength of the screen, an additional platoon of light tanks (M5 "Stuarts" with machine guns and 37mm cannons) was attached and placed in position with the 3d Platoon. Armored cars (four-wheeled M8s, also with machine guns and 37mm cannons) and tanks were dug in hull-down. Wire communications, supplemented by radio, connected all units, and also established liaison with the 100th Division's 399th Infantry Regiment on the left.

The consensus was that everything possible had been done.

From the 117th Cavalry's After Action Report, one can follow exactly what happened as the German assault unfolded:

| Date/Time | Action |
|---|---|
| 31 2310 Dec | Troop B reports heavy German traffic on the main road due east of Bitche. |
| 01 0015 Jan | Troop B reports a telephone message from an outpost of the 399th Infantry that they are surrounded by the enemy. |
| 01 0030 | 3d Platoon, Troop B reports they are under attack. |
| 01 0100 | Troop C, 117th Cavalry, and Troop D, 94th Cavalry, report they are engaged by the enemy. |
| 01 0200 | Lieutenant Colonel Hodge requests reinforcements from Headquarters, TF Hudelson. He commits Company B, 540th Engineers. |
| | Troop B calls for artillery fire within twenty-five yards of their positions. |
| 01 0330 | Reports from Troop B indicate that enemy is infiltrating between their positions; positions are deemed untenable. Hodge orders the entire squadron to withdraw to a delay position 2.5 kilometers behind the main line of resistance. Many vehicles and four 4.2-inch mortars are abandoned, as German forces had cut the roads behind them. |
| 01 0430 | One platoon of tank destroyers from the 645th TDs and six light tanks from Troop F, 117th Cavalry are placed in position to support the withdrawal. |
| 01 0500 | A second delay position is established 400 yards behind the first, and is occupied until 0700. |

| | |
|---|---|
| 01 0930 | The 19th Armored Infantry Battalion, detached from the 14th Armored Division, is sent forward by Colonel Hudelson to counterattack to restore the positions of the 117th Cavalry. |
| 01 1330 | Baerenthal, the location of the command post of Task Force Hudelson, comes under German fire. Without reserves, Hudelson requests Hodge send elements to protect the Task Force CP. |
| 01 1400 | Hodge believes right flank of TF Hudelson is collapsing. Hodge orders 94th Cavalry, now attached to him for command and control, to send one troop to Baerenthal, while one troop keeps open the Fourneau Neuf-Reipertswiller road. The remaining forces under his command are to withdraw from their "second delay position" to the Mouterhouse-Lemberg road. 117th Cavalry to delay toward Lemberg; 19th Armored Infantry to delay to Sarreinsberg. |
| 01 1530 | Both troops of the 94th Cavalry arrive at Mouterhouse and receive artillery and small arms fire. Unable to fight their way out to the east, they also withdraw toward Lemberg. |
| 01 1700 | 19th Armored Infantry Battalion and Troop C, 117th Cavalry arrive just to the southwest of Mouterhouse, then withdraw to Sarreinsberg.<br>117th Squadron command post with is established in Wingen-sur-Moder. Unable to make radio contact the headquarters of TF Hudelson, Hodge proceeds to Bouxwiller (fifteen kilometers to the rear, straight-line distance), to report to the commanding general of the 14th Armored Division, ands requests instructions.<br>After learning that the TF Hudelson command post has been reestablished at Reipertswiller (forward of his own command post), Hodge proceeds there to receive the order from Colonel Hudelson to hold the line between Reipertswiller and Sarreinsberg with the remaining forces of the 94th Cavalry Squadron and the 19th Armored Infantry Battalion, in addition to his own 117th Squadron. |

During the first day of *NORDWIND*, the 117th Cavalry Squadron fell back over nine kilometers; in the process, they sustained one soldier killed, one officer and twelve enlisted men wounded, and one officer and twenty-four enlisted men missing. They lost more vehicles than they did men, abandoning or otherwise losing twelve M8 armored cars, six M5 light tanks, two half-tracks, and thirty-eight jeeps.

On the right flank of Task Force Hudelson, elements of the 45th Infantry Division's 2d Battalion, 157th Infantry Regiment successfully defended Dambach against the combined assault of the *Grenadier Regiments 456* and *481* of the *256th VGD*. On the left flank, the 399th Infantry stood fast against the assaults of the *559th VGD*, until the withdrawal of the 117th Cavalry left the right flank of the 399th Infantry (and, therefore, the entire XV Corps) hanging in space. Although the 117th Cavalry reported its initial withdrawal to Major Lawrence Conrey, the S-3 of the 399th Infantry, their withdrawal was conducted so precipitously that the infantry could not react. Subsequent withdrawals to the second delay line and beyond were not reported to the 399th at all.[63] As a result, by the evening of 1 January, Major General Burress, the commanding general of the 100th Infantry Division, had to peel back his division's right flank all the way to Lemberg, facing no longer northeast, but due east.

## -III-
## At the End of the Day

On the German side, *Generalmajor* Philippi could be satisfied with the results achieved by his *361st VGD*. His regiments had reached their objectives for the day. Baerenthal was in their hands, and there was a good basis for continuing the attack to the south. His men's acquaintance with the terrain through which they had passed during their withdrawal in December had stood them in good stead when they headed back over it in the attack. His men were rested on the eve of the operation, and the Maginot Line had been to their backs from the beginning.

*Generalmajor* Philippi could also not rightfully complain about the achievements of his neighbor to the right, the *257th VGD* of *Generalmajor* Erich Seidel. Their advance had taken them to Mouterhouse, abreast of the *361st*. However, he was legitimately concerned with the capabilities of his neighbor to the left, namely the *256th VGD* of *Generalmajor* Gerhard Franz; its regiments had taken neither Dambach nor Philippsbourg. Thus, the right flank of the *361st* was entirely exposed, meaning that forces vital for continuing the attack southward would have to be deployed to cover the gap with the *256th*.

Now, as the second day loomed near, Philippi's men were stressed from the exertions of the day, and they lacked proper winter clothing. Also, his assault gun company had lost several vehicles to American fighter-bombers during the assault on Baerenthal.[64]

Somewhat consoling for Philippi was that the *LXXXIX Corps* commander, *Generalleutnant* Gustav Höhne—when visiting his command post on the evening of 1 January—had given Philippi tactical control over the advance elements of the *6th SS Gebirgs-Division NORD*. These seasoned troops, equipped for winter warfare and highly experienced in forest combat in cold weather, were just what was urgently required for the *361st* to continue its offensive momentum.

When briefing *Generalleutnant* Höhne in detail, Philippi requested more armor support to make up the day's losses; only with mobile, hard-hitting armor could he assure himself of the combat power and flexibility he would need for the next day's success. Höhne promised to do what he could with *1st Army* and *Army Group G*—he had no armored reserves under his own command, and would have to get support from either the tanks, tank destroyers, and assault guns supporting the *XIII SS Corps* attack in the west, or receive detachments from the *Army Group G* operational reserve, the *21st Panzer* or *25th Panzer-Grenadier* divisions.[65]

To the right of Philippi's division, *Generalmajor* Seidel and his *Ia*, *Oberstleutnant i.G.* Ernst Linke, were not quite as pleased with the results of the *257th VGD*'s day of fighting. The reports of progress from their units coming into their command post just east of the *Camp de Bitche* were not all good.

On the positive side, *GR 457* had seized Mouterhouse from the 117th and 94th Cavalry Squadrons. On the other side of the ledger, *GR 477* had failed to take the key crossroads in Lemberg. Elements of the 100th Infantry Division's 399th Infantry had defended Lemberg fiercely, taking advantage of the town's natural defensive posture—it sits on a hill, dominating the approaches to all sides. This physical domination prevented the *477th* from side-stepping the town and pushing on to Goetzenbruck-Sarreinsberg, too, as fire could be brought on any German units trying to get around the area.

At Lemberg, Seidel's *grenadiers* could have used some help from their right neighbor, namely *Generalmajor* Kurt Freiherr von der Mühlen's *559th VGD*. Both, after all, were part of *General der Infanterie* Erich Petersen's *XC Corps*. One should have thought that a combined effort of both divisions would have yielded the desired results, that is, seizure of the key terrain of Lemberg. Yet apparently, the *559th* had its hands full, too.

To add extra impetus to his attacks for the next day, *Generalmajor* Seidel requested that *General* Petersen release his corps reserve, namely the third regiment of the *257th*, *GR 466*. Seidel proposed using this regiment to seize Goetzenbruck-Sarreinsberg while the rest of his division attacked Lemberg. After the *257th* secured Mouterhouse, Petersen reassigned the *466th* to its

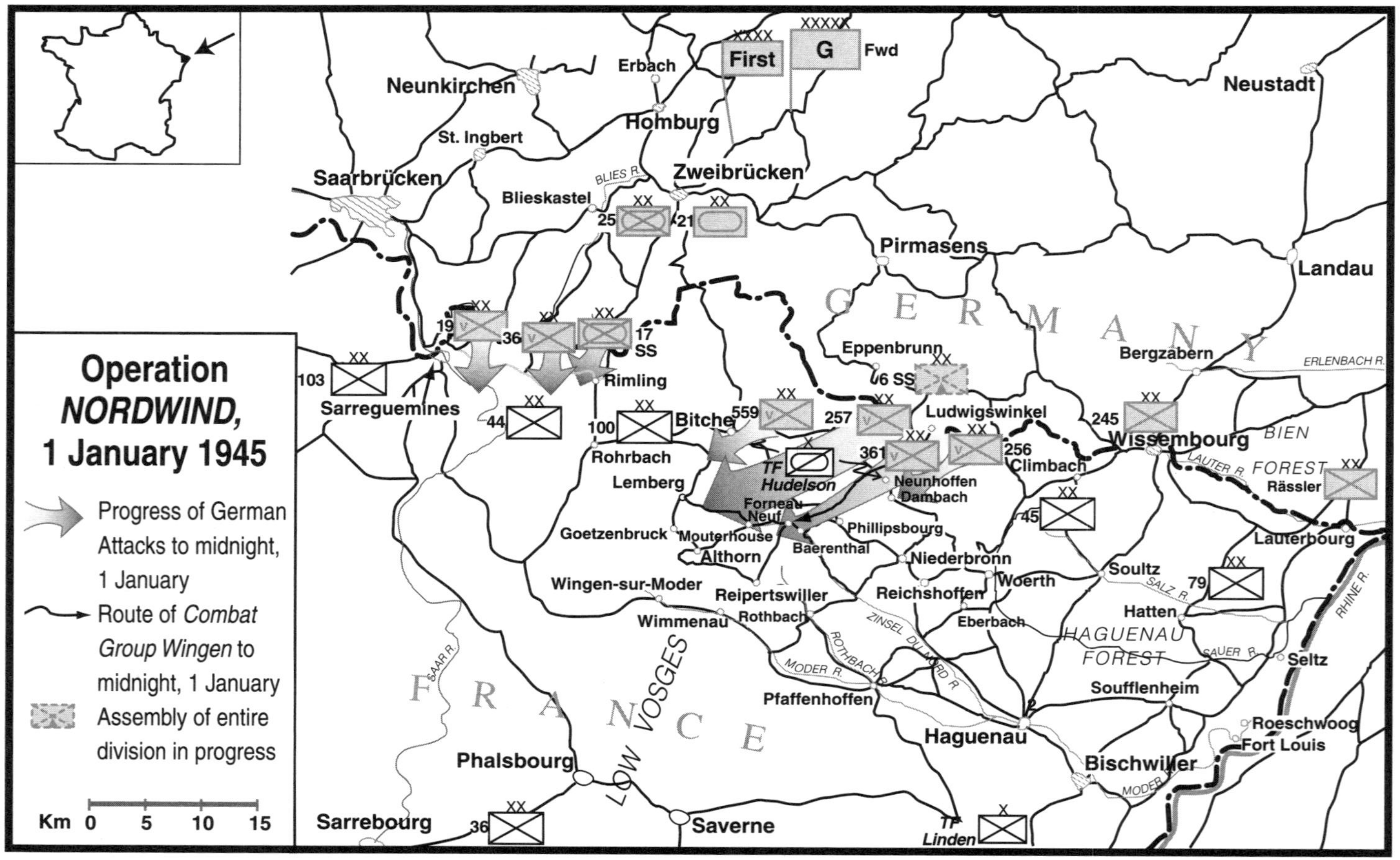
Operation NORDWIND, 1 January 1945
Progress of German Attacks to midnight, 1 January
Route of Combat Group Wingen to midnight, 1 January
Assembly of entire division in progress
Km 0 5 10 15
GERMANY
FRANCE
LOW VOSGES
BIEN FOREST
HAGUENAU FOREST
RHINE R.
ERLENBACH R.
LAUTER R.
SAUER R.
SALZ R.
MODER R.
ZINSEL DU NORD R.
ROTHBACH R.
SAAR R.
BLIES R.
First
G
Fwd
Neunkirchen
Erbach
Homburg
St. Ingbert
Saarbrücken
Zweibrücken
Blieskastel
Neustadt
Pirmasens
Landau
Sarreguemines
Rimling
17 SS
6 SS
Eppenbrunn
Bergzabern
Ludwigswinkel
Bitche
Rohrbach
Lemberg
TF Hudelson
Neunhoffen
Dambach
Climbach
Wissembourg
Rässler
Forneau Neuf
Goetzenbruck
Mouterhouse
Phillipsbourg
Baerenthal
Althorn
Niederbronn
Lauterbourg
Soultz
Woerth
Wingen-sur-Moder
Reipertswiller
Reichshoffen
Wimmenau
Rothbach
Eberbach
Hatten
Seltz
Soufflenheim
Pfaffenhoffen
Haguenau
Roeschwoog
Fort Louis
Bischwiller
Phalsbourg
Sarrebourg
Saverne
TF Linden
103
19
36
25
21
44
100
559
257
361
256
245
45
79
36

parent division, and the *466th* set off on a night approach march to its assembly area north of Alt-Schmel, three kilometers northwest of Mouterhouse.* The *466th* would thus participate in the continuation of the attacks to the west and southwest on the morrow.

The least progress of all German divisions in the Low Vosges on that first day of the new year was made by the *256th VGD. Generalmajor* Franz and his *Ia, Oberstleutnant i.G.* Bernhard Kögel, had cause to be concerned about their division's posture as the day ended. While their units had indeed succeeded in taking Lieschbach and Neunhoffen from TF Hudelson's 62d Armored Infantry Battalion, they were still not in position to seize Dambach from the 157th Infantry, nor Philippsbourg from the 275th Infantry.

The reasons for this inadequate performance, which seriously jeopardized the *361st*'s ability to perform its mission on the morrow, were manifold. The *256th VGD* had been shifted from its previous defensive positions between Wissembourg and the Rhine to assembly areas around Hinterweidenthal, Dahn, and Hauenstein, and on the night of 30–31 December, its *Landsers* had to march on foot from there to attack positions to the south of Ludwigswinkel—distances of over twenty-five kilometers, over hilly terrain, in frosty weather. Most units only arrived in their positions late on New Year's Eve, and so had no time to pause before going directly into the attack.

Furthermore, for reasons of operational security, the battalion and company commanders in the *256th* were apprised of their orders as late as a few hours before the commencement of the attack, on the evening of 31 December. For intelligence on the enemy and terrain, they had to rely on ultra-short briefings from their counterparts in the *361st VGD* upon their arrival in the attack positions. There was no time or opportunity for reconnaissance or other planning or preparations of their own.

To make matters worse for Franz's men, in their zone, the fortifications of the Maginot Line were in American hands. These would have to be dealt with before any of the day's objectives could be seized.

Finally, the personnel situation in the *256th* was the least promising of all the divisions in the *NORDWIND* offensive. Besides being significantly

*Tactical information from Petersen, 23–24.

Petersen was originally an infantry officer, who volunteered to serve in the paratroops in 1941. In the German armed forces, nearly all parachute troops were in the *Luftwaffe*, so Petersen had transferred to that service, and saw action on the East Front as commanding general of the *7th Fallschirm-Division*. In 1944, he was given command of the *IV Luftwaffe Field Corps*, and as such, directed the fight of numerous German infantry formations in the High Vosges in October and November 1944. When his headquarters was removed from the Colmar Pocket after the American penetration of the High Vosges passes, it was renamed *XC* (Army) *Corps*, and *General der Flieger* Petersen and his staff reverted to Army ranks and Army uniforms (Bonn, 84).

understrength, the units had been supplemented by men of low physical stamina, who were of limited use in strenuous mountain combat. The training afforded the division had been too little to condition these men for the rigors of offensive operations. Only one of the regimental commanders had sufficient experience for his posting, and the battalion and company commanders, though willing, were too young and inexperienced for the demands of their billets. As *Oberstleutnant* Kögel put it, by the time of *NORDWIND*, the division was only "fit for defense."[66]

The results on the American side were similarly mixed as the first day of *NORDWIND* came to a close. While the infantry had stood their ground—the 399th at Lemberg, the 157th at Dambach, and even the green 275th at Philippsbourg, the units of the ad hoc TF Hudelson had yielded to the German onslaught, albeit unevenly. That is, the cavalry had given ground quickly, while the 62d Armored Infantry had only more stubbornly given way, and even then mainly because the cavalry to their west were exposing their left flank.

Task Force Hudelson has received "bad press" for their performance on 1 January, which is only partly justified. By training and equipment, mechanized cavalry is never meant to "stand fast," to defend a line of resistance to the last cartridge. Their higher headquarters had chosen to employ them in this role, hoping that they would not be attacked in a sector unsuitable for a major attack. When Major General Brooks decided to employ his cavalry in this fashion, he was accepting risk, and could only have hoped that the terrain in the Low Vosges between Bitche and Neunhoffen would slow any enemy attack long enough for him to rush reinforcements to the rescue.

This is exactly what he did, releasing the 19th Armored Infantry Battalion from his reserve (the two remaining combat commands of the 14th Armored Division) in an attempt to restore the situation. Unfortunately for the Americans, this force arrived too late to shore up the defenses, and lacked the strength to successfully counterattack. Nevertheless, over the next week, forces would be continuously fed into the battle in the Low Vosges and during the next days of *NORDWIND*, the American situation would improve significantly.

Nevertheless, the precipitous, and ultimately deep, withdrawal of the 117th Cavalry, with practically no notice given to its neighbor on the left, the 399th Infantry, left the right flank of the XV Corps wide open. The hole left in the lines by this action opened the door for the German attack on Wingen-sur-Moder!

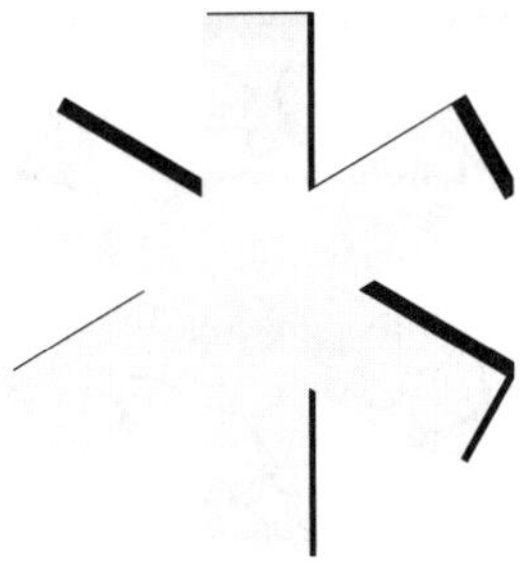

# The Second Day: First Contact

## -I-
## A Quiet Beginning

Those few members of the *3d Battalion, SS-Mountain Infantry Regiment 12* who were lucky enough to be able to sleep in any position, under any conditions, were awakened around 0400. The night had been bitterly cold and there was fresh snow on the ground. Only the steep slopes of the draw turning off the Lindelthal Road had protected the battalion, and kept out the icy wind.

Ersatz coffee was served, and everyone still had a bite of bread, which had been issued with the hot meal around midnight. As the battalion formed in march order under the supervision of the NCOs, *Hauptsturmführer* Kreuzinger called the company commanders together and briefed them on the day's mission. Melch had to be reached by first light. All we knew from the map we had been issued by *Major* Ehlers, the *Ia*, was how to find Melch, which seemed to be a hamlet higher up in the mountains, with a single access road from the south. Nobody in the *361st* knew what to expect at Melch, but they had warned us to be wary of enemy stragglers, scattered small units from American forces that had retreated in the face of the German attack during the previous afternoon.

Order of march this morning was a scouting party, then the main body, then the battalion trains—our *Bergstaffel*, or mountain support echelon. I was to lead the scout element, with the only map we had, and the bulk of the battalion would follow in single file, combat-ready.

Shortly after 0430, I left the draw with the scouts and turned right onto the dirt road along the Lindelthal. With first light only coming at 0730, we had three hours to march the six kilometers to the outskirts of Melch. So long as nothing happened along the way, this was ample time, even in the pitch dark.

Soon our dirt road joined the main road linking Mouterhouse and Baerenthal, about six kilometers apart; both towns had been in German

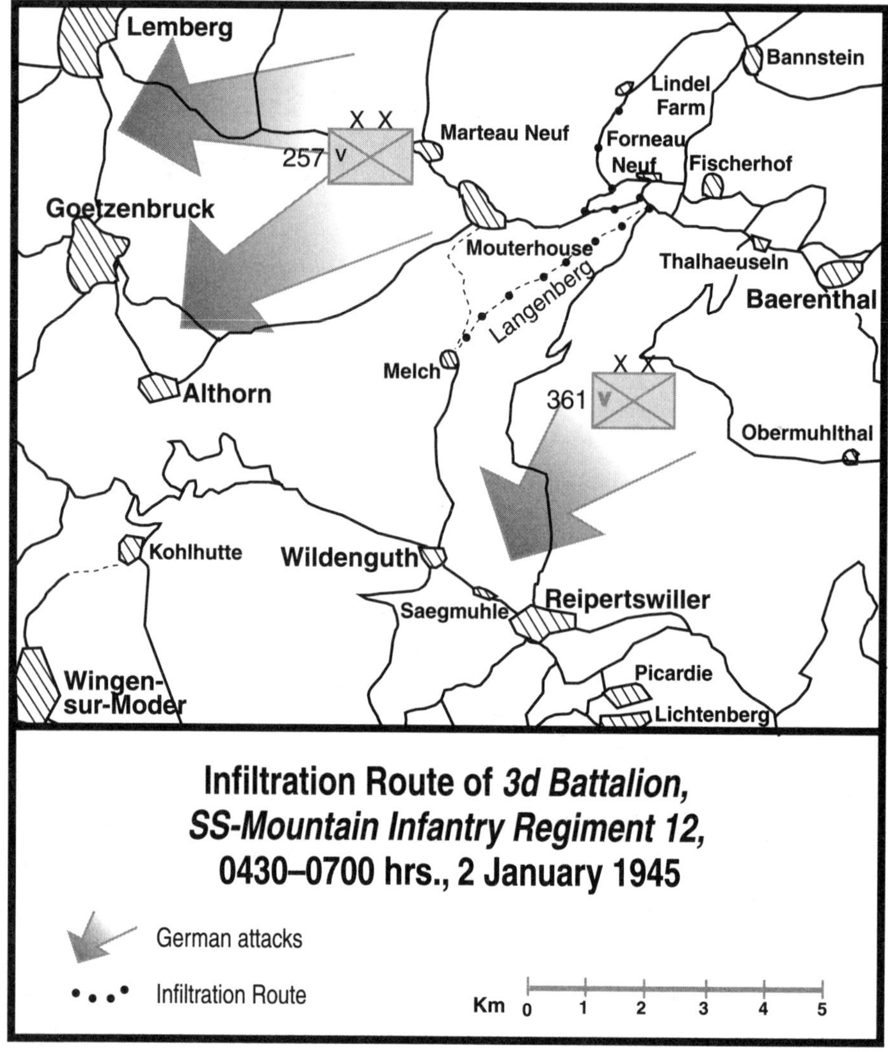


**Infiltration Route of *3d Battalion, SS-Mountain Infantry Regiment 12,* 0430–0700 hrs., 2 January 1945**

hands since the late hours of 1 January. After crossing the bridge over the Zintselbach, we had a clear view to the right, where the sky was flickering brightly from the fires in Mouterhouse. But that did not concern us presently; we had to turn in the other direction. Bypassing Forneau Neuf on our left, and marching on the main road, we reached the toe of the Langenberg, exactly on the corner where the road to Reipertswiller turns off in a southerly direction. We did not take this road, instead choosing to climb the steep path, which eventually led us to the crest of the Langenberg.

Two kilometers done, four to go!

Before reaching the more gentle ridge, there was steep climbing for the first kilometer and a half along the way, where we had to negotiate a gradient averaging ten percent. It must have been around 0600 when we came to the crest and our footpath seemed to flatten out in front of us, always in a generally southwesterly direction.

There were no certain markings on this trail, the ground being covered by snow. But we had the stars twinkling over us for orientation and in case of doubt, got assistance from the compass. Moving in single file, each man took care to be absolutely silent. There was a strict "no smoking" order in effect, as the glow of a cigarette was likely to be seen 500 meters away.

After another hour, we came to a clearing. Crouching low and moving cautiously to the edge of the wood, I could make out a basin-shaped valley before us to the south. There were a few buildings down below, the nearest one being about 200 meters from our position. This was Melch, the morning's objective, and it was still shrouded in early morning mountain darkness.

It took our companies until 0730 or 0745 to reach the forest's edge. No one was to leave the cover of the woods. By all indications, it would be a bright and sunny day, and with that, we had to expect aircraft at any time. So far, so good, though; we had reached our objective by daybreak, undetected.

## *Frays in the Fabric of NORDWIND*

Although our battalion was advancing south on its solitary route through some of the most rugged terrain in the Low Vosges, it was by no means operating in a vacuum. The *361st VGD*, to which *Combat Group Schreiber* (and therefore we) was attached, was under the control of *LXXXIX Corps*, and was operating mostly to our left rear. The *257th VGD*, operating to our right rear, was under the control of *XC Corps*. As a result, we were operating not only in advance of our neighbors on either side, but also were on the boundary between two corps. Many of the problems we encountered over the next few days resulted directly or indirectly from this situation.

The missions of the organic and attached units of the *361st VGD* for 2 January were as follows:

- *GR 953* (reinforced by the *2d Battalion, GR 951*) was to conduct the main attack and seize Reipertswiller and subsequently Wimmenau;
- *GR 952* (less one battalion) was to support them by seizing Lichtenberg, and then reconnoiter the zone up to Rothbach and Ingwiller;
- a battalion of *GR 952* was to remain in place in the vicinity of Baerenthal to block the approaches to Zintsel Creek Valley from the west; and

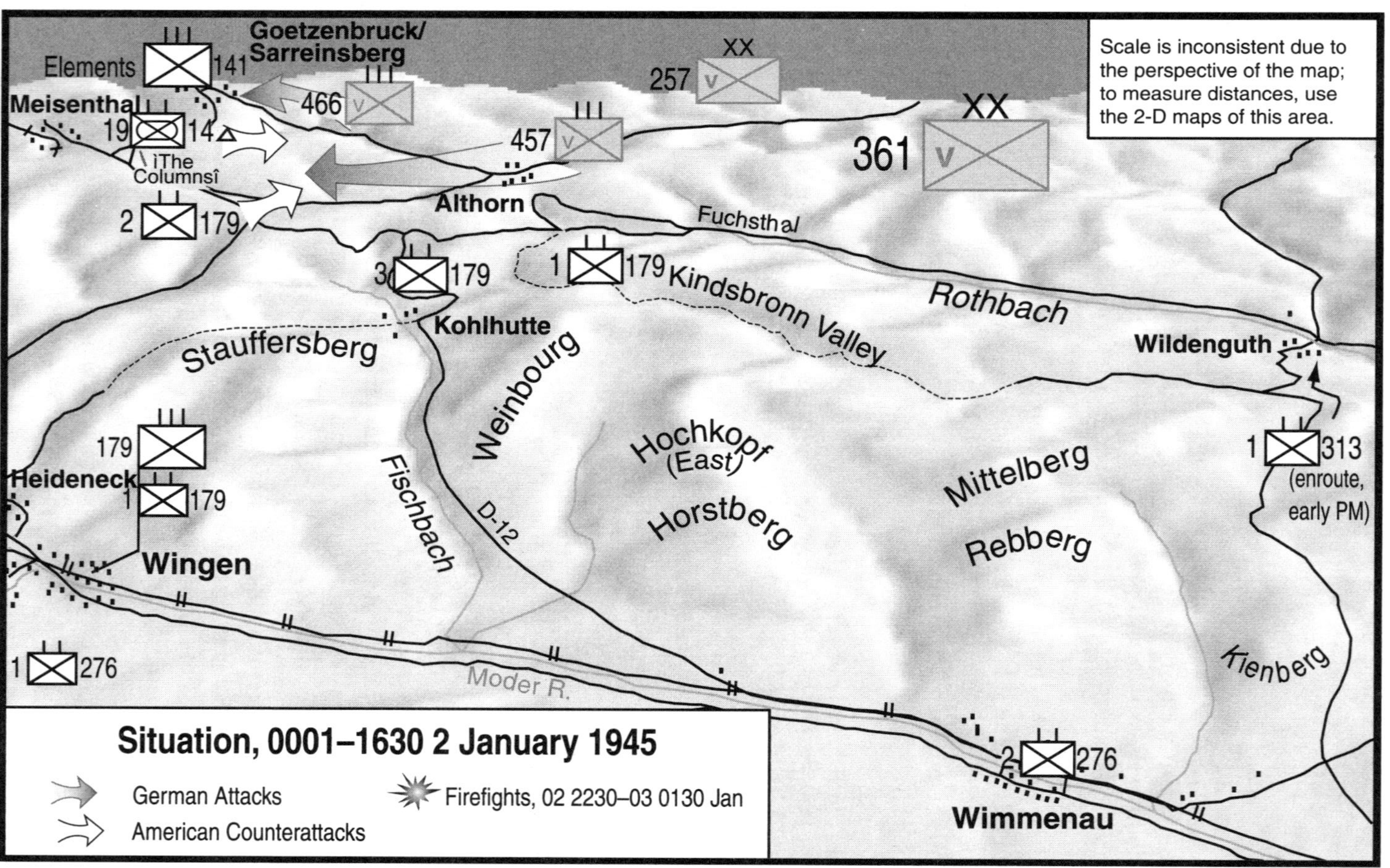
Scale is inconsistent due to the perspective of the map; to measure distances, use the 2-D maps of this area.
Goetzenbruck/ Sarreinsberg
Elements
141
Meisenthal
19
14
ìThe Columnsî
466
257
XX
457
XX
361
2
179
Althorn
Fuchsthal
3
179
1
179
Kindsbronn Valley
Rothbach
Kohlhutte
Stauffersberg
Wildenguth
Weinbourg
Hochkopf (East)
179
Heideneck
1
179
1
313
(enroute, early PM)
Mittelberg
Fischbach
D-12
Horstberg
Rebberg
Wingen
1
276
Moder R.
Kienberg
2
276
Wimmenau
Situation, 0001–1630 2 January 1945
German Attacks
Firefights, 02 2230–03 0130 Jan
American Counterattacks

* elements of *Combat Group Schreiber* were to seize Wingen.[67]

Philippi started his day on 2 January by driving to the command post of *GR 953* in the dark at 0700. He found the regimental commander in his command post at the highest point north of Reipertswiller, next to the road. The two battalions of the *953d* had reached their respective assembly areas on the hills north of Saegmuhle and Reipertswiller only after an exhausting night march. Philippi noticed deep fatigue on the faces of his grenadiers, especially the young ones who had not been fully conditioned for this kind of warfare.

The reinforcing battalion, namely, the *2d Battalion of GR 951*, was still on the march, and the artillery battalion assigned to support the *953d* was not yet in position. Although the rest of the division's artillery regiment was ready to fire at 0700, there were no communications between the forward observers and the guns. Only two assault guns had reached the assembly area, as two others had failed mechanically during the movement from Baerenthal. As a result of these conditions, the regimental commander postponed the attack on Reipertswiller until the direct support artillery battalion was in place, and solid wire and radio communications established with all fire support elements. The attack was now rescheduled for 1400, in broad daylight. Reconnaissance elements had yet to contact the enemy in the vicinity of the objective.[68]

## -II-
## Actions and Reactions

*Generalmajor* Philippi was not wrong at the end of this day when he stated that, "the enemy had shifted new forces to the battlefield." These forces would vastly complicate and significantly hinder the already difficult operations of *XC* and *LXXXIX Corps*.

The events of Day Two of *NORDWIND* proved how promptly the higher headquarters of the US Seventh Army in this sector reacted to the new threat. The intent of the Seventh Army commanding general was to effectively block all pass roads from the Vosges Mountains leading south, to deny German forces access to the Alsatian Plain. Thus, 2 January became the "Day of the Great Shift."

On the far right of the XV Corps sector, just to the west of the boundary between XV and VI Corps, the 100th Infantry Division's 399th Infantry Regiment tenaciously defended Lemberg against the attacks of the *559th VGD*. This anchor-point was reinforced as the day went on by the 3d

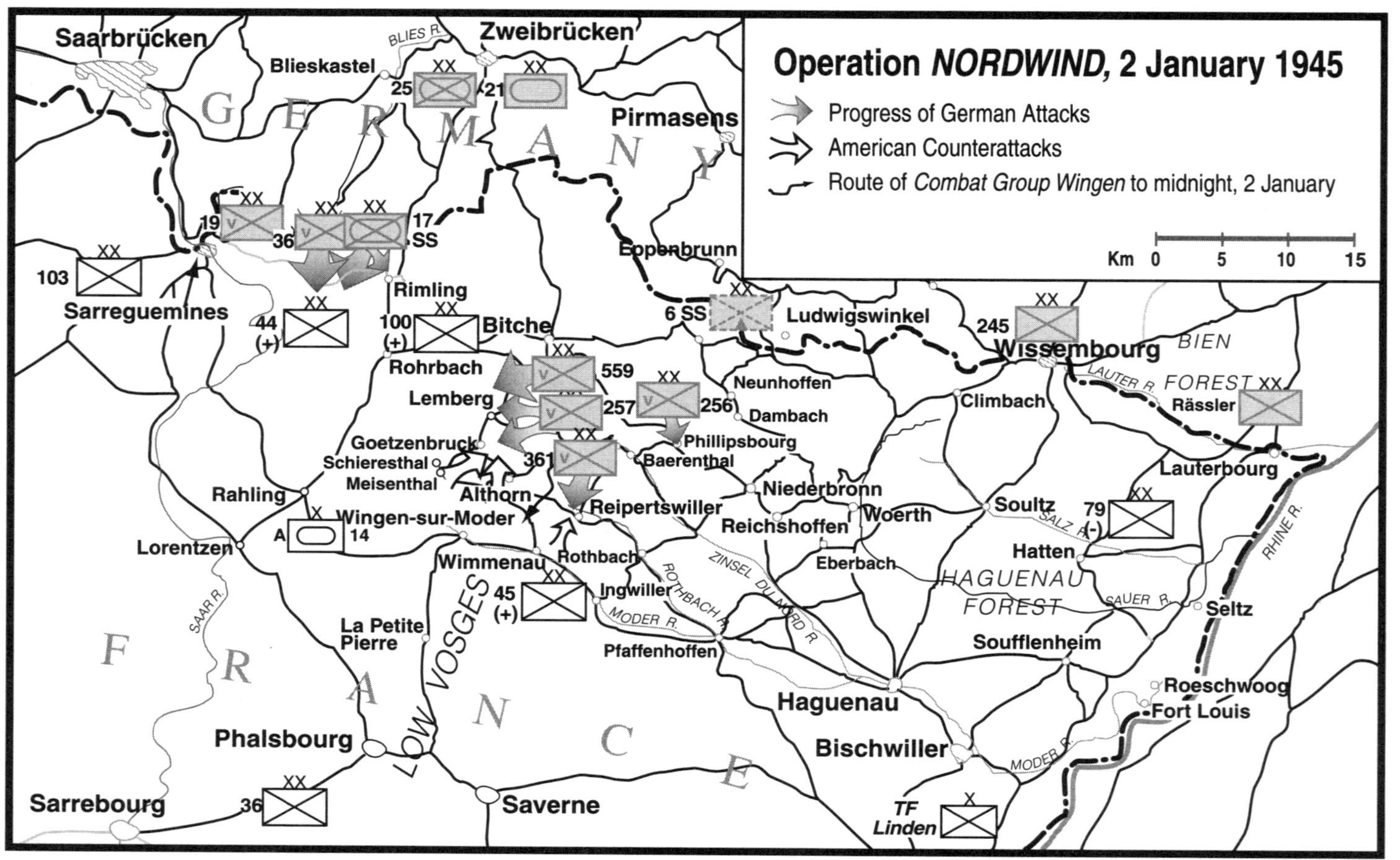
Operation NORDWIND, 2 January 1945
Progress of German Attacks
American Counterattacks
Route of Combat Group Wingen to midnight, 2 January
Km 0 5 10 15
GERMANY
FRANCE
Saarbrücken
Blieskastel
BLIES R.
Zweibrücken
Pirmasens
Eppenbrunn
Ludwigswinkel
Sarreguemines
Rimling
Bitche
Rohrbach
Lemberg
Goetzenbruck
Schieresthal
Meisenthal
Althorn
Rahling
Wingen-sur-Moder
Lorentzen
SAAR R.
Wimmenau
Rothbach
Ingwiller
MODER R.
ROTHBACH R.
Pfaffenhoffen
La Petite Pierre
LOW VOSGES
Phalsbourg
Sarrebourg
Saverne
Reipertswiller
Baerenthal
Phillipsbourg
Neunhoffen
Dambach
Niederbronn
Reichshoffen
Woerth
Eberbach
ZINSEL DU NORD R.
Haguenau
Bischwiller
TF Linden
Wissembourg
BIEN FOREST
LAUTER R.
Rässler
Climbach
Lauterbourg
RHINE R.
Soultz
SALZ R.
Hatten
HAGUENAU FOREST
SAUER R.
Seltz
Soufflenheim
Roeschwoog
Fort Louis
103
19
36
17 SS
25
21
44 (+)
100 (+)
6 SS
559
257
256
361
245
79 (-)
45 (+)
A 14
36

Battalion, 255th Infantry Regiment of Task Force Harris,* and the 141st Regimental Combat Team of the highly-experienced 36th Infantry Division.

The 45th Infantry Division was most directly concerned with this major transfer of forces. Along with the elements of the 36th Infantry Division arriving in the Goetzenbruck area, the "Thunderbirds" were the most seasoned American troops in the Vosges in this sector. The division had participated in the campaigns in the mountains of Sicily and mainland Italy, as well as the invasion of southern France, the push on the Saverne Gap, and most recently, the attack on the *Westwall.*

During this Second Day, the left boundary of the 45th Infantry Division was shifted twice by order of the commanding general of VI Corps. By evening, it included Soucht and the southeast portion of Lemberg, terminating southeast of Bitche. Thus, the 45th, as the westernmost major unit of the VI Corps of the US Seventh Army, was now extended over a continuous front line of some fifty kilometers from Niederschlettenbach in Germany on its right (east) to the highland forests of the Lower Vosges on its left (west), tying in there with elements of the XV Corps' 100th Infantry Division.

To enable Major General Robert T. Frederick, commanding general, 45th Infantry Division, to operate over such a long front line, Major General Edward H. Brooks, the commanding general, VI Corps, placed numerous units of other divisions under Frederick's command. Frederick placed the 36th Engineer (Combat) Regiment on his far right, in the least endangered sector, abutting elements of the 79th Infantry Division; to more threatened sectors, he committed the 274th, 275th, and 276th Infantry Regiments of the newly arrived Task Force Herren,† and elements of the 79th Infantry Division, including the 313th Infantry (less the 3d Battalion), the 1st Battalion, 314th Infantry, and the 1st Battalion, 315th Infantry Regiments.[69]

In his own sector, *Generalmajor* Philippi and his *361st VGD* were opposed by elements of the 313th Infantry Regiment which defended Reipertswiller,

*Task Force Harris, commanded by Brigadier General Frederick M. Harris, Assistant Division Commander of the 63d Infantry Division, consisted of the three infantry regiments of the 63d, namely the 253d, 254th and 255th Infantry. The remainder of the division, that is, the division artillery, engineer battalion, medical battalion, and so on, was still enroute to France and would not arrive in time to participate in combat in *NORDWIND.* The third unit in this predicament was Task Force Linden, commanded by Brigadier General Henning Linden, which consisted of the three infantry regiments of the 42d Infantry Divison, that is, 222d, 232d, and 242d Infantry Regiments. This latter unit would also have a brutal baptism of fire starting 5 January, while attached to the 79th Infantry Division in the defense of the Rhine Plain.

†Task Force Herren, commanded by Brigadier General Thomas Herren, and consisting of the three infantry regiments of the 70th Infantry Division, was one of three such "task forces" present in the Seventh Army order of battle. Like Task Force Harris, it was without the benefit of remainder of the division for the duration of *NORDWIND.*

established a roadblock at Wildenguth with its 1st Battalion, and counterattacked Philippi's troops during the afternoon hours with its 2d Battalion.

Further northwest, the battle centered on the twin town of Goetzenbruck-Sarreinsberg, whose easterly outskirts were attacked all day by the *257th VGD*, but defended by the 19th Armored Infantry Battalion, reinforced by the remnants of Troop C, 117th Cavalry Reconnaissance Squadron (Mecz).* Only during the later hours of the day, the 45th's 2d Battalion, 179th Infantry Regiment, as part of the Great Shift, arrived near Goetzenbruck-Sarreinsberg to improve the defenders' situation.

The Great Shift had its genesis in the afternoon hours of 1 January, when Colonel Murphy, the commanding officer of the 179th Infantry Regiment, accompanied by his S-2 (intelligence officer), Captain Watkins, reported to General Frederick at his 45th Division command post in Langensoultzbach. There, they were briefed on the general situation and the missions awaiting the 179th in the sector to which they would shift on the morrow.

In the meantime, the relief of the 179th Infantry Regiment was being conducted by Colonel Boatner's 36th Engineer (Combat) Regiment.

During the night of 1/2 January, the men of the 179th were shuttled by truck from their last sector in Germany northwest of Wissembourg in the following sequence: 2d, then 3d, then 1st Battalion. On 0300 hours on 2 January, Colonel Murphy, his battalion commanders, his S-3 (Captain Williams), and S-2 (Captain Watkins), left the regimental interim command post at Lembach and proceeded to Wingen-sur-Moder. From then, the action went like this:

| Date/Time | Action |
|---|---|
| 02 0520 Jan | Captain Williams arrives at the command post of the 117th Cavalry Reconnaissance Squadron at Wingen-sur-Moder, where he is briefed on the situation by Captain Brown. |
| 02 0640 | Colonel Murphy arrives with his staff officers at the 117th Squadron command post, and is briefed there by the squadron commander, Lieutenant Colonel Hodge. Subsequently, Colonel Murphy issues the following verbal orders:<br>—1st Battalion: Assemble in Kohlhutte.<br>—2d Battalion: Assemble in the vicinity of Sarreinsberg and be prepared to attack or counterattack.<br>—3d Battalion: Assemble north of Wingen and attack northeast to seize Mouterhouse. |

*Mechanized was abbreviated in 1944 as Mecz.

| | |
|---|---|
| 02 0830 | 179th Infantry Regiment establishes its command post in Wingen. |
| 02 0955 | Captain Williams leaves the command post to visit the battalions and pass Colonel Murphy's orders to the respective battalion commanders. |
| 02 1105 | Captain Schmid of the 1st Battalion receives orders to block the crossroads from Wildenguth and Reipertswiller in the forest northeast of Wimmenau with one company (B), and to block the forest road climbing up from the Rothbach Valley northeast of Kohlhutte with another company (C).[70] |

## Combat Group Wingen at Its First Objective

Oblivious to the ominous developments elsewhere, outside Melch, after I reported to the battalion commander, we used our field glasses to systematically sweep all buildings and their surroundings for any sign of life. Although the sun was already shining between the tree trunks to our left, we could not detect anything. Melch seemed to be devoid of human life.

I offered to reconnoiter Melch, and chose one of the runners from our battalion staff messenger section to come with me. Warily, we approached the first building; it was locked and seemingly empty. Only in the third building (of the dozen total) did we finally find an old man. Leaving my runner outside for security, I went in to interview the old fellow, who leisurely smoked one of those bent pipes so common with the mountain people.

Of course, he was a local Alsatian, about seventy years old. His dialect was strange to me at first, but easy to understand. His story was short; he was the last inhabitant of Melch! All the others had left by noon on the day before, headed to some town in the south to lodge with relatives to "avoid the trouble of war" once more. No, there were no longer any "Amis" (German slang for Americans) in Melch, but a small group of some ten or twelve had come the night before—obviously stragglers. They had departed shortly before our arrival, but not before liberating the old man's pocket watch.

Together with my runner, we checked some other houses, but found them all locked, which corroborated the story of the old chap. We had to cut our tour short, as somewhere from the south we heard the distinctive sound of an approaching light aircraft. We made for the nearest edge of the forest, and, crouching low next to a large tree, observed an aircraft which might have been a light reconnaissance machine belonging to an artillery unit. The pilot circled over Melch and the forest around the hamlet. He must have seen something or at least suspected our presence in the woods north of Melch, as a little while after the plane left, we received several rounds of medium caliber artillery fire. Scattered about the area, the only damage done by the fire was to one of the empty houses.

I had just reported my findings to Kreuzinger when our "Franz" appeared, *Standartenführer* Schreiber, our regimental commander. He was accompanied by his aide-de-camp (*Ordonnanzoffizier*) and a runner, and had come up the same trail that we had used three hours before. We had seen him last on New Year's Eve when reporting to his makeshift command post, still on the German side of the border. Kreuzinger briefed him succinctly, at the end repeating what I had just reported after returning from the reconnaissance of Melch.

Schreiber called for the company commanders, and while he sat on a tree stump and we crouched under cover of the trees, he gave us a summary of what had happened during the last twenty-four hours. He explained the highlights of our temporary organizational situation—the composition of *Combat Group Schreiber*, and so on. Next, he explained that we would be joined later that afternoon by the *1st Battalion*, and that our two-battalion force, under the command of the senior officer present, *Hauptsturmführer* Alois Burgstaller (the *1st Battalion*'s commander), would be designated *Combat Group Wingen* (*"Kampfgruppe Wingen."*)

The mission of *Combat Group Wingen* was to seize the town of Wingen-sur-Moder and block the main road running east-west to interdict enemy traffic. The *3d Battalion* of our *Artillery Regiment* would support our attack, and a forward observer would accompany our battalion.

Parallel to and concurrently with our advance on Wingen, *SS-Panzer-Grenadier Battalion 506* (employed dismounted from their halftracks), reinforced by a battalion of *GR 951* (*361st VGD*) would seize Wimmenau, about four kilometers down the road to the Alsatian Plain.

After securing the first objective and establishing a bridgehead over the Moder River, we would be reinforced *inter alia* with a battalion of assault guns. We were to prepare to subsequently seize La Petite Pierre, and from there be ready to push on to the Saverne Pass, to open access to the Rhine Valley for our armored forces.

Little was known about the enemy between Melch and Wingen. Since the start of *NORDWIND*, the enemy—at least in this particular sector—had been routed and was on the run. It had consisted of motorized reconnaissance elements only. The limited intelligence available indicated that there might be a higher command post (perhaps a division) at Wingen. One had to expect that Wingen, therefore, would be defended appropriately—that is, that there would be a line of resistance north of the town.

Schreiber warned us not to depend too much on lasting chaos within the American forces. We had to assume that they had the potential to establish control over their currently confused situation in a very short time. Furthermore, we had to figure that soon they would be bringing reserves up to block our advance. Our success, therefore, hinged on surprising and "outsmarting" the American adversary!

*Standartenführer* Schreiber concluded his talk by announcing that he would now establish his command post at Melch. He departed with this entourage to link up with the rest of his headquarters.

The leaders of the *3d Battalion* immediately began our terrain analysis for the upcoming operation. From the map, we could tell that the Rothbach ("Red Brook") runs generally west-east about three kilometers south of Melch. With its sources south of Althorn, it goes through the villages of Wildenguth and Reipertswiller, then changes its direction to run southeast to the Alsatian Plain at the town that bears its name, Rothbach. For our immediate task, the best avenue of approach to our objective seemed to be through the western part of the Rothbach Valley; it was seemingly devoid of settlements, save the local forester's house. The valley was rather narrow, hemmed in by densely-wooded mountains climbing steeply on both sides. The westernmost part of the Rothbach Valley was rimmed in by a mountain ridge called the "Weinbourg," culminating at an elevation of 380 meters. It was 140 meters higher than the floor of the valley through which we would be advancing. From the valley, the forest road climbed up in narrow serpentines to a pass at the northern end of the Weinbourg Heights. As we "wargamed" the situation, trying to imagine what the enemy would do in defense of Wingen, we could imagine that he would regard the road pass on the Weinbourg ridge as a convenient choke point for checking any advance toward Wingen from our direction. We would have to pay special attention to that spot during our approach later in the day, and take great care coming to this road pass!

Behind and to the west of the Weinbourg ridge, there was a district road, which we would have to cross *en route* to the objective. It connected Bitche to the north with the towns of the Moder Valley to the south, and intersected with the Moder Valley road between Wingen and Wimmenau. This would definitely be a danger area, to be crossed carefully and swiftly.

The town of Wingen-sur-Moder itself was clearly key terrain in this vicinity, being a transportation nexus amid heavily wooded, snow-covered mountains. Besides the district road, there was a more significant one that led from the Saar Valley in the west to the Alsatian Plain in the east. It connected the important cities of Sarre-Union, Ingwiller, Haguenau, and ultimately, Strasbourg. Also, there was another road, which entered Wingen from the south, from Saverne, the greatest gateway to the Rhine Valley. Finally, there was a railroad junction in Wingen as well. The main line from Saarbrücken to Strasbourg runs through the town, and in those days, there was a branch line that connected Wingen with St. Louis-les-Bitche as well. The railroad station was on the northern end of town.

The inhabitants of Wingen, which we estimated to be about 1,000 in number, seemed to be divided into two settlements. Besides Wingen proper, there was a sort of suburb to the northwest, which the map identified as Heideneck ("Pagan's Corner"). The whole area was surrounded by hills that towered 100 to 150 meters above the town.

This was the extent of our map analysis; we had to prepare for our infiltration. Our men, who had established a security screen around the edge of the forest, had enjoyed the rest. They basked in the bright winter sun, and had munched slices of ham they had brought with them from Denmark . . . Denmark! It already seemed as if we had been there years ago.*

## The First Serious Setbacks

In the late morning, *Generalmajor* Philippi met the *2d Battalion* of *GR 952* on a mountain path three kilometers south of Baerenthal. The men were manually dragging their heavy weapons up the steep inclines, as neither the horses nor the vehicles assigned to them could make it. This battalion would not be available for the attack on Lichtenberg at any time on 2 January![71]

As *Generalmajor* Philippi himself wrote in 1947 while in American custody, all of this proved the difficulties implicit in mountain warfare in terrain practically devoid of roads and paths, especially for incompletely-trained units. It also indicates the importance—for both sides—of controlling what few roads existed, such as the one from Forneau Neuf to Reipertswiller and beyond to the Moder Valley. It took on the importance of a key mountain pass.[72]

Around 1300, the *953d* reported the results of its reconnaissance. Wildenguth and Saegmuhle were clear of the enemy, and Saegmuhle was now occupied by the *2d Battalion*, *GR 951*. Reipertswiller, however, was defended by an enemy unit.

*Grenadier Regiment 953*'s attack kicked off punctually at 1400. The *2d Battalion* penetrated Reipertswiller on its first rush. Before it could consolidate its position, however, the enemy counterattacked sharply, supported by tanks, and forced them out. After sustaining heavy losses, the *2d Battalion* withdrew from the town, and the regiment regrouped in the woods to the north. The battalion in Saegmuhle arrived too late to support the attack on Reipertswiller.

The unit left in Baerenthal, *1st Battalion, GR 952,* had repulsed a noontime enemy thrust, and was still holding its blocking position.

*The halt in the sunny, quiet wood near Melch was one of the fondest and most vivid memories of many of the men of *Combat Group Wingen,* even decades later.

Thus, at the end of 2 January, none of the day's missions had been successful. Fire support had been inadequate, and the armor support was impotent. Worse, the enemy was increasing his artillery and mortar fire, and fighter-bomber activity had increased throughout the day. The opportunities for success, so promising in the morning, were now gone.

As he attempted to prepare for the next day's operations, the commanding general of *LXXXIX Corps*, *Generalleutnant* Höhne, was frustrated by the absence of *Luftwaffe* aerial reconnaissance. Thus, he was forced to base his estimates of enemy activity on the short-range reconnoitering of his ground combat elements, interrogation of American prisoners of war, and limited signals intercepts by *1st Army* and *Army Group G* intelligence assets.[73] Nevertheless, he and his *Corps* chief of staff, *Oberst i.G.* Karl Emmerich, agreed with Philippi that the rapid seizure of Reipertswiller and Lichtenberg was essential for the continued progress of the *361st VGD*—and the safety of *Combat Group Wingen*, lest it should be outflanked![74]

On the right of *Combat Group Wingen*, *Generalmajor* Seidel's *257th VGD* had experienced somewhat more success, but had also been unable to attain its objectives for the day.[75] On 2 January, Seidel's main effort was against Lemberg, to which end he not only attacked Lemberg itself, but attempted to outflank the American defenders by seizing the high ground around St. Louis-les-Bitche. To the north, he expected the *559th VGD* to support this effort as well. As a secondary effort, Seidel wanted to seize Goetzenbruck-Sarreinsberg, to control the key crossroads there.

On the right of the *257th*'s sector, by its boundary with the *559th VGD*, *GR 477* attacked Lemberg, but could not secure Hill 404, the critical road junction south of the town. There was still no assistance from any other *XC Corps* units. *GR 466* attacked down the road toward Lemberg, reached Unterbildmuhle, and turned south to the northeast of Goetzenbruck, where it halted for the night. *GR 457* attacked along the road southwest from Mouterhouse, took Althorn, and linked up with *GR 466* on its right in the eastern outskirts of Sarreinsberg. Ultimately, by the end of the day on 2 January, elements of *GR 457* established a roadblock at the crossroads one kilometer south-southeast of Meisenthal, near the site of two ancient Roman columns.*

*The *Tagesmeldung* and the *Kriegstagebuch* (*KTB*) of the *257th* for 2 January indicate that the *457th* reached the "road junction south of Kaesberg" at 1600, and at 1700 the road junction "one kilometer north of Kohlhutte." This could only have been with patrols, such as the one met in the morning hours of 3 January on the latter road junction, but certainly not by establishing an MLR south of the Kaesberg, as claimed in the *KTB* for that day. On 3 January, we did not encounter any German unit on or near the Kaesberg, besides the lone patrol. This erroneous claim is repeated graphically on the map for 2.1.–3.1.45, in what could have been only a mistaken report or a case of wishful thinking!

The *257th VGD* reported counterattacks by US troops out of Meisenthal at 1400 and 1430, each reportedly conducted with approximately 200 men, supported by ten tanks. Also in the afternoon hours, the regiment beat back several counterattacks from the southeast along the road from Wimmenau, conducted by US troops who were transported to the scene on trucks.

All these attacks were repulsed by concentrated artillery fire, reported the *Ia* of the *257th VGD* that evening, who claimed high losses for the enemy. In its Daily Report to headquarters, *XC Corps*, the division claimed "approximately 400 enemy killed in action," with high materiel losses inflicted on the enemy east of Meisenthal. These casualties constituted "wishful thinking" on the part of the staff of the *257th*, as the casualty reports for the units engaged (namely, the 2d Battalion, 179th Infantry; the 19th Armored Infantry Battalion; and the 141st Infantry Regiment), combined for 3 and 4 January, do not amount to ten percent of this total.[76]

On a less optimistic note, the *257th*'s *Ia* also mentioned continuous American fighter-bomber attacks during most of the afternoon, especially against the division's artillery positions, but also against the *257th*'s infantry, impeding their movements.

## Combat Group Wingen Presses On

At 1500, there was still no sign of our sister battalion. As we later found out, they had bivouacked in the vicinity of Schweizerländel during the previous night, and had commenced their march, as ordered, at 1300. Fortune did not smile on the *1st Battalion* during their march. The radio car assigned to accompany them, from the *3d Company* of *SS-Signal Battalion 6 NORD*, broke contact with the column, missed the Forneau Neuf turnoff, drove six kilometers further, and ran into an American roadblock north of Philippsbourg. At 1400, they were captured by the 3d Battalion, 275th Infantry, and earned the dubious honor of being the first members of *NORD* to be captured by the Americans. The absence of this critical long-range communications asset would have far-reaching effects on the course of the coming battle at Wingen.

Turning off on the road to the southwest at Bannstein, the *1st Battalion* column (minus the radio car) was attacked by American fighter-bombers on the road north of Fourneau Neuf.* The ensuing havoc caused yet another delay, and it was long after dark when the *1st Battalion*, *SS-Mountain Infantry Regiment 12* arrived in Melch, over the same trail we had used on the night before. *Standartenführer* Schreiber was fuming, and refused to accept any excuse for the delay.

*"We are deeply impressed by the enormous American air superiority . . ." wrote Hans-Hermann Carlau, *Adjutant* of the *1st Battalion,* in his personal diary that day.

Despite their late arrival, Schreiber ordered them to proceed to Wingen and seize it. They would just have to catch up to our *3d Battalion*, which was already four hours ahead.

We had left at 1630, close to sunset. Avoiding the straight dirt road to the south, we were taking the steep mountain trails in the west of the Melch Valley, which offered us ample coverage from overhanging branches. The first leg of about five kilometers would take us to the Rothbach Valley. The lead company pushed out a leading screen of scouts, and the entire battalion would follow in single file. The *Bergstaffel*, with its pack horses, was second to last in the order of march, with a line company bringing up the rear. There was to be absolutely no talking or smoking, and noise discipline was to be strictly enforced for man and beast.

The march in the gathering darkness was uneventful for about two hours, when the lead company reached the Rothbach Valley. Kreuzinger and I were with the *11th Company* at the head of the column. We dispatched a patrol under *Unterscharführer* Budt, with the mission of reconnoitering along the valley road to the east to "ferret out the Ami." The remainder of the battalion halted in the forest along the road and rested.

## The Opposition Presses On, Too

Across the front to our south, the Americans of the 179th Infantry Regiment had been busily redeploying to close just the gap through which we hoped to move toward Wingen.

| Date/Time | Action |
|---|---|
| 02 1815 | Colonel Murphy orders Captain Schmid to recon the road for moving his 1st Battalion, less Company C, to Meisenthal, and thence to the west of Goetzenbruck-Sarreinsberg. |
| 02 1900 | Captain Schmid reports to the Regiment that trucks carrying rolls of concertina wire to Company C received small arms fire on the road east of Kohlhutte. Company C ordered to check the situation there by patrol.* |
| 02 2150 | Lieutenant Bogart, liaison officer from the 276th Infantry Regiment of Task Force Herren, reports to the 179th Infantry Regiment command. He reports that the 1st Battalion/276th Infantry is assembled around Wingen, with the 2d Battalion at Wimmenau. (Already before this day, the 3d Battalion, 276th Infantry was |

*This fire may have come from the *Pioneer Platoon* of *GR 457* of the *257th VGD*, mentioned in the next chapter.

deployed in the vicinity of Rosteig.) The command post of the 276th Infantry Regiment is at Zittersheim.

02 2335 Colonel Morgan, the commanding officer of the 276th Infantry Regiment, visits Colonel Murphy at his command post, and informs him that the 276th is blocking all roads in the "vicinity of Ingwiller-Wimmenau-Wingen to the northeast." Colonel Murphy requests the 276th Infantry Regiment make contact and establish liaison with the 313th Infantry Regiment (mainly in Reipertswiller and vicinity).

Company C engaged in firefight.

## Firefight at the Weinbourg Pass

The patrol left at 1900 and returned ninety minutes later. Budt reported the road to be clear to the east all the way to the junction in Wildenguth, where the Melch road ends. They found the houses beyond the road junction to be occupied by Americans (with hindsight, these were probably from the 1st Battalion, 313th Infantry of the 79th Infantry Division).* When dogs started to bark at Budt and his men, American soldiers ran out of the houses, trying to locate the source of the dogs' consternation.[77] Budt and his men turned around to return to the main body.

During the return trip, the men almost collided with a party coming up the road. Approaching the turnoff to Melch, Budt and his men saw movement in the darkness ahead. Believing no Germans to be in the vicinity—his own men were still 2,000 meters away—Budt gave the order to his machine gunner, "*Feuer frei!*"†

The bolt jammed.

Fortunately for all concerned, by the time the gunner cleared the stoppage, the shadows in the woods identified themselves . . . as *Untersturmführer* Hans-Hermann Carlau, the *1st Battalion*'s adjutant, *Obersturmführer* Hans Jacobs, the commanding officer of *3d Company*, and their messenger. They were looking for a way to lead their men down to the valley floor. Thus, when *Unterscharführer* Budt's patrol returned, they not only had cleared the danger area, but also had made first contact with our sister battalion.

We conferred with the *1st Battalion* party in the protective darkness of the woods. We agreed to lead the march west, with the *1st Battalion* following. Two messengers were dispatched to Melch to report to *Standartenführer* Schreiber of our link up, and also to pass the intelligence that Wildenguth

*This unit had repulsed an attack by a company of *GR 953* earlier in the day.

†"Fire at will."

was in American hands. We passed the battalion through the *11th Company*, which now became the rearguard, charged with maintaining contact with the *1st Battalion*. The *12th Company* took over the lead. It was 2130 hours.

The darkness was truly deep by now, as there was a low, thick cloud cover. Not a single star was visible, much less the moon. The only illumination was provided by the snow, which reflected the weak light that permeated the clouds. Although this made navigating harder, it also made us more difficult for the Americans to detect. The other advantage of the weather was, if the clouds held through the day, we wouldn't have to worry about enemy air strikes.

At first, the route of the next leg was a simple one—just follow the forest road along the foot of the Rothbach Valley. According to our map, after about 2.5 kilometers, we would encounter the serpentine route that would lead us to the pass into the north end of the valley that ended at Wingen to the south. *Obersturmführer* Schindler, the commanding officer of the *12th Company*, warned his scouts of the danger that could be expected from the Weinbourg heights, to which the road was climbing. The men grew more wary as they trekked higher into the pass.

Then, all suspense ended; we heard the first shots up front, higher up on the road! Up front with Schindler and Kreuzinger, I sent a messenger to *Hauptsturmführer* Bruno Schütze, commanding the *13th Company*, to *Oberscharführer* Willi Heuer, the acting commander of the *11th Company*, and to *Hauptsturmführer* Burgstaller, commanding the *1st Battalion*. It was 2230.

Schindler passed the word he had received from his NCO with the scouts—there seemed to be an American unit dug in close to the Weinbourg. It is hard to say whether it was an outpost, or whether we had hit the main line of resistance. Kreuzinger quickly gave orders:

* *13th Company* climbs the mountain on its left; upon reaching the summit, advance along the ridge line to the west and (hopefully) attack the right flank of the enemy.
* *12th Company* advances carefully abreast, selecting advantageous terrain from which to attack, but under no circumstances does it attack before the *13th Company* assault begins.
* *11th Company* secures the right and supports the *12th Company* with machine-gun fire.
* Our *Bergstaffel* and the *1st Battalion* should stand fast along the road.*

The company commanders quickly returned to their units and passed the orders for the hasty attack. Our scouts had withdrawn, and deprived the

*Attentive readers will recognize this tactic; it closely resembles the plan at Muonio, on the night of 28/29 October 1944.

enemy of targets; the shooting from the American lines died down. We were not unhappy at this development, as we wanted to give the impression that the contact had only been a recon patrol, which was now scurrying away into the night with information about the whereabouts of the American positions.

In thirty minutes, all hell broke loose! On the mountain to the left, the *13th Company* was attacking. Almost simultaneously, the *12th Company* started frontally up the hill, straddling the winding forest road. It was 2320 hours.

After twenty minutes, I found myself taking cover in a ditch shortly below the crest of the pass, with the men of *12th Company*. Although the small arms fire had abated somewhat, the Americans were hitting us with mortar fire and were pinning us down. With us in the ditch were the first dozen American prisoners, also seeking cover from their own mortars.

It was close to midnight. The *13th Company* had reached the top of the pass, where the terrain was flat and the space between the trees was wider. The men tried to dig in, because the small arms fire was picking up again. Obviously, the Americans had rallied after being pushed back 500 meters from their initial positions. Someone from the American side called out in passable German, proposing a ten-minute cease fire to care for the wounded. Schütze agreed at once. The medics met in "No Man's Land," and evacuated the wounded to their respective sides.

We were stunned. No event could have illustrated more clearly the difference between fighting the Americans and fighting the Russians, to whom such a truce would have been inconceivable.*

## - III -
## Battle Analysis

At the end of the second day, terrain had been gained, but the day's objectives could not be reached, namely the dominating hills on both sides of St. Louis-les-Bitche, Lemberg, and Goetzenbruck-Sarreinsberg. Still greater was the danger of the extended right flank, which required valuable forces to defend against possible American counterattacks from continuously-reinforced enemy strong points at Lemberg, Goetzenbruck-Sarreinsberg, and Meisenthal. The enemy forces in Lemberg were a particular nuisance, as they were binding an entire regiment (*GR 477*), which otherwise could have been used against Goetzenbruck-Sarreinsberg.

The disappointing German situation by the end of the second full day of *NORDWIND* can be attributed to several factors.

*Decades later, this incident still amazes some of the men of the *3d Battalion* who fought that night.

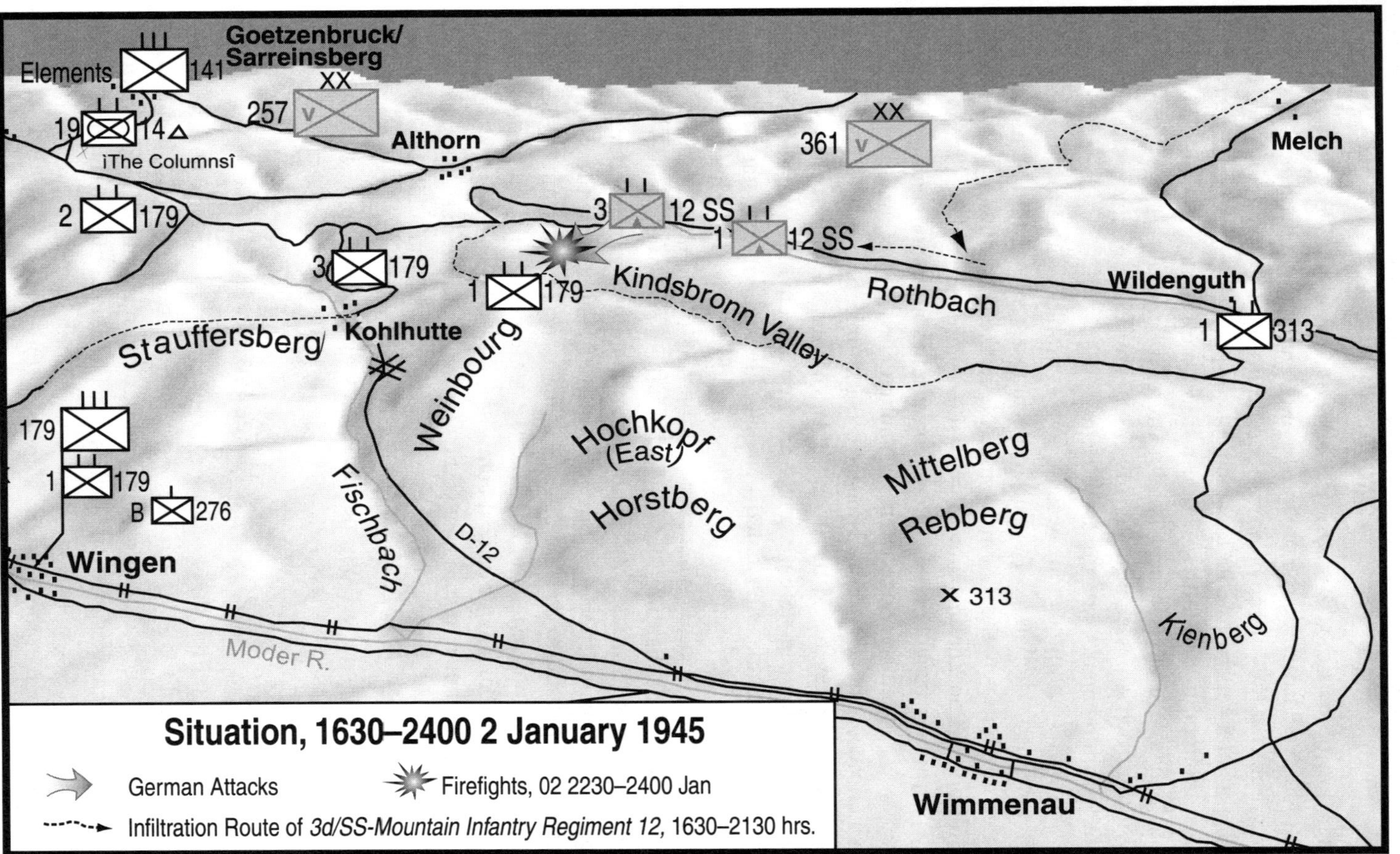


**Situation, 1630–2400 2 January 1945**

## Communications

The loss of the radio car was the day's major disaster for *Combat Group Wingen*. Although we lamented the separation of the radio car at the time—not knowing then that the car and crew had been captured by the enemy—we had no idea what a central role its loss would later play. When we experienced the insurmountable difficulties of transmitting the simple message "Wingen in our hands!" to any German headquarters, its criticality came home to us. Without such a message from us to Schreiber or Philippi, there would be neither reinforcements, nor any assault guns!

Overall, communications became a great problem for us for the remainder of our time in the Vosges. Actually, it became a significant problem for everyone, not only on the German side. Nevertheless, although *Generalmajor* Philippi was not the first and only division commander who had to grudgingly postpone a vital operation due to communications shortcomings, his problem was particularly severe: the six-hour delay in the attack on Reipertswiller, necessitated by the absence of communications with his supporting artillery, afforded the 2d Battalion, 313th Infantry Regiment enough time to properly organize its defense. Thus, one key objective was not taken on time.

Radio communication failed generally throughout this stage of *NORDWIND* due to the peculiarities of the rugged terrain—a fact hard to comprehend fifty years later. Whenever possible, field telephones, connected by wire, had to be substituted for FM radio in the Low Vosges. Not only was the preparation of a wire network time consuming, but it was exceptionally difficult to maintain in the face of enemy artillery and mortar fire. Sometimes, units had to resort to messengers, and at least one German unit in the Vosges devised an elaborate network of message centers to facilitate this most primitive and slow means of tactical communications.[78] German radio sets were generally cumbersome and heavy; the German forces were lacking the sort of "walkie-talkie" equipment possessed by many American units. In Germany, the development of two-way, portable radio technology had been significantly retarded during the 1930s, perhaps partly due to the ban on amateur radio communications.

## Intelligence

The lack of solid intelligence about the enemy was also problematic for us. On the Arctic Front, we had become accustomed to a very high and dense degree of intelligence on everything pertaining to the enemy. We consistently knew the exact designation of all enemy elements before us, and how they were deployed, at a minimum. We could not understand the profound lack of such intelligence in the Western Theater of Operations.

Although the front here had been largely static for about two weeks prior to the commencement of *NORDWIND*, our questions about the enemy forces were answered rather vaguely. True, there had been limited intelligence successes, such as the *361st*'s capture of Lieutenant Middlebrook of the 117th Cavalry, but such *coups* were too few to yield the kind of sharp picture which we needed to optimize our chances for success. Fortunately, the staff and commanders of the *361st VGD*, to which *Combat Group Schreiber* was attached, were at least familiar with the terrain from their previous defensive and retrograde experience there during December. (The other divisions of *LXXXIX* and *XC Corps* did not even have this advantage, having moved into their attack positions only shortly before the commencement of *NORDWIND*.) However, the overall lack of intelligence about enemy forces still persisted, and was due at least in part to the operational orders of *Generaloberst* Johannes Blaskowitz, commanding general of *Army Group G*.

To maintain operational security—that is, to maximize the chances of surprising the American defenders—Blaskowitz forbade reconnaissance of the attack zones prior to the commencement of *NORDWIND*. In his operation order for *NORDWIND*, the Army Group commander specified that only routine reconnaissance should be carried out, to "give the impression of a quiet front."[79] Coupled with little or no effective reconnaissance support from the *Luftwaffe*, this order effectively blinded the commanders of the attacking forces until *NORDWIND* was launched in the last hour of 1944. By then, it was too late for the *grenadiers* in the initial assault, many of whom surged directly into American minefields and well-laid-out fields of fire. The heavy losses they sustained in this way was one of the reasons for the failure of the *559th* and *257th VGD*s to take Lemberg, the corollary effects of which in turn adversely affected the entire *LXXXIX* and *XC Corps*' offensive efforts.

Finally, what little intelligence there may have been to pass on may have been further hampered by the absence of intelligence personnel in some of the German units participating in *NORDWIND*. In the *6th SS-Mountain Division*, for example, there were no intelligence officers (*Ic*) below the division level! In our *3d Battalion, SS-Mountain Infantry Regiment 12*, there had not been one since October 1943!

On the other hand, commanders of the enemy units seem to have been astonishingly well informed about their adversaries. Two reasons may account for this differential. Thanks to the comparatively fresh manpower situation of the US side, there were officers and NCOs assigned at every level, down through battalion headquarters, to intelligence billets. Thus, the Americans maintained intact their system for collecting and analyzing information, and converting it to useful intelligence, through all levels of command.

Also, by this stage in the war, upon capture by the Americans, many German prisoners started to get rather talkative, commensurate with their very personal assessments of the war situation. In most instances, the German soldier felt glad that the war was finally over for him, and that his captors were Americans, and not the dreaded Reds.

## Weather

The severe weather, that is, cold and snow, had little appreciable impact on the men of *Combat Group Schreiber*. We had experienced far worse in northern Karelia, and were also equipped to deal with the elements for protracted periods. Many of the *volks-grenadier* units were not at all prepared for extended operations in this weather, however, either by equipment, training, or experience. By the end of the second day of *NORDWIND*—and, in the case of *Generalmajor* Philippi and the *361st*, at the end of the *first day*—the leaders of several of the *VGD*s had noted a significant decline in the physical capabilities of their men.[80]

The assault guns that could have been so helpful in the delayed assault on Reipertswiller were further hampered by icy road conditions. After losing several of the precious armored vehicles to American fighter-bombers on the first day, Philippi was further deprived of this important support by mechanical failure of two more *en route* from Baerenthal to Reipertswiller.[81]

Finally, the road conditions so delayed the approach march of the *2d Battalion* of *GR 952* that the assault on Lichtenberg had to be postponed by a full day.

## American Command and Control

There can be no question that the swift and decisive reaction of US higher headquarters to the onslaught of *NORDWIND* was a major factor in the results of the Second Day. From the very outset, Generals Patch, Brooks, and Haislip rapidly shuffled units in the northeast sector of VI Corps, and moved them to the endangered sectors during the night from 1 to 2 January.

In reference to the flexibility and spirit of the 45th Infantry Division—the division mostly burdened by the "Great Shift," Lieutenant General Jacob L. Devers, the commanding general of the Sixth Army Group, rightly expressed these sentiments of commendation,

> Ordered on the night of January 1/2 to shift your forces from the Siegfried Line to take over a sector from another unit [Task Force Hudelson], you completed the movement in considerably less time than could reasonably be expected. Arriving in the new sector, you

> found an exceedingly confused situation in the area being overrun by the enemy. With the steady coolness that has already made the 45th famous, you immediately stemmed the main enemy advance and deepest penetration.[82]

Such decisions were not without risk at that time, as they partly stripped VI Corps' "Rhine Front" of troops. Had Himmler's *Army Group Upper Rhine* not waited until 5 January to conduct its landing across the Rhine at Gambsheim, but instead attacked on 2 January, they would have met with only light resistance and might well have helped the *Army Group G* effort in *NORDWIND* to a more favorable result . . . but Himmler had his own ambitious plans and plots.

Himmler was none too keen to see Blaskowitz succeed with *NORDWIND*, and thus earn Hitler's praise. Instead, he planned (plotted) to achieve a much more substantial success by action of his own—an encirclement of the Allied forces on the Alsatian Plain by his *Army Group Upper Rhine* and the *19th Army* in the Colmar Pocket. Such an action would also restore Strasbourg to German control, and thus allow Himmler bring it to Hitler "on a platter" as a present for the twelfth anniversary of his accession to power on 30 January.

## Coordination of Effort

Due to the almost complete absence of the German *Luftwaffe*, the major movements of American troops on roads within the VI Corps sector could have just as well been executed during daytime, instead of during the night. The situation during the first week of January on the American side, which had full command of all roads in the Rhine Valley Plain—limited only by the weather—as well the road net in the Moder Valley and its routes to the north and south, resembled the situation we encountered on Arctic Front between 1941 and 1944. The Soviet Army had full command of the Murmansk Railway, not only for the shipment of Lend-Lease goods from the United States to the inner Soviet Union, but also for laterally shifting their forces at will from one sector of the front to another.

The Germans, on the other hand, had to clear routes for a road net that would support the passage of armor to the Alsatian Plain. There were essentially three routes that were suitable for the passage of the armored assets of the *Army Group* operational reserve to the Alsatian Plain: Bitche-Niederbronn, Rohrbach-Lemberg-Zinswiller, and Rohrbach-Lemberg-Goetzenbruck-Wingen-Ingwiller. As an expedient, if the attack of *XIII SS Corps* failed and Rohrbach remained in the hands of the 100th Infantry Division—as it remained on 2 January—the armor could be routed from Bitche to Lemberg, and thence to the Alsatian Plain via Zinswiller. Either way, however, control of Lemberg was essential to using either of the two more southerly routes.

By the end of the first day, the Bitche-Niederbronn route did not appear likely to open, as the *256th VGD* failed to open the route beyond Phillipsbourg. Thus, Lemberg, which *XC Corps* was to have seized on 1 January, became a key to the success of *NORDWIND*; the other key to unlock the route to the Rhine Plain was Wingen.

The problem at Lemberg seems to be more than a case of neglected coordination within the *XC Corps*, commanded by *General der Infanterie* Petersen. Lemberg was near the divisional boundary between the *559th VGD* and the *257th VGD*, both belonging to the *XC Corps*, and was clearly a priority objective. Here begins the "Lemberg Riddle!"

At first glance, it seems that both *Generaloberst* Blaskowitz and *General der Infanterie* von Obstfelder were of the opinion that the *XC Corps* had tasked *Generalmajor* von der Mühlen's *559th VGD* with the mission of seizing Lemberg. Von der Mühlen certainly thought so, and ordered *GR 1126* to take the town.[83] At the same time, there is an abundance of evidence that suggests that *Generalmajor* Seidel also believed he was to seize Lemberg; he even assigned the mission to *GR 477*.

This redundant and uncoordinated situation was made even more confused by the alteration of the division boundaries within the *XC Corps* early on 2 January by *Headquarters, Army Group G*; this switch placed Lemberg clearly in the zone of the *257th VGD*. Subsequently, at the request of the commanding general of the *257th* at 0340 on 3 January, the boundary was changed back by *Army Group*, and Lemberg again became a *559th VGD* problem . . . although it is clear from a conversation between the *Army Group G* chief of staff and and the *XC Corps* chief of staff that the tactical intent was for the *559th* simply to prevent a counterattack from the Americans in that region, and that Lemberg was no longer a viable offensive objective.*

This obscure riddle, in which two divisions of the same corps failed to orchestrate a coordinated attack on a common objective can in part perhaps be explained by the extraordinary security measures under which Blaskowitz issued the orders *NORDWIND*, that is, only the division commanders and

*The *Army Group G KTB* records a conversation between the *Army Group* Chief of Staff and Blaskowitz on the night of 1 January in which it is clear that the boundary between the *559th* and *257th* is to be shifted north, to bring Lemberg into the *257th*'s zone. The text of the *257th*'s *KTB*, the accompanying situation map, and the *XC Corps* daily report for 3 January all indicate the requests by the *257th* to change it back, which was approved by *Army Group* effective 0340 on 3 January! At 2310 on 2 January, the Chief of Staff, *Army Group G* and *Oberst* Reinhard, the Chief of Staff of the *XC Corps*, conferred and agreed that the *559th* should assume a defensive posture in the vicinity of Lemberg. (From *Army Group G KTB* for 2 January) their *Ia*s knew about the content of the order before 31 December. One should assume, however, that during the no fewer than three mission briefings on 28 and 29 December at *Headquarters, XC Corps,* the tactical boundaries and primary objectives should have been clear to all concerned.

The otherwise successful *257th VGD* tried for two days in vain to take Lemberg. An encirclement with the assistance of elements of the *559th VGD* on the first day would have been helpful and probably would have solved the case. Failing that, both the *559th* and *257th VGD*s each found themselves in the disadvantageous situation of being forced to tie down one entire regiment at Lemberg, to prevent the US forces there from counterattacking into the otherwise open right flank. In particular, the regiment of the *257th* was urgently needed for the already initiated strong southwesterly push of the *257th Division*!

With American troops in control of Lemberg, two of the major east-west routes of advance for the *Army Group G* exploitation forces (the *21st Panzer* and *25th Panzer-Grenadier divisions*) would be interdicted. This realistically left only the road net, which broke out on the Alsatian Plain at Ingwiller . . . on which Wingen was a major intersection available for German exploitation.

Thus, as Day Two ended, athough we of *Combat Group Wingen* could not have known it, the mission to seize Wingen was one on which the success of *NORDWIND* now hinged almost entirely!

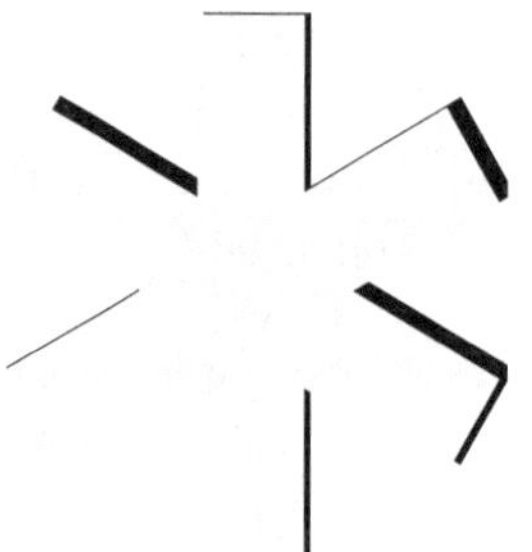

# The Third Day: The Order to Attack

## -I- Desperate Plans

The Third Day's attacks would prove to be crucial, and no one was more aware of this than *Generalmajor* Philippi. In fact, he assessed it as the very last opportunity for a breakthrough. Failing this, not only would the physical strength of his troops be unequal to further exertions, but their materiel support would also be inadequate. That was reason enough for Philippi to make some definitive decisions.

One option he considered was to concentrate his assault forces in a narrow frontal attack on Reipertswiller. For this, he would need armor support, which he did not have in sufficient quantities or strength.

Another option was to attack not only Reipertswiller, but also Lichtenberg, simultaneously. This he could not do, because his *GR 952* had only one battalion at his disposal, as the second one was still bound at Baerenthal. To use the available battalion in an envelopment against Reipertswiller from the east was not feasible because of the danger of being flanked by enemy forces at Lichtenberg.

A third option was to attack Reipertswiller in a wide, multi-pronged envelopment, including outflanking the enemy from the west through the forest. Since the enemy did not yet seem to have established a definite and coherent main line of resistance, this appeared to be a feasible way to tackle the problem. If he could establish a blocking position on the route from Ingwiller and Rothbach, and thus prevent American reinforcement of their elements in Reipertswiller, then enemy resistance there should quickly terminate.

This last option was accepted by the *361st VGD*. For any other, more promising action, Philippi would have needed full control of *SS-Mountain Infantry Regiment 12*, but that was earmarked by higher headquarters solely for its assault on Wingen, partly in consideration of the *257th VGD*'s plight.

After this comparison of competing courses of action had yielded its results, *Generalmajor* Philippi formulated his field orders for 3 January:

- ✠ Elements of *SS-Mountain Infantry Regiment 12* to seize Wingen.
- ✠ *1st Battalion, GR 952* defends in the vicinity of Baerenthal to prevent an American attack into the left (east) shoulder of the division's salient.
- ✠ Supported by *2d Battalion, GR 951, GR 953* proceeds from Wildenguth. *2d Battalion, GR 951* attacks Wimmenau-East, and blocks the roads leading from Wimmenau and Ingwiller to Reipertswiller. *2d Battalion, GR 953* attacks Reipertswiller from the west. *1st Battalion, GR 953* attacks Reipertswiller from the north astride the road, supported by assault guns.
- ✠ *2d Battalion, GR 952* blocks the road leading from Rothbach to Reipertswiller at a point two kilometers east of Reipertswiller. [In view of the extreme difficulties of moving heavy weapons in this part of the Rothbach sector, Philippi did not order an attack on Picardie, a decision that would later have a momentous impact on the course of the battle!]
- ✠ Artillery Regiment *361* moves another battalion into position east of Melch. The most important task, though, was to prepare reliable wire connections (radio connections failed almost entirely!) to the forward observers supporting the assaults—responsive artillery support was of the utmost importance for the success of these operations.

To realize the success of *Army Group G*'s concept of sending its armored operational reserve onto the Plain of Alsace, *Generalmajor* Seidel's *257th VGD* also had to accomplish its missions for the day. Now that the commander and staff of *Army Group G* had given up on taking Lemberg, *GR 477* was freed from its task there by the new change to the boundary with the *559th VGD*. The *559th* was to tie down the American forces at Lemberg, while the *257th* bypassed it and attacked further to the southwest.

*Generalmajor* Seidel ordered his division to accomplish its mission this way on Day Three:

- ✠ Upon relief in the vicinity of Lemberg by elements of the *559th VGD*, *GR 477* attacks across Hill 409 [northwest of Goetzenbruck] and seize Schieresthal.
- ✠ *GR 466* attacks to seize Goetzenbruck-Sarreinsberg and Meisenthal.
- ✠ *GR 457* secures the division's right flank; upon seizure of the above objectives, *GR 457* attacks to secure the line Rosteig-Heideneck.

## -II-
## We Learn About the Americans

Even as Philippi and Seidel were formulating their orders for the Third Day, our medics were gathering the last of the wounded while the precious moments of truce ticked away. As soon as the ten minutes' cease-fire ended, the shooting started again on both sides of the pass above Wingen, and continued throughout the night.

From the prisoners we had taken, we knew that during most of the firefight, our adversaries were from Company C, 179th Infantry Regiment. In a report to its battalion command post, the company estimated our force to number 300, so the commander of 1st Battalion, 179th Infantry took no chances. He moved up his Company B as a backstop, to give depth to the defense.* Further, Colonel Murphy, regimental commander of the 179th Infantry, requested and received a rifle platoon from Company I, 276th Infantry, which the 1st Battalion's commander placed in battalion reserve.

As our attack developed to the east, attempting to outflank the defenders, we ran into elements of 3d Battalion, 179th Infantry around 0345. This was fortuitous, as the S-3 of 1st Battalion had recently requested, through the regimental S-3, that 3d Battalion counterattack to relieve the pressure we were putting on his battalion. As a result of our contact, the commander of 3d Battalion reported that his unit was under attack, and he could not fulfill this request. Our contact with the 179th continued until at least 0500.†

Gradually, the intensity of the firing faded, and stopped altogether just before first light. When the gray dawn of the new day slowly allowed us to recognize our surroundings, we discovered to our astonishment that we had lost contact with the enemy, obviously some time ago.

The 45th Infantry Division (the "Thunderbirds") was an outfit with many battlewise and hardened soldiers, veterans of considerable mountain fighting before this night. Except for some periods during the advance up the Rhône following the invasion of southern France in August of 1944, the "Thunderbirds" had seen action in little territory *other* than mountains: they had fought in the mountains of Sicily in 1943; in the Apennines in 1943 and 1944; and

*This was not a bad estimate, considering they were being engaged by most of a 400-man battalion, and were making the estimate literally "in the dark."

†Interestingly, the report from 3d Battalion at 0400 alleged that they were receiving "considerable enemy artillery and mortar fire." Since our FO was out of contact with our supporting artillery, and we didn't even have our mortars with us, this can only have been friendly fire.

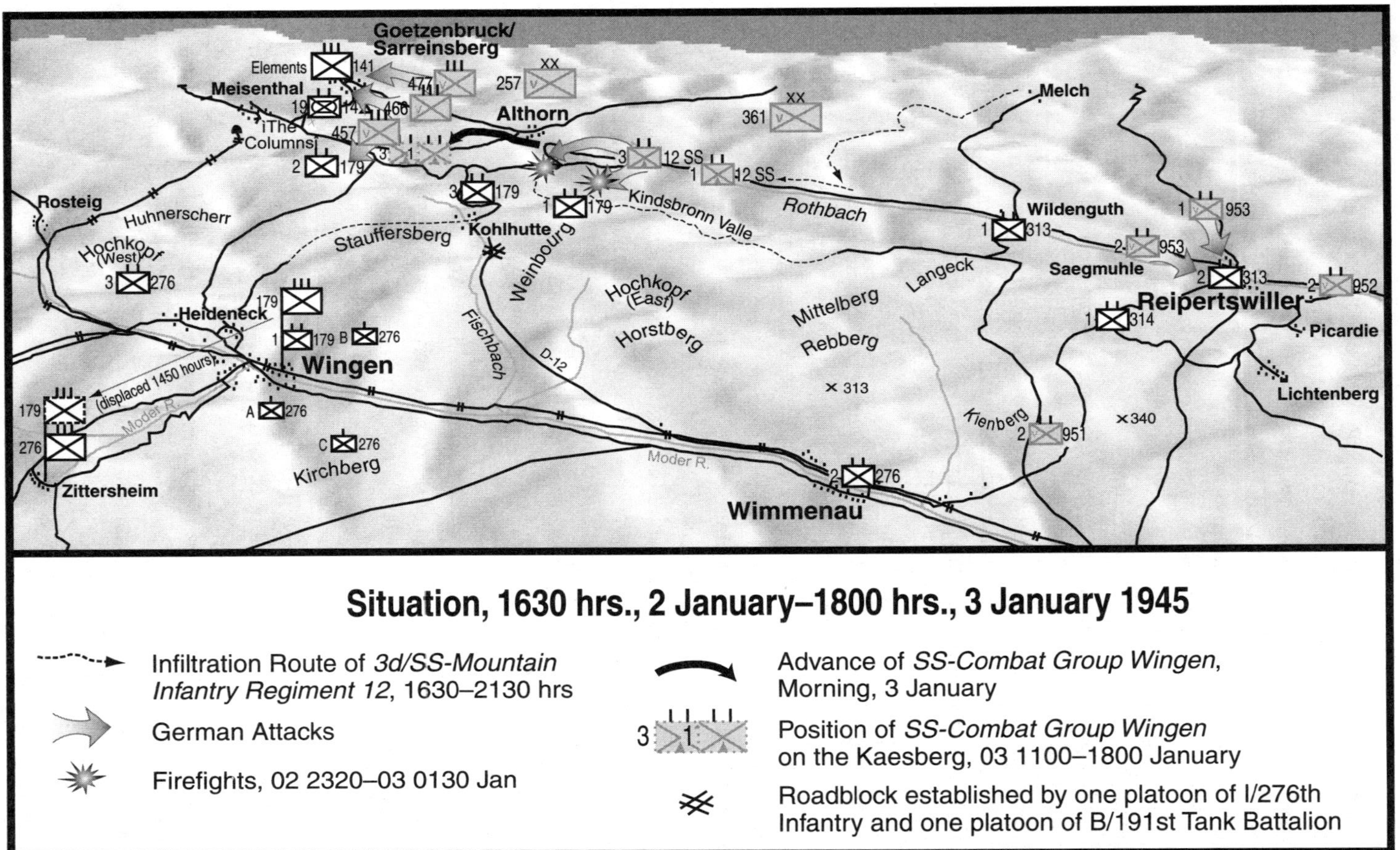


## Situation, 1630 hrs., 2 January–1800 hrs., 3 January 1945

they had fought in the foothills of the High Vosges in October. Just before *NORDWIND*, they had been putting their experience in cracking fortified positions of the innumerable German defensive lines in Italy into use in their assaults on the *Westwall* positions near Reisdorf and Bundenthal. Although it was a conventionally-organized US Army infantry division, it had far more experience in actual mountain warfare than we did!

During the night, I tried to gather information from our men, and to determine our exact situation. The results were of varying quality, but were nevertheless interesting and revealing.[84]

One platoon of the *13th Company* had been surprised to find ten to twelve American soldiers fast asleep in their sleeping bags beyond the top of the pass. When questioned on their way to our prisoner of war (POW) collection point (which we had established in the side ditch of the road), they justified their being asleep by complaining that they had been "on the march all day yesterday for sixteen hours," and being dead tired when finally coming here; they simply slept through the fracas.

Most of the Americans' foxholes were empty, their occupants having left in time to avoid capture. Knowing by heart what to expect in a Red Army foxhole, our men were curious about what American foxholes contained. As these were the first ones, they searched them thoroughly. They found unbelievable riches, including lots of cigarettes! But what was the lengthy brown box covered with waxed paper? On first sight, it looked like a pack of dynamite. But then somebody took heart and bravely explored further. He was rewarded for his courage—to his great enjoyment it contained food of the highest quality! It was an American "K-ration." Only the continuous cursing of their commanding officer could make the men cease stuffing their jackets full of this bounty, abandon further searching, and move on in the fight.

Having no support from heavy weapons, one platoon leader had invented one. He took his signal pistol and loaded it with "whistling charges," per regulation used to aurally indicate "Tank Warning." By chance, he had his pockets full of them. Instead of shooting vertically, he employed them on a horizontal trajectory, straight through the woods. They made a terrible, unearthly noise and had a greatly demoralizing effect on the enemy. Later, the men of the 179th Infantry Regiment reported that our assault had been supported by "sledge-hammer shelling."[85]

Not all events during that night were rewarding or amusing. For instance, when a squad of the *13th Company* advanced after the firefight had already died down and most American foxholes were abandoned, they found one that was still occupied. Standing around the hole, cock-sure that their quarries would surrender at their appearance, their squad leader demanded that the three defenders give up. After all, the Americans had been surprised by our arrival, and seemed to fade away during the night in the face of our attack. As an answer to the German entreaties, one of the American soldiers shot and killed the old squad leader, *Unterscharführer* Walter Rieger (he had been a basic training instructor for many of our men back in 1942). He was the first killed in action that night.

When convinced that sure annihilation was near, the three Americans finally came out, but only after they had pulled Red Cross brassards over the sleeves of their field jackets. Trying to convince their captors that they were medics; they repeatedly pointed at them when they finally emerged from their hole.[86] We were not fooled; we simply took them captive and sent them to the rear like the combatants they were.

Experiences like these perplexed our men; they had only a short while before, for the first time in their military lives, witnessed a cease-fire observed to care for the wounded. They felt happy that the Red Cross seemed to be recognized here on the Western Front, contrary to the rough customs of the Soviets. Yet now, the Red Cross was used in a coarse ruse. They wondered aloud what they had to expect from this point forward: Red Cross as a respected sign of helping the helpless—or Red Cross as ruse to avoid capture?

Around first light, the three *Jäger* companies of the *3d Battalion* moved on in search of the enemy. When we came down the forest road to its Y-junction with the district road (D-12), to our surprise we met with a German element: it was part of a pioneer platoon belonging to *GR 457* of the *257th VGD*! They seemed to be following an obscure and garbled combat order, and walked away into the brightening woods.[87]

The order of advance saw the *13th Company* moving forward in a westerly direction with its left platoon along the district road. Both other companies were abreast and to the right, slowly climbing a mountain, the Kaesberg (elevation 418 meters). Occasionally we received small arms fire, mostly from the south (left side). When the Kaesberg was in our hands, the companies were ordered to stop their advance and to dig in for the day.

The enemy was mostly to the south across the district road, obviously in the vicinity of Kohlhutte—and it was more than only one company. But now, we also could discern American troops beyond the western slope of the Kaesberg. They were manning an antitank gun that was shooting at irregular intervals. More troublesome for our men in their dugouts was the high-angle mortar fire they received from the south, even though the American artillery also eventually zeroed in on our positions.

## *The Ferocious Fight at Reipertswiller*

While we were fighting on the Weinbourg and Kaesberg, most of the organic units of the *361st VGD* were locked in an assault against the enemy at Reipertswiller, the "thorn in the side" of this division.*

The operations against Reipertswiller started on time at 0700, with *2d Battalion, GR 953* jumping off from Saegmuhle, gaining the mountain west of Reipertswiller, and bringing its heavy weapons into position. Simultaneously, *2d Battalion, GR 952* cut the road from Rothbach, using abatis and mines to establish a roadblock. Although the men manning this blocking position turned back several American armored reconnaissance vehicles, this action did not entirely cut off Reipertswiller from the east—patrols from *2d Battalion, GR 952* found that Picardie, to the south, was occupied by enemy troops. This was an ominous discovery.

Nevertheless, the rest of the operation to isolate Reipertswiller went on exactly as planned when *2d Battalion, GR 951* (also known as "*Combat Group Stämmle*") started down the road leading from Wildenguth to Saegmuhle at 0700, and then followed the dirt road leading due south, just east of the Langeck Mountain. After 2.5 kilometers, the battalion crossed over the Kienberg, then left the road to approach Wimmenau from the northeast. Except for the unexpected forces at Picardie, the American defenders of Reipertswiller were now cut off.

At 0900, the leaders in *2d Battalion, GR 953* fired colored flares indicating the completion of their preparations for the attack. Almost immediately after

*This and the following account from Philippi, 35–44.

Philippi wrote the text of his MS B-428 during his US Army custody at Allendorf two years after the action, and closed it on 22 February 1947. Being elaborate on many details in his text, he must have forgotten on the other hand some likewise important facts. For instance, that the *3d Battalion/SS-Mountain Infantry Regiment 12* was attached to his *361st VGD* as part of *Combat Group Schreiber* since the start of *NORDWIND*, and had already at the close of the Second Day made its first contact with US forces. In his manuscript, he does not make any mention of this, or the subsequent action of *Combat Group Wingen* on the Kaesberg during the same day. Instead he wrote (38), "At 0700 (3 January), two *SS* battalions . . . cross the road on both side of Wildenguth and disappear in the forest," a sentence often quoted in historical treatises, albeit wrong and misleading.

As shown earlier in this chapter, by 0700, both battalions had already done most of their day's work, and were at this hour in a fierce fight with elements of two US battalions, the 1st and the 3d Battalions, 179th Infantry. They had "crossed the road . . . of Wildenguth" at least *ten hours* earlier. Of course, all this must have been known to Philippi, who was in communication with Schreiber, as shown in this chapter already.

In his account, Philippi is not firm with the time element, and more than once is erroneous in citing days. To rectify this, it has proven beneficial to have primary US sources, such as the G/S-2 and G/S-3 journals of the engaged elements of the 45th Infantry Division.

this coded confirmation of readiness, all tubes of *Artillery Regiment 361* fired a five-minute preparation of the objective. As soon as the barrage lifted, both battalions of *GR 953* attacked the Americans at Reipertswiller. The *Landsers* of *2d Battalion, GR 953* assaulted the western part of the town, while *1st Battalion, GR 953* advanced to the south on both sides of the road, supported by the assault guns. The assault guns ground their way down the icy road, on line with the infantry. Pressing on despite heavy American artillery and mortar fire, the leading elements of *1st Battalion, GR 953* reached the first houses on the north edge of Reipertswiller, where they were met by heavy enemy machine-gun fire at close range. Then calamities began to occur.

Upon reaching the northern entrance to the town, the leading assault gun's tracks slipped on the ice and the entire vehicle slewed ninety degrees, effectively blocking the road for the following vehicles. Under incessant shelling, there was no way to recover the vehicle during daylight. Shortly after the armor was rendered useless, the commanding officer of *1st Battalion, GR 953* was killed by enemy fire. The battalion's attack ground to halt.

When *2d Battalion, GR 953* descended from the mountain to the west of Reipertswiller, it was enfiladed with small arms fire from the south, and fire from tanks positioned on the road southwest of the town. In view of the rapidly mounting losses, the experienced and reliable battalion commander stopped the attack and withdrew his battalion to the rim of the forest west of Reipertswiller.

Around 1400 the commander of *GR 953* reported that his regiment failed to take Reipertswiller; that its assault had been stopped by strong enemy fire which had inflicted heavy casualties; and that a repetition of the attack with the same forces would be senseless. Philippi accepted this opinion.

By 1030, even before the German attack was called off, Headquarters, 313th Infantry Regiment was reporting the successful repulse of the German efforts to seize Reipertswiller to the G-2 of the 45th Division:

> A 3-column attack (on Reipertswiller) this morning was stopped, 1 tank and 1 Flak wagon destroyed. The attack came from the north into town in battalion strength; from the west trying to envelop Reipertswiller. They came along the south of the stream. The attack from NW also was estimated to have been in battalion strength. 1st Battalion, 314th Infantry Regiment moved to [the] Boxenberg [500 meters in the south of Reipertswiller] to protect flank.*

*Ibid., 03 1030 (3). The "tank" referred to in this report is in fact one of the assault guns of the *361st*'s *Panzerjäger Battalion*; many GIs typically referred to any German tracked vehicle that mounted a cannon as a "tank," just as they classified almost all German artillery as "88s."

The enemy in Reipertswiller, which consisted of the 2d Battalion, 313th Infantry Regiment, reinforced by Company B, 313th, had not only expected the attack by the *GR 953*, but had *been forewarned of it in detail*, giving them ample opportunity to prepare their defenses. During the night, elements of the 313th Infantry Regiment captured a captain from *GR 953*, with his messenger. A search of his map case revealed a map with arrows pointing not only to Reipertswiller from different sides, but also to Wildenguth and Wimmenau, clearly indicating the impending German attacks![88]

*****

Not all American units in the fight in this area had the advantage of superb intelligence, however. The vanguard of *2d Battalion, GR 951* arrived north of the prominent road junction where the road coming from Reipertswiller joined their own road and promptly knocked out an American 57mm antitank gun and its crew there. The gun had only very recently been emplaced—just a few hours before, in fact. Its crew, attached to the 276th's 2d Battalion, belonged to Antitank Company, 276th Infantry Regiment of Task Force Herren. This battalion, which had arrived during the night of 2/3 January, was in turn attached to the 313th Infantry Regiment.

To the officers and men of the newly-arrived 276th Infantry, this was the *first* indication of hostile forces so far south.[89] Apparently, during the all-night move from assembly areas on the Alsatian Plain, the "word" of the impending German activity derived from the captured documents had not been passed to the incoming reinforcements! Other American forces in the Low Vosges were far better informed, however.

*****

While the 313th Infantry was announcing its repulse of the attack on Reipertswiller, the S-3 of the 179th Infantry Regiment in Wingen received word from his 1st Battalion that Company A (in the process of being relieved by the 276th Infantry near Wimmenau) had captured a German soldier of *8th Company, 2d Battalion, GR 951* with interesting and important information. This man, who became separated from his unit and had wandered into the Americans' lines near the Wimmenau railroad station, told his captors that his battalion's mission was to cut the road between Wimmenau and Wingen.[90] The Americans were quick to piece together the picture, and began taking effective countermeasures.

In the late morning, the 1st Battalion, 314th Infantry, another 79th Infantry Division unit that had been attached to the 45th Division as part of the Great Shift, moved out of Picardie, heading west. After the assault on Reipertswiller had been repulsed, Companies A and B of this battalion occupied the Boxenberg Ridge, south of Reipertswiller. At 1430, 1st Battalion continued the attack, and seized the ridge 500 meters south of the town against "moderate resistance," probably from flank elements of *2d Battalion, GR 953*. The Americans, so recently cut off in Reipertswiller, had now opened a tenuous route through the hamlet of Picardie, whence a mountain road ran down to the valley road leading to Ingwiller. The forces in Reipertswiller were far from safe, however. The American units there watched as the dogged German attackers dug in at the edge of the forest to the north and west of Reipertswiller, and they knew that the road between Wildenguth and Reipertswiller was cut. Although Reipertswiller was still in American hands, it was still partially surrounded, as were the elements of 1st Battalion, 313th in Wildenguth.[91]

At 1445, Major Large of the 45th Division Artillery sent a report to the commanding general of the 45th Division that confirmed this development:

> 313th Inf reported enemy NE-NW-SW of Reipertswiller dug in on high ground. Two companies of friendly infantry [A & B, 313th Infantry] cut off in Wildenguth. Communication out and cannot be serviced. Plans captured indicate enemy to continue E from high ground N of Reipertswiller, then S and cut the road to E. Request air reconnaissance over the sector if possible.[92]

Other developments helped the Americans grasp the situation more precisely, while that of the German command grew foggier. From its position on the Kienberg, *2d Battalion, GR 951* sent a radio message to the *361st VGD* headquarters at about noon. Unfortunately for both sender and receiver, the message was garbled. As Philippi and his staff strained to comprehend the transmission, they could make out that Stämmle and his battalion had reached the edge of the forest north of Wimmenau, and found the town to be in enemy hands. Through the static and electromagnetic fuzz, they also understood that Stämmle was convinced that his own forces would be unable to seize Wimmenau without further reinforcement. Before the signal disappeared completely, the operations staff of the *361st* finally understood that the battalion would remain on the Kienberg. "Reading between the lines," Philippi believed the message was essentially a call for help.[93]

The Americans were also listening, and perhaps heard the message even better than the intended receivers. Throughout the day, multiple radio intercepts by the US VI Corps indicated the presence of these German forces on the Kienberg. Their content seemed to infer that these forces would be soon reinforced, probably by *SS-Mountain Regiment 12*, which they believed to have orders to attack Wimmenau from the north. Corps G-2 relayed this intelligence to the 45th Division as it came in, between 1630 and 1920 hours.[94]

Other information contributed to the clear intelligence picture forming about the situation on the Kienberg. Not only had the Americans captured the plans for the attack on Reipertswiller early that morning, but they again inherited an intelligence windfall later that same evening! The detailed intentions of the commander of the *361st VGD* fell into the hands of the 45th Infantry Division G-2 when the Adjutant of *2d Battalion, GR 951* was captured. On his person were found marked maps and other documents outlining the latest orders for his battalion. They clearly indicated that Wingen, the Hochkopf (East), and the Kienberg were to be taken and held.[95] The Americans were reading the *361st*'s mail, and Philippi's men had no idea of it!

## Frustration on the Kaesberg: The Impact of Poor Communications

As misfortunes were accumulating for the battalions around Reipertswiller and Wimmenau, we were faced with problems of our own. Despite the shelter provided by our deep foxholes, our casualties began to mount. It was a frustrating and dangerous situation, because there was nothing we could do in retaliation. The forward observer of the *3d Battalion, SS-Mountain Artillery Regiment 6* who accompanied us could not make radio contact with his own artillery battery!

Shortly after noon, we got the sad message that *Obersturmführer* Schindler, the commanding officer of our *12th Company*, had been killed by a mortar round that landed directly in his foxhole. Schindler was a South-Tyrolean, one of the born mountaineers. He had been wounded during the night 28–29 October 1944 in the battle for Muonio against the 50th Finnish Infantry Regiment. Not waiting for his wound to heal properly, he pressed to be sent back to his company, which he joined again on Christmas Day in Denmark, joyfully greeted by his men. Command of the *12th Company* devolved upon *Hauptscharführer* Schüler, the senior NCO in the company.

The companies of both battalions dug in, forming a large "hedgehog" position, or all-around defense. Our *3d Battalion* faced south and west, while the *1st Battalion* defended to the north and east. Both battalion commanders established their command posts in the same dugout, half-way down a reverse slope close to the center of the Kaesberg. Their adjutants and messengers occupied foxholes nearby. All communications to the companies had to be by runners, as the time of our intended stay here was too short to warrant laying field wire. We *did* have radios with us, but only the large, cumbersome "Berta" boxes, operated by a couple of signal men. "Walkie-talkies" or something of their ilk would certainly have been convenient—and much safer for the runners—at this point.

Over the course of the day, the American infantry never attacked us on the Kaesberg. Acknowledging the fact that we forced them to withdraw 600 yards, the G-2 of the 45th US Division classified us on this day as appearing "determined and well organized."*

Here our men experienced for the first time the very pronounced tendency of the US Army to use heavy weapons to preserve their infantrymen's lives. Our casualties from artillery and mortar fragments on this day were higher than those we had sustained from small arms fire on the night before.

While we crouched in our holes on the Kaesberg, completely unbeknownst to us, *GR 457* was hanging on stoically to the gains it had made on Day Two, less than a kilometer from our positions! Although we could not hear it over the thunder of the American artillery rounds crashing around us, there must have been quite a racket coming from the north. The *477th*'s advance toward Schieresthal was halted by heavy small arms fire from the 141st Regimental Combat Team on the heights south of Lemberg. Soon thereafter, it was obliged to turn back a vicious American counterattack, as the *559th VGD* was unequal to the task by itself. Under these circumstances, the seizure of Schieresthal was out of the question for the *477th*.

This began a disastrous chain reaction because without securing Schieresthal, *GR 466* did not have any hope of taking Goetzenbruck-Sarreinsberg or Meisenthal. Even though Goetzenbruck received intermittent German artillery fire from the morning on (200 rounds in all), from the commanding heights around the town, the American defenders from the 2d Battalion, 179th Infantry, reinforced by the 19th Armored Infantry Battalion and Troop C, 117th Cavalry, enjoyed excellent fields of fire and observation. They smothered the *466th*'s assault with withering small arms and artillery fires. Although Meisenthal took a much heavier pasting (about 1,000 rounds during the day), *GR 466* never got close to this, its deepest objective. Even a much more experienced and well-trained regiment than the *466th* would have been hard-pressed to accomplish such a demanding mission.

Without these successes, our neighbors to the north, *GR 457*, had no choice but to hunker down and defend themselves against the 45th Division's attempts to dislodge them, which seemed to grow fiercer as time

*45th Infantry Division, G-2 Journal for 3 January, 1. Withdrawal listed as occurring at 0005. Although no subsequent rearward movement of the 1st Battalion of the 179th was documented in this source, sometime after 0005 and before 1000, this element was forced to withdrawal of roughly 1,000 meters further.

went on. Of course, being out of radio contact with our higher headquarters, we were operating in a vacuum, and had no idea of what was happening even a kilometer away.

As this failure within *XC Corps* was unfolding, around 1430, *Untersturmführer* Oldenburg, the commanding officer of the regimental signal platoon, appeared at our command post with two messengers. He had been ordered by Schreiber to convey personally the attack order from *Generalmajor* Philippi of the *361st VGD* to our two battalions. For our attack on Wingen, we were to take the road via the Huhnerscherr, which branches off to the south opposite the Kaesberg: we were to open and clear this road, and take both parts of the town. The *1st Battalion* was ordered to seize Heideneck, while our *3d Battalion* was to take Wingen proper. The main road running through Wingen and Heideneck-Hochberg was to be blocked.

Additionally, a bridgehead was to be established over the Moder, which was rather more of a creek than a river at this point. After we took Wingen, *Generalmajor* Philippi promised that we would be reinforced by a battalion of assault guns to allow us to continue our advance in the direction of Saverne. Thus and there, access to the Rhine Valley Plains would be opened, as a prerequisite for the employment of the *21st Panzer* and *25th Panzer-Grenadier Divisions*!

Carlau and I summoned our respective company commanders by sending runners to them. After a short while, all company commanders were assembled around both battalion commanders in their dugout, along with a few messengers. In the presence of Oldenburg, the order just received was repeated to the company commanders, and then discussed.

Considered in the light of what we had experienced during the last fifteen hours, all company commanders declared that a frontal attack along the Huhnerscherr Road without artillery support was impossible. According to our limited intelligence, the enemy infantry was obviously straddling that particular road, perhaps even massed in depth.

The commanders discussed other potential avenues of approach to Wingen. At one point in the discussion—with the ceaseless enemy mortar and artillery fire as background noise—I offered the following course of action as a solution to our problem: Return to the vicinity of the forest road pass, which our *3d Battalion* had crossed last night and where the positions of Company C of the 179th Infantry Regiment had been located. Follow one of the mountain trails to the southwest, approximately on the ridge of the Weinbourg mountain; then cross the district road and the Fischbach creek below the road. Finally, climb the wooded mountain to the north of Wingen ("Heidenfels"), and split up for the attack: the *1st Battalion* to the west, toward Heidenneck, and our *3d Battalion* to the south, toward Wingen.

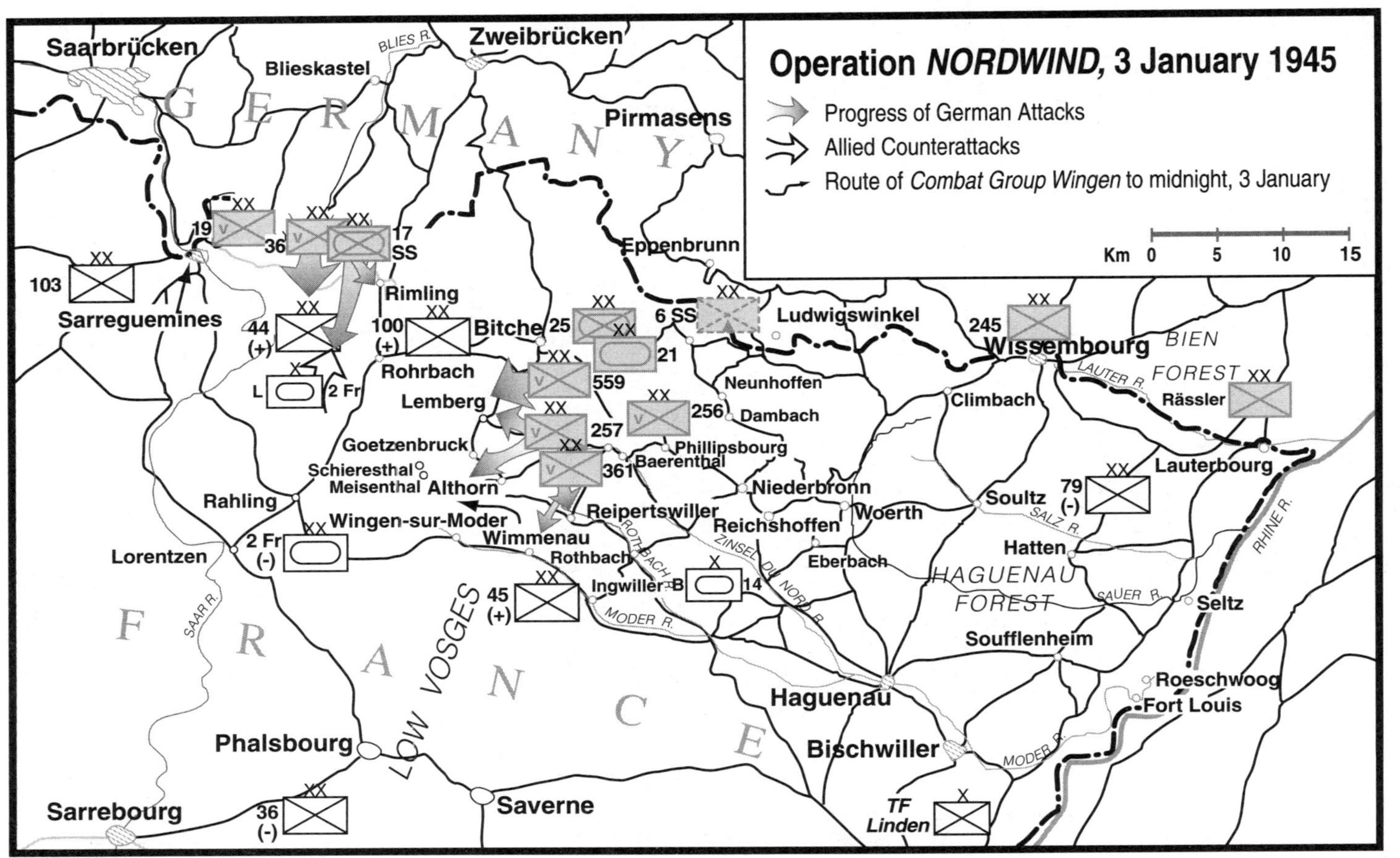

Operation NORDWIND, 3 January 1945
Progress of German Attacks
Allied Counterattacks
Route of Combat Group Wingen to midnight, 3 January
Km 0 5 10 15
GERMANY
FRANCE
BIEN FOREST
HAGUENAU FOREST
LOW VOSGES
RHINE R.
LAUTER R.
SAUER R.
SALZ R.
MODER R.
ZINSEL DU NORD R.
ROTHBACH R.
BLIES R.
SAAR R.
Saarbrücken
Zweibrücken
Blieskastel
Pirmasens
Eppenbrunn
Sarreguemines
Rimling
Bitche
Rohrbach
Lemberg
Goetzenbruck
Schieresthal
Meisenthal
Althorn
Rahling
Wingen-sur-Moder
Wimmenau
Rothbach
Reipertswiller
Ingwiller
Lorentzen
Ludwigswinkel
Neunhoffen
Dambach
Phillipsbourg
Baerenthal
Niederbronn
Reichshoffen
Woerth
Eberbach
Wissembourg
Climbach
Rässler
Lauterbourg
Soultz
Hatten
Seltz
Soufflenheim
Roeschwoog
Fort Louis
Haguenau
Bischwiller
Phalsbourg
Saverne
Sarrebourg
103
19
36
17 SS
44 (+)
L
2 Fr
100 (+)
25
21
559
257
256
361
6 SS
245
79 (-)
B
14
45 (+)
2 Fr (-)
36 (-)
TF Linden

Very quickly. I substantiated my proposal with arguments that were actually self-evident to everybody in attendance. This course of action avoided the enemy to the right and the left of the Huhnerscherr Road, most probably massed there in depth. With utmost silence, we would have a fair chance during the coming night to infiltrate through possible outposts on our new path. In the German Army, taking such a round-about route to deceive the enemy was called a "*Horizontenschleicher*," literally, to sneak along the horizon—it is the true opposite of a frontal approach.

The combat group's combined leadership discussed the pros and cons of this proposal. Everyone agreed that this would give us a far better chance of reaching our respective objectives than the course of action ordered by our higher headquarters. The battalion commanders asked Oldenburg to return to Schreiber at his command post in Melch and explain our counterproposal, the development of which he had followed from the start.[96]

Oldenburg and his runners left us around 1600. He had four to five kilometers to cover to Schreiber's command post of the *SS-Mountain Infantry Regiment 12* just west of Melch, so we knew that there was no way he could be back on the Kaesberg before two to three hours, and only then if he didn't run into trouble.

As soon as Oldenburg left, the company commanders returned to their units. Both battalion commanders were once again alone with their adjutants and runners in the CP. Now, everything depended on whether "higher command" would agree to dispense with its highly-prescriptive original order to advance along the confounded Huhnerscherr Road, and instead give higher priority to seizing the objective, regardless of *how* it would be accomplished.

## The Reipertswiller Riposte

While Oldenburg trudged quickly through the snow back to Melch, and as the 1st Battalion, 314th Infantry was attacking to clear the southern and southwestern approaches to Reipertswiller, 2d Battalion, 313th Infantry, supported by armor, counterattacked from the town itself along the northbound road. This attack inflicted severe casualties on the elements of *1st Battalion, GR 953*, which were still in position behind the Rothbach, and surprised the companies of *2d Battalion, GR 953* at Saegmuhle. The three remaining German assault guns were too late to be of use in opposing this attack. Only in the dark was it possible for the rest of the *1st Battalion, GR 953* to withdraw from the low area around the creek to more suitable defensive positions on higher ground north of Reipertswiller. By now, the combat strength of the *1st Battalion, GR 953*, which had gone into combat two days before with about 400 men, had sunk to 150.

Under these circumstances, it would have been irresponsible to leave *2d Battalion, GR 953* in its now fully-exposed positions west of Reipertswiller. Consequently, this battalion was also withdrawn into the positions from which they had started the day. It reported Saegmuhle free of enemy troops, and occupied it during the evening.[97] The Americans in Reipertswiller had all but erased any chances of being cut off by the Germans, and had significantly weakened the attackers in the process.

## We Prepare to Press Forward

As the picture became clearer to the American command, we were still "in the dark" about the acceptability of our proposed plan for seizing Wingen by infiltration. Since it seemed to be definite that no matter what, we would not spend the night on the Kaesberg, we used the time to prepare everything for onward movement. There was a "safe" trail from our Kaesberg-Hedgehog to the hamlet of Althorn, about 1.5 kilometers away, and from there we could send elements along the road to Mouterhouse, where our service and supply units, and the motorized valley echelons of both battalions were located. At least one of our aid stations was also in Mouterhouse, so we saw to it that all wounded were transported there quickly. We decided that if they were deemed unfit to endure the stress of the upcoming night march across the mountains, even the more lightly wounded would be evacuated.

We also transported our American prisoners to the rear, and all surplus baggage of any sort was taken care of by the *Bergstaffel.* While in Althorn, the *Bergstaffel* picked up ammunition and other supplies, and brought them back to the Kaesberg.

By the time Oldenburg returned, it was already dark, around 1900. Despite the demanding march over the mountains in snow, he wore an optimistic face as he approached us—he seemed to have done it!

Philippi's revised order for our *1st* and *3d Battalions* was much more practical and simple, "Penetrate to Wingen, by-passing enemy resistance! Take and hold Wingen, establish bridgehead over Moder!"

Substantively, that was the higher headquarters' blessing of our counterproposal. We were a bit relieved, even if the task facing us still seemed highly daunting, that is, that two weakened mountain infantry battalions—without any heavy weapons or other support—against the cream of the American Army.

The orders for the infiltration and attack, already prepared in anticipation of their approval, were quickly conveyed to the companies:

* Under cover of darkness, each company will carefully disengage by platoon, at short intervals.

- ✱ All companies will reassemble near the center of the Kaesberg to conduct resupply of ammunition and food. Each man was issued a half a loaf of bread and a few tubes of cream cheese spread. Anticipating that it might be difficult to be resupplied again in the near future, we resolved ourselves to gain the next food resupply from "the Ami." We took all the ammunition we could carry, however.

  Here, standardization really paid off: we only had to take two types of ammunition, that is, 7.92mm for rifles and machine guns and 9mm for pistols and submachine guns. Our heaviest weapons were the MG-42 light machine guns and *panzerfausts*. We also took rifle grenades and hand grenades (the "potato masher"-type with the wooden handle), although our pioneers carried some Teller-mines* for use against armored vehicles.
- ✱ Every NCO, every man will be informed about the nature of our upcoming march, and is to be instructed not to talk, not to make noise, to wind some cloth around metal (such as the gas mask container), not to smoke, and—as vital as everything else—not to lose contact with the man in front! Only complete silence and unsevered connection from one man to the next gives us even a bit of a chance to infiltrate stealthily between the American units dispersed in locations unknown to us.

As usually happens in the dark, these vital preparations for the infiltration took more time than we had anticipated. It was past 2200 when the first of our companies disengaged itself from the enemy, and it took until midnight for both battalions to assemble in the depression in the center of the Kaesberg, behind a thin screen still left in our previous foxholes. Our men were ready to go, everybody had received his orders, and all knew the importance of our mission.

## At the End of the Day

At the close of the Third Day, Philippi assessed the efforts of his division rather gloomily. All offensive activities in the *361st VGD* had come to a stop. The *953d*'s attack against Reipertswiller had failed, and the unit had sustained irreplaceable casualties. The garbled radio message from his *2d Battalion, GR 951* in Wimmenau, in which he thought he understood that they were requesting reinforcements, bode more bad news. Besides, it now appeared that rather than cutting off the Americans in Reipertswiller, it was the enemy who was close to cutting off *2d Battalion, GR 951* on the Kienberg.

*So-called because they were truncated cylinders which vaguely resembled a dinner plate (*Teller*).

Philippi appreciated that *SS-Panzer-Grenadier Battalion 506* (operating dismounted) had at best reached the Hochkopf (East) only shortly before midnight; it would laager there for the night. This unit still had not physically contacted the hard-pressed *2d Battalion, GR 951* on the Kienberg, two kilometers to the southeast, but would attempt to link with them on the morrow. Barring changes to the situation, both battalions would attack Wimmenau.

Overall, the actions of this day's offensive operations had ended in fiasco. and it was obvious that the enemy had reinforced his positions with fresh troops. To make things worse, the batteries of Philippi's *Artillery Regiment 361* were receiving increased attention from enemy *Jabos* and artillery.

The whole situation had been complicated by the instructions he had received earlier in the day. At about noon, in his CP in the forester's house in Bannstein, *Generalmajor* Philippi received a distinguished visitor in the person of *Generaloberst* Hans von Obstfelder, the commanding general of *1st Army*. During this conference, they decided to relieve *1st Battalion, GR 952* at Baerenthal during the coming night with elements of the *256th VGD*; with the completion of the relief, Baerenthal would pass into the responsibility of the *256th VGD*. Philippi, who had hoped for exactly such a possibility to concentrate his forces, rejoiced prematurely; von Obstfelder promptly ordered Philippi to use this battalion to attack toward Zinswiller, to open the road from there to Baerenthal for the possible use of the German armored reserve, the *21st Panzer-Division* and the *25th Panzer-Grenadier Division*. To reinforce the *361st VGD* in his mission against Reipertswiller and Lichtenberg, von Obstfelder promised Philippi an infantry regiment from the *257th VGD*, its right neighbor. Furthermore, Philippi received the promise that his future attacks would be supported also by the artillery of *both* his neighbors. Until the regiment from the *257th VGD* appeared, von Obstfelder gave his consent for the *361st* to assume a defensive posture.[98] *Generalmajor* Philippi was not the only division commander in the Low Vosges to be visited by a VIP that day. The commanding general of *Army Group G*, *Generaloberst* Johannes Blaskowitz, visited *Generalmajor* Seidel at the *257th*'s command post to inform the division commander of the progress of Operation *NORDWIND* and of the tasks laying ahead during the coming days.

* * * * *

As Philippi, Seidel and their staffs worked through the night to formulate plans that might yet secure success for *NORDWIND*, they would have been deeply disheartened to know what was going on in the command posts of their counterparts across the line of contact.

Although not crisp and complete, by midnight on January 3/4, the staff of the 45th Infantry Division had a fair idea of what was coming on the Fourth

Day. At their new command post, the operations and intelligence officers and NCOs worked through the night to process new information into meaningful intelligence. Although Major Bishop, the 45th's acting G-2, was somewhat off target when he wrote his intelligence summary for the day, misidentifying the unit on the Kaesberg as being from the *257th VGD*, overestimating the presence of NORD units (he believed that *SS-Mountain Infantry Regiments 11* and *12* were present) and mistaking their mission (an attack on Reipertswiller and Wimmenau), the picture cleared up as the Fourth Day approached.*

First, at 2115, Major Bishop received a call from Colonel Langevin (VI Corps G-2) who had evaluated the German map captured with the Adjutant of *2d Battalion, GR 951* north of Wimmenau. Colonel Langevin cautioned Major Bishop that this map showed *inter alia* an arrow indicating an impending attack on Wingen.[99]

Next, Bishop received a report of the results of a prisoner interrogation at the 179th Infantry command post. A German captured by Company A, 179th to the northwest of Kohlhutte—probably from the confused patrol from the *257th* we'd run into early in the day—told his captors of seeing "an *SS* unit" on the Kaesberg Mountain. Reported to division at 2255, this was the first indication to the 45th that the "stubborn defenders" on the mountain three kilometers north of Wingen could be from *NORD*.[100]

From this information, then, the staff of the 45th knew that some elements of *NORD* were near the Kaesberg earlier in the day, and that an attack on Wingen was likely in the near future. While this probably concerned them, they must have felt that they were prepared for this eventuality. During the day, the 1st Battalion, 276th Infantry of Task Force Herren had been deployed in the vicinity of Wingen. Company B took up positions on the forested heights overlooking Wingen from the north, while the Companies A and C were disposed south of the town, thus intermingling with the companies of its sister battalion, the 3d, to which Company C was attached at 1335, with the mission of taking over the right sector of Company I.[101] Thus, Wingen seemed to be well-protected by three infantry battalions, with 1st Battalion, 179th Infantry defending on line to the north and northeast; 3d Battalion, 179th defending to the north and northwest, and 3d Battation of the 276th Infantry in position to the west/northwest, on the Hochkopf (West). The roads from the German side were blocked or at least could be taken under direct and indirect fire, and 1st Battalion, 276th was in position south of Wingen to react to any unexpected developments. Yes, Wingen seemed secure.

*45th Infantry Division G-2 Journal, 3 January, 5, 1800 hours. *SS-Mountain Infantry Regiment 11* was still enroute, and would not be in the battle for almost another week.

*****

On the freezing, snow-swept Kaesberg, both battalion commanders and their adjutants had one last meeting before moving out. Kreuzinger convinced Burgstaller that this time it was the *1st Battalion*'s turn to take the lead. Gathered under a blanket to maintain light security, the precious maps of both battalions (one each) were compared a final time, and consensus was reached after a short discussion about the best avenues of approach to the objective. We also agreed that both battalions should arrive at their assembly areas north of Wingen not later than daybreak, as we wanted to assault Wingen right after first light. There being no more preparations to make, we bade each other a final blessing, "God be with you."

So ended Day Three for *Combat Group Wingen*.

## - III -
## Battle Analysis

An analysis of the events of the Third Day sheds further light on the factors contributing to the outcome of *NORDWIND* in the Low Vosges. It also reveals some of the characteristics of the tactics, techniques, and procedures in use on the German side. Finally, it reveals certain strengths of the American opposition.

### *Command and Control*

Certainly, this is one of the most important considerations of any campaign; on the third full day of *NORDWIND*, it was not decisive, but there were nevertheless clear indications about its efficacy—on each side.

Neither Blaskowitz nor von Obstfelder could be faulted for not trying to influence the action with their personal presence. Each visited the headquarters of their two most successful divisions to this point in the offensive, and tried to reinforce and encourage their success on the following day. On the other hand, whether the respective corps commanders were bypassed and, to some extent, obviated, is unknown, since none of the existing records specifically mention the roles of Höhne and Petersen in these visits.

At the division level, we know that Philippi's order to us regarding the plan for the attack on Wingen was overly prescriptive and directive; we also know that he possessed the flexibility to change his instructions in the light of the alternative plan we formulated in our dugout on the Kaesberg and forwarded to him via courier. In retrospect, what is peculiar and even disturbing is why we got an order that was so restrictive in the first place. Unbeknownst to us at the time, on 27 December 1944, *Generaloberst* Blaskowitz directed *General* von Obstfelder to use our unit in exactly the fashion we suggested in our "counterproposal" to Philippi:

> The *Combat Group* of the *6th SS-Mountain Division* is to be employed in such a way that it makes use of the mountainous terrain to bypass the enemy—who will mainly stick to the roads—breach his lines and thus give momentum to the entire assault operation [of *NORDWIND*].[102]

The five-hour delay caused by the requirement to evaluate the plan, formulate an alternative, send a messenger by foot over snowy mountains, and receive permission resulted in unnecessary exposure to further casualties on the Kaesberg, and a much later start toward Wingen than would have been the case if we had gotten simple, mission-oriented orders—or at least ones which reflected the *Army Group* commander's intent—via radio at noon, when *Untersturmführer* Oldenburg presumably received them before beginning his trek.

There were other problems caused by the communications breakdown. All higher commanders' knowledge of the moment-to-moment actions of *Combat Group Wingen* was poor, due to the continued complete absence of radio or wire communications. Even though we were within direct, face-to-face contact with our support echelon at Althorn and Mouterhouse, the lost communications assets were never replaced. Obviously, this communications lapse had already had severe consequences for our operations (lack of artillery support, no passage of intelligence updates, delay of orders, and so on), and these would only be compounded over the next several days.

On the American side, while we did not know about their commanders' presence at forward positions or other such personal activities, it is obvious that higher-level commanders were able quickly and deftly to shuffle forces to fulfill the tactical requirements of the day. During Day Three, the 45th Infantry Division, already controlling major elements of the 79th Infantry Division, was now controlling an additional three regiments, namely those of Task Force Herren. Major General Brooks and his staff at VI Corps, and Major General Frederick and his staff in the 45th must be credited with outstandingly quick reactions to Operation *NORDWIND*, most remarkably their rapid shifting of forces to the most endangered points. While the commander and staff of *Army Group G* certainly anticipated a strong American reaction, they never thought it would be so swift!

Of course, the American's ability to route convoys of trucks and even sometimes DUKWs* full of soldiers and supplies to critical points was

*An amphibious vehicle based on the ubiquitous 2fi-ton cargo truck.

absolutely unhindered by the *Luftwaffe*. Even given this advantageous capability, however, VI Corps had been unable to close the gap left by the disintegration of Task Force Hudelson on Day One. From the late morning of Day One forward, the two sides raced to take appropriate action regarding the sixteen-kilometer gap yawning in the ravines and snow-covered hilltops of the Low Vosges between Bitche and Neunhoffen.

Major General Frederick almost won the race. By Day Three, there was only one important gap still open in the American line, namely the gap along the upper Rothbach Valley between Wildenguth in the east and the Weinbourg Heights in the west. This was an opening in the American defense of some four kilometers' width and a depth of at least five kilometers, southward clear down to the Moder Valley. No coherent defense had yet been established. The only American unit in the area was a single battalion at Wimmenau (2d Battalion, 276th Infantry).*

By the end of the Third Day, this gash in the American lines had already been used by four German battalions: the two battalions of *Combat Group Wingen*; the *2d Battalion, GR 951;* and, on this very evening, *SS-Panzer-Grenadier Battalion 506*. Of these four German battalions, only one had been recognized and identified so far by the Americans.

Of the "cornerstones," or shoulders of the gap, only the western one, held by 1st and 3d Battalions of the 179th Infantry Regiment, could be regarded as relatively secure. The eastern cornerstone at Wildenguth, its crossroads occupied by Companies A and C of the 313th Infantry Regiment, was less solid, both companies being already cut off by elements of the *361st VGD* on the third day. If that cornerstone failed, Reipertswiller would be the next secure American position, thus widening the gap to five or six kilometers. Frederick and his staff officers in the 45th Division were well aware of this precarious situation and did their utmost to change it to the better as fast as possible.

## Training and Organization for Combat

By the end of Day Three, the *XC* and *LXXXIX Corps* drives had lost their initial momentum. A major reason was the inadequate training of the assault echelons. This was compounded by the unsuitability of the *Volks-Grenadier*

*The vigilant reader will remember that on the First Day, the commanding officer of 117th Cavalry Reconnaissance Squadron, Lieutenant Colonel Hodge, in the late afternoon of 1 January had received orders from Colonel Hudelson at his command post in Reipertswiller to "establish and hold the present line between Reipertswiller and Sarreinsberg." A short look on the map will prove that this "line" in the Rothbach Valley is identical with the wide gap which is the subject of this paragraph. Task Force Hudelson was disbanded on 2 January, and the entire region was taken over by the 45th Infantry Division.

*Division* organization for offensive operations. Although highly motivated by the success of the Ardennes offensive to the north,[103] most of the reclassified airmen, naval ratings, and former industrial technicians who comprised the majority of the *Landsers* in the *559th, 257th, 361st,* and *256th VGD*s simply had not been trained for attacking in mountainous terrain, much less in the depths of a particularly ferocious winter.[104]

The difficulties which arose from this lack of training were exacerbated by the abbreviated nature of *volks-grenadier* regimental and, in the case of the *559th,* divisional organizations. In the regiments of a typical *VGD*—including those in the Vosges—each regiment only possessed two battalions, instead of the three included on the rolls of previous German infantry formations. To attack on a regimental-sized front required the commitment of both battalions, and there could be no reserve, without unduly crippling one of the assault battalions. Thus, there was little or no opportunity to rotate attack responsibilities, and no force with which to exploit success. *All duties*—attack, security, local defense, and so on—were performed *all the time* by *all the infantrymen* in the regiment, without the chance for respite which "reserve" status brings, however briefly. In this way, the marginally-trained and conditioned men of the other divisions of *XC* and *LXXXIX Corps* could not possibly maintain the high tempo of operations requisite for offensive operations for long, even in the best meteorological conditions.

In the case of *Generalmajor* von der Mühlen's *559th VGD,* of course, this problem was made more acute by the presence of only two *grenadier* regiments in his division, namely the *1126th* and *1127th*. After the tough time the four battalions of this division had against elements of the 100th Infantry Division west and southwest of Bitche, and certainly before Lemberg, a third regiment would have provided crucial combat power, and the opportunity to rest some units. In Philippi's *361st,* one of the regiments (*GR 951*) had only *one* battalion, due to a previous combat loss. This left Philippi—not to mention the regimental commander—with a completely untenable organizational situation.

## Casualties and the Materiel Situation

The manifold shortcomings and challenges faced by the *VGD*s and their subunits were only aggravated by the losses of the Third Day. Most of the *volks-grenadier* battalions were commanded by captains, or even by lieutenants. When any of these men—who may or may not have been qualified to lead formations of this size in the first place—were killed or became otherwise *hors de combat*, there was no one to take their place.[105] The units simply did not possess the "depth" of key personnel to make good these losses. In this regard, *Combat Group Wingen* was in the same situation, although its impact had not yet particularly manifested itself by Day Three.

The impact of the inexperienced leadership within the *VGD*s can be seen in many ways on this day, however. Two captains were captured carrying critical operational information, which allowed the Americans to divine Philippi's intentions and take decisive counteractions. Patrols, such as the one from the *257th* we encountered in the morning of this day, became lost, got captured, and revealed further information to the Americans. The impact of six years of war on the officer manpower situation of the German Army was obvious in the Low Vosges.

On the other hand, better trained German units avoided these problems. As of Day Three, the Americans had yet to identify the exact location or intent of *Combat Group Wingen*—they knew that some units of *NORD* had arrived, and they suspected an attack on Wingen, but other than the information divulged by a single prisoner from the *257th* that he had seen "*SS* troops in the area [of the Kaesberg]," the Americans did not possess about our operations anything like the detailed, precise knowledge they had of the activities of the other units under Philippi's command. Up to this point, other than the communications vehicle and crew lost on Day One, the Americans had captured no one from *Combat Group Wingen*. Also, after all firefights, we had gathered our dead and taken them with us, preventing the Americans from gaining any information from their uniforms or personal items. Thus, we still maintained at least some element of surprise, and used it to maximum advantage on Day Four.

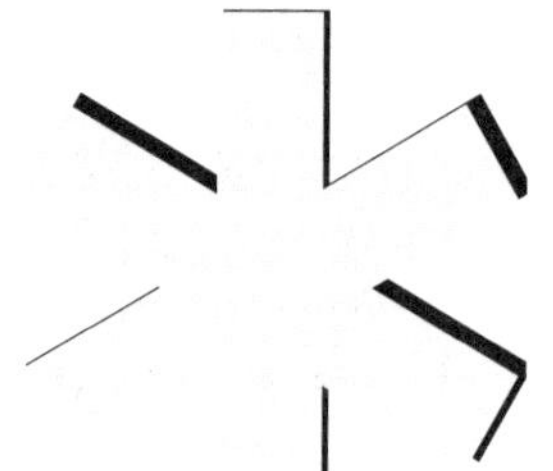

# The Fourth Day: The Attack on Wingen

## -I- One Way Out

By the Fourth Day of *NORDWIND*, most of the hopes for success in the Low Vosges devolved on *Combat Group Wingen* and its co-combatants in *General der Infanterie* Höhne's *LXXXIX Corps. XIII SS Corps* had failed to break through to Rohrbach, which had been one of the intended jump-off points for the exploitation actions of the *Army Group G* armored reserve. By the end of 3 January, *Army Group G* no longer expected any further progress in their zone, and late on the fourth day, had ordered the *36th Volks-Grenadier Division* to disengage, march east, and in several days, join *LXXXIX Corps*, whose attacks still held prospects for success.[106] The *XC Corps* attacks of 3 January had repeatedly failed to seize the several key crossroads in or near Lemberg. This corps went over to the defensive on 4 January, with *GR 477* of the *257th VGD* also being transferred to *LXXXIX Corps*, to reinforce the last hope for success in its zone.[107]

There were still two possible routes for the deployment of the *21st Panzer* and *25th Panzer-Grenadier Divisions* to the Alsatian Plain. If Wingen could be seized and held, and the route to Ingwiller cleared, then the *21st* and *25th* could wend their way south from Bitche over the spider's web of mountain roads between Bitche and Wingen, to ultimately gain the excellent road to Ingwiller. An alternate possibility was the seizure of Reipertswiller and the clearance of secondary roads to the east, reaching the Low Vosges exit at Rothbach. Given the nature of the roads, the former was clearly the preferable choice. To open this route, however, *Combat Group Wingen* would have to accomplish its mission, and *Combat Group Stämmle* (*2d Battalion* of *GR 951*), after linking up with *SS-Panzer-Grenadier Battalion 506*, would have to seize Wimmenau.

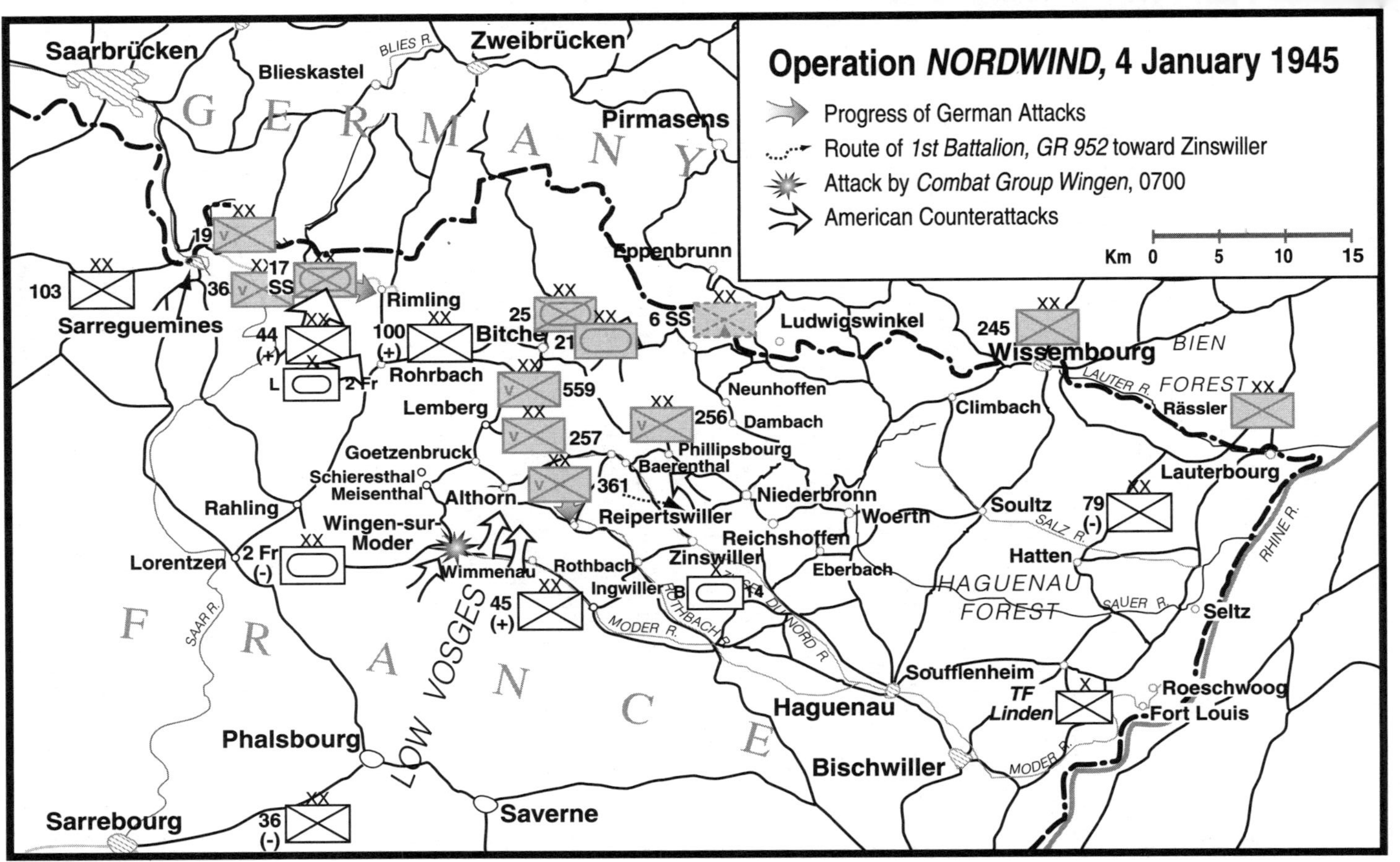

Operation NORDWIND, 4 January 1945
Progress of German Attacks
Route of 1st Battalion, GR 952 toward Zinswiller
Attack by Combat Group Wingen, 0700
American Counterattacks
Km 0 5 10 15
GERMANY
FRANCE
LOW VOSGES
BIEN FOREST
HAGUENAU FOREST
RHINE R.
LAUTER R.
SALZ R.
SAUER R.
MODER R.
ROTHBACH R.
DU NORD R.
SAAR R.
BLIES R.
Saarbrücken
Blieskastel
Zweibrücken
Pirmasens
Eppenbrunn
Sarreguemines
Rimling
Bitche
Rohrbach
Lemberg
Goetzenbruck
Schieresthal
Meisenthal
Althorn
Rahling
Wingen-sur-Moder
Lorentzen
Wimmenau
Rothbach
Ingwiller
Zinswiller
Reipertswiller
Baerenthal
Phillipsbourg
Dambach
Neunhoffen
Ludwigswinkel
Niederbronn
Reichshoffen
Woerth
Eberbach
Climbach
Wissembourg
Rässler
Lauterbourg
Soultz
Hatten
Seltz
Soufflenheim
Haguenau
Bischwiller
Roeschwoog
Fort Louis
Phalsbourg
Saverne
Sarrebourg
103
19
36
17 SS
44 (+)
L
2 Fr
100 (+)
25
21
6 SS
559
257
256
361
245
79 (-)
2 Fr (-)
45 (+)
B
14
TF Linden
36 (-)

## - II -
## On to Wingen!

The advance screen of scouts of the leading *3d Company* (*1st Battalion*) left the depression near the center of the Kaesberg Mountain early after midnight traveling in an easterly direction, almost as if returning to where we had come from twenty-four hours before. *Untersturmführer* Carlau, the adjutant of the *1st Battalion,* led the long column with the aid of a map and compass from behind the scout screen, together with *Obersturmführer* Jacobs, the CO of the *3d Company. Hauptsturmführer* Burgstaller, the *1st Battalion* commander (and CO of our *Combat Group Wingen* as well),* marched behind that company, but was often up front.

Our *3d Battalion,* with its four companies moving in single file, followed the *1st Battalion.* In total, a serpent-like column of some 2,000- to 2,500-meters' length snaked over the mountain ridges and through the woods during this night. It was cold and snowing. The vegetation in the forest was of variable density. Between the cloud cover and the forest canopy, it was pitch dark. The darkness concealed our movement to the eye, and the falling snow, coupled with that already on the ground, muffled what little sound we made as we approached our objective.

Our men conducted themselves in a perfect manner. Everybody knew that the success of our mission depended solely on surprising the enemy—surprise and shock were the heaviest (albeit psychological) weapons that we carried with us to Wingen.

Slowly, another problem arose on the march with which everyone had to cope: sheer exhaustion from sleeplessness during the last days threatened to overwhelm us. Every little stop on the march (and there were many) were used to sleep—leaning against a tree, crouching, sitting, even standing erect. This was very dangerous, as just one man failing to recognize that the man before him had started marching again could cause a disastrous break in contact—it was *that* dark. Every squad leader constantly passed up and down the single file of his men to guard against this sort of catastrophe.

After we reached the crossroads at the Weinbourg Pass, where we encountered the enemy on the previous night, the column turned first southeast, then later to the southwest. At one time on our march we crossed the narrow Kindsbronn Valley with a stony brook. Soon after crossing the valley, one

*Alois Burgstaller was almost two years senior in age to Kurt Kreuzinger. At the time of this report, both had the rank of *Hauptsturmführer* (captain). Burgstaller was promoted to *Sturmbannführer* (major) on 30 January 1945. Schreiber, our regimental CO, had appointed Burgstaller as commander of our two-battalion *Combat Team Wingen.*

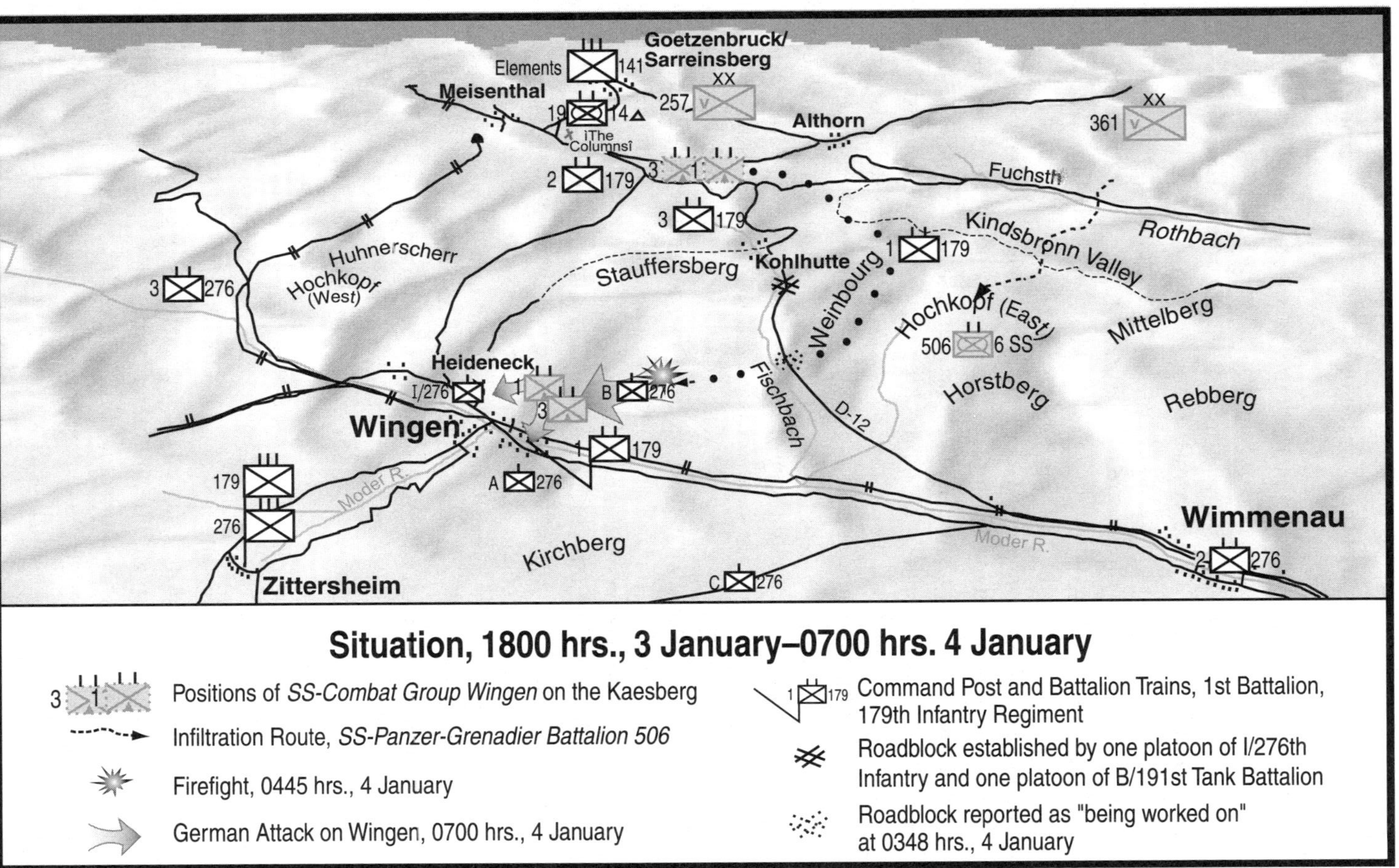
Goetzenbruck/
Sarreinsberg
Elements
141
Meisenthal
19
14
The Columns
257
XX
Althorn
361
XX
Fuchsth
Rothbach
Kindsbronn Valley
Mittelberg
Rebberg
Hochkopf (East)
506
6 SS
Horstberg
Weinbourg
Kohlhutte
Stauffersberg
Huhnerscherr
Hochkopf (West)
Heideneck
I/276
Wingen
Fischbach
D-12
Moder R.
Kirchberg
Zittersheim
Wimmenau
179
276
Situation, 1800 hrs., 3 January–0700 hrs. 4 January
Positions of SS-Combat Group Wingen on the Kaesberg
Infiltration Route, SS-Panzer-Grenadier Battalion 506
Firefight, 0445 hrs., 4 January
German Attack on Wingen, 0700 hrs., 4 January
Command Post and Battalion Trains, 1st Battalion, 179th Infantry Regiment
Roadblock established by one platoon of I/276th Infantry and one platoon of B/191st Tank Battalion
Roadblock reported as "being worked on" at 0348 hrs., 4 January

could perceive gentle slopes on both sides of the mountain—we had reached the footpath on the crest of the Weinbourg Heights. There was no sign of the enemy.

We slowly and meticulously picked our way ahead. Many halts were necessary. We often had to stop, look, and listen for indications of the enemy's presence. Further, in the deep darkness of the mountain winter night virtually no terrain features were visible, *Untersturmführer* Carlau was essentially navigating by dead reckoning, so he had to make frequent azimuth and distance checks. Finally, there were the natural "stop and go" irregularities inherent to a serpentine column of 750 to 800 men in single file. After another hour and many halts, the head of our marching column reached the district road (D-12), which connected Goetzenbruck in the north with the Moder Valley and Wimmenau in the south. Time: about 0400. The first two companies of the *1st Battalion* had crossed the road in single-file when we suddenly heard the engine noise of an approaching motor vehicle, coming from the north. The last men still on the road cleared it fast. Everybody else on both sides of the road remained rigidly frozen wherever they were. Now the vehicle (a jeep with three men) appeared around the last corner, its lights doused. Suddenly, the vehicle halted almost exactly where we were hiding in the woods. Our men who had already crossed the road had left a tell-tale dark band on the road in the new snow! When the crew of the American jeep saw this, two of them bravely climbed out to investigate, suspecting there might be mines on the road, then climbed into the jeep again and left the scene in a hurry, in the direction of Wimmenau.

We heaved a sigh of relief! Later, on second consideration, we felt a sort of remorse. What if these Americans had perceived that the "dark band" must have been made by a column of soldiers? At least on the edges of that band, single boot prints must have showed. And what if they reported this as soon as they returned to their unit, alarming the entire garrison? We should have overpowered and taken all three, but that would have risked that a shot or two would have rung out. (Instead, we should have relaxed. There is no evidence on record that these men reported what they had seen during their trip!)[108]

After getting back our breath, the rest of us—and that was the majority—also crossed the road to the southwest.

Now we had to negotiate a steep, wooded decline down into the Fischbach Valley. The Fisch-Bach is a creek of close to two-meters' width, running in a bare valley some eighty to 100 meters wide, down to the Moder River, which it joins 1,500 meters from our crossing place. The creek was not frozen, and jumping over the stones in the creek and getting wet feet (which we didn't feel in the strain we were under), we crossed this obstacle and entered the

Left: The author as a twenty-year old junior noncommissioned officer in *SS-NORD*, prior to attending the *SS-Junkerschule Bad Tölz*. (Author's collection)

Above: The author's strongly built, well-camouflaged billet in the Karelian taiga, 1944. (Author's collection)

Forward observers of *SS-Artillery Regiment 6* in northern Karelia, 1942. The author served in this regiment throughout the *NORD Division*'s battles in 1941 and 1942, until he attended the *SS-Junkerschule at Bad Tölz*. Following graduation and commissioning as an infantry officer, he returned to *NORD* to assume his new duties in *SS-Mountain Infantry Regiment 12*. (Author's collection)

An officer of *SS-NORD* after a long period of combat. Except that they wore their ski caps and, in some cases, long overcoats during the Wingen mission, veterans of the both sides of the battle agree that members of *Combat Group Wingen* resembled the soldier in this photo, in equipment and attitude. The photo is actually of *Obersturmführer* Karl-Hans Scheu, *SS-Reconnaissance Battalion 6*, a veteran of many long-range patrols behind Soviet lines in the wilderness of northern Karelia. Here he enjoys a cigarette after just returning from one such operation in 1943. (Photo graciously provided by *Obersturmführer* Scheu's granddaughter, Sabine Sebald of Hannover, and used by kind permission of Herr Patrick Agte, Munin Verlag, Pluwig, Rheinland-Pfalz, Germany).

Old enemies, new friends: Orville Ellis, Company C, 276th Infantry and former President of the 70th Infantry Division Association (left) and the author exchange a bottle of wine at one of the first joint gatherings of veterans of their respective wartime units. (Author's collection)

beechwood forest again beyond the valley. Under the shield of the tall trees we assembled our forces again, and straightened them out.

After this short halt, we continued our march up the steep incline, to an evenly-forested plateau of (according to our map) about 1,000- to 1,200-meters' breadth from east to west, and some fifty meters higher than the surrounding valley. This plateau rises in the north to the Heidenfels summit ("Pagans Rock," elevation 350 meters) and ends in the south with a slope down to the marshaling yard of the Wingen railroad station.

As before, the *1st Battalion* was leading, our *3d* was following. It might have been some twenty minutes after the last man had crossed the Fischbach when up on the wooded plateau the first salvoes of our submachine guns rang out. Elements of the *1st Battalion* had made contact with the enemy, probably an outpost stationed in this wooded terrain, obviously charged with securing Wingen from the north.*

What now ensued in the darkness of the early day and the dense forest was a stubborn small arms firefight which lasted probably no longer than twenty minutes, but seemed to us rather like hours on end. It was much too loud, too. It was exactly what we had desperately wanted to avoid, realizing that only with surprise would we have any chance to overwhelm the enemy in Wingen! On our side, units of both battalions were involved. Both sides sustained casualties before we overpowered and silenced this company-strong outpost, and were able to move on toward Wingen. Time: approximately 0515.†

On the evening before (1800, 3 January), in their headquarters at Zittersheim, the commander and staff of the 276th Infantry Regiment of Task Force Herren (attached to the 45th Infantry Division), were notified that a hostile attack was to be expected. They subsequently alerted their 1st Battalion, which had arrived in the vicinity of Wingen on the afternoon of 2 January and had been placed in reserve. Of its four companies, three had been committed to that point: Company A was in position on the northern slope of the Kirchberg Heights, facing Wingen from the south, with the .30-caliber heavy machine guns of Company D nearby and to its west. Company C had been placed under the command of 3d Battalion, 276th Infantry in the area, and had positions to the east of Company A, in the eastern part of the Kirchberg.[109]

*Carlau (7) says it was his *4th* (HMG) *Company* that first came into contact with the enemy outpost, which was manned by Company B of the 276th Infantry Regiment.

†Meininghaus (10, 11) was seriously wounded here, but with the assistance of another wounded soldier of his *13th Company*, reached friendly lines southwest of Melch. Also: Zoepf I, 28.

Uncommitted so far was Company B, commanded by Lieutenant Ivan Stone. This company originally had dug positions in the north of Wingen, overlooking the railroad embankment, but later in the evening was ordered to establish positions to outpost the forested heights further to the north, after extra belts of machine-gun ammunition and hand grenades had been issued.

Lieutenant Stone chose positions almost in the center of the aforementioned plateau, approximately 600 meters west of the Fischbach Valley, 500 meters to the east of the forest edge overlooking Heideneck, but only 400 meters north of the Wingen railroad station. He ordered a tent pitched to house his command post, and told his platoons not to dig in—should there be Germans around, he reasoned, the noise of digging might give away their position. Most of the men fell asleep on blankets laid on the frozen ground.

In retrospect decades after this event, the American veterans of the ensuing fight are still impressed by the immense firepower generated by the Germans' automatic weapons (MG-42 machine guns and MP-40 machine pistols). They relate episodes such as this, "The Germans would walk to a tree, put their hand on it, lay their burp guns on their arm, and say, 'All right, Americans: *Fire!* So we can see where you are!' If you did, they would get you every time."*

In short, Company B was totally routed during the early hours of this day, the majority killed or wounded, with some dispersed and taken prisoner later during the morning. Only a few (of the 2d platoon) made an orderly

*This anecdote is related by Mr. Richard Struthers of Company B if the 276th Infantry Regiment, in Wallace R. Cheves' *Snow, Ridges and Pillboxes*. In fact, a German mountain rifle company *did* possess greater firepower than its American infantry counterpart, and it was especially evident in close range engagements. The MP-40 submachine gun (GIs called it the "burp gun," due to the distinctive sound it made when fired), with which all officers and NCOs were equipped, sprayed 9mm pistol ammunition at a high rate of fire, and was very effective under 100 meters' range; several of the NCOs still carried Finnish-made submachine guns which were even more effective, due to their large-capacity, drum-type magazines. Although the rank and file German mountain infantryman, still armed with the Kar 98 Mauser bolt-action rifle could not match the volume of fire attained by his American counterpart, armed with the M1 Garand, the much higher proportion of submachine guns on the German side helped even the odds. The German firepower superiority noticed in this vignette stemmed mainly from the overwhelming proportion of machine guns: while each US rifle company had two organic .30-caliber air-cooled machine guns, and nine Browning automatic rifles (firing from twenty-round magazines), each German *Jäger* company disposed twelve belt-fed MG-42 machine guns! The fire from these, combined with the fifteen to twenty submachine guns that must have been present in each *Jäger* company, accounted for the German firepower advantage . . . as long as ammunition lasted!

withdrawal to the west, where in Heideneck they made contact with elements of the 45th Division's 3d Battalion, 179th Infantry, remaining with them for the next several days.

The first word of this debacle soon reached the command post of the 179th Infantry Regiment at Zittersheim, four kilometers to the southwest, and is duly noted in its Operations Journal for 4 January. At 0450, the staff of 3d Battalion, 179th Infantry informed their regimental CP that they could hear small arms fire to their right (east); at 0512, the regimental S-3 passed the information to the 45th's G-3.

Inexplicably, it took the 276th Infantry Regiment much longer to notify the 179th Infantry Regiment CP, even though its CP was also located in Zittersheim. Even when the report did come through, it was grossly inaccurate. At 0630 when "Pagan 3" (the callsign of the S-3, 179th Infantry Regiment) was informed by "Wriggle 3" (S-3, 276th Infantry) of the details of the firing of over 100 minutes before, they were told that Company B, 276th Infantry had been "hit by [an] enemy patrol (20-24 men)."*

*****

During the firefight in the dark forest, the two battalions of *Combat Group Wingen* broke contact with one another for some time, but restored unit integrity when both battalion commanders and their adjutants met after the heaviest combat was over. After the disaster of our running into this American outpost and the firefight following it, we were almost certain that we had lost the element of surprise—our only hope. We now expected the garrison of Wingen, of which we know next to nil, now to be on full alert, waiting for us to come. We therefore had no time to lose with long discussions.

We could not have known it at the time—in fact, we would not have dreamt of such good fortune—but even after the 3d Battalion, 179th Infantry reported small arms fire "to their right" at 0450 (meaning the outpost position of Company B, 276th Infantry), and even after a twenty-minute firefight within 600 meters of the CP of 1st Battalion, 179th Infantry, the duty officer in the 1st Battalion CP reported from Wingen to the regimental duty officer "ALL QUIET" at 0500.[110]

*These quotations from 179th Infantry Regiment Operations Journal for 4 January 1945. When examining the Operations Journal of the 179th Infantry, the researcher must be careful to realize that the 179th's radio operators and other CP personnel often misinterpreted the spelling of the 276th's callsigns—there are many references to "Regal 3," which should have been "Wriggle 3," the correct callsign of the 276th's S-3. There were no stations using "Regal" anywhere near this area of operations.

Consensus was reached quickly regarding the respective assembly areas, and also about H-hour: sunrise was expected at 0822, with daylight approximately one hour before—say shortly after 0700. All we needed was enough light to see our objective, the streets and houses of Wingen, to avoid getting misoriented, and to delineate the objectives for the individual companies. So we set the H-hour for our joint attack at 0700.

We then split up again, the *1st Battalion* continuing in a westerly direction through the woods against Heideneck ("Pagans Corner"), the western part of Wingen. Our *3d Battalion* assembled on the southern edge of the forest, facing the main part of the town. Not being able to see much in the darkness of the early day, we had agreed to take the connecting line between both churches—which we had made out on the map—as the general boundary between our two battalions. Within the built-up area west of this line would be the *1st Battalion*, east of it our *3d Battalion*. Part of our joint forces would be left in the woods to effect a perimeter defense in all directions, in the event of an American counterattack while our assault was taking place.

It was close to 0630 when the companies of our *3d Battalion* reached the southern end of the mountain slope. The four company leaders assembled around the battalion commander. We were staying inside the forest but had a clear view over the town, thanks to the slowly developing dawn. Directly to our front was a steep decline that terminated at the level of the marshaling yard, with its six or seven tracks and the railroad station diagonally to our left. Beyond the station area were the buildings of the town proper. Already easy to recognize was the Catholic church with its prominent spire, not 300 meters from the station.

Scrutinizing all features before us with our field glasses, we were astonished to see not a single sign of human life. All we saw was some smoke rising straight up into the brightening blue morning sky from the chimneys of the houses, lending the picture a peaceful appearance. Could everyone stationed here have missed the noises of combat, not two hours ago? Weren't any guards here on duty to wake the rest? Could everybody really still be sleeping? We could not trust our eyes, and passed the word to be extra wary, and suspect an ambush waiting for our entrance on the stage.

Orders were quickly issued:

* *13th Company* attacks on the right flank with two platoons, along the boundary with the *1st Battalion,* to claim the southern bank of the Moder River, and establish a bridgehead beyond it. The third platoon attacks east along the railway as far as the last houses of the town.
* *12th* and *11th Companies* establish the northern arm of our perimeter defense on the forested heights we had just passed through in

positions that would permit sustained defense against enemy attacks from the north. *12th Company* deploys to the east, to include a factory of sorts,* located north of the railroad line.

✱ The combat engineer platoon (organic to our battalion headquarters company) accompanies the *3d Battalion* into Wingen, its specific mission depending on our achievement within the next few hours.

We had just come to the end of our orders' issue when we heard the typical muffled staccato firing of mortars, obviously coming from beyond the southern part of the town.[†] Moments later we started receiving mortar fire, the first salvo a bit too far behind us, but the following coming nearer to our area. H-hour was coming up, and some of us were not unhappy for this prodding, which made it so much easier for us. There was no more time to lose! The attack had to commence *now*, so we took heart and began running down the steep slope toward our objective.

## Actions on the Objective

In no time, we were between the tracks of the marshaling yard and across, without drawing as much as a single rifle shot. With his *13th Company* headquarters section, *Hauptsturmführer* Schütze ran to the station building, where they took the very first American prisoners. Meanwhile, his two platoons went down the street past the church[‡] towards the Moder bridge. Leaving the last houses in the south of Wingen behind them, they now had to cross the sloping meadows which rolled up to the forest edge of the Kirchberg Heights, bordering the Moder Valley in the south.

Although to this point we had not received organized resistance from the town's garrison, the two platoons of the *13th Company* now took machine-gun and rifle fire from the edge of the woods, both in front and flanking from their right. Very soon, the small arms fire was also supported by mortar fire. All this action by the enemy[§] proved rather effective, and pinned our men down on the meadows, which were bare of any cover. Not being in a position to retaliate in kind, the platoon leaders did the only sensible thing—they ordered their men back to the cover of the row of houses, before their platoons sustained substantial losses.

*This factory marked on the map turned out to be the renowned Lalique glass- and crystal-works.

[†]This mortar fire may have come from Company D, 276th Infantry, although there is no record of it.

[‡]This larger church close to the railroad station turned out to be the Roman Catholic church of St. Félix, built during the German administration before World War I.

[§]Company A, 276th Infantry Regiment (Lowry, 40, 41).

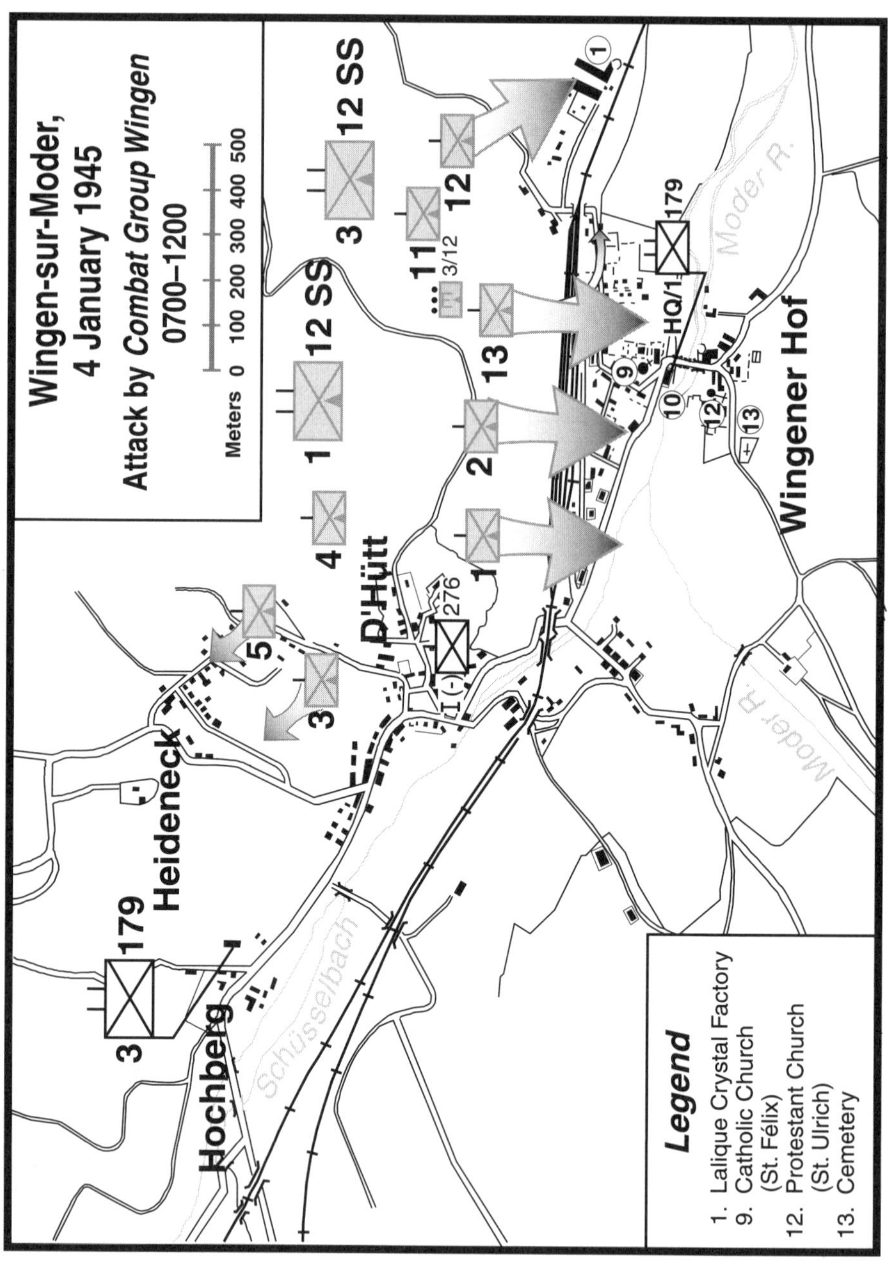


Meanwhile, the third platoon of the *13th Company* had occupied the eastern-most part of the town without substantial resistance. The *11th* and *12th* Companies also reported that they had reconnoitered suitable positions north of the railroad line, both on the forested heights and in the northeast suburb of Wingen, with its factory. They were now about to quickly dig in, with most of their foxholes and machine-gun positions facing north, as part of the intended overall perimeter defense. Some of their machine guns would, however, be positioned on the *southern* edge of the woods overlooking the town, to render fire support to our elements in Wingen proper against the expected American counterattack.

After the battalions had parted in the dark of the early day, the *1st Battalion* had moved to the western side of the plateau and assembled its companies under the cover of the forest. *1st* and *2d Companies* were to establish a bridgehead beyond the Moder River; the *3d* and *5th Companies* were to seize and occupy Heideneck.* Only the heavy machine-gun company (*4th*) remained in the woods, to support the attack of the line companies by fire.

The *1st Battalion* jumped off from its assembly area at the same time as ours, and two of its companies crossed the western part of the marshaling yard without drawing fire, clearing the houses of American soldiers, which they literally surprised *in their beds*. The *4th Company* had positioned its heavy machine guns on the southern and western edge of the forest, overlooking most of the town, and had already opened fire on American soldiers who tried to run to the safety of the woods in the south and the west.

The *3d* and the *5th Companies* both attacked in a westerly direction. The *5th Company*, under *Untersturmführer* Paul Kürten, cleared the houses in Heideneck, north of the railroad embankment, while the *3d* under *Obersturmführer* Hans Jacobs, climbed the hilly area south of the same embankment and occupied the houses on the westerly edge of the mountainous forest, which stretched all the way to Puberg.

At the same time, the *1st* and *2d Companies* attacked south, crossing the town and the Moder River to establish a bridgehead beyond. One of the near objectives of the *1st Company* was the town's cemetery on the hilly outskirts to the south of the town. This cemetery was rectangular and enclosed on all four sides by a stone wall about four- to five-feet high, ideal for covering and concealing machine-gun positions. A short distance beyond the cemetery, climbing up to the wooded height of the Kirchberg, to their astonishment, men of the *1st Company* discovered freshly dug foxholes, unoccupied. They had been dug in the evening before by men of Company A, 276th Infantry, which had left them to stay in the cover of the woods over night. Now the *Gebirgsjäger* of the *1st Battalion* occupied their foxholes before the builders were able to reoccupy them![111]

*The *5th Company* was the headquarters company of the *1st Battalion*, and consisted for this mission of only two platoons, namely the engineer platoon and the signal platoon. The leader of the latter, Paul Kürten, was commanding this abbreviated formation.

The American reaction to our attack was strangely slow to develop. At 0730—as Wingen was being overrun—the S-3 of the 276th Infantry informed his counterpart in the 179th that "enemy patrols [are] still active in [the] B Company sector" *400 meters north of the town*, and that the 276th's S-3 "believes [the] enemy to be in Wingen." By 0805, "Wriggle 3" updated this appraisal of German activity: "[The] Enemy [is] definitely in WINGEN, firefight reported."

Incredibly, no report was forthcoming from the 1st Battalion, 179th Infantry's own command post. The closest thing to a report of our attack was a message, also received at the 179th's regimental CP at 0805, from the executive officer (XO) of the 157th Infantry Regiment, far to the east. He reported that the 157th's liaison officer with the 1st Battalion, 179th Infantry CP in Wingen had transmitted a message that there were German soldiers fighting in the town itself. Apparently, the command post personnel of 1st Battalion, 179th were largely paralyzed by our assault. The first recorded message from this battalion about our attack was at 0850, when a Sergeant Mills (of Headquarters Company, 1st Battalion, 179th) informed the S-3 of his Regiment, "enemy [is] in WINGEN in strength of about 40-45 men [*sic*!] [who] came into town from [the] NE, sniping at first and developing into a fight in front of [the] 1st Bn CP."

Even before this belated confirmation from his subordinate headquarters, the CO of the 179th Infantry, Colonel Murphy, quickly decided not to withdraw elements of his own regiment to restore the situation, but rather to leave them in place, forward (to the north) along the regimental MLR. Instead, he called on the combat novices of the 276th Infantry to recover the ground their 1st Battalion had so recently lost. This decision was reflected in a message transmitted at 0840 from the 179th's CP to the commanders of the regiment's 1st and 3d Battalions, strangely, using the fire coordination net of the supporting 160th Field Artillery (FA) Battalion.

The unusual means by which this call was transmitted probably demonstrates that at this hour there were no *reliable* communications between the 179th Infantry Regiment CP at Zittersheim and its 3d Battalion CP at Hochberg, just to the west of Wingen. Of course, all communications with the CP of its 1st Battalion in Wingen had been severed an hour before. Fortunately for the 179th Infantry, the radio communications of the supporting artillery functioned well, linking their liaison party in Zittersheim with their forward observers and liaison officers with both infantry battalions. Subsequent entries in the 179th's Operations log show that the regimental operations staff relied extensively on the artillery net to communicate with the 3d Battalion, 179th Infantry CP in Hochberg.

The appraisals of the situation by the staff of 3d Battalion, 179th Infantry were no more accurate than those of 1st Battalion, 179th Infantry in Wingen.

At 0930, the artillery liaison officer at the 3d Battalion, 179th Infantry CP reported that forty-five Germans had attacked Heideneck. That the area was under attack was confirmed via radio directly from the 3d Battalion's CO ten minutes later, although his message was even less illuminating regarding the gravity of the situation.

Between 1010 and 1130, there was a conference at the 179th CP in Zittersheim—just three kilometers from Wingen—about what to do next. Colonel Murphy conferred with Lieutenant Colonel Adams, the G-3 of the 45th Infantry Division, as well as Lieutenant Colonel Embry, the CO of the 160th Field Artillery Battalion, and Major Riggs, the commander of 3d Battalion, 179th Infantry. Brigadier General Thomas Herren, CO of Task Force Herren, arrived last from his CP at La Petite Pierre, around 1115.

As the American battalion, regimental, and task force leaders conferred, the commander of Company A, 276th Infantry, Captain Dean M. Hendrickson, led his company forward to regain the positions they had abandoned during the previous night for the safety of the woods, and to reestablish contact with Company B. Hendrickson was in a difficult position: his own battalion commander had fled raving into the forest earlier that morning, shouting, "Take to the hills, men, the Germans are coming."[112] To add to the confusion, he had been briefed by the 276th's S-2 that there were no more than "thirty to fifty German soldiers in and around Wingen, that they were nearly out of ammunition and food, and probably ready to surrender (!)"[113]

As Captain Hendrickson and his men soon found out, the actual situation was somewhat different. From the very positions prepared by Company A, 276th Infantry, but left unoccupied during the night for the safety of the woods, the *Gebirgsjäger* of *1st Company* oriented their full attention southwards, to repel attempts against their bridgehead over the Moder River. Without a battalion commander or inter-company communications of any kind, Captain Hendrickson nevertheless sallied forth with his company toward Wingen.

It took Company A's 2d and 3d Platoons most of the day to fight their way back into their original forward positions, located some 100 meters beyond the fringe of the woods on the snow-covered, bare slope. In doing so, they had to overcome not only the German opponents in their own foxholes, but also the German machine-gun fire from the cemetery, which enfiladed their every move. It was Company A's very first contact with any enemy, and it was a brutal baptism of fire. By the afternoon, they had finally regained their former positions, by virtue of individual bravery and hand grenades, and the support of their weapons platoon's 60mm mortars and .30-caliber air-cooled machine guns. In the process, the company's 2d and 3d Platoons suffered large numbers of casualties, many of which were sustained as they attempted to improve their fighting positions by additional excavation in full sight of the enemy. Company A lost their first officer in this action, Lieutenant Richard L. McClintock, the 3d platoon leader, who was killed in the attempt to single-handedly silence the German machine gun at the cemetery.

The *1st Company* must have tried to gain better positions in the south several times by infiltrating through Company A lines, with their last attempt made in the darkness of the evening. But it was already too late for *1st Company*. Having learned their lessons the hard way, Company A men were on full alert, and repulsed each attempt.

After having complied with the first part of his mission, Captain Hendrickson wanted to also fulfill the second part: he sent a squad-sized patrol under the 1st Platoon Leader, Lieutenant William Doenges, to make contact with Company B across the valley. Doenges left sometime during the night, first in an easterly direction on the reverse slope of the Kirchberg woods, then crossing the Moder Valley and entering the forested heights overlooking Wingen from the north. Needless to say, he was unable to find or contact any US elements, and returned to the Company A CP during the morning of next day.[114]

## Closing the Gap

Unknown to the men of *Combat Group Wingen*, but also concealed from the US Army elements trying to defend the town, a major operation was under way on this very morning, not one mile distant from the center of the heavy fighting at Wingen. While elements of the 179th Infantry Regiment were being routed or taken into German custody as prisoners of war, the 180th Infantry had arrived in the early morning hours in its entirety and detrucked on the road leading from Eckartswiller to Wimmenau, to the east and southeast of le Kirchberg.

Belonging to the later echelons of the "Great Shift" within the US VI Corps, the 180th Infantry Regiment had been relieved during 3 January by elements of its sister regiment, the 157th Infantry, and the 36th Engineer Combat Regiment (attached to the 45th Infantry) in its previous positions on the Maginot Line, and had been trucked for close to 100 kilometers through the Alsatian Plain on a roundabout route until they reached their assembly area south of Wimmenau. Detrucking at 0100 (2d Battalion), 0245 (1st Battalion) and 1000 (3d Battalion), the troops of the 1st and 2d Battalions were given rest until 0900.[115]

In strict accordance with 180th Infantry Regiment Field Order no. 79 of 3 January,[116] the two battalions chosen for the attack crossed the line of departure (the railroad line between Wingen and Wimmenau) heading north at 1005 (2d Battalion, 180th Infantry on the right) and 1025 (1st Battalion, 180th Infantry on the left). Their immediate orders were to close the still existing

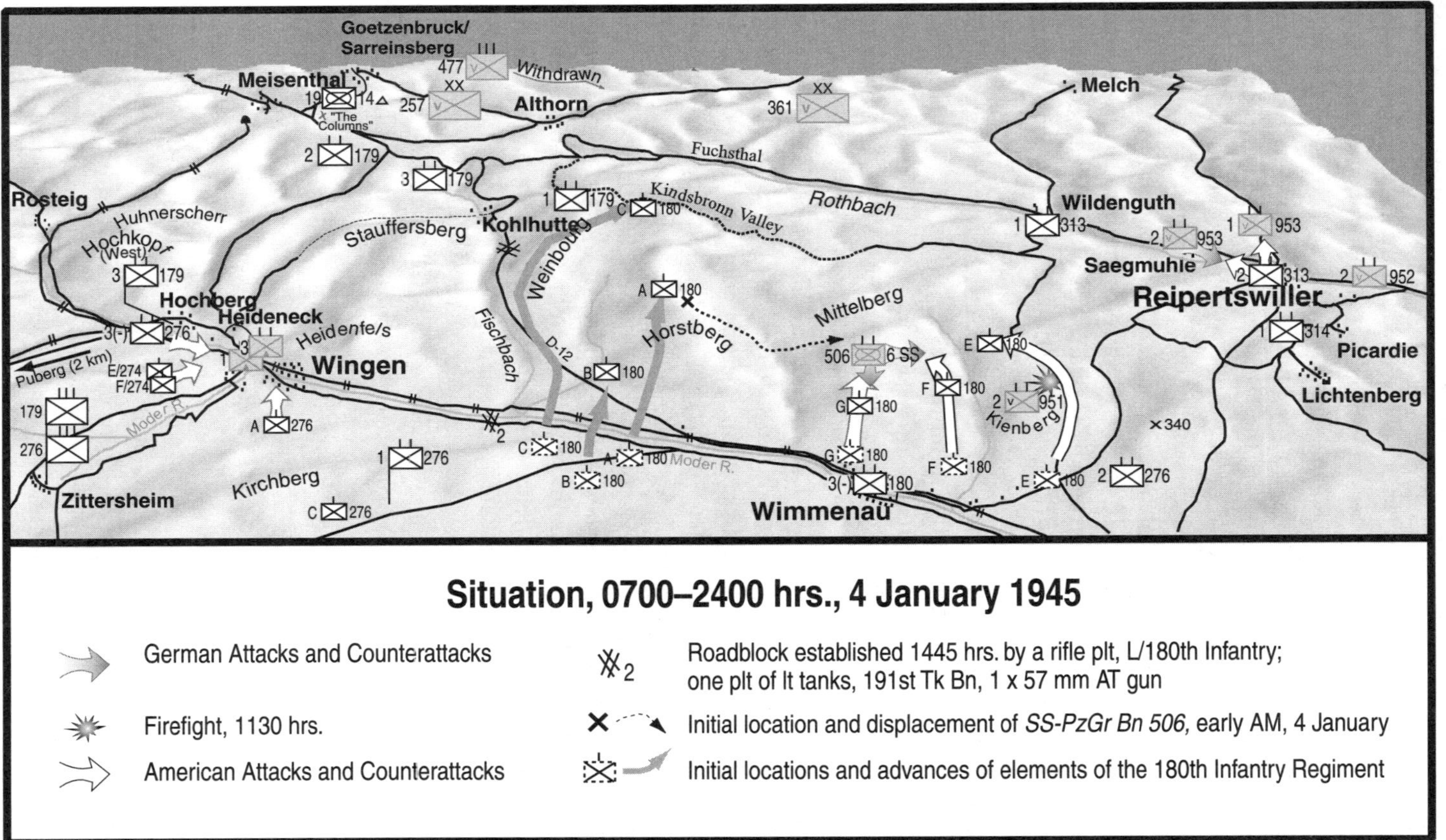
Goetzenbruck/
Sarreinsberg
Withdrawn
Meisenthal
"The Columns"
Althorn
Melch
Fuchsthal
Rosteig
Huhnerscherr
Hochkopf (West)
Kindsbronn Valley
Rothbach
Wildenguth
Stauffersberg
Kohlhutte
Weinbourg
Saegmuhle
Reipertswiller
Hochberg
Heideneck
Heidenfels
Wingen
Fischbach
D-12
Horstberg
Mittelberg
Picardie
Lichtenberg
Puberg (2 km)
Moder R.
Kienberg
Kirchberg
Zittersheim
Wimmenau
Situation, 0700–2400 hrs., 4 January 1945
German Attacks and Counterattacks
Firefight, 1130 hrs.
American Attacks and Counterattacks
Roadblock established 1445 hrs. by a rifle plt, L/180th Infantry; one plt of lt tanks, 191st Tk Bn, 1 x 57 mm AT gun
Initial location and displacement of SS-PzGr Bn 506, early AM, 4 January
Initial locations and advances of elements of the 180th Infantry Regiment

four-kilometer gap between Wildenguth in the east and the Kaesberg in the west, that is, the gap between elements of the 313th Infantry Regiment and the 179th. The 3d Battalion was to remain in reserve in the vicinity of Wimmenau, as the regiment advanced in the classic "two-up, one-back" formation.

When the two assault battalions of the 180th Infantry began their advance, their combat-wise soldiers heard small arms fire in Wingen to their left, as the fate of the 179th Infantry's elements in the town was being sealed. The commanding general of the 45th Infantry Division, Major General Frederick, had decided against using the newly arrived 180th to counterattack the German troops that had infiltrated Wingen, and instead kept the 180th strictly on its mission to close the last part of the gap in the Low Vosges. To regain control of Wingen, Frederick ordered the attached 276th Infantry Regiment of Task Force Herren to attack and clear the town of German troops. He attached Company B(-), 781st Tank Battalion for this task.[117]

The primary German units in this gap between the Kaesberg and Wildenguth were *Combat Group Stämmle* (*2d Battalion, GR 951*), still cut off and occupying the Kienberg, north of Wimmenau, and the unit sent to relieve and reinforce them, *SS-Panzer-Grenadier Battalion 506*, of *Combat Group Schreiber*. Finding it impossible to raise *Combat Group Stämmle* by radio, the commander of the *506th* had sent out a patrol under *Standarten-Oberjunker* Grütz to make physical contact with it early on the morning of 4 January. After linking up with a patrol of Stämmle's outfit near the Kienberg, Grütz's patrol was captured by the Americans.[118] Knowing that they would find *Combat Group Stämmle* somewhere to the southeast, the rest of *SS-Panzer-Grenadier Battalion 506* moved out of their assembly area on the Hochkopf (East) soon after its patrol's departure. After traversing this mountainous region for only about two kilometers, they began preparing entrenched positions on the Rebberg and across the draw to the east toward the Kienberg. It was here they expected to join up with *2d Battalion, GR 951*, which had hopefully already been contacted by *Standarten-Oberjunker* Grütz and his patrol. After linking up, they intended to join with *Combat Group Stämmle* in an attack on Wimmenau, as ordered.

The 180th Infantry Regiment was not the last one to arrive at the scene on this morning. Still later, another element reinforced the American forces in the immediate vicinity of Wingen, a unit that during the coming days would play a decisive role in clearing Wingen from the German intruders: the 2d Battalion, 274th Infantry Regiment, commanded by Lieutenant Colonel Wallace R. ("Bob") Cheves.

This battalion had left its positions near Drusenheim close to the Rhine River after being relieved by elements of the Task Force Linden during the late hours of 3 January. Early on 4 January, the motorized column of the 2d Battalion, 274th Infantry had reached the command post of Task Force Herren at La Petite Pierre, only to pick up a guide for reaching Puberg, a mountain village some ten kilometers to the north. They subsequently arrived at Puberg at 1100. Here Cheves received the first vague information about the German raid on Wingen from Colonel Samuel Conley, his regimental commander. The talk was about "only a few Germans."[119]

## Consolidating Gains

Even while the 180th Infantry was closing on its assembly area east of Wingen, the *5th Company* of *1st Battalion, SS-Mountain Infantry Regiment 12*, under *Untersturmführer* Paul Kürten, was closing on its own objectives on the right flank of *1st Battalion*, namely the communities of Heideneck and d'Hütt. After leaving its assembly area at the western edge of the woods, this company had no problem overwhelming a squad of eight to ten American soldiers asleep on the ground in their sleeping bags. This outpost was the first contingent of American prisoners of war taken by the *1st Battalion*, and they were escorted into Wingen.

During the morning hours Kürten and his men cleared a good portion of the houses along the village streets, until they reached a two-story house beyond a building which he identified as a "water mill." From the occupants of this house, he received the first substantial resistance, and suffered his first casualties. Kürten wrote,

> After a while [the occupants] waved white sheets, signaling surrender. We waited for them to leave the house. But suddenly they dropped the white sheets and resumed their resistance. Soon we could make out the reason: from the attic of their house they had recognized a column of American tanks on their way towards Wingen.[120]

After arriving on the scene, the tanks shot up the houses occupied by Kürten's company, thus ending his company's advance to the west. The tanks eventually forced him and his men to withdraw through the waters of the adjoining Schusselbach to the south, under a steady stream of machine gun and 76mm fire.

At 1100, *Untersturmführer* Carlau and a messenger walked to the west along the southern slope of the railroad embankment, to reach the *3d Company* of *Obersturmführer* Jacobs, which had full control of that part of town. Upon arriving at Kürten's positions, Carlau found them under continuous fire, with no way of retaliating. The tanks were standing off at a distance greater than that at which they might have been prey to our *panzerfausts*. After a joint evaluation of the situation, both Carlau and Kürten decided further occupation of this exposed position was pointless—the company had already suffered several men killed, and could only stop the fruitless loss of life by withdrawing to a more protected position. Kürten repositioned the men of his *5th Company* to the railroad-embankment, to form a linear connection between the *4th Company*, on the wooded heights north of Wingen, and the *3d Company*.[121]

In the center of Wingen, the *1st Battalion*'s men cleared the houses of American soldiers whom they had found fast asleep in their beds. In one of these houses next to the tracks, the battalion established its command post. It was the residence of the railroad stationmaster, now empty.

The adjoining house to the south was the school building. Here the *1st Battalion* surgeon, *Hauptsturmführer* Dr. Hans Lautenschlager found the 1st Battalion, 179th Infantry's battalion aid station fully intact with some twenty litter cases, two US medical officers (a captain and a lieutenant) and twelve American medics. In addition—at least of equal importance—he discovered a supply of medical materials and drugs in an astonishing abundance. Dr. Lautenschlager declared this house as the joint dressing station for friend and foe alike, taking command of his American colleagues and their medical helpers.[122]

Before noon, all houses in the sectors of both the *1st* and *3d Battalions* had been cleared.

Only a few men from the elements we had surprised in Wingen escaped and eventually reached friendly lines.* In their haste, they had not bothered to take many of their vehicles, choosing instead to get away on foot. As a result, many vehicles were standing on the town's streets: jeeps, 2fi-ton trucks, a number of trailers, and even two assault guns and one fully-tracked recovery vehicle. Two of our NCOs with some tank experience manned one of the assault guns—an M8 self-propelled 75mm howitzer evidently left behind by elements of Task Force Hudelson—started it, and then drove along the main street in broad daylight. They even went through the first underpass into the western part of Wingen, trying to assist the men of the *1st Battalion*, while they were being shelled by American tanks. This brave and innovative maneuver met quickly with misfortune, however, as the captured assault gun—equipped with a low-velocity, short-barreled 75mm howitzer—was engaged by the M4A3E8 Shermans of Company B, 781st Tank Battalion. Their 76mm high-velocity main guns far outranged the weapon of their reappropriated "sister," and the American tankers made "short work" of the

*3d Battalion, 180th Infantry (in regimental reserve south and west of Wimmenau) had established straggler collection points for those men who escaped from Wingen, 180th Infantry S-3 Journal 4 January, no. 48.

vehicle, hitting it almost immediately. Both our NCOs lost their lives in this unequal fight.[123]

We established our *3d Battalion* CP in the *"Hotel de la Gare,"* just south of the railway station. I designated the Roman Catholic church of Saint Félix as the prisoner collection point, and ordered its parsonage on the same property to be used to confine the eight officers in our custody (ranking from lieutenant to lieutenant colonel), in keeping with the internationally-recognized policy of separating officers from enlisted prisoners.

When passing this church in the earlier morning hours, men of the *3d Platoon, 13th Company* had received rifle fire, obviously originating from an American sniper who had hidden in the church. *Scharführer* Linus Maier, the platoon leader, advanced up the stairs leading to the steeple, but found its door locked. Maier had with him one of the American prisoners of war who, as a child of German emigrants, spoke fluent German. He asked him to call to his comrade in the spire and request his immediate surrender. Instead of complying, the sniper continued shooting, forcing everybody in the street to take cover.

Somewhat later, in one of the houses next to the church, Maier went up to its attic and removed some of the roof tiles to observe the field to the south. There he saw for the first time that a few American tanks had arrived and posted themselves on the rim of the Kirchberg forest, facing the town. Between the tanks he saw American soldiers standing, seemingly oblivious to the danger to which they exposed themselves. Maier took a '98 Mauser rifle with a telescopic sight and tried some shots through the opening in the roof. He must have hit his target: one of the Americans went to the ground and was quickly taken by his comrades to a safer place behind the tanks. No soldiers were subsequently seen between the tanks.

Understandably suspecting that the accurate incoming rifle fire had come from the steeple, one of the tanks started firing at the apex of the spire. It took him only a few trial shots to hit it, leaving a large hole in its tile roofing and thereby killing his compatriot. Maier concluded his story with a respectful remark for the American sniper in the church: "*Das muß ein ganz schneidiger Kerl gewesen sein*!" (That must have been one very gutsy guy!)[124]

By about noon, the exchange of small arms fire had stopped in most of Wingen, and could be heard only in its western parts. It had been replaced by mortar fire coming from the American side, and very effective fire from the tanks positioned on the northern edge of the Kirchberg forest. The tanks' machine guns first poured lead into the windows of the buildings in Wingen, and then started to shoot at the houses with their main guns. Combined with occasional hits from mortars on the same buildings, this tactic was effective in limiting our return fire and observation of the battlefield. During the same time, American artillery fire covered the wooded heights north of Wingen where they correctly expected German troops to be occupying positions overlooking the town. Needless to say, there was nothing with which we could retaliate in kind. Both our battalions had entered Wingen without their mortars, and the forward observer of the *3d Battalion, Artillery Regiment 6 Nord* was vainly trying to get a connection by radio to one of his batteries.[125]

Our *Pioneer Platoon*, part of the *Signal Platoon*, the *11th Company*, and two platoons of the *12th Company* were digging foxholes in the southern part of the Heidenfels forest, each element trying to make an effective "hedgehog" position by itself. They divided their forces' fields of fire between south, down into Wingen, and north, to shield themselves against American attacks through the forest. The more fortunate men of the *13th* and part of the *12th Company* had already looked for billets in the buildings of the eastern part of the town. All men were absolutely exhausted from the long period they had endured without real sleep; almost all were now well into their fourth consecutive sleepless day. Just as they had been when we took our first American position on the Weinbourg Heights near the pass, our men were again surprised at the luxurious nature of the American rations they seized from caches in some of the buildings. Of course, the abundance of American cigarettes pleased them as well. But they likewise enjoyed finding stores of new underclothes and socks, which they happily donned as they peeled off their old, torn, and soaked stuff.

Roadblocks had been established at all entrances to Wingen, and patrols scheduled for the coming night. It went without saying or ordering that these guard and patrol details were manned sparingly, to allow the bulk of the men at least some urgently required, too long postponed rest. In our *3d Battalion*, the casualties on this day so far had not been extensive, and were extremely low during the morning assault, but they were rising now due to mortar, artillery, and tank fire.

After most administrative and logistical things were put to order, I took charge of our command post, the railroad hotel, which had 2fi stories, plus a vaulted cellar with extremely stout, strong outer walls. Having established a guard routine at the entrance to the hotel, I went rummaging through its rooms. It did not take me long to find what I was looking for: two rooms on the second floor, which appeared to be makeshift offices, were filled with neatly stacked files. There were even desks in the room, which I used to systematically make a short inventory of some of the files. In 1945, my English was typical high school stuff, rusty by forced neglect during more than three years on the Arctic front. But notwithstanding my poor English, I understood enough from the files to find that this office had been used only hours ago by Service Company of the 179th Infantry, which I surmised belonged to the 45th Infantry Division.

Although I could not have known it at the time, after the displacement of the 179th's regimental CP to Zittersheim during the afternoon hours of 3 January, the following US Army elements comprised the roughly 350 men of the Wingen garrison on the morning of 4 January:

- The CP and staff of 1st Battalion, 179th Infantry, in the Hotel Wenk;
- Headquarters Company, 1st Battalion, 179th Infantry;
- Service Company, 179th Infantry, with other service units;
- Battalion Aid Station, 1st Battalion, 179th Infantry;
- Elements of the 36th Engineer Combat Regiment;
- Liaison officer, 157th Infantry Regiment, 45th Infantry Division; and
- Headquarters section and one rifle platoon, Company I, 276th Infantry.

During my prowl through the US Army documents, I realized the reason for our easy victory during this morning's attack: our adversaries had been mostly service and support soldiers, unused to combat. In the hours and days ahead, we most certainly would meet American combat troops who made our life harder and proved their combat worthiness.

## Counterattacks

By 1300, the 3d Battalion, 276th Infantry was ready to jump off, in accordance with Brigadier General Herren's written order, issued late that morning, to "counterattack, drive enemy to NW, restore situation at Wingen." In his order, Brigadier General Herren stressed that it was "imperative that enemy be kept NW of road Ingwiller to Volksberg." He promised the commander of the 276th Infantry one company of medium tanks, less one platoon, to support the assault. These were the tanks from Company B, 781st Tank Battalion.

At that time, Colonel A. C. Morgan, commanding the 276th Infantry Regiment, had only his 1st and 3d Battalions at his disposal. The 2d Battalion, in the vicinity of Wimmenau, had been attached to the 313th Infantry.

The situation was not as rosy as it sounded. The 1st Battalion had lost most of its Company B during the morning, and in addition, a significant proportion of Company A—as well as the battalion commander. Company C was attached to the 3d Battalion. So the orders Colonel Morgan issued on the morning of 4 January were received by a very shaken and seriously understrength 1st Battalion.

The regimental commander's plan concentrated, therefore, on using the 3d Battalion, commanded by Lieutenant Colonel Sidney E. Iverson, who received the instructions at his CP next to the main road west of Hochberg and north of Puberg. This battalion, however, had also been weakened during the morning's action. In the information vacuum of the morning, the battalion executive officer, Major Robert Natzel, had gone forward to investigate the situation. Taking a squad of ten to twelve men from Company I, he ultimately advanced through the railway underpass ("RR Underpass West–3"), only to be captured by the Germans waiting for them on the other side. While Major Natzel was escorted to the Catholic church, we subsequently used the captured American enlisted men as litter bearers; and several of them sustained wounds from fire by their own men.[126] Thus Iverson was without his "right-hand man" to coordinate the support of the upcoming operation, and Company I was shy a squad.

But Company I's problems did not end there. Elements of *Combat Group Wingen* overran the Company I CP in Wingen during the morning, and all headquarters personnel had been captured, along with the Company's 1st Platoon. Most of the men of the 2d and Weapons Platoons of Item Company had escaped, assembling in the western part of Wingen. The 3d Platoon was manning a roadblock elsewhere, under the control of 180th Infantry.[127]

Iverson's Company K had been detached to form part of the VI Corps reserve, along with two squads of Company L.[128] In partial compensation, he had received control of Company C, 276th Infantry, which had its CP south of the Kirchberg. However, this company was south of Wingen on the afternoon of 4 January, and was therefore out of position to participate in the assault.

Thus, for the initial counterattack on Wingen, Lieutenant Colonel Iverson could effectively employ one understrength rifle company (Company L, with two rifle platoons and one squad of another); one rifle platoon and the Weapons Platoon of Company I (without their company command section); and his heavy weapons company (Company M). He also had at his disposal a small number of stragglers from the routed Company B.

With this quite modest force, Lieutenant Colonel Iverson was to execute the mission he received at 1030 from Colonel Morgan:

> Have Reserve Company [Company L, 276th Infantry had been held in regimental reserve] with I Company launch coordinated attack on Wingen from west, generally astride RR. 1st Bn will support by fire from south and east. Clean out town. 1 platoon medium tanks attached to you; have guide meet them at your CP in an hour. Reorganize after cleaning out town.[129]

Probably due to the suspected presence of 179th personnel in Wingen as prisoners, a request from the 276th Infantry Regiment for artillery fire in the center of Wingen had been refused by the 45th Infantry Division G-3. Instead, the 276th's regimental S-3 was advised to "make plans to bomb

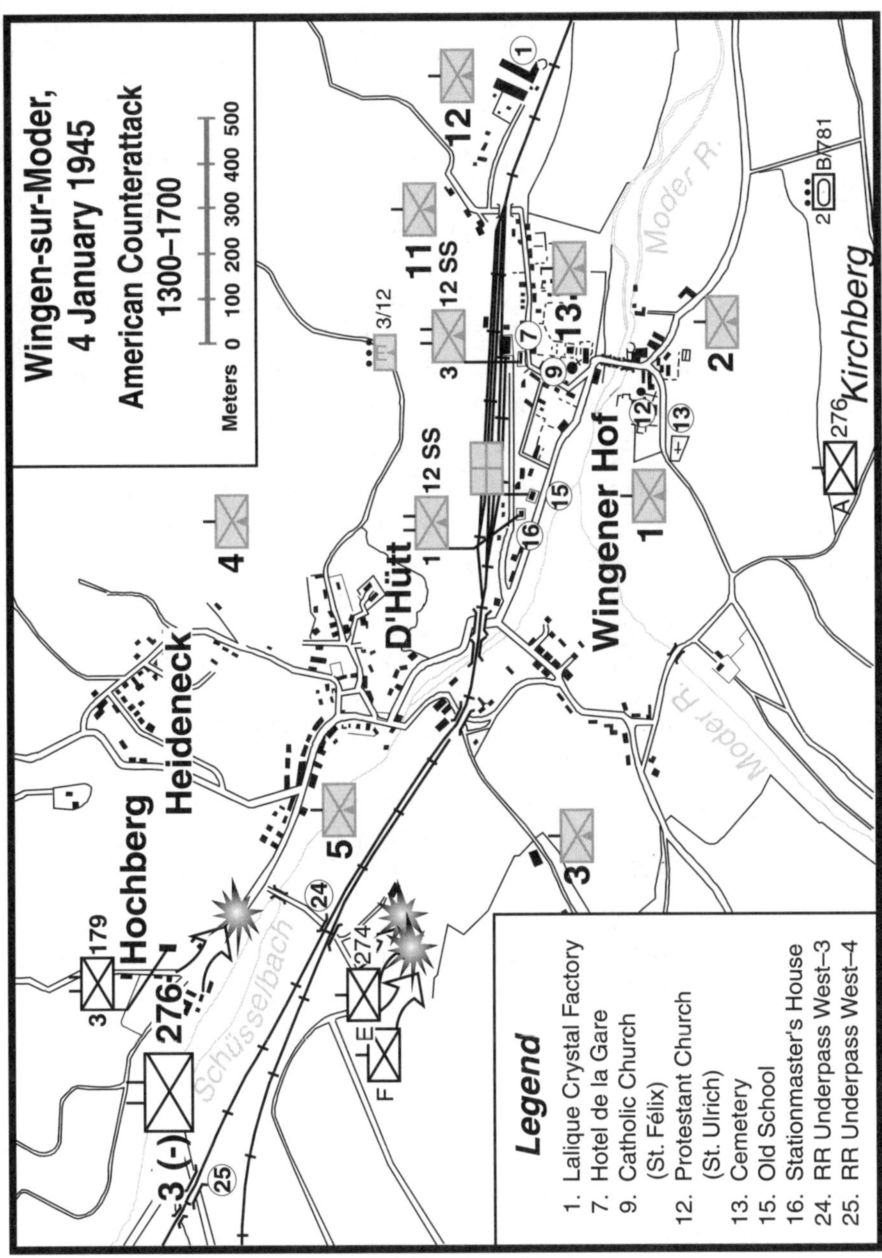


Wingen, when our troops are out of there."[130] Thus, no artillery support was forthcoming to support the counterattack.

After one platoon of Company B, 781st Tank Battalion reported to Lieutenant Colonel Iverson at his CP, he led his force toward Wingen, supported by two 81mm mortars from Company M. The attack started at 1330.

In an attempt to avoid fratricide, the medium tanks were restricted to machine-gun fire only; use of their main guns was prohibited during the operation "due to insufficient information which houses were occupied by enemy or friendly troops."[131]

After the American attackers passed down through the railway underpass ("RR Underpass West–4"), *4th* and *5th Companies* of the *1st Battalion* pinned down the advancing American infantrymen with rifle and machine-gun fire. The heavy machine guns of *4th Company* wreaked particular havoc on Company L, enfilading them from positions in the western edge of the forest. The two leading tanks were hit by rockets from *panzerfausts* sited on the high ground north of the road, which Iverson and his men believed to be held by friendly infantry.[132] The commander of 3d Battalion, 276th Infantry later wrote about this attack,

> It was decided to move through the west part of the town and attack the hill north of the railroad tracks. . . . L Company was committed toward the hill without preceding artillery preparation, and made good progress at first, cleared the houses to the woods, and then started up the hill. Everything seemed OK, but the Germans were waiting in the trees, and all hell broke loose! The Company CO and a lieutenant were killed along with several others. The Germans really had L Company pinned down, but we managed to hold on through the night.[133]
>
> Except for the company executive officer, who was directing support of the company from the rear, all the officers of Company L were killed in the afternoon attack.[134]

The same unit tried to attack again at 1630, right down the same route, but the supporting tanks' advance was blocked by the two previously disabled tanks next to the underpass. This forced the rest of the tanks to withdraw for the night to Zittersheim, and the attack faded away.[135]

*****

As Lieutenant Colonel Iverson's men were preparing to attack from the northwest, elements of Lieutenant Colonel Cheves' 2d Battalion, 274th Infantry were digging foxholes to defend the mountain village of Puberg, three kilometers to the west-southwest. Their regimental commander, Colonel Conley, arrived shortly before noon.

Colonel Samuel ("Shooting Sam") Conley had promised his colleague, Colonel Morgan, the CO of the 276th Infantry Regiment, to "clear the woods between Puberg and Wingen of any Germans" that might have gotten as far to the west as the forest leading to Puberg. Colonel Conley was eager to take personal command of this clearing action, and talked Cheves into giving him two rifle companies and Major Buford Boyd, the battalion's executive officer.

Colonel Conley and Major Boyd took off for this attack around 1310, with Companies E and F abreast, moving east through the forested mountains on snow covered trails, down the steep hillside toward Wingen.

Upon reaching the eastern edge of the forest, Conley and his men saw Germans digging in around Wingen. Both sides opened fire. It was the first time the 2d Battalion men heard German machine guns. "It fires about twice as fast as our gun, and when the bullets zip in your direction, it is scary as hell," wrote one of the 274th's men later.[136] To Cheves, the German (MG-42) machine gun "seemed deadlier." At about 1100 rounds per minute (cyclic rate), it certainly was exactly twice as fast as the Americans' Brownings, but it consumed ammunition at a 100 percent greater rate as well. This was an important consideration for a unit such as ours, which was cut off from our supply lines.

Shortly after this skirmish, which had cost both 2d Battalion's companies their first casualties—one killed, three wounded—darkness set in and the action was proclaimed finished at 1700. The force returned the four-kilometer long way back to Puberg, very much to the disgust of Colonel Morgan, commander of the 276th Infantry Regiment, who wanted them back at the forest edge, with "eyes on" Wingen, observing the activity in the town from the heights to the south, and ready to again attack or support an attack.[137]

Their attack had been met and repelled by our *3d Company*. This company sustained similar casualties. The one severely wounded German soldier taken by the Americans to Puberg for questioning died *en route.*

*****

In the zone of the 180th Infantry, almost immediately to the east of Wingen, by late morning, the Americans were well on their way to sealing off the remaining gap in their lines to *Combat Group Wingen*'s northeast. Major Fry, commander of 1st Battalion, 180th Infantry, configured his unit's advance in the two-up, one-back formation, with Company C on the left, Company A on the right, and Company B in reserve.

To the west, Company C advanced on the far left of the battalion (and, therefore, the regiment) with one platoon hugging the district road (D-12), and the remainder of the company in the adjacent draw, parallel to the district road and some 500 to 600 meters offset to the east. Both components of Company C made good progress, undisturbed by the enemy. At 1350, the platoon along the road had reached the bend in the rear of an already existing roadblock (occupied by one platoon each of Company I, 276th Infantry, and Company B, 191st Tank Battalion), where it remained for the night. This platoon of Company C, 180th Infantry, was by now augmented by fifty-seven stragglers from the 179th Infantry and ten men from Company B, 276th Infantry, flushed out of their positions earlier in the morning by the attack of *Combat Group Wingen*.[138]

The main body of Company C, supported by two tanks, advanced unimpeded as far as the southern rim of the Kindsbronn Valley, which it reached at 1730. Along the way, it crossed the route by which *Combat Group Wingen* had infiltrated only nine hours before, thereby further cutting off our tenuous line of communication with our higher headquarters. At the edge of the Kindsbronn Valley, Company C, 180th Infantry made contact with Company B, 179th Infantry on its left.[139] Of all six companies that participated in the attack, Company C made the best progress during the day, and was the only one that reached its designated limit of advance that day.

After crossing the line of departure, Company A, 180th Infantry climbed the ridges to the north, the Horstberg being the first of them. By 1130, this company, supported by one tank, reached the Hochkopf (East), and reported it clear of enemy. Of course, only a few hours before, it had been the assembly area of *SS-Panzer-Grenadier Battalion 506*. There is no evidence of any reports rendered by Company A indicating they recognized that this area had been recently occupied.

Company B started its advance in the afternoon, covering the left rear flank of its sister companies against possible German attackers emerging from Wingen, and, at the end of the day, had established blocking positions in the draw south of and between the Weinbourg and the Horstberg.

Things did not go so smoothly for 2d Battalion, 180th Infantry, advancing on the right. The density of the vegetation, coupled with the deeply-compartmented nature of the terrain, combined to force the battalion commander to advance all three of his companies on line, with Company E, on the battalion's right, Company F in the center, and Company G on the left.

Company E moved forward along the road leading out of Wimmenau to the northeast after the main road junction in the forest, turned to the north, toward Wildenguth.

Company F advanced up the draw between Kienberg and Rebberg, in the center of the battalion. Company G on the left flank (and along the battalion's boundary with the 1st Battalion), went straight for the hills to the north of Wimmenau, passing the first mountain (Hill 313) without difficulties.

At no time during this day was the width of the advancing 2d Battalion wider than 1,500 meters.

A platoon of Company E that had been set off to the west from its company's main body, was the first one that got into a small arms skirmish on the Kienberg, at about 1130. One hour later, the commander of 2d Battalion,

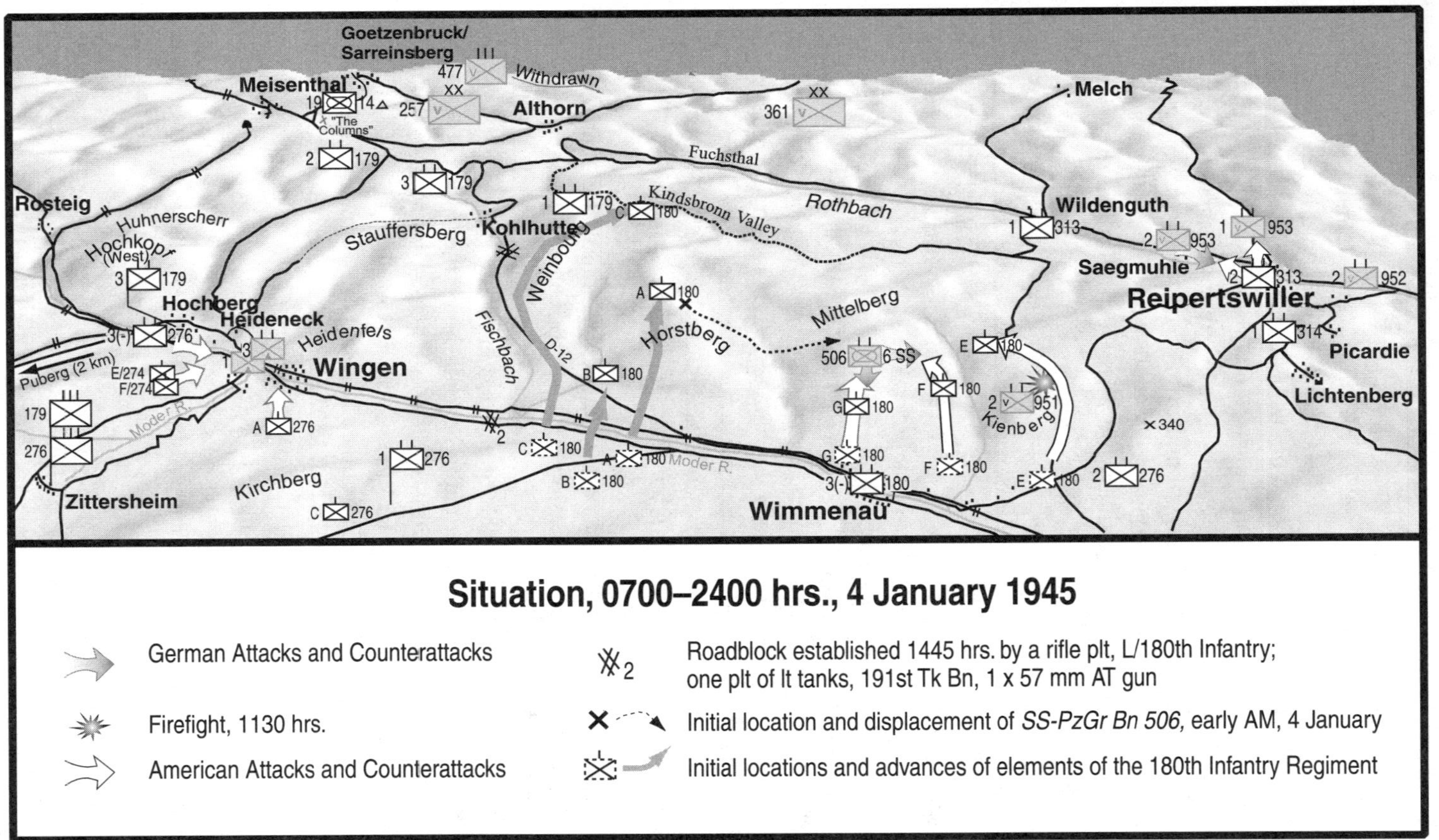
Goetzenbruck/
Sarreinsberg
477
Withdrawn
Meisenthal
19
14
"The Columns"
XX
257
Althorn
XX
361
Melch
2 179
3 179
Fuchsthal
Rosteig
Huhnerscherr
Hochkopf (West)
3 179
1 179
C 180
Kindsbronn Valley
Rothbach
Kohlhutte
Stauffersberg
Weinbourg
1 313
Wildenguth
2 953
1 953
Saegmuhle
2 313
2 952
Reipertswiller
1 314
Picardie
Lichtenberg
Hochberg
Heideneck
3(-) 276
3
Heidenfels
Wingen
Puberg (2 km)
E/274
F/274
179
276
Moder R.
A 276
Fischbach
D-12
A 180
B 180
Horstberg
Mittelberg
506 6 SS
E 180
F 180
G 180
2 951
Kienberg
×340
2
C 180
A 180
B 180
G 180
F 180
E 180
2 276
1 276
3(-) 180
Kirchberg
C 276
Zittersheim
Wimmenau
Situation, 0700–2400 hrs., 4 January 1945
German Attacks and Counterattacks
Firefight, 1130 hrs.
American Attacks and Counterattacks
Roadblock established 1445 hrs. by a rifle plt, L/180th Infantry; one plt of lt tanks, 191st Tk Bn, 1 x 57 mm AT gun
Initial location and displacement of SS-PzGr Bn 506, early AM, 4 January
Initial locations and advances of elements of the 180th Infantry Regiment

180th Infantry reported to regiment this platoon was "held up short of the crest of the ridge line, [where] 50 Germans [are] dug in." The main body of Easy Company,* with tanks and tank destroyers attached, had already advanced on the "good road," and was past the Kienberg, when it received artillery fire. It seemed to be directed by German observers on Hill 340 (about halfway between Wimmenau and Reipertswiller, west of the Kienberg, but at a slightly higher elevation). The commanding officer of 2d Battalion requested that his regimental executive officer take action against the enemy on Hill 340, since that was beyond the regimental boundary, but whose accurate direction of artillery fire was nevertheless pinning down his right flank company.[140]

During the same field telephone conversation, the CO of the 2d Battalion reported the first prisoners. They were from *SS-Panzer-Grenadier Battalion 506, 6th SS-Mountain Division.*

As the afternoon wore on, all three 2d Battalion companies were counter-attacked by *SS-Panzer-Grenadier Battalion 506*, each time in approximately company strength, supported by artillery fire. All these counterattacks were repulsed after long firefights.[141] Despite its efforts to dislodge the *SS panzer grenadiers* defending its crest, at the end of the day, Company G was still not on top of the Rebberg, which was three meters higher than any other terrain in the vicinity and afforded good observation over the area. Company G had lost four wounded. On the other hand, the enemy in front of Company F, also from the *506th*, seemed to be routed. This company had lost three killed and eight wounded.[142]

Company E had lost one officer and an unknown number of enlisted men, not only to mortar fire directed from Hill 340, but also from small arms fire from *2d Battalion, GR 951* on the Kienberg. Although the small arms fire was eventually silenced, they still felt threatened in their advance by the enemy on Hill 340 which, by virtue of being beyond their zone, they could neither physically attack nor engage with artillery fire. Although Colonel Dulaney, the CO of the 180th Infantry Regiment, had procured an order from Major Charles Gallaway, S-3 of the 276th Infantry Regiment (signed at 1455) for its 2d Battalion to "occupy and hold Hill 340 at once," at the days end, Dulaney complained that not much action had come from his right neighbor, the 2d Battalion, 276th Infantry.[143] Since 2d Battalion was attached to the 313th Infantry at the time, and was therefore not under the control of the 276th Infantry Regiment, this complaint was as groundless as Major Gallaway's order was meaningless.

*Companies were often referred to by the communications pro-words that represent their companies' letter designation: A: Able; B: Baker; C: Charlie; D: Dog; E: Easy; F: Fox; G: George; H: How; I: Item; K: King; L: Love; and M: Mike.

Although all three companies of the 2d Battalion had reached a common line by the end of the day (albeit separated from each other by deep draws), they were still some 1500 meters short of the days' designated limit of advance. According to the 45th Infantry Division's Operations Journal, "the enemy [had] resisted bitterly."[144] The gap ripped in the American lines on 1 January with the rout of Task Force Hudelson, although now smaller, was still there above the Kienberg and west of Wildenguth.

Closer to Wingen to the west, Major Fry, commanding 1st Battalion, 180th Infantry, ordered Company A, his right flank unit, to remain on the Hochkopf (East) for the night, in view of his insecure right flank. The failure of Company G to reach the assigned phase line and the enemy resistance it encountered left Fry's right flank open. Bringing Company A further to the north would only have widened the distance to its right neighbor, and would thus have endangered its own right flank. To this end, Major Fry got his regimental commander to agree to leave Company A shy of the limit of advance.

To maintain security, patrols from each company in 1st Battalion, 180th Infantry operated constantly. They maintained contact with Company G on the right and units from 1st Battalion, 179th Infantry on the left.

Still in regimental reserve, 3d Battalion, 180th Infantry remained deployed in depth behind the two forward battalions. With two rifle companies and the battalion command post in Wimmenau, its third rifle company established and maintained a blocking position astride the Moder Valley road to block egress of *Combat Group Wingen* to the east, toward the Alsatian Plain.[145] This roadblock, erected between 1300 and 1445, consisted of one platoon of Company L, 180th Infantry, one section of light tanks from the 191st Tank Battalion, and one 57mm antitank gun.[146] With the 180th Infantry to our east and northeast, 2d Battalion, 274th Infantry to the southwest, the 179th Infantry to our north and northwest, and elements of the 276th Infantry to our south and west, we were pretty much boxed in to our perimeter in Wingen by nightfall of the Fourth Day.

## Disaster Averted

It was already dark, not only outside, but also in the room upstairs in our command post building when I closed the American files. A short while before, there had been a concentrated American artillery strike on the wooded heights behind us, and also on the town itself. Our hotel building had received a couple of hits. Now, a sort of tranquillity seemed to reign outside, as if today's bloody business had been closed for the night, for both sides to regain strength in anticipation of the coming day. Being increasingly on edge, both physically and psychically, we were more than grateful for this respite.

After dark, we could move freely within the southern part of Wingen, going from one company's position to the other. There were no American attacks, neither from infantry nor from tanks. Save for occasional artillery fire into the woods north of Wingen, this evening was quiet, almost tranquil.

After informing my battalion commander, *Hauptsturmführer* Kreuzinger, about my findings as result of the file studies, he agreed that I should attempt to make contact with our *1st Battalion.* Since we had no wire communication, I walked down the *Rue de la Gare* toward their positions, about 300 meters away. Entering the house through the veranda, I only found Dr. Lautenschlager inside by a glowing, red-hot stove. Going by the smell, lots of paper had been burned there during the last hour.

Dr. Lautenschlager informed me of what had happened. During the artillery barrage around 1700, a messenger had appeared, reporting that the enemy had not only attacked again, but that this time they had broken through the lines of the *1st Battalion.* Thereupon, orders had been sent to the *3d* and *5th* Companies to withdraw and assemble in the Heidenfels forest beyond the railroad tracks. While the battalion headquarters personnel scrambled to rush to the north, Carlau and his messenger section had burned all papers which were in his map case.

Hearing this, I hastened back to our own command post. So far, we had no indication that there were no German rifle units to our west between our CP and the Americans—our position was seriously exposed! When entering our CP building, I was relieved to find *Hauptsturmführer* Burgstaller talking with Kreuzinger. As it turned out, the information that the Americans had penetrated our lines had not been properly substantiated, and was subsequently proved wrong. Burgstaller had already revoked his orders to the *3d* and *5th* Companies of his battalion, and they were on their way back from the woods to the north to their previous positions in the west of the town. Carlau has also found his way to our CP and had joined us. He reported that after leaving their positions, the *1st Battalion* elements temporarily lost contact with one another in the woods.[147] Burgstaller was ashamed that such panic could happen in his battalion, and expressed his shame in front of Kreuzinger, who was two years junior to him in date of rank.

Now that the potentially dangerous situation was being restored, we tried to forget the vicissitudes of the past hours, and were talking about the outlook of our affairs. We had attained an easy victory in the morning, with a minimum of casualties. On the other hand, we had experienced the steadily growing resistance of the American forces during the afternoon hours, after they obviously had overcome their original disorganization and began trying to regain control. We also suspected that unlike us, cut off from our support, there was no shortage of personnel or materiel on the American side.

All day long we had been fully aware of the necessity of reporting our success to higher headquarters, preferably to *Standartenführer* Schreiber or, failing that, to *Generalmajor* Philippi of the *361st VGD*. We had passed the brief text of our intended message to the communications men of both battalions, and to the artillery forward observer as well. Each had encoded it and had been trying continuously to contact one of the German radio stations for which they had the frequencies and call signs. All efforts were in vain! They were not able to make themselves heard.

Without announcing the news of our success, so urgently awaited by our higher headquarters, we would not receive reinforcements, let alone the promised assault-gun battalion.

After we had lost hope of getting by through by radio, we decided to send a patrol back to the German lines. Carlau was prepared to dispatch one of his bright NCOs who possessed a superior sense of direction and navigational skills. He was to reach German lines and make his report to the first German officer he contacted—for this, he would not need a written message.

Unknown to us in Wingen, German headquarters had already received word of our success anyway, albeit in a roundabout fashion: During the morning of 4 January, German signals intelligence assets intercepted American radio traffic about our attack. At the *LXXXIX Corps'* CP, *Major* Schuster reported to *Oberst i.G.* Emmerich, the *Ia* of *1st Army*, that "300 German soldiers are in Wingen since 0900," and quoted his own signals intercepts as the source.[148]

*****

At the end of this day, *Combat Group Wingen* had accomplished its mission to seize Wingen and establish a bridgehead over the Moder River. A perimeter defense around Wingen had been established; it had reached its greatest girth between 1100 and 1400, but after that, it shrank due to American counterattacks in the south and the west. The *1st Battalion*, holding most of the bridgehead, had absorbed most of those counterattacks, and had consequently suffered the heaviest casualties.

During the day, the following Americans were captured: 256 enlisted men, including NCOs, in the church; 8 officers in the nearby parsonage; and 2 medical officers, 10 medics, 20 sick cases, and approximately 10 wounded: in the dressing station. Thus, the prisoner count was approximately 306.[149] We had not taken time to count the dead Americans, but could only assume that there were between 35 and 50.

Besides the two self-propelled tank destroyers and the one recovery vehicle, we captured numerous trucks, trailers, and jeeps. We also captured many machine guns, complete with their ammunition, and set them aside; these came in handy during the coming days when the ammunition for our MG-42s was all expended. Much more important at the moment, however, were the American rations!

## -III-
## Impacts on the Citizens of Wingen

Soldiers were not the only ones affected by the harsh fighting in the village of Wingen on this cold January day.

The town's civilian population had suffered the effects of war since early December 1944, when the *361st VGD* and the US 100th Infantry Division clashed in and around the town on 3–5 December. For two days, in the western parts of Wingen, north of the railroad tracks, d'Hütt and Heideneck had been the target of heavy bombardment by American artillery, as the infantrymen of the 398th Infantry Regiment vainly attempted to drive out the *361st*'s defenders. The events of 3 December were especially tragic for the civilian population, when a building received a direct hit by a heavy artillery projectile which went clear down into its vaulted cellar before detonating there, in the midst of civilian refugees; eleven people were killed, including two children. In addition, six others were severely wounded. They had fled to this house during the start of the bombardment to find shelter in its arched basement. Another woman was killed by artillery when she emerged from her house.

In the wee hours of the morning of 4 December, after entering the town around last light, practically all of Company A, 398th Infantry was captured in Wingen by elements of the *361st*, and combat action continued through the next day.[150] The worst difficulties for the civilian population ended only on 5 December when the elements of the *361st* withdrew and other elements of the 100th's 398th Infantry Regiment finally moved into Wingen.[151] However, some problems persisted in the aftermath of the "First Battle for Wingen."

Since this winter was exceptionally cold and rich in snow, the population suffered greatly, because most dwelling houses had lost their windowpanes in the artillery bombardment, and many doors had been smashed in during clearing operations by the 398th Infantry.

The first American garrison of Wingen moved in on 5 December and stayed until shortly before year's end. For the greater part they were lodged in the Hotel Wenk, between both churches. The occupants of Hotel Wenk changed twice thereafter; it seems to have housed the CP of the 179th

Infantry Regiment and later, its 1st Battalion CP. Since some of the Americans spoke German, and others French, there were no problems communicating with the citizens of the town.

On or around New Years Day, the town's population was warned against defeatist rumors, and threatened with arrest by French police authorities. This situation caused unrest, and a number of inhabitants left Wingen, especially those who lived in the western parts of Wingen who still vividly remembered their harrowing experiences of only a few weeks before. On 3 January, as the hammering sound of machine-gun fire drew nearer, the town's mayor, the French police, and the town priest left Wingen. In their stead, new American combat troops arrived during the afternoon, causing renewed trepidation among the civilians.

Unlike the population of the western part of town, most of whom had left with what few belongings they could pack aboard hand-drawn sleds, the inhabitants of eastern Wingen, who had not experienced the horrors of war in early December, mainly stayed in their homes. This was especially true of families with sick members, or livestock to take care of in their sheds.

The Hotel Wenk owner's family and their neighbors looking for shelter had assembled in the spacious cellar of the hotel for the night. On the morning of 4 January, the turmoil started with the rapid fire from German automatic weapons. The roughly 200 American soldiers billeted in Hotel Wenk were taken by surprise in their sleep. After they were overwhelmed by the *Gebirgsjäger* of *Combat Group Wingen*, they were lined up on the street and brought to the nearby Catholic church.

Our men entered each house in succession, searching for hidden American soldiers. They positioned machine guns in windows, although some of those machine guns were silenced subsequently by hits from the American tanks on the northern slopes of the Kirchberg, beyond the Moder River.[152]

A reasonable estimate of the civilian population remaining in the town during this Second Battle for Wingen would be perhaps thirty-five to forty.

## -IV-
## Battle Analysis

Although far from inducing euphoria, the events of 4 January provided hope to the high commands of both sides that they would be successful in their respective missions. On the German side, commanders from *Generaloberst* Blaskowitz, on down knew that Wingen was in the hands of *Combat Group Wingen*, and that *SS-Panzer-Grenadier Battalion 506* had linked up with *2d Battalion, GR 951* (*Combat Group Stämmle*) near the Kienberg. They also were aware that reinforcements, *GR 477* and the *36th VGD*, were on the way from *XC* and *XIII SS Corps*, respectively. Although the Americans had shifted reinforcements to the periphery of the salient created by *XC* and *LXXXIX Corps* on New Year's Day, there was still a gap in the US lines.

On the American side, General Patch and his subordinates knew that they had contained the attacks of *XIII SS* and *XC Corps*, and had made significant progress in closing the ten-kilometer hole left by the collapse of Task Force Hudelson on the first day of *NORDWIND*. On the other hand, they recognized that they had neither succeeded in closing the gap altogether, nor had they yet encountered the German armored reserve they knew to be assembled north of the "Bitche Salient." Further, they now had a German force of indeterminate size behind their lines, controlling the key crossroads in the town of Wingen.

The factors accounting for these developments bear analysis, as they shed light on issues greater than the immediate tactical milieu in which they appear.

## Command and Control

The initially weak American response to our seizure of Wingen was due primarily to a lapse of effective command and control. This lapse seems to have been due mostly to a poor understanding of the situation around the town.

The 45th Infantry Division G-2 summarized the events of 4 January 1945 in his G-2 Periodic Report this way:

> Continuing to evidence aggressiveness, enemy penetrated to Wingen in undetermined strength, [which he] occupied and remained [in] throughout the period.
>
> Farther east, 2d Bn of 951 Rgt attacking toward Wimmenau met the 180th Infantry head on. The attack became 3 counterattacks . . . all of which were repulsed.[153]

Even by 5 January, the 45th Division's G-2 did not yet recognize the identity of the enemy units in Wingen. This was in spite of the fact that the first correct identification on record was made by 3d Battalion, 276th Infantry on 5 January; its Unit Report 8 for 1800/3 January to 1800/5 January:

> Interrogation of prisoner of war captured at Wingen at 1800/4 January indicated that the village and surrounding hills are held by *1st* and *3d Bns, 12th Regiment, 6th SS-Mountain Division.*

Other lower-echelon intelligence reports contributed to obscuration of the situation, however. For example, during the late morning of 4 January, the

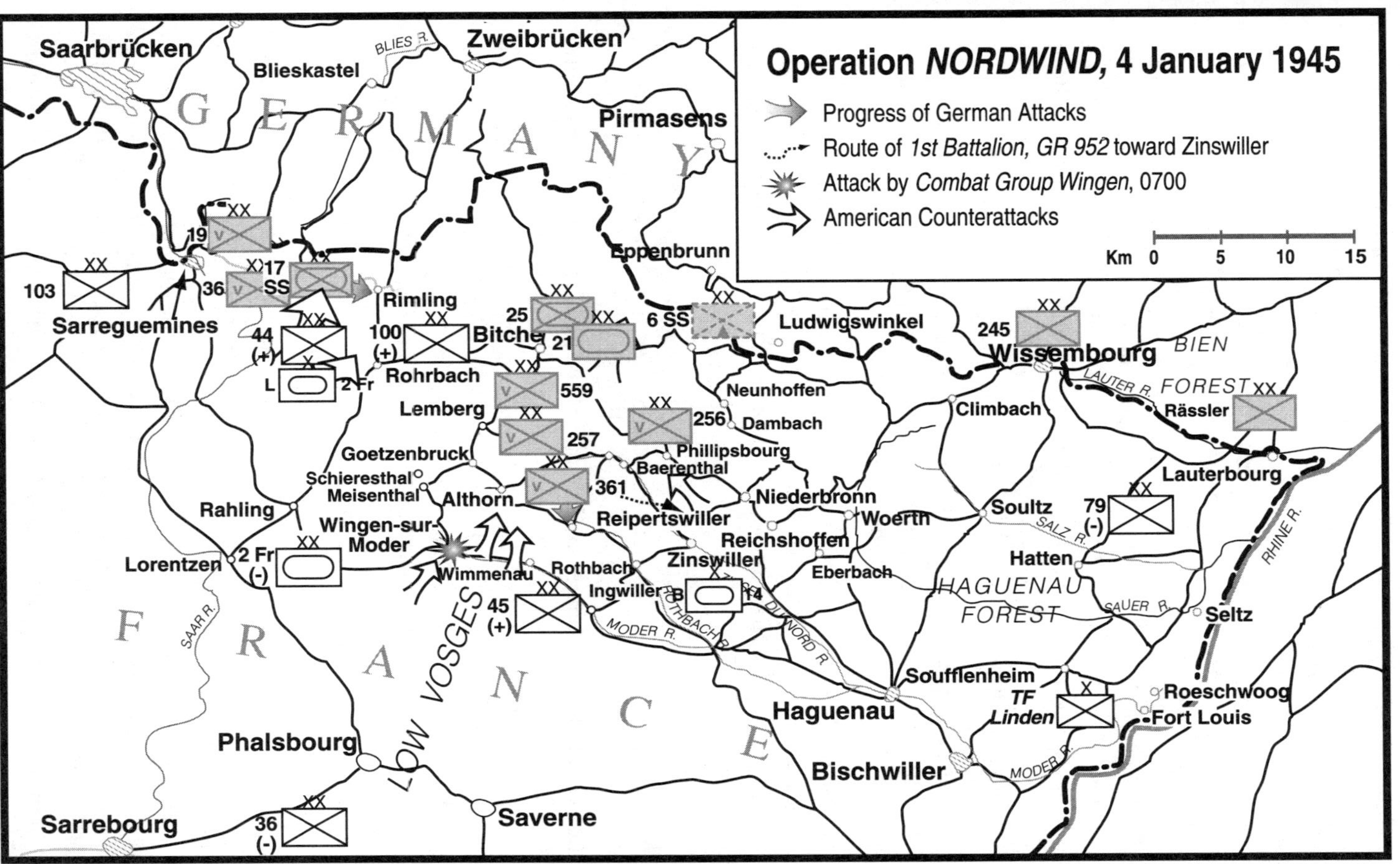
Operation NORDWIND, 4 January 1945
Progress of German Attacks
Route of 1st Battalion, GR 952 toward Zinswiller
Attack by Combat Group Wingen, 0700
American Counterattacks
Km 0 5 10 15
GERMANY
FRANCE
LOW VOSGES
BIEN FOREST
HAGUENAU FOREST
RHINE R.
LAUTER R.
SAUER R.
SALZ R.
MODER R.
ROTHBACH R.
SAAR R.
BLIES R.
Saarbrücken
Blieskastel
Zweibrücken
Pirmasens
Eppenbrunn
Ludwigswinkel
Wissembourg
Rässler
Lauterbourg
Seltz
Roeschwoog
Fort Louis
Sarreguemines
Rimling
Rohrbach
Bitche
Lemberg
Neunhoffen
Dambach
Phillipsbourg
Baerenthal
Niederbronn
Reichshoffen
Reipertswiller
Climbach
Soultz
Hatten
Woerth
Eberbach
Zinswiller
Rothbach
Ingwiller
Goetzenbruck
Althorn
Schieresthal
Meisenthal
Wingen-sur-Moder
Wimmenau
Rahling
Lorentzen
Soufflenheim
Haguenau
Bischwiller
Saverne
Phalsbourg
Sarrebourg
TF Linden
19
36
17 SS
44 (+)
L
2 Fr
100 (+)
25
21
6 SS
245
256
559
257
361
79 (-)
14
B
45 (+)
2 Fr (-)
36 (-)
103

regimental S-2 of the 276th Infantry disseminated information to his companies that there were not more than thirty to fifty German soldiers in and around Wingen; that they were nearly out of ammunition and food; and were probably ready to surrender.[154]

Oddly, the G-2 Journal of the 45th Division indicated that the 276th had sized up the situation differently, although still inaccurately. At 1130, their G-2 Journal records:

> Information from 276th Rgt: B Company at (N of Wingen) had enemy come into their rear, approx. 200, have had no contact with the Company. Enemy is bringing one company of tanks to assist in fight in WINGEN. . . . TF Herren reports 200 enemy in WINGEN at 0945; also company was ambushed N of WINGEN.[155]

Later during the same day, the 276th Regiment in its Unit Report 8 (3 to 5 January) offered a vastly different opinion, but one congruent with its previous report to its higher headquarters:

> [Enemy] has taken the town of Wingen, strength estimated at 200 men with excessive amounts of automatic weapons. Enemy appeared very aggressive and well equipped. . . . Morale of troops (mountain division) seems very high.

Besides the omnipresent fog of war, this clear intelligence gaffe is probably indicative of the enormous responsibilities thrust upon the staff of the 45th Infantry Division by the commanding general, VI Corps. In executing the "Great Shift," Lieutenant General Brooks had little choice but to burden the commander and staff of the 45th Infantry Division with a very significant command and control challenge. In its operations narrative, the 45th Infantry Division proudly registered that by 4 January, it had "more than 26 infantry battalions [with nine in and around Wingen], and 10 artillery battalions under its command" to defend a sector from the Corps boundary at Rosteig in the west to Niederschlettenbach (Germany) in the east, a straight line distance of twenty-two kilometers, but an MLR length of more than twice that distance. All information generated by the activities in this huge area had to be collected, collated, analyzed, and synthesized into intelligence by a G-2 staff designed to perform its mission in a much more limited area, with only about one-third as many subordinate units. The resultant slow recognition of the dangers of the capture of Wingen can probably be attributed chiefly to this, as well as the information vacuum created by the precipitous loss of the CP of 1st Battalion, 179th Infantry, and the loss of the commanding officer of the other battalion directly affected by the attack, 1st Battalion, 276th Infantry.

The German command and control situation was also less than optimal, although for different reasons. Having succeeded in seizing Wingen only by infiltrating down obscure mountain trails, *Combat Group Wingen* had to be reinforced soon. The promised "assault gun battalion" would have been especially useful in repelling the attacks of American armor, yet such hopes on our part were in vain. Even if such battalion had been actually available (which it obviously was not), a prerequisite for its arrival would have been that at least one of the two roads leading from the north into Wingen had been cleared (and kept open) by *Combat Group Wingen*. Under the circumstances, this was impossible.

The same argument holds true for the missing radio vehicle. Even if its crew had not taken a wrong turn and been captured, it could have reached Wingen only on a firm road, and all of these were sealed by 1st and 3d Battalions, 179th Infantry.* Practically all of our command and control problems resulted from the inability to communicate with our higher headquarters, adjacent units, and our supporting artillery. This deficiency prevented us from understanding what was happening around us in a real-time fashion, and severely degraded our intelligence about the enemy.

With over 300 prisoners in custody, including eight officers, it may appear odd that we did not obtain more information about our situation from them. In fact, not one of them was properly interrogated. The reason for this neglect may sound trivial, but it was nevertheless true. In the rush from Scandinavia, we were not prepared for combat against American troops, and we had not one soldier or officer (including me) whose spoken command of the English language was adequate for interrogation. Of course, the use of our captured son of German emigrants was out of the question, as we could not judge the reliability of his translations. Almost the entire intelligence picture we had of the enemy in and around Wingen was based on the file studies which I undertook on the afternoon of this 4 January, using my atrophied high school English reading skills!

## Tactical Employment of Troops

Although the men of *Combat Group Wingen* were hardened, disciplined, and highly experienced in forest warfare, it is a simple fact that our infiltration and subsequent successful attack would have been compromised—and our mission's accomplishment therefore jeopardized—by more effective American tactical countermeasures. When ordered to establish defensive positions for his unit, a company commander receives general directions for the orientation of his fields of fire, the location of the friendly units on the right and left, and information about the character of his support, such as

*It should be noted that these reflections are in retrospect only, and were never discussed during our days in Wingen.

reserves and indirect fires. It is the responsibility of the company commander to reconnoiter the terrain thoroughly and select optimal positions for his platoons and squads, all commensurate with his order.[156]

The first US Army unit to have an opportunity to stop our infiltration long before we reached Wingen was Charlie Company, 179th Infantry Regiment, at the pass on the Weinbourg Heights. This unit was deployed on the geographical crest of the pass, and slightly forward on the slope facing the Rothbach Valley, astride the pass (forest) road. To this extent, the company's position facilitated the mission of blocking ingress on this avenue of approach to Wingen and points south. Its drawback was that due to the vegetation, none of the men could observe down the valley road from the level of their foxholes. An approaching enemy could be first noticed only at very close ranges.

An observation/listening post in a place which afforded good observation of the valley road, equipped with functioning communications to the company commander, would have certainly detected the long marching column of the two battalions using the valley road, and could have warned the company. In turn, what became an inconclusive night meeting engagement from which *Combat Group Wingen* emerged relatively unscathed, could have been a successful ambush.

After it was ordered to support its sister company in depth, the positions assumed by Company B, 179th Infantry on the afternoon of 3 January again only seemingly enabled the blockage of the advance of an enemy coming from the north toward Wingen. Had its right platoon been extended to the northeast by only 200 meters, its men would have gained the opportunity to observe the Kindsbronn Valley, and the night march of some 800 German soldiers could not have passed undetected.

These mistakes, committed by commanders of a veteran unit, are of course easy to see in hindsight. It is almost equally possible that our highly-experienced advanced scouts may have detected these units' dispositions anyway, and the situation may have developed similarly after all. In the pitch black and snow of a mountain winter night, many things can happen.

The situation of elements of 1st Battalion, 276th Infantry is a very different one, however. The mission of 1st Battalion was "to outpost [the] high ground [north of Wingen], and establish [a] roadblock" on the D-12 road, about halfway between Kohlhutte and Wimmenau. This mission was received by the 1st Battalion CP at 2100 on 3 January.

The commanding officer of the 1st Battalion ordered his Company B to establish the outpost in the forest north of Wingen. We can only assume the same company was also to establish the roadblock a mere 500 meters to the east of its main position. At 0348, the 1st Battalion CP reported that its men were "Working on [the] roadblock."[157]

It was indeed either a very lucky guess or the result of outstandingly prescient analysis by the staff of the 45th Infantry Division to order a roadblock at this location. The G-3 of the 45th Infantry Division ordered a roadblock erected *exactly* on the very spot where, only seven hours after his orders were received by the executing unit, the two battalions of *Combat Group Wingen* crossed the district road! In fact, this crossing took place only *minutes* after 1st Battalion, 276th Infantry reported they were "working on" establishing the roadblock.*

That we did not run into *any* US soldiers whatever at this point could only mean that the roadblock had not been established at all, or that it was in the wrong place altogether. Either way, 1st Battalion, 276th Infantry rendered an inaccurate report to its higher headquarters, thereby engendering a sense of false security. Whether the report was intentionally false, and the battalion and/or company commanders and/or platoon leader were allowing their cold, tired, hungry, and tense men to sleep, or whether the roadblock was sited in a grossly incorrect location, the impact is clear. The nearly 800 men of *Combat Group Wingen* passed the intended site of the roadblock *en route* to their objective unhampered and unchallenged, while higher headquarters was warmed by the confidence imparted by a false sense of security. In return for some extra, probably fitful, sleep in the snow, or as a result of incompetent navigation, numerous men of Company B died within two hours of our unimpeded passage.

While this was the first combat engagement for all elements of Task Force Herren, lapses in judgment by numerous leaders plagued 1st Battalion, 276th Infantry to a significant degree. The deployment of the remainder of Company B in the center of a heavily-wooded plateau, without fields of fire or observation, was senseless and absurd. It totally obviated the effectiveness of the deployment in depth of 1st Battalion, 276th Infantry, which was the last line of resistance for the occupants of Wingen, who were mostly service troops depending on the protection of this unit. That Company B men were told *not* to dig in only added to their sad, predestined fate.

The deployment of Company A, 276th Infantry on the unprotected forward slope of the hill overlooking the Moder River and Wingen from the south is another example of poor judgment in the selection of defensive positions. By preparing their fighting positions some 100 meters forward of the forest edge on the entirely exposed, bare northern slope of the Kirchberg on the afternoon of 3 January, and subsequently abandoning those positions at

*The unwelcome encounter on the district road with the jeep and its crew discussed earlier may be reinterpreted now: this could have been a patrol in search of the roadblock squad.

night—the only time when they would not be starkly obvious against the background of the newly-fallen snow—seems the height of tactical folly. No benefit was gained by those forward positions, and their disadvantages were overwhelming. The positions were obvious to attackers, especially from the protection of the cemetery walls, but allowed only limited fields of fire and observation. On the other hand, the view from positions on the rim of the woods behind the company was perfect, and so were the prospects of concealment in the forest. Foxholes dug there could be easily occupied and reinforced, should such need arise. Still more absurd seems to be the order to reoccupy these problematic foxholes after the enemy had been chased out of them, and to then excavate them to a "proper" depth, all under heavy enemy small arms fire. It would have been far more effective and much safer to use the much more advantageous positions on the rim of the forest.

A similarly odd decision seems to have been made by Colonel Conley, commander of the 274th Infantry Regiment after leading his abortive counterattack with Companies E and F, 274th Infantry. Withdrawing all the way to Puberg after being repulsed near the western corner of Wingen was senseless. Colonel Morgan, CO of the 276th Infantry Regiment, seems fully justified in having been irate at losing the opportunity to exert additional pressure on *Combat Group Wingen* by having another battalion of infantry in close proximity to the western edge of town.

Combined, these instances of lapsed leadership and seriously faulty judgment demonstrate the disadvantages of committing incompletely-trained units to combat. The 70th Infantry Division (of which Task Force Herren represented the three infantry regiments, separately deployed) was incompletely trained, as a result of repeated "strippings" of soldiers—overwhelmingly infantrymen—to serve as replacements in US Army units already in combat elsewhere. This repeated excision of large proportions of the combat "muscle" of the division during its predeployment training prevented the units from ever conducting collective training above the company level. Combined with the effects of adding large proportions of soldiers who had been recently reclassified from positions in the US Army Air Forces, antiaircraft units, and the classrooms of the Army Specialized Training Program (ASTP), this incomplete training bore its distasteful fruit in the snowy woods outside Wingen on the fourth day of *NORDWIND*.[158] Just as equally serious training inadequacies handicapped the *Volks-Grenadier* units of *LXXXIX* and *XC Corps*—or *SS-Division NORD* in the summer of 1941, at the Soviet fortress at Salla, for that matter. This did nothing to restrain the gallantry of the individual soldiers, whether German or American.

Perhaps this unimpressive performance by the elements of the 276th Infantry played a part in Major General Frederick's decision to employ them to counterattack Wingen, rather than redirecting the 180th Infantry to perform this mission. While this may sound counterintuitive, that is, why employ a troubled unit to eject an elite German unit from a stronghold behind one's lines when a much more experienced unit could be employed, the totality of the 45th's responsibilities to VI Corps and Seventh Army must be considered.

After receiving reports from its diverse elements in and around Wingen that German troops had infiltrated and had taken possession of the town in the morning hours of 4 January, Major General Frederick and his staff officers of the 45th Infantry Division must have been, at least for a while, in a dilemma. Not one mile from Wingen was the better part of the crack 180th Infantry Regiment, after having been trucked into this region during the night. With two German armored divisions in assembly areas less than an hour's drive away, General Frederick clearly thought priority had to be given to the establishment of a solid, coherent MLR north of Wingen. Accordingly, he gave priority to the already scheduled attack to the north, with the first goal being to close the still existing gap between Goetzenbruck and Wildenguth.

As a result, the newly arrived, uninitiated battalions of Task Force Herren (70th Infantry Division) were ordered to attack the German enemy in Wingen and restore the situation there. In the coming years, veterans of the 276th and 2d Battalion, 274th Infantry would question why—since the 1st Battalion, 179th Infantry had allowed *Combat Group Wingen* to successfully infiltrate through their lines on the night of 3/4 January—did elements of Task Force Herren have to retake Wingen? And since the CP of the veteran 1st Battalion, 179th Infantry and associated service personnel were literally asleep as the *Gebirgsjäger* swept into the town, why did the greenest troops in the theater have to rescue them, at a frightful cost of their own buddies' lives?

Although General Frederick's exact thoughts are lost to history, this was a sensible, if morally difficult, decision. While the infiltration of several hundred German mountain infantrymen through the MLR south of the Bitche Salient was certainly troubling, it was not likely to be *decisive.* Frederick had confidence that his veterans in the line units of the 179th Infantry Regiment could hold on and retain their forward focus, even with German units in their immediate rear.

Allowing the Goetzenbruck-Wildenguth gap to remain open could have been considered by German forces as an invitation to additional infiltration. Such infiltration in force could have enabled the Germans to encircle and subsequently eliminate the critical American blocking positions at Wildenguth, Reipertswiller, and even Wimmenau. The collapse of these as yet unconnected strongpoints would have enabled the deployment of the armored reserves Frederick knew to be assembled to the north. (In fact, *Generaloberst* Blaskowitz and his staff were just waiting for the exits from the Low Vosges to be opened before sending the *21st Panzer* and *25th Panzer-Grenadier Divisions* roaring through to the Alsatian Plain.) Frederick would have been strategically and tactically irresponsible to risk such a disaster.

On the other hand, Frederick knew that by virtue of its very location, it would not be difficult to seal off *Combat Group Wingen* in town. The field order already issued to both the 179th and 180th Infantry Regiments to restore an unbroken line of resistance in the north would also make further infiltrations by the enemy impossible. Such a situation would deprive *Combat Group Wingen* of reinforcements and supplies. This "thorn in the side" would soon be forced to succumb to counterattacks or alternatively have to attempt a breakout or exfiltration. Either way, their presence *alone* could not prevent Frederick from accomplishing his mission.

Major General Frederick trusted his seasoned 180th Infantry Regiment to accomplish this critical mission. In conjunction with the 179th Infantry, he ordered the 180th to restore the pre-New Year situation south and east of Bitche. Closing the gap was the first task of this mission.

At 0900, when Frederick had to make his final decision, the most recent reports received at 45th Division headquarters indicated the maximum strength of the German elements in Wingen to be fifty soldiers. This may have made it easy for Frederick to decide. Putting his confidence in his most experienced infantry, he continued on with his chosen course of action for his two organic regiments to restore the situation up north, and issued the order to the attached Task Force Herren to counterattack Wingen.

For Frederick, it was not a matter of assigning blame for the fall of Wingen to a specific party. Clearly, elements of the veteran 45th Division and novice Task Force Herren shared liability for his fiasco. It was, rather, a matter of mission priorities, and the degree of faith he had in the different units under his command.

The misapprehension of the size of *Combat Group Wingen* must have also played a part in the decisions by the commanders of the 274th and 276th Infantry to counterattack with such small units on the afternoon of 4 January. Both counterattacks—that of Lieutenant Colonel Iverson's fragmented 3d Battalion, 276th Infantry, and that of Companies E and F under Colonel Conley—especially unsupported by artillery, had no realistic chance of regaining Wingen from a force of over 750 Germans. However, this is connected to a historical point that must be made. Strangely, some American records claim several counterattacks *in addition to* these two ill-fated attempts on the afternoon of 4 January.

Parallel to the tank-supported attack of 3d Battalion, 276th Infantry from west to east, there was supposedly another attack during the later afternoon, from east to west, starting on the road between Wingen and Wimmenau. According to the regimental S-3 Journal of the 276th Infantry, it was mounted by the Intelligence and Reconnaissance (I&R) Platoon, together with "10 tanks with heavy mortar support." The attack allegedly jumped off at 1720 "down the valley thru town and now moving forward."[159] Another source (CO, 3d Battalion, 180th Infantry who was in close contact with the 1st Battalion, 276th Infantry) reported to his regiment that this east-west attack was mounted by Companies A and D, 276th Infantry; but according to later reports, by Company C, 276th Infantry, supported by four light tanks. According to this source, the attack started around 1630, and returned before 1900:

> This outfit that went into the town from C Co (276th Infantry) ran out of ammunition; one bunch got [as] far as the church, and one bunch got far as the RR station. The only fire they got was from outside the town, they shot up their ammo and pulled back out of the town.[160]

These reports are completely inaccurate. Having been in the *Hotel de la Gare* during the exact time of this alleged penetration, it would have been impossible for me to miss an attack by a tank-supported infantry company across the street. As for the other attack, the one supposedly prosecuted by the I&R platoon with ten tanks, it is strange that no one in *Combat Group Wingen* noticed the better part of a company of Shermans attacking our positions. Further, it would have been an at least equally odd use, on the part of Colonel Morgan, of the precious intelligence-gathering asset that is a regimental I&R platoon. These reports of non-existent counterattacks are probably indicative of the confusion of the moment, the sort that can be severely exacerbated by inexperience, fear, and exhaustion. Such wildly inaccurate perceptions of reality were by no means limited to the American side.

The withdrawal of the *1st Battalion, SS-Mountain Infantry Regiment 12*, which literally took to the hills on the unsupported and untrue report of a messenger, is a perfect example of this phenomenon occurring in a highly-experienced organization. Had American troops in the west or southwest of Wingen aggressively maintained contact with the enemy—had Colonel Conley not pulled Companies E and F of the 274th all the way back to Puberg, for example—they might have discovered that for the better part of two hours on this evening there was not a single German soldier west of the railroad station or the church.

This reaction on the German side can best be explained by the profound sleep deprivation experienced by practically all of the men of *Combat Group Wingen*, and the corollary utter fatigue after an extremely long and eventful day.

The coming days would be no less exhausting, however.

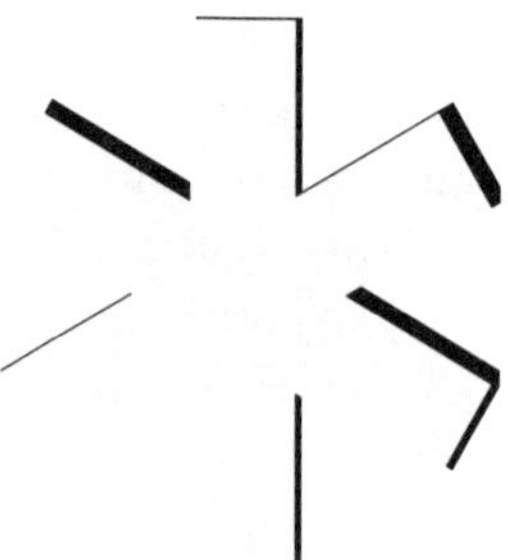

# The Fifth Day: Defense

## -I-
## The Last Hopes for *NORDWIND*

The fifth day of *NORDWIND* continued the trend of the last four days. The grossly overstressed and thoroughly fatigued German infantrymen of most of the formations of *LXXXIX* and *XC Corps* became increasingly worn out. Not only were most of them ill-trained and inexperienced in forest warfare, but the weather conditions also were becoming unbearable for such men living in the open. The armored operational reserves were still held out of the action, while Hitler awaited the seizure of a pass to the Alsatian Plain. The armored reconnaissance battalion of the *21st Panzer Division* was, however, sent toward Wissembourg to reconnoiter the American positions to the south on the Rhine Plain.[161] Artillery ammunition resupply became even more problematic, and the dwindling fire support was compounded by the frequent inadequacy of radio communications between forward observers and firing batteries. These nightmares and more contributed to the mounting anxiety among German commanders at all tactical levels.

On the western end of the Low Vosges salient, in its second day of defensive combat, the *257th VGD* was trying to fend off attacks of increasing size and intensity by elements of the US 45th and 100th Infantry Divisions (the latter of which controlled the 141st Infantry Regiment and elements of Task Force Harris). Despite a shortened MLR, the *257th*'s defensive efforts actually became more difficult; after higher German headquarters consented to *Generalmajor* Seidel's request to go over to the defensive, they almost immediately rejoined that permission with the detachment of key combat assets. Seidel lost a supporting artillery battalion to the *559th VGD* in its struggle between Lemberg and Reyersviller, and also had to detach *GR 477*, one of his three two-battalion regiments. Redesignated as *1st Army* reserve, the men of *GR 477* were already trudging through the snow in the vicinity of Fourneau Neuf, on their way to assisting the *361st VGD*.[162]

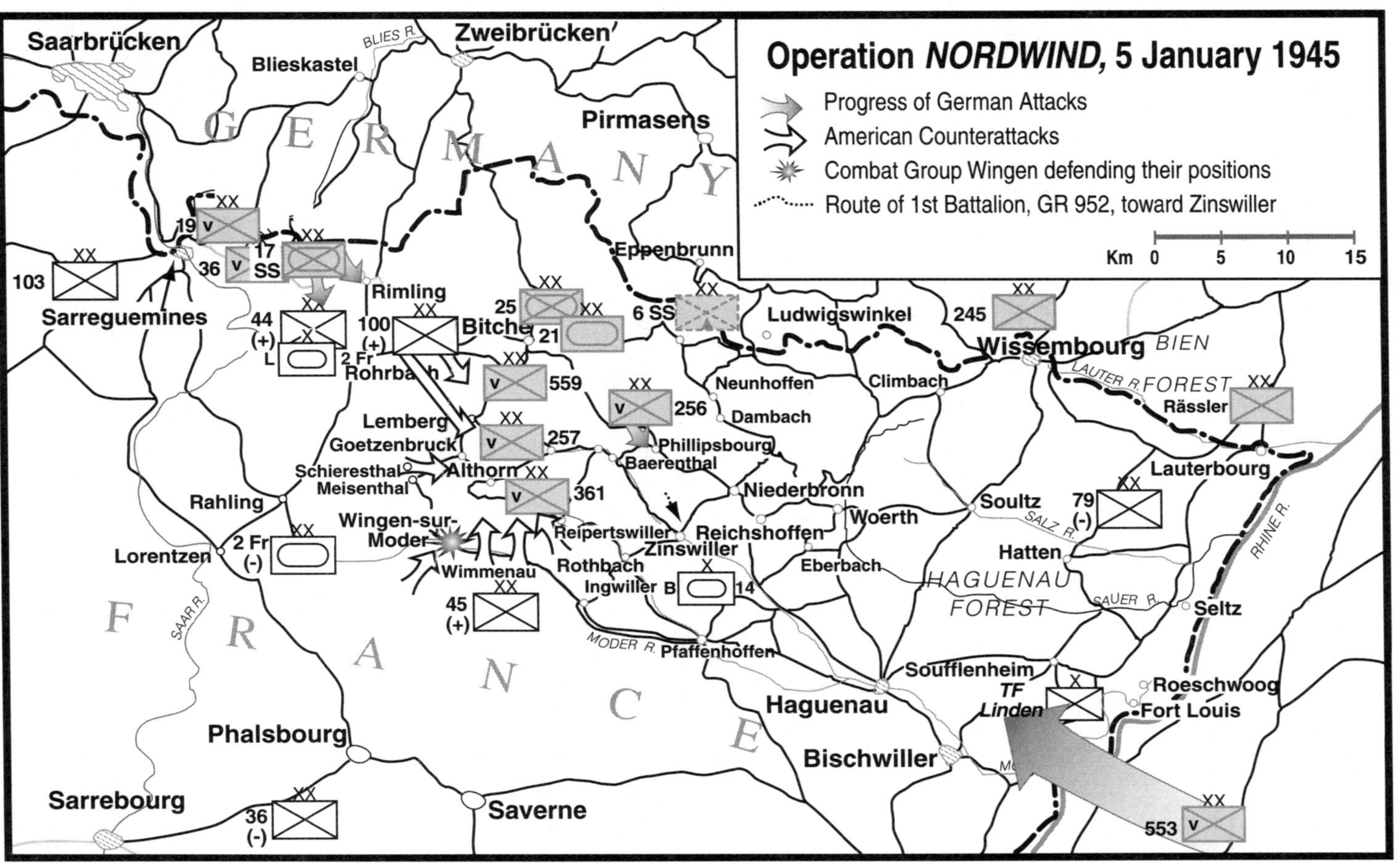
Operation *NORDWIND*, 5 January 1945
Progress of German Attacks
American Counterattacks
Combat Group Wingen defending their positions
Route of 1st Battalion, GR 952, toward Zinswiller
Km 0 5 10 15
G E R M A N Y
F R A N C E
Saarbrücken
Blieskastel
BLIES R.
Zweibrücken
Pirmasens
Eppenbrunn
Sarreguemines
Rimling
Bitche
Rohrbach
Lemberg
Goetzenbruck
Schieresthal
Meisenthal
Althorn
Rahling
Lorentzen
Wingen-sur-Moder
Wimmenau
Reipertswiller
Rothbach
Ingwiller
Zinswiller
Reichshoffen
Niederbronn
Baerenthal
Phillipsbourg
Neunhoffen
Dambach
Ludwigswinkel
Climbach
Wissembourg
BIEN FOREST
LAUTER R.
Rässler
Lauterbourg
Soultz
SALZ R.
Woerth
Eberbach
Hatten
HAGUENAU FOREST
SAUER R.
Seltz
RHINE R.
MODER R.
Pfaffenhoffen
Haguenau
Soufflenheim
TF Linden
Roeschwoog
Fort Louis
Bischwiller
SAAR R.
Phalsbourg
Saverne
Sarrebourg
103
19
36
17 SS
44 (+)
L
2 Fr
100 (+)
25
21
6 SS
245
559
256
257
361
79 (-)
2 Fr (-)
45 (+)
B
14
36 (-)
553

*Generalmajor* Philippi, commanding general of the *361st VGD*, expected the arrival of this reinforcement during the course of 5 January. The regimental commander eventually reported to him at the *361st*'s command post with the frustrating news that the lead company was only at Mouterhouse, still ten kilometers away from its intended assembly area near Saegmuhle. Compounding the disappointment was that the two battalions' average company strength was only 100 men, all deeply fatigued from the last four days' combat. They would require rest after their approach march to be fit for the offensive action Philippi had in mind for them.

As a result, Philippi dispensed with the idea of yet another attack on the American forces dug in at Reipertswiller. Besides, the enemy there had demonstrated that it was on full alert. Instead, Philippi chose to attack the medieval castle at Lichtenberg as an intermediate objective; seizing Lichtenberg would facilitate a further attack on Reipertswiller from a different direction. Also, the high ground on which the castle was situated would provide excellent fields of observation for his artillery observers, as well as more suitable transmission sites for their FM radios. Finally, the seizure of Lichtenberg would at least open the stretch of road between Lichtenberg and the Ingwiller exit from the Low Vosges. If Reipertswiller could then be taken, Philippi would provide the *Army Group G* armored reserve one tenuous route to the Plain of Alsace.

Philippi planned to tie down the American forces at Reipertswiller with a supporting attack by his own right (western) flank units, then envelop them with his left, after seizing Lichtenberg. In gaining permission for this concept of operations, he not only received the concurrence of *General der Infanterie* Höhne, the *LXXXIX Corps* commander, but also received the welcome news that his units' efforts would be supported by three or four additional artillery battalions, as well as a battalion of rocket launchers. Given the extensive "reshuffling" of his forces and coordination that all of this would require, Philippi set the attack for 7 January.[163] Even if all went as planned, it would be a few more days before the Americans could be ejected from Reipertswiller and the road to the Zinswiller exit opened.

After the war, *Generalmajor* Philippi lamented that on this fifth day of *NORDWIND*, he still could not communicate with the battalions in the Moder Valley, because both patrols and radio contact had failed. "With continuing concern and apprehension, the division thinks of the battalions isolated and left to themselves in the Moder Valley!"[164]

While stagnation or lengthy delays reigned on the entire *NORDWIND* front, in the higher German command echelons, all eyes turned to the two battalions that had made the deepest penetrations of the American front on the day before, namely *Combat Group Wingen*. If there was a flicker of hope left for success in breaking through to the excellent road leading to the Ingwiller exit from the Low Vosges, it seemed to be in Wingen. Yet so little was known.

## -II-
## Blood and Fire

The order which had caused elements of the *1st Battalion* of *Combat Group Wingen* to withdraw during the previous evening had been the result of a report by a messenger whose nerves were clearly frayed by sleeplessness and stress. During the long mountain winter night, the *3d*, *4th*, and *6th Companies* of *1st Battalion, SS-Mountain Infantry Regiment 12* of *Combat Group Wingen* reoccupied the same positions they had so recently vacated in the west and northwest sections of Wingen, without their American opponents ever realizing they had left.

Otherwise, the night was quiet, and we cherished what seemed to be the American "custom" of using the night to sleep. Actually, the enemy around Wingen was licking his wounds from his first day of action, while we veterans of a thousand arctic nights of combat got our first rest of the year 1945.

Just at 0800, however, the Americans brought some of their heavy weapons to bear. Tanks blazed away from the Kirchberg heights, and mortars and artillery opened fire from behind the hills around Wingen. The Americans did not seem to be constrained by ammunition shortages, and threw in what seemed to be endless quantities of high explosive shells.

We had still not established wire communications between the command posts of the *1st* and *3d Battalions* (and never managed it throughout the duration of our presence in Wingen). We had no short-range radios like the American "walkie-talkie," either. Therefore, all detailed communications had to be conducted in person. I recommended to *Hauptsturmführer* Kreuzinger, my battalion commander, that it would be wise to have a knowledgeable liaison at the *1st Battalion* command post, and I volunteered to go. Based on our experience of the previous day, the Americans seemed most likely to attack in the *1st Battalion*'s sector again, and Kreuzinger had to maintain awareness of the action there.

I went alone, not seeing the need to take a messenger with me. For the first 200 to 300 meters, I didn't have a problem—buildings, fences, and hedges provided concealment from enemy observation from the south. The further I proceeded, though, the more critical the situation became as any keen observer with decent field glasses should have been able to spot me as I darted between gaps in the cover.

I wasn't surprised at all when an American machine gunner opened up on me.

The last ten meters of my journey to the gate in front of the building housing the *1st Battalion* CP was covered by a pile of firewood, the likes of which is customary in these villages. When I leapt into the cover provided by this stack, the American gunner followed me with a line of bullets, but ceased firing when he realized that further shooting would just create a lot of wood chips, and be a waste of ammunition.

Shielded behind the woodpile, I tried to reconnoiter my last bound. The little gate to the property was half open, and there was a steep slope going down from the street up which I'd come so far. I had to negotiate a few flagstone steps, then sprint over fifteen meters in the sights of the American gunner, in position somewhere on the heights of the Kirchberg to the south.

I was in no rush. I decided to remain behind the perfect cover of the woodpile long enough to eventually unnerve my opponent, making him inattentive, or hoping he would lose interest in me and engage another target. In the meantime, I observed a crew of medics carefully making their way down the steep street from the railroad embankment to the road, waving a Red Cross flag all the way. They were headed to the combined aid station in the former schoolhouse, just beyond the *1st Battalion* CP. No one fired at them.

As soon as the litter party was out of sight, and therefore out of the line of fire, I made a run for it. My timing was good—the American gunner only started shooting at the moment I jumped onto the porch, and into the house.

Inside, I found *Hauptsturmführer* Burgstaller, the battalion commander, and Carlau, his adjutant, in the main room of the house, together with a few of their messengers, as well as the forward observer from *3d Battalion, SS-Artillery Regiment 6*. They welcomed me as they had so many times in north Karelia and Finland.*

While we were exchanging information about the action in our respective sectors, the American tankers on the southern slope of the Kirchberg blasted the building and its immediate environs with their tanks' main guns. We sprinted down into the cellar for safety. Evidently, by observing the comings and goings of several messengers and officers, the enemy (accurately) concluded that this was some sort of a command post or message center. This intermittent, concentrated fire not only interrupted the message traffic and command and control of the battle, but also interdicted the transportation of wounded to the nearby aid station. Thus, evacuation of casualties was suspended during daylight hours.

*After the war, we learned that the house belonged to the railroad company, and was the residence of the Wingen station master, who had left the village with so many other inhabitants before the battle began.

With messenger communication with the companies cut off, to monitor operational developments, the commander and staff of *1st Battalion* had to rely on changes to the noise of battle and the reports from a few lookouts observing from covered and concealed locations in the immediate vicinity of the CP. This was clearly an unfavorable situation, but all that could be managed in the absence of wire or radio communications.

Dr. Lautenschlager, the surgeon of the *1st Battalion,* braved the whirlwind of shrapnel outside and joined us in the cellar. He reported that the aid station he had established, or more accurately, taken over in the adjacent building, was rapidly filling with casualties. When he and his medics had first arrived, two American medical officers, a captain and a lieutenant, and ten of their medics were caring for about twenty bed-ridden cases. Most of these American soldiers were sick, but there had been a few wounded, too. Now, the battle for Wingen was adding many new wounded—from both sides.

Dr. Lautenschlager was full of praise for the professional cooperation he was receiving from his two American colleagues, and further related that the American medical personnel had joined forces with his own German medics. He was further astonished by the lavish medical supply situation in this American facility. His concern about being limited to the medical supplies he and his medics brought with them—limited to minimal essential surgical equipment and paper bandages—was replaced by his wonder at the stocks of antibiotics and especially blood plasma present in the aid station. Many lives had already been saved by the administration of the precious plasma.

Despite this unexpected good fortune, Dr. Lautenschlager was worried about the steadily increasing influx of casualties from all companies. In his report, he mentioned that a number of them were in critical condition, urgently in need of a major surgical operation—in other circumstances, they would have been immediately evacuated to hospitals in the rear. Now, cut off several kilometers behind American lines, there seemed to be no way to evacuate these severely wounded men—or was there? Contrary to the rough and inhuman customs of the Red Army, the Americans seemed to respect the Red Cross. Perhaps the Americans would be willing to accept the most seriously wounded, and evacuate them to one of their well-equipped hospitals for further treatment.

To discuss this possibility in earnest, the American assistant surgeon was summoned from the aid station. He concurred with the dire prognoses of our own surgeon, and agreed with the necessity of evacuating a number of the most seriously wounded men as soon as possible. He also said that he thought the American troops surrounding us might be willing to accept them for evacuation—he thought we should at least try. On the other hand, he refused to conduct the negotiations himself. *Untersturmführer* Carlau was fuming.

After sending the American medical officer back to the aid station to attend to his duties, we discussed this urgent topic further. Dr. Lautenschlager proposed sending one of his medics who spoke English to parlay, accompanied by one of the American medics. We attached a very high priority to this issue and decided to offer the American side an even exchange of their men whom we had taken as prisoners—that is, we would send back as many Americans as we would Germans.[165]

* * * * *

As we strained to acoustically follow the course of the battle outside our cellar refuge, a group of soldiers on "the other side of the hill" were trying to visually ascertain our locations in preparation for a major attack.

The failure of the largely uncoordinated assaults of the day before left Colonel Morgan frustrated and upset by several aspects of the unsuccessful operation. The lack of coordination among his regiment's organic units bothered him, as did the withdrawal of 2d Battalion, 274th Infantry after its brief entry into the battle during the previous afternoon. This battalion could do little to assist in the recapture of Wingen from its positions near Puberg.

The commander of 2d Battalion, 274th Infantry, Lieutenant Colonel Cheves, was also in a frustrating position: His boss, Colonel Conley, had personally led two of his three rifle companies forward to Wingen and back during the previous afternoon. Colonel Murphy, commander of the 179th Infantry, wanted Cheves to move his battalion into position to provide better depth to his regiment's defenses north of Wingen. At the same time, Colonel Morgan wanted him to send two companies back to the western outskirts of Wingen, whence they had just come. Respectfully refusing Colonel Murphy's desires, Cheves' dilemma was partially solved by an order from Brigadier General Herren, conveyed by Lieutenant Colonel Jim Richardson, the Task Force Herren G-3: Cheves was to detach a rifle company to the 276th immediately. Lieutenant Colonel Cheves dispatched his Company G, under the command of First Lieutenant Fred "Casey" Cassidy, to link up with elements of the 276th on the western edge of Wingen. Sometime around midnight, Company G trudged off through the snow, following its charismatic commander, who had only assumed command a few days before.[166]

During the night, Colonel Morgan ordered most of the 1st and 3d Battalions of his 276th Infantry Regiment—and the attached company from the 274th Infantry—into an attack to eject the German defenders of Wingen. These concerted attacks were to commence simultaneously at 0800, after an artillery preparation on suspected German positions in the wooded heights north of the town by the 105mm howitzers of the 45th Infantry Division's

160th Field Artillery Battalion. The concept of the operation, a semi-concentric attack made feasible only by Wingen's bowl-like valley location, called for the following:

- Company A, 276th Infantry attacks from the south
- Company G, 274th Infantry (attached) attacks from the southwest
- Company C, 276th Infantry attacks from the north
- Elements of 3d Battalion, 276th Infantry attack Wingen from the west[167]

Since a recon patrol dispatched earlier in the morning had still not returned, the commanding officer of Company A, 276th Infantry, Captain Dean Hendrickson, ordered his executive officer, Lieutenant Arnest, to reconnoiter using two squads of the company's 1st Platoon. Hendrickson believed that such a force would suffice to smoke out the "50-odd" Germans reported by TF Herren's G-2 to have infiltrated into the town.

Arnest led the two squads allotted for his mission around the left flank of the Company A position on the forward slope of the Kirchberg, to the road coming into Wingen from Zittersheim, which lay to the southwest. At first, the patrol met no opposition, and it "looked like a picnic."[168] But when the men came to the first intersection south of the railroad underpass, they were met on three sides by a storm of intense, close-range small arms fire from cellar and second-story windows. Although they sustained two casualties, the patrol was nevertheless able to occupy houses on both sides of the street at the intersection. The intensity of the fire convinced Lieutenant Arnest that there must be a lot more Germans in the town than the handful of which he had been apprised, so he sent a runner to inform Captain Hendrickson.

Hendrickson, in turn, was of the opinion that his entrenched 2d and 3d Platoons were already fixing the majority of all German forces in the town by engaging them in a firefight. He couldn't understand what was delaying Arnest and his two-squad patrol. Growing impatient, Hendrickson personally took a squad from the 2d Platoon and his company messenger and worked his way along the ditch to the side of the Zittersheim road, following the same route used by Arnest and his patrol. At the road, Captain Hendrickson's patrol was joined by a medium tank of Company B, 781st Tank Battalion. This crew and its vehicle had arrived from the assembly area north of Zittersheim too late to support Lieutenant Arnest and his men, so it was now joining Captain Hendrickson's small force. The tank commander made it clear that he would not enter Wingen unless he received adequate protection from the infantry, and insisted on continuous security measures being taken by the accompanying foot soldiers to guard against engagement by *panzerfausts*.[169]

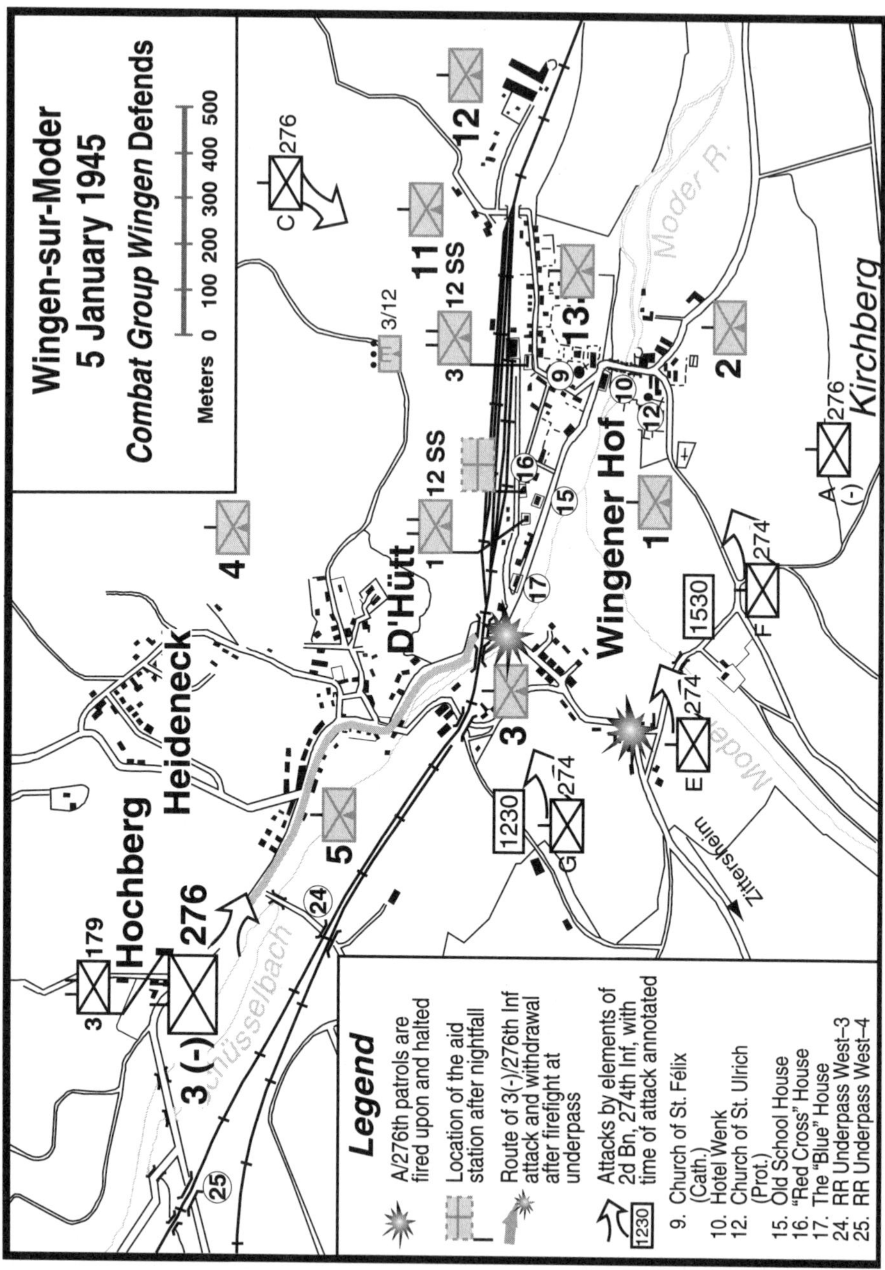


When this small infantry-armor force reached the intersection at which Arnest's men had already run into trouble, they, too, received automatic weapons fire from the buildings on both sides of the street. Linking up with

Arnest's men, Hendrickson demanded to know what was holding up their progress further into Wingen. "Germans and machine guns," answered the soldiers from the 1st Platoon.

It was not the answer Dean Hendrickson wanted to hear.[170]

After a frontal assault by his squad from his 2d Platoon failed to materialize under the hail of German automatic weapons fire, Captain Hendrickson must have decided to set an example of personal bravery, and started running toward the intersection himself. He was hit in the chest after a few paces. Several more of his men became casualties in the process of rescuing him.[171]

*****

Even as Able Company, 276th Infantry was having difficulty getting its attack off the ground, shortly after daybreak, the tired men of George Company, 274th Infantry were arriving at the edge of the same woods in which they had had the short firefight during the previous afternoon. In front of them was a grove of evergreens. When they started in that direction, a German machine gun opened up—its gunner had cannily waited for his targets to expose themselves before commencing fire at close range. In the ensuing engagement, a brave American sergeant knocked out the German gun with a hand grenade, but was fatally hit immediately thereafter.

The Company G advance slowed and then stopped altogether, as well dug-in Germans continued to rake the area with machine-gun fire. To Lieutenant Cassidy, it was obvious that the defenders clearly possessed fire superiority and evidently intended to hold their positions. Only after Cassidy brought his 60mm mortars to bear could his men subsequently attack the German position in the grove and drive them back—the enemy was finally on the run. With this obstruction cleared, George could move forward to the verge of the forest, from which they enjoyed an unobstructed view of Wingen-sur-Moder.[172]

At 1230, Company G began its advance towards the town.[173]

*****

In the original concept of operations for arraying its forces around Wingen on 3 January, Company C, 276th Infantry (commanded by Captain Bill Greenwalt) was in reserve, to the southeast of the Kirchberg, somewhere to the right of the Able Company positions. It was the last company of the regiment to receive its baptism of fire on this day. In the dark hours of early morning, its men received their ammunition, rations, and their exceptionally simple instructions: prepare for a long march followed by an attack.[174]

Skirting the edge of Wingen, the 160 men of Charlie Company warily crossed the railroad tracks about halfway between Wimmenau and Wingen at 0720.[175] Turning counterclockwise further north of the railroad line, the men came unexpectedly upon the bodies of many men on top of a wooded ridge, "scattered about, frozen in the snow where they fell." Jack Herman, one of the survivors of that attack, recalled, "They were almost all in American uniforms. We did not count the dead, but the numbers overwhelmed us; there could easily have been fifty to one hundred, or even more GIs, and only a few—maybe five or six Germans. . . . Weapons, ammunition, and rations had been removed." In this way, the men of Charlie Company discovered the battlefield of twenty-seven hours previously, where most of their sister unit, Company B, 276th Infantry, had been wiped out.

It took the men from Company C until 0940 to make contact with *Combat Group Wingen*, specifically our *3d Battalion*'s *Pioneer Platoon* and *11th Company* which they found to be well dug-in on one of the more prominent east-west ridges on the wooded heights north of Wingen. At 0941, the Regimental S-3 Journal laconically notes, "Company C held up by small arms fire from Hill N of town. Will take care of it by themselves."

After his company's first attack was repulsed by the German hedgehog position, Captain Greenwalt employed the two machine guns and three mortars of his weapons platoon in preparation for the second attack. Herman writes,

> At the blast of a whistle, the rifle platoons started downhill and back up the [German] defended hill. The Germans joined in the firing and soon dominated it; their machine-gun fire was unbelievably loud and intense and seemed to echo from all directions. . . . The scene was total confusion. . . . Finally it came clear to everyone that we weren't accomplishing anything and the word came to pull out. We went back the way we came, under fire. . . . I remember feeling hopelessly that the Germans were indeed supermen, and that we were incompetent amateurs who had fooled ourselves into believing that we were capable of fighting them.[176]

Herman believes that during those two attacks, in addition to a higher number of wounded, Company C lost twelve men killed, including his platoon leader, Lieutenant Robert H. Wardell.

The hedgehog position attacked vainly by Charlie Company was manned by the *Pioneer Platoon, 15th (headquarters) Company*, and by elements of *11th Company*, both of our *3d Battalion, SS-Mountain Infantry Regiment 12*.

By Colonel Morgan's order, the fourth force that was supposed to participate in the concerted attack to rid Wingen of the "fifty members" of the German raiding party was the 3d Battalion, 276th Infantry, commanded by Lieutenant Colonel Sid Iverson. Supported by tanks from Company B, 781st Tank Battalion, Colonel Iverson's battalion was to conduct a reprise of the previous day's action from the westernmost fringe of Wingen through Hochberg, and into the town.

Company L, which had led the attack on the day before, had remained in its positions overnight. On this day, its men would be spared the dangers of leading the attack. With about fifty stragglers from the ill-fated Baker Company under First Sergeant Woodrow Barnett attached, Company I would lead the assault. Company K, the 3d Battalion's remaining rifle company, remained in VI Corps reserve in positions between Rosteig and Volksberg.[177]

After requesting two ten-minute artillery preparations from the 45th Infantry Division's 160th Field Artillery Battalion, the 276th's S-3 apprised Headquarters, Task Force Herren, that the 3d Battalion's attack had jumped off at 0840. At 0900, the S-3 of 3d Battalion requested an additional ten minutes' firing, at 200-yards'-greater range.[178] The targets were the wooded heights overlooking Wingen from the north, and the vicinity of the two western railroad underpasses.

The tanks supporting the 3d Battalion's assault were from 2d Platoon, Company B, 781st Tank Battalion. Despite this armored support and Colonel Morgan's presence at the 3d Battalion's CP, the attack made slow progress. The effort by the joint armor-infantry team soon suffered heavy losses. Both the tankers and the infantry had been told that the high ground to their left (north) was held by American forces—Colonel Morgan and Lieutenant Colonel Iverson evidently believed Charlie Company's earlier attack there was successful. But the men attacking through the underpass soon learned otherwise. As the leading tank ground its way forward, "a German bazooka team was hidden behind a house, waiting until it was at close range, and then opened fire. The tank was disabled."[179]

Then-Private First Class Frank Lowry of Company A, 276th Infantry, recalls the appearance of the German defenses from the American perspective,

> The German troops were well entrenched on the steep hill north of Wingen, with positions that commanded a clear view of the north entrance to (both) underpass(es). The Germans destroyed both tanks and inflicted many casualties before the attacking companies turned back.[180]

As one of the participating Company B riflemen, Private First Class John Hartman, later remarked,

> The Krauts saw us coming a mile away and waited until we were all in range, then blasted the hell out of us from both sides. We didn't have a chance.[181]

Monitoring developments around Wingen, General Herren sent a message to Colonel Morgan at 1200, "Drive enemy out of Wingen and high ground in North by 1500 today! Use artillery with forward observer and tank support. Be prepared to repel counterattack."[182] To add emphasis to this exhortation, Herren left his CP at La Petite Pierre and drove to Colonel Morgan's CP, arriving at 1340, where he demanded a full situation briefing. He spoke with Colonel Morgan and his staff for the next forty minutes.

*** * * * ***

On the German side in Wingen, during the night, *Untersturmführer* Kürten had led the men of his *6th (headquarters) Company, 1st Battalion*, namely the *Pioneer* and *Signal Platoons* (employed as riflemen), through the westernmost railroad underpass to the houses at the western end of Wingen, south of the high railroad embankment. He and his men were occupying the homes facing this underpass when the first American attack materialized that morning.

Kürten and his men did their best to turn back the combined tank-infantry assault, and finally succeeded by separating the tanks from the foot soldiers. He wrote, "the infantry left the work to the better-suited American tanks."[183] Unprotected by infantry, the tanks began firing into the houses where they suspected German positions. While these homes were being destroyed by the fire from the tanks' main guns, Kürten and his men took to the cellars, whence they could still observe the action—the cellar windows were below the angle to which the tankers could depress their main guns.

Kürten described an incident that could have ended with more serious consequences for him and his men. Sharing their meager rations (fruit preserves found in the cellar of the abandoned house) was an American prisoner whom they had been incapable of evacuating to the church, given the fire from the tanks outside. When the shelling ceased, Kürten and his men discovered—to their great consternation—that the American still had two hand grenades in his pockets. The men of *6th Company* had taken away the prisoner's rifle, but had not bothered to search him further.

Kürten and his men must have lacked *panzerfausts*, unlike the men at the *1st Battalion* CP further to the east. At 1200, one of the men at an observation post near the CP reported two American tanks on the lower road, the one on which the schoolhouse with the joint aid station was located. As one of the tanks rolled toward the school, a few American prisoners (sick cases, not battle casualties) appeared outside with a German medic. The medic waved a

Red Cross flag at the tank, and stepped forward to warn him of the presence of an aid station in the school building. It was all to no avail—the tank crew opened fire on the school building at point-blank range, killing some of the American prisoners who had ventured outside.[184]

Carlau recalled, "A most hectic half-hour follows. Our commander, Rutschmann (the CO of *4th Company*), Mathes (a platoon leader), one of the artillery forward observers, and I are armed with *panzerfausts* and are posted behind the house and its chicken-coop." A tank unaccompanied by infantry is rather vulnerable. Mathes registered a direct hit on the American tank from thirty meters. The crew clambered out and ran for the safety of the aid station. Carlau noted that there was "great jubilation" on the German side.[185]

Shortly after 1500, two more approaching Shermans were reported by our lookout, who kept up a running commentary on the tanks' actions. One turned off on a side street, but the other kept coming, again toward the school building. Rutschmann made the "kill" this time, firing his *panzerfaust* from an attic window only eight meters away from the tank. Again, the crew survived and disembarked.*

During the afternoon, while the tank attacks were being made and turned back, our delegation sent to negotiate the turnover of wounded and captured personnel returned from their parlay with the attackers. Accompanied by an American medic, *Rottenführer* Heinz Mochner—one of Dr. Lautenschlager's medics who possessed an above-average command of the English language—had traveled the short distance to the American lines in a captured jeep under a large white flag. Coming back, Mochner reported correct treatment at the hands of the Americans. Our proposal—repatriation of American POWs presently in our custody, including both American medical officers, in exchange for expedited evacuation of our more seriously wounded men to an appropriate treatment facility—had not been accepted. *Rottenführer* Mochner had, however, received medical supplies for use in our "joint" aid station. Mochner had not been blindfolded, and reported that he had observed a larger number of tanks than we had previously recognized. Perhaps out of confidence, perhaps out of bluster, and perhaps to justify their refusal to accept our terms, one of the American officers had assured him that Wingen would be in American hands before the day ended. If he really believed this, perhaps he and his comrades believed that the delay that would be necessitated by procedures inevitably accompanying the exchange would only "burn daylight," and deprive his side of the most convenient time for the "final attack." Although this confidence was clearly overly-optimistic, at least we received

*After the previous night's panic within the *1st Battalion*, Carlau remarked in his memoir that this destruction of two American tanks "redeemed" the *Battalion*'s reputation (Carlau, 13).

much needed plasma and sulfa for treating the casualties that were steadily piling up in the aid station.

The projectile from the tank that had been fired at the aid station passed cleanly through the large classroom of the old schoolhouse, not exploding but certainly causing panic among the wounded lying on the floor. (The crew must have fired an antitank projectile, that is, solid shot; a high explosive round would have caused far more damage.) There were at least 100 wounded—from both sides—crowded in the building; many corpses had already been taken outside to make room for the living. It was a horrid scene. Together with *Untersturmführer* Carlau, Dr. Lautenschlager decided to move the aid station to a larger building that was less exposed than the schoolhouse. Between the refusal of the Americans to accept the wounded and the distinctly unpleasant experience of being fired upon by tanks, this seemed a sound decision indeed.

There was a larger building higher up, not 100 meters away, which housed the post office. With the assistance of the remaining local inhabitants, all wounded were transferred from the school building to this larger house under cover of darkness. The residents there were preparing four large Red Cross flags which were later fastened to the outside of the edifice, one on each wall.[186] During the same night, a detail from *Combat Group Wingen*, accompanied by representatives of the townsfolk, scoured the abandoned residences for food. This effort turned up mostly preserves, stored in the cellars of the houses. They had to do for now; we had used up all of the captured American rations, and long ago consumed the meager rations we had carried with us.

In the chaos of combat, not all wounded were fortunate enough to be delivered to the aid station run by Dr. Lautenschlager and his associates from both sides. Some could be brought only to the safety of the nearest house or cellar.

Private First Class Arthur Stelzer of the Communications Platoon, Headquarters Company, 1st Battalion, 179th Infantry Regiment, has been on the chow line when *Combat Group Wingen* assaulted the town on the previous day. Taking to the woods, he was hit by small arms fire, which broke his femur. Bleeding and in awful pain, Stelzer laid in the snow undetected for over thirty-six hours, near a forest path, sheltered by a wall of snow. On the night of 5 January, he was found by two soldiers of *Combat Group Wingen*, who brought him back to the nearest shelter. Apprehensive about being captured by any Germans—let alone by *SS* troops—Stelzer (who is Jewish, and whose dog tags clearly indicated his religious preference) was surprised when he was treated and left unmolested. Of the men who captured him, Stelzer later wrote to the author, "They saved my life."[187]

Howard Sylvester of Company C, 276th Infantry, was taking part in the attacks on the hedgehog positions on the Fifth Day when he was hit seven times by German machine-gun fire. He refused rescue by his buddies lest they, too, be hit. Instead, he tried to crawl back to friendly lines after darkness settled into the valley of the Moder. He failed, and was taken prisoner by some of our men, who carried him down into the cellar of a house, where they cut away his uniform and wrapped his wounds in paper bandages. According to Sylvester, there were roughly ten to fifteen wounded Germans in the same cellar—he was the only American.

"They treated me well, considering what they had to work with," Sylvester later remarked. "There was a big keg in the basement and when I asked for a drink, the medic would draw me a stein of beer from it. Days later, the German medic who saved me told me they were pulling back and would I speak for his German [wounded] comrades. He shook my hand and said, 'God bless you!' Later, on 7 January, Sylvester was rescued by men of his own outfit, Captain Greenwalt's Charlie Company, and was swiftly evacuated through medical channels. He spent the next two years in hospitals, recovering from his extensive wounds.[188]

*****

On the Zittersheim road, Lieutenant Arnest had assumed command of Company A, 276th Infantry, and had succeeded in evacuating his wounded CO, Captain Hendrickson, as well as the other victims of the day's intense combat in the vicinity of the intersection near the center railroad underpass. Able Company on this day alone had lost eight men killed in action and numerous wounded.

Lieutenant Arnest took over Able Company at a most critical moment. The company was split, with three squads fighting in the town, under his immediate control, and the rest in defensive positions outside and to the south of town. He had communications with neither his CP nor his other platoons; they were out of range of the SCR 536 walkie-talkies.

After the casualties were evacuated, Arnest again tried to move his three squads across the intersection. Together with the supporting tank, they worked out a sort of standard procedure. Some of the riflemen would point out important targets to the tank commander, while others would watch and fire into the cellar windows. Still others would watch the first and second floor windows and fire at any signs of activity there. Thus the enemy was occupied while the tank tried to fire at the targets indicated for them. In spite of this teamwork, "the men were outnumbered, outgunned, and most of the time pinned down," according to Lowry.[189]

Nevertheless, they persevered, and with hand grenades and small arms fire, the Able Company element finally succeeded in driving out and capturing thirteen members of *Combat Group Wingen* from one of the houses near the intersection. They surrendered only after firing up the last of their ammunition and in the face of certain death. Most were already wounded. To the Americans, all appeared confident and even arrogant. They were dispatched to the Able Company CP under the guard of two men.[190]

When the supporting tank turned to the rear, the small remaining force from Company A also decided to return to their original positions.* They were replaced by elements of the 2d Battalion, 274th Infantry Regiment.

Upon rejoining the rest of the company, the survivors of the fight around the intersection talked about their first experience of close combat. Lowry wrote, "Every doughboy had to admit that the Germans were damn good soldiers. One of the men remarked, 'If we live through this and ever fight another war, let's hope the Germans are on our side.' "[191]

The unit which replaced the Company A forward element, namely the 2d Battalion, 274th Infantry, under the command of Lieutenant Colonel Cheves, now had all three rifle companies forward. All of them had been ordered to "try to work their way into town [by] any way possible."[192]

The arrival of these reinforcements immediately tipped the balance at the intersection in favor of the attackers. Carlau described the combat on the Zittersheim road in his personal diary,

> In the later afternoon, we witness the attack of an American company against our *2d Company*. Two other companies, supported by tanks, outflank *Platoon Hafner* [*3d Company*]. After an hour-long fight, the remainder of the platoon is eventually taken prisoner and led away. We cannot help; we do not have reserves.[193]

The reinforcements from 2d Battalion, 274th Infantry—not part of the original plan for the day's operations—arrived as a result of the mounting pressure for success at Wingen within the American chain of command. It must have been during this disappointing and inconclusive afternoon that Brigadier General Herren came to the end of his patience and decided that only something drastic could remedy the situation at Wingen-sur-Moder. With steadily increasing demands for results, not only from the commanding general of the 45th Infantry Division—to whom he was answerable as commander of the attached task force that bore his name—but from the commanding general of VI Corps as well, Herren realized that unusual measure might be in order. The deadline for "driving out the enemy" by 1500 hours had passed without appreciable progress toward mission accomplishment.

*To the men of the 276th Infantry, it seemed standard procedure that the tankers of Company B, 781st Tank Battalion did not fight after dark, but typically returned to their assembly area at Zittersheim.

Thus, Herren was ready to change the command structure to try to find a commander who could get the job done.

During the morning, Lieutenant Colonel Cheves and his S-3, Captain Boyea, had gone up to the TF Herren CP at La Petite Pierre. After he had committed his Company G, Cheves wanted to gain a more accurate picture of the situation in and around Wingen, something he obviously felt he could not get at the 274th's regimental command post at Weiterswiller, even further away.

Colonel Richardson, the TF Herren G-3, not only welcomed the visitors cordially, but provided all requested information. After being shown the situation map, Cheves recalled, "It was then for the first time that we realized the precarious position of the American forces."[194]

As Cheves and Boyea prepared to depart, Brigadier General Herren appeared and spoke with Cheves, requesting that he give Colonel Morgan "all the help you possibly can." During the conversation, Herren apprised Cheves that Major General Brooks, commanding general of VI Corps, was "very anxious to have that situation cleaned up right away."

Returning to his CP at Puberg in the early afternoon, Cheves committed his remaining two rifle companies, Easy and Fox, and dispatched them to the east through the forest to follow George Company.

Overlooking Wingen from his vantage point from the southwest before they advanced, Cheves described what he saw,

> On the left of town was the railroad track, and a steep cliff rose sharply to a thick, dark woods. It was there that the Germans were firmly implanted and poured devastating fire onto everything below. They were also in the town, but it was impossible to distinguish which buildings they were occupying. . . . The battle in and around town increased in tempo. My men tried to edge forward. It was impossible to tell friendly fire from foe. An American tank on the road to Zittersheim, about 300 yards away, slowly turned its muzzle in our direction; and as I watched almost petrified, it let go with a broadside into the trees all around us. It was a terrible feeling to lie there hugging the ground while that monster blasted away. Finally it ceased, and I called [Lieutenant] Colonel Iverson on the radio: 'For God's sake, stop that tank from firing![195]

Cheves plea succeeded and the tank ceased firing in their direction.

During the afternoon, a squad of Company G, 274th Infantry worked its way into the first houses along the edge of the town, eventually linking up with the element of Company A, 276th Infantry that was fighting near the intersection. This linkup was rather dramatic, according to Frank Lowry,

> The 2d Battalion, 274th Infantry was ordered to attack Wingen from the west and apparently the forward elements were not informed that Company A had a platoon locked in combat inside the town. They ceased firing on the Company A men only after some of the GIs on the street swore at them in colorful English, using terminology that only a GI could use and recognize. Fortunately, there were no GI casualties in the village from this friendly fire. The men had already suffered enough bloodshed from unfriendly fire.
>
> No one could ever adequately put into words what those weary men felt as they watched the reinforcements [the three rifle companies of 2d Battalion, 274th Infantry] arrive. It was their prayers answered. They were so deeply committed that they would have been unable to successfully disengage themselves from the enemy.[196]

The same situation was described by Cheves, "It was fortunate that a serious firefight did not develop between the men of [these two companies]. Neither company knew the location and the plans of the other. This was all part of the general confusion which prevailed."[197]

* * * * *

By the end of the day on 5 January, Colonel Morgan's coordinated, four-pronged assault had accomplished something less than its goal of retaking Wingen:

- Company A, 276th Infantry never launched a full company attack, but rather pushed piecemeal reconnaissance elements into the edge of town, eventually relinquishing their toe-hold to Company G, 274th Infantry.
- Company C, 276th Infantry was repulsed in its two attempts to penetrate the hedgehog positions on the dominating heights north of Wingen, and had been withdrawn.
- Company I, 276th Infantry, with an attached platoon-sized element of survivors Company B, 276th Infantry, supported by Sherman tanks from Company B, 781st Tank Battalion, reached both railroad underpasses, but were driven off, losing both tanks.
- Only the three rifle companies of 2d Battalion, 274th Infantry remained in Wingen overnight, occupying part of the southwestern quadrant of the town.

Of this last accomplishment, Lieutenant Colonel Cheves wrote, "My battalion had accomplished virtually nothing other than to reach a location where we would be readily available for a continuation in the morning."[198]

*****

While discussing the importance of the operations on the morrow with his company commanders at his CP in Puberg, Lieutenant Colonel Cheves was summoned to meet with Brigadier General Herren and Colonel Morgan at the 276th's CP in Zittersheim. Again accompanied by his S-3, Captain Boyea, it took Cheves a full hour by jeep to negotiate the treacherously icy four kilometers of road in the deep mountain darkness.

Not wasting any time, Herren asked Cheves if he believed he could "chase those Germans out of Wingen." Receiving Cheves' affirmative answer, Herren placed Cheves "in full command of the entire operation." Confirming his belief that there were "not more than fifty Germans in town," Herren nevertheless attached the entire 276th Infantry Regiment (minus the 2d Battalion, still attached to the 313th Infantry further east) to Cheves, plus a company of tanks.*

In an attempt to leave as little as possible to chance during operations on 6 January, General Herren issued quite specific orders:

- The attack would begin at 0800, and proceed only from west to east.
- Cheves was not to direct artillery fire against the two buildings in Wingen believed to be housing American POWs in German custody (the Catholic church and the "Red Cross House"); the American prisoners were to be liberated "as soon as possible."
- Cheves was to ensure that all of his men had hand grenades and was to organize flamethrower teams.
- Cheves was to ensure his men ate a hot meal before initiating the attack.
- In addition to the fires from Cannon Company, 276th Infantry, a forward observer from the 45th Infantry Division would be available to direct "all the support you [Cheves] need."

Herren promised to join Cheves at 0600 the following morning, and departed the 276th's CP only after communicating with the commanding general, VI Corps, by telephone—and promising that Wingen would be "cleaned up" by 1100 on 6 January.[199]

*According to the 276th Regimental S-3 Journal, Brigadier General Herren was at their Zittersheim CP from 1756 until 2225 hours. Herren was joined there by Lieutenant Colonels Cheves and Iverson (CO, 3d Battalion, 276th Infantry) at 2025. Iverson departed at 2242, and Cheves at 2250. During the same time, Herren issued his orders at 2100—these subsequently became known in the journal as "Fragmentary Order by CG, TF Herren."

After Herren's departure, Cheves—who had been thoroughly surprised by the unexpected turn of events—was temporarily at a loss. Nevertheless, he quickly regained his wits, and asked to be informed about the situation throughout the 276th Infantry Regiment area of operations. Lieutenant Colonel Dan Russell, the 276th Infantry's regimental executive officer, brought Cheves up to date:

- 1st Battalion, now commanded by Captain Curtis Brooks, occupied defensive positions south of Wingen, and had effectively lost its Company B.
- 2d Battalion, under Lieutenant Colonel Cole, was still attached to the 313th Infantry Regiment, and was defending the Moder River line near Wimmenau. It was, therefore, unavailable for operations the next day.
- 3d Battalion, under Lieutenant Colonel Sid Iverson, was disposed generally north of the railroad, and had suffered heavy casualties; also, its Company K was still being held in VI Corps reserve. Iverson's battalion could muster only the equivalent of one and a half companies of riflemen.[200]

One hour before midnight, Cheves and his S-3 left the 276th regimental CP in Zittersheim and headed back to Puberg.[201]

With the direction of this highly unorthodox command arrangement, Herren did something unheard of in the US Army of World War II, and possibly unknown in any of that Army's combat since 1775: He bypassed two regimental commanders and charged a battalion commander with the accomplishment of a mission that gave him command of all of the available combat assets of a sister regiment. This unprecedented situation was made even more unusual in that Herren did not relieve either regimental commander, but rather chose to simply obviate their roles in the coming day's operations. Clearly, he did not possess faith in their abilities to carry out the impending mission, but for reasons unrecorded chose to allow them to remain officially in command of their units. Thomas Herren, a forty-nine-year old World War I combat veteran, must have been thoroughly frustrated with the course of events over the last two days, and with two major generals "breathing down his neck," made a decision based on the immediate exigencies of the situation. Thus, he must also have been very sure of Cheves' ability to accomplish the mission.

Returning to his CP in Puberg in the wee hours, Cheves called together his company commanders and staff for formulating and issuing the orders for the next day's attack. He had already made up his mind regarding the general concept of the operation:

- 2d Battalion, 274th Infantry attacks from its current positions on the southwest edge of town.
- 3d Battalion, 276th Infantry(-), but with Company C, 276th Infantry attached, renews its previous attack against the Germans positioned on the commanding ground which "loomed like a tower" [Cheves' description] on the north side of town, commencing at the same time and tied in with the attack of 2d Battalion, 274th Infantry.[202]
- 1st Battalion, 276th Infantry (minus Company C) constitutes the reserve, remaining in its current positions southeast of Wingen; it is to be prepared to repel a German counterattack.

Based on a nagging doubt about the accuracy of the estimate of "fifty Germans" in Wingen, Cheves elected to advance with one company leading the 2d Battalion, 274th Infantry attack; since the locations of the Germans were still largely uncertain, this formation gave him maximum flexibility to maneuver with his other two line companies. He chose Company F to lead the attack. Its CO, Captain Davenport, was the most experienced of the line company commanders in the battalion, and the Fox Company men were still fresh, to the extent that they were unbloodied in combat.

At the end of this sleepless night, Cheves ordered Captain Eugene Sisson's Company E to keep to the right of Fox for support, and retained First Lieutenant Cassidy's Company G in reserve. Everyone then left the CP to issue the necessary orders and make other preparations for the attack.

* * * * *

In Wingen, the commanders and staffs of *Combat Group Wingen* were making preparations of their own for the next day's expected onslaught. Under cover of darkness, all American POWs were escorted to the Church of St. Félix. *Obersturmführer* Hans Jacobs, commanding *3d Company*, and *Untersturmführer* Paul Kürten, the CO of *6th Company*, were summoned to the 1st Battalion CP. In integrated positions in houses south of the railroad embankment between the two westerly underpasses, they had beaten back three American attacks during the day. Both of these companies, as well as the supporting *4th (heavy machine-gun) Company*, had sustained severe casualties in the last twelve hours. *Hauptsturmführer* Burgstaller, the *1st Battalion* CO, decided to move the battered *3d* and *6th Companies* from their exposed forward positions during the night to the road fork adjacent to and to the east of the central railroad underpass, forward of the *1st Battalion* CP. Here, the house at the corner (called the "Blue House" in American accounts), was to be fortified as a bulwark, with field expedient anti-tank obstacles. Jacobs would take overall command of the forces of both companies in this decisive sector.[203]

Carlau and the leader of his messenger section were looking for a new, less exposed battalion command post, but were unable to locate a suitable site. The houses in the preferred locations were either too weakly built, didn't have cellars, or had been badly damaged by enemy artillery and mortar fire.

At dusk, I returned to the *3d Battalion*'s CP, and briefed *Hauptsturmführer* Kreuzinger on the day's events in the *1st Battalion* sector. I learned about the events which had transpired in the *3d Battalion* area, hearing all about the American (Company C, 276th Infantry) attacks on the hedgehog position of the *11th Company* and the *Pioneer Platoon* on the north edge of town. Things had been dicey there for a while. At one point, it had been necessary to send the *3d Battalion's* reserve, *Scharführer* Linus Maier's *3d Platoon* of *13th Company*, to assist in the defense.

During the evening, Carlau joined us in our sturdy cellar, with its vaulted ceiling. Together, we pondered the events of the coming day. We were anxiously awaiting the reinforcements we had been promised in the order we received on 3 January. Our combat strength was dwindling, and we urgently required replacements; we were also severely in need of ammunition and ration resupply. There had been several instances during the day when we believed we could hear the noise of combat not far away, and hoped that our reinforcements were already on the way.

This turned out to be a *fata morgana*, or wishful thinking.

## - III -
## The Door Slowly Closes

What we heard had probably been the firefights engaged in by the elements of the 45th Infantry Division and German units east and north of Wingen.

The night of 4/5 January had passed rather quietly for 1st and 3d Battalions of the 179th Infantry Regiment north of Wingen. The night had also been peaceful for the 180th Infantry Regiment's battalions which had advanced north from the Wingen-Wimmenau road to close the gap left by the disintegration of Task Force Hudelson on New Year's Day.

The only significant event in the sector of the 179th Infantry near Wingen was an attempted infiltration by German troops which was reported between 0415 and 0510, which was repulsed.[204] This could have been one of the patrols ordered by *Standartenführer* Schreiber to resupply *Combat Group Wingen*. The remainder of the day was spent quietly, both waiting to defend against further German advances in sector, and preparing to attack to the north in concert with the 180th Infantry on the coming day (6 January).

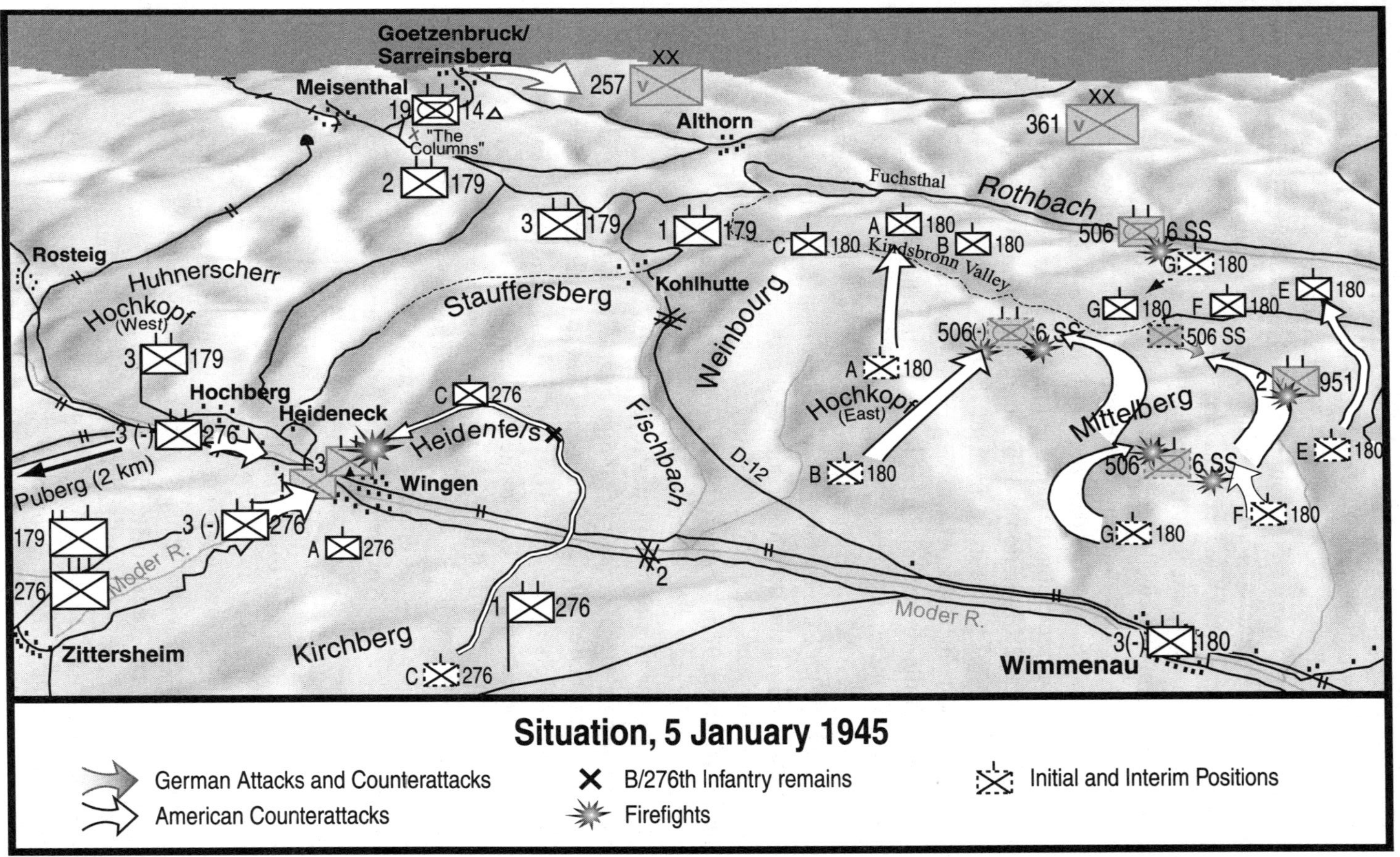
Goetzenbruck/
Sarreinsberg
Meisenthal
"The Columns"
257
XX
361
XX
Althorn
Fuchsthal
Rothbach
Kindsbronn Valley
Rosteig
Huhnerscherr
Hochkopf
(West)
Stauffersberg
Kohlhutte
Weinbourg
Hochberg
Heideneck
Heidenfels
Wingen
Fischbach
D-12
Hochkopf
(East)
Mittelberg
506 SS
6 SS
951
Puberg (2 km)
Moder R.
Zittersheim
Kirchberg
Wimmenau
Situation, 5 January 1945
German Attacks and Counterattacks
American Counterattacks
B/276th Infantry remains
Firefights
Initial and Interim Positions

Before that coordinated offensive operation could take place, however, the 1st and 2d Battalions of the 180th had a full day of combat ahead of them.

Despite the efforts of Company G, 180th Infantry to drive elements of *SS-Panzer-Grenadier Battalion 506* from their firmly entrenched positions on the Rebberg (one kilometer north of Wimmenau) on 4 January, the Germans were still there. The *SS panzer grenadiers* continued to defend their hilltop positions with the utmost tenacity, despite heavy losses.

The Americans renewed their assault at 0800 on 5 January. The 180th's 2d Battalion attempted a double envelopment of the Rebberg, with Company G swinging out to the left to attack the hill from the west, and a rifle platoon from Company F attacking the same hill from the east. After fifty minutes of this attempt, the 2d Battalion S-3 informed his regimental counterpart that Company G, "still has stuff in front of them." Only at 0915 could the 2d Battalion report that Company G was on top of the Rebberg, preparing to move through the draw to the next hill to the north, namely the Mittelberg (Elevation 353 meters).[205]

Advancing east of the Rebberg and Mittelberg later that same morning, Company F, 180th Infantry encountered the remainder of the German forces in the area. During this action, the men of the 180th's Fox Company captured forty-eight Germans, and counted thirty-six dead in the same area. Most of the POWs were from *Combat Group Stämmle* (*2d Battalion, GR 951, 361st VGD*). From interrogation of the prisoners, the American concluded that this battalion was for all intents now destroyed. Seven of the forty-eight prisoners were from *SS-Panzer-Grenadier Battalion 506*. These prisoners revealed that they believed the remainder of their battalion to have withdrawn to Hill 340 about 1,000 meters to the northwest, south of the Kindsbronn Valley.[206]

During the afternoon, Companies G and B, 180th Infantry, reported "terrific fire-fights" with the *SS panzer grenadiers* on Hill 340, where they were ensconced in well-concealed positions. They apparently held their fire until the advancing Thunderbirds were very close, then opened a devastating fire at close range. Nevertheless, the Americans pressed forward, having killed an estimated sixty Germans; captured thirty-one more (of whom eight were evacuated through medical channels); and seized one 81mm mortar, fifteen machine guns, and three (destroyed) German radios in their fighting against both *SS-Panzer-Grenadier Battalion 506* and *2d Battalion, GR 951*.[207]

At the same time, Company F was counterattacked on the Mittelberg by a German force estimated at platoon strength, although it may actually have been a company, given the casualties the German forces had sustained to this point. Fox Company killed fifteen of the attackers before the remainder withdrew. The CO of Company F, 180th Infantry reported that the German attackers fought "like paratroopers: a number of the counterattacking

German soldiers were wounded but instead of calling for help they kept firing."[208]

After Company G cleared Hill 340, they continued their advance 1,100 meters to the northeast, crossing the Kindsbronn Valley, and climbing Hill 330. Here, about 1,100 meters west of Wildenguth, they encountered not only "a couple of heavy MGs," but also a German counterattack in company strength from the valley to their rear; this counterattack "kicked them back to the road" along the Kindsbronn Valley, a distance of about 600 meters.[209]

During this engagement, First Lieutenant Pollar, the CO of Company G, 180th Infantry, was killed along with four or five of his men. Apparently, the *SS panzer grenadiers* waited for the men of George Company to pull abreast of them, then enfiladed the American flank at close range.[210] In the fading light of another winter afternoon, it was unlikely that the Americans could adequately identify the German positions. The remainder of Company G broke off its advance and dug in for the swiftly-falling night.

Of 2d Battalion, 180th Infantry's three rifle companies, Company E experienced the fewest problems, and made the most progress toward closing the gap in the southern edge of the Bitche Salient. After covering about 1,500 meters, it arrived at dusk next to the clearing just west of Wildenguth.

To the left (west) of 2d Battalion, 180th Infantry, their sister 1st Battalion had much easier going until early afternoon, when their Company B (which had been in reserve throughout the previous day) joined the firefight with Company G on Hill 340 against *SS-Panzer-Grenadier Battalion 506*.[211]

Company A crossed the Kindsbronner Valley before 1530, and by the end of the day was in positions on the forward (northern) slope of the hill halfway between the Kindsbronner Valley and the road in the Rothbach Valley, which lay only 500 meters away. They were ordered to establish a roadblock there.

Company C consolidated its positions on this day, displacing slightly to the northwest to the pass at the western end of the Rothbach Valley, and occupying the same positions held by Company C, 179th Infantry, before being dislodged by *Combat Group Wingen*. Company C, 180th Infantry was reinforced by a platoon from Company C, 179th.

At the end of the second day of the attack, Colonel Dulaney, CO of the 180th Infantry, could declare that his men had now reached the Phase Line set for the *first* day of his regiment's attack. The thickly-forested, deeply-scored, snow-bound terrain had combined with the tenacious defense of the German battalions to delay the complete closure of the gap in the Bitche Salient one more day. For while the 180th Infantry Regiment was now tied in with the 179th on their left and the 313th Infantry (with the attached 1st Battalion, 314th Infantry) on their right, they had by no means established a continuous, unbroken line of defense. There was a gap of about 1,500 meters—almost a mile—between the leftmost (westernmost) company of 2d Battalion, 180th Infantry and the rightmost (easternmost) company of 1st Battalion, 180th Infantry. In the densely-vegetated mountain terrain of the Low Vosges, this constituted an avenue of approach through which a large enemy force could still move undetected, especially at night. Colonel Dulaney was rather concerned about this and ordered the area patrolled and outposted during the coming night.[212] These measures did not succeed, however.

At 1740 hours, Colonel Dulaney issued regimental Field Order no. 180 at his CP, now on the eastern edge of Wimmenau, north of the railroad tracks. It dictated the continuation of the attack on the morrow, commencing at 0900. The 3d Battalion, in reserve throughout the last two days' actions, would relieve the 2d Battalion, and would advance on the right (east) while 1st Battalion continued the advance on the western flank of the regimental front. With these two battalions abreast, the regiment was to gain the second phase line, the ridge beyond the Rothbach Valley, between Wildenguth to the east and Melch to the west. At this point, the line would be shortened, and the 180th would be tied in with the 1st Battalion, 314th Infantry (attached to the 313th Infantry, itself attached to the 45th Infantry Division) on the right, and the 179th Infantry on the left.[213]

At nightfall, only Company G remained in contact with German forces, namely elements of *SS-Panzer-Grenadier Battalion 506*, on top of Hill 330. Upon reaching the Rothbach stream, a patrol from Company C heard the Germans chopping wood and digging in on the other side of the valley road. Company E reported at midnight that they, too, could discern the sound of the Germans digging in opposite their sector.[214]

Around 2100, Colonel Dulaney and his S-3 had some second thoughts about passing 3d Battalion through 2d Battalion in the morning. So that 3d Battalion wouldn't "have to worry" about the German resistance in front of Company G, and would not be forced to bypass the enemy pocket clearly forming to the right (east), Dulaney ordered his 2d Battalion CO to attack early in the morning to "clean out" the German forces to his front as far down as the road in the Rothbach Valley; 3d Battalion would pass through further to the east, through Company E.[215]

Although we had no way of knowing the details of the fighting to our east and north—and were praying that it was the approach of our desperately-needed reinforcements—we of *Combat Group Wingen* could not assume that help was on the way. More than once, rumors had circulated through the hard-pressed German troops in Wingen that reinforcements were fighting their way through to relieve us! There were two basic versions of the rumor. Our *2d Battalion, SS-Mountain Infantry Regiment 12* had finally arrived and was now approaching. Alternatively, some believed it was *SS-Panzer-Grenadier Battalion 506*.

There was still no word from the patrol sent back by our *1st Battalion* twenty-four hours earlier. We had no idea what had become of it. Our radiomen could still not establish contact with any German station. On the night of 5 January, we were literally and figuratively still in the dark.

Together with Carlau, we came to the decision that our situation warranted sending another patrol back to the German lines, this time, one from our *3d Battalion*. Again, the leader of the patrol was to report to the first German officer he could find, and his report should include an accurate report of our situation. We wanted the urgency of our needs to be clearly conveyed that to avoid the problems of security posed by a written report, a verbal summary had to suffice. *Hauptsturmführer* Schütze was to provide an NCO from his *13th Company* who was qualified for this task. In no time, *Unterscharführer* Karl Keefer reported to be briefed for the risky mission. We left it to him to choose two men to accompany him.

He would be exfiltrating through an enemy fully alert to the possibilities of just such an attempt. Around 1800 hours, the CP of the 179th Infantry began reporting that, "it looks as though the Krauts are trying to pull out to the north of Wingen." At the same time, the 179th assured the 180th that they, "have a company there that will try to keep them from doing it."[216] The 180th's CP passed the information to its battalions for their information and appropriate action.

## - IV -

## The Continuing Ordeal for the Citizens of Wingen

The plight of the civilian inhabitants of Wingen worsened as the fury of battle intensified with each passing hour. Many of the town's houses had already been severely damaged by American artillery, tank, and mortar fire, rendering a number unfit for continued habitation. Their occupants were forced to move to other homes to ask for shelter.[217]

Madame Annie Mathié wrote, "We learned the names of the German soldiers who walked in and out of our basement. We shared our provisions with them, since they had received no supplies."[218] On the evening of 5 January, the Mathié family had to evacuate their house, which was needed for military purposes. In the gloomy blackness, they moved to another house, in the eastern part of town, north of the eastern railroad underpass.

> With us was the brother of the former director of the [Lalique] glass factory. He was on a visit, but was trapped by the events and unable to leave the village. We headed for his brother's house [north of the railroad tracks], stumbling over fences, wires, bricks, and other debris in the darkness. Bullets whizzed around our heads, fire rushed through the sky, and smoke and flames filled the night. We had reached the underpass [to the east] which led to the house, when my grandmother said, "I can't go on anymore," and fell down. After a few gasps, she died.
>
> With great efforts, we managed to drag her up the hill to the house, where soldiers with rifles and bazookas were running around. "Where are you going?" they shouted. "Don't you know this house is under constant fire?" We were so exhausted, it didn't matter. The soldiers led us to the cellar where we stepped over dead and wounded Germans by the light of a candle. My grandmother was brought by the soldiers to the laundry room.
>
> We slumped down on a pile of coal, trying to recover from our horrors, but the freezing cold air coming through the broken cellar windows forced us to search for a better place. We found a niche under the stairway where we huddled together. We had barely settled there when a shell crashed through the wall and landed in the coal pile where we had been only a minute before. Pieces of coal slashed around the dark room, and there was a gaping hole in the wall. We had narrowly escaped death again.[219]

On 5 January, in the cellar of the Hotel Wenk with her sick mother, relatives, and neighbors, Madame Paula Felden wrote,

> After the first assault [4 January] by the Germans, the combat soon began again; machine guns barked without rest. A medic showed up in our cellar to see if there were any wounded people in it, but he could not help our mother. He said, "We are establishing a bridgehead over here [the Moder River], but if we don't receive reinforcements, we will be encircled and finished." He added that he had been with the attack on Poland and also on Russia, [and] Norway, but had never seen anything like this battle before." He said that they had come from Finland to Wingen.
>
> On 5 January, after a relatively quiet night, the shooting started all over again. That evening, more neighbors joined us after they had managed to extinguish a fire that had broken out in their house. Now, there were about 26 people in our cellar. We still had light because we owned our own generator since about 1920. This source of electricity allowed us to listen to the radio and follow the battle of Wingen. Suddenly the

lights went out, and we were in the dark except for some candlelight. The air was full of tension and fear, and whenever the shooting stopped, we could hear my mother moaning. Then, the bells of the Protestant Church began to toll. We interpreted this as a sign of an armistice and were relieved the fighting had ended. But, we were regrettably wrong. The battle went on. Apparently one of the bells had been hit and caused the other bell to toll.[220]

# - V -
# Battle Analysis

## *Communications*

By 5 January, the inability of the leaders of *Combat Group Wingen* to communicate with their higher headquarters was the decisive factor in practically every aspect of the battle for Wingen. Without communications, neither *Standartenführer* Schreiber nor *Generalmajor* Philippi could comprehend the situation in Wingen. All they knew—by virtue of a single intercepted American radio signal—was that "German troops are in Wingen." For our part, as our communicators' continued attempts to contact the outside world failed, we could not know that reinforcements were not forthcoming. The only hope for receiving instructions now rested with the patrols dispatched to the rear over the last twenty-four hours. Without communications, there would be no hope of relief, reinforcements, or resupply of ammunition and food. Even between battalions within Wingen, we relied on messengers to pass information from one end of town to the other.

Difficulties with communications were by no means limited to the German side of this battle, although the Americans' problems were not nearly so profound. In this mountainous terrain, their communications also sometimes failed, and they consequently relied heavily on wire communications. Radio turned out to be good, at best, at the short ranges between company commanders and platoon leaders, and even here sometimes failed over otherwise normal ranges.

After receiving Field Order no. 80 from Colonel Dulaney on 5 January, the CO of 3d Battalion, 180th Infantry took pains to order the stringing of a wire to his intended forward CP during the night before his attack the next morning. He clearly hoped this redundancy would facilitate uninterrupted communications during the next morning's attack.[221]

American attempts to maintain effective wire communications were hampered by a number of factors. The 180th's regimental communications officer complained that there was a dire shortage of wire—the maximum he could obtain from division was 7.2 kilometers per day for the entire regiment. This was clearly insufficient for the installation of lines to all battalions, especially in the hilly terrain of his regiment's zone, and it was not nearly enough to satisfy the needs of the battalion, which had to run wire to the companies. Also, all echelons had to maintain the lines under constant artillery and mortar fire, which repeatedly cut the lines.[222]

Establishing wire communications was also a major activity for the 276th Infantry Regiment although perhaps because of their recent commitment, they seemed to have had far more wire on hand for use. In the Narrative Report of the regiment's operations for the month of January 1945, the regimental commander noted:

> In the course of the operations at Wingen, the regimental and battalion communication platoons of the 276th Infantry overcame the loss of their principal wire lines with the fall of Wingen, and maintained uninterrupted service throughout the battle. Wires from all battalions, going to the CP at Zittersheim, had been channelized through the town of Wingen. When that point was taken by the enemy it was necessary to lay wire back through La Petite Pierre and then north to the CPs at Wimmenau and Rosteig. . . a total of 250 miles of wire was laid by the Regiment during the Wingen action. Tanks and artillery fire destroyed wire constantly, necessitating 24-hour duty by the wire crews. In addition, 150 messages a day were transmitted by radio. . . .
>
> The tide of the battle put the routes of communication in the hands of the enemy . . . an example of the hazards of carrying messages was the case of one mounted messenger who counted 10 bullet holes in his 1/4-ton vehicle [jeep] following a dispatch trip.[223]

## American Tactical Trends

After long experience on the Northern Front, we of *Combat Group Wingen* believed we knew everything there was to know about the tactics and techniques employed by the Red Army, but we were still definitely learning about our new adversaries.

What greatly impressed us from the first contact with American troops was their tendency (and their capability) to use materiel to break enemy resistance, before risking infantry. The Americans seemed to be have no shortage of artillery or mortar ammunition, and every day, our adversaries brought their armor to bear with adequate quantities of ammunition for their tanks' various weapons. Only when they believed an objective—such as a building occupied by stubborn German defenders—had been shelled to the extent that effective resistance had been neutralized, would the infantry be committed to follow up for the intended *coup de grâce*.

This certainly was a tactic we, too, had learned long ago, but were incapable of using in Wingen, due to the absence of indirect fire support—without communications of any sort with the rear, there was no German artillery or mortar fire during the battle for Wingen. Even if we had had it, it is unlikely that we could have counted on barrages sufficient to neutralize many objectives; there just wasn't enough ammunition to go around by that stage of the war.

We were particularly amazed by the almost complete absence of American reconnaissance patrols in and around Wingen. The resultant lack of "human intelligence" led to seriously mistaken assessments of the German strength in the town, and probably caused the underallocation of American forces for the mission of clearing Wingen of German defenders. Obviously, the prospects of driving out the better part of two battalions of experienced mountain infantry with attacks by little more than one inexperienced battalion at a time were dim. Had the American command been aware of the far greater German strength in Wingen, it must be assumed that they would have devoted significantly greater resources to the attacks against us.

The Americans' attacks certainly did not indicate a lack of resolve on the part of individual soldiers or leaders. If anything, there were some indications of naïveté about the effects of gunfire. Captain Hendrickson's dash across the intersection, and the charge of Company C of the 276th Infantry's men toward the bristling hedgehog position north of town—eerily reminiscent of the Great War, in that it was initiated at the shriek of a *whistle*—may certainly be interpreted as validating this. There is no doubt that manifestation of personal courage in the face of the enemy does credit to any officer. Sometimes, there is just no other way to spur men to action, to break a deadlock, or motivate them to the actions that will bring victory within their grasp. But sometimes, ill-advised valorous actions can have deleterious results, and can actually detract from mission accomplishment, especially when more casualties are suffered retrieving a gallant leader than are saved by his actions.

Although completely conversant with the rigors and requisites of night operations from our years of fighting the Soviets (it was dark for almost whole winter weeks at sixty-eight degrees north latitude!), we continued to profit from the lack of American activity during the hours of darkness. Just as they did, we planned, redistributed our dwindling ammunition, reorganized forces, and rested for about twelve hours on the nights of 4/5 and 5/6 January. Many of our men, however, had the good fortune to use the shelter of the houses we chose for our defensive positions, while most of the Americans spent the night in the snow. Perhaps this reliance on daylight operations was a function of our antagonists' inexperience. In any case, we continued to welcome the respite, and were glad for it.

## *Placement of the Joint Aid Station*

It is difficult to judge why the American tank fired on the aid station. An inadvertent, or unintentional, shot must be discounted, given the warning from American POWs and a German medic, who waved a Red Cross flag at the gunner and tank commander. Perhaps they suspected a *ruse de guerre*; maybe they simply interpreted the protestation as meaning that the gunner should not shoot directly at *them*. In any case, Dr. Lautenschlager and his American assistants clearly concluded that the building was both too exposed to direct fire *and* insufficiently clearly marked to identify it as an aid station and, therefore, a non-combatant edifice. Their previous hopes—that because the same building had been used by 1st Battalion, 179th Infantry as their aid station—were dashed with the main gun round that penetrated and exited the building, fortunately without exploding.

Dr. Lautenschlager learned from his experiences in the first location. When his facility was established in its new building, closer to the center of town, it was lavishly and unmistakable marked with Red Cross flags on all four exterior walls.

It was providential that the new facility was thus appropriately marked—it would do a lot of business on the morrow.

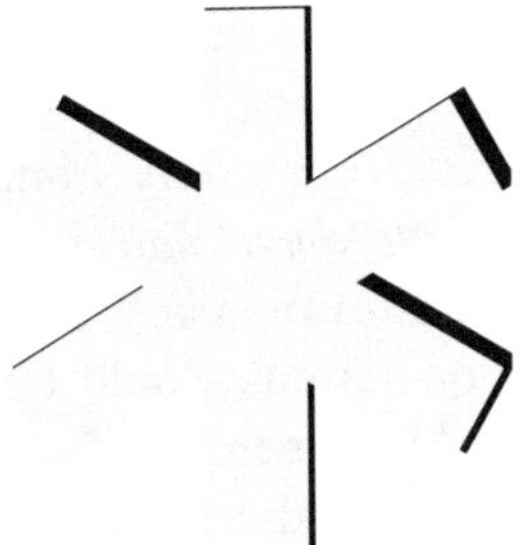

# The Sixth Day: Inferno

## - I -
## A Shift of Focus

Throughout the *Army Group G/1st Army* area, 6 January was a day of consolidation—and also a day of decision. Despite the tenuous hold on the Vosges exit at Zinswiller by *1st Battalion, GR 952* of the *361st VGD*, the icy, narrow roads leading to it were unsuitable for mass armored traffic. Instead, the *21st Panzer Division* was assembled north of Wissembourg for commitment on the Plain of Alsace. To command the upcoming thrust east of the Low Vosges, the headquarters of *XXXIX Panzer Corps* was transferred from west of Bastogne to the *1st Army*. This corps headquarters was to lead the *21st Panzer Division* and the *25th Panzer-Grenadier Division*, both of which had been withheld in *Army Group G* reserve. Later, the *10th SS-Panzer Division "Frundsberg"* would also be added to its order of battle.

Some of these decisions were prompted by *Generalleutnant* Winter, of the *Wehrmachtsführungsstab OKW* (Supreme Armed Forces Command), who had spend a day at *Generaloberst* Blaskowitz' *Army Group G* headquarters. In his report to the *Wehrmachtsführungsstab*, Winter concluded that the situation on 6 January constituted an "equilibrium of forces" between both sides in the Low Vosges. The efficiency of the infantry elements of *LXXXIX* and *XC Corps* had sunk considerably, and there was a general fatigue due to the severe weather, the difficult terrain, and plain physical exhaustion. In the region north of Wingen, the enemy was slowly gaining the upper hand. The enemy now seemed to intend to retain control of Lower Alsace.

Based on this estimate, *Generalleutnant* Winter did not believe it possible to continue the offensive out of the Lower Vosges without new reinforcements. Any success in Lower Alsace could only come with the commitment of an attack by *XXXIX Panzer Corps*. Should that armored push not materially alter the situation, Winter believed that the high command should consider seeking a decision in a battle in the region of Haguenau, employing all available mobile and infantry elements.[224]

During the early morning hours, *Army Group G* received orders from *Oberbefehlshaber West* (Supreme Command West, *Generalfeldmarschall* von Rundstedt) for its further operation against the "Anglo-American" [*sic*] forces, pointing out that the individual details of the operations would be ordered by the *Führer* himself. First, all enemy forces "between the Low Vosges and the Rhine" were to be destroyed. To prepare for the following assault operations, it would be necessary to seize the western exits of the Low Vosges, and subsequently to press through to the Saverne region, blocking the Saverne-Sarrebourg highway. The latter operation was to be executed with the utmost swiftness, and with ruthless employment of men and all available materiel. *Army Group G* was to assemble additional forces north and east of Saarbrücken in such a way that they could be employed either in a southerly direction, or via Bitche with either the *XIII SS Corps* or *XC Corps*.[225]

On this sixth day, Blaskowitz and his staff commenced the withdrawal of the *36th VGD* from the *XIII SS Corps* zone to employ it on the left flank of *LXXXIX Corps*; they also sought to move the *256th VGD* to the same corps' right flank after its relief by the *36th*. This would take several days, however, as the *36th* had only begun to disengage from its six-day-old attack against the enemy lines just east of Sarreguemines, then had to march over sixty kilometers to its new zone to relieve the undermanned and exhausted *256th VGD*. The *21st Panzer Division* was to breach the Maginot Line south of Wissembourg, and to attack toward Saverne via Soultz-sous-Forêts with the mission of blocking the Saverne Gap.

*Army Group "Oberrhein"* also scored a success on this day by widening the bridgehead beyond the Rhine River, although Drusenheim could not yet be secured from elements of Task Force Linden under the control of the 79th Infantry Division. Also, enemy resistance increased against the bridgehead established by *XIV SS-Corps* at Offendorf, as elements of Task Force Linden counterattacked near Gambsheim.[226]

## - II -
## A Crushing Blow

I must have dozed off, crouched in a corner of the cellar that belonged to the *Hotel de la Gare*, the railway hotel in Wingen which was our battalion command post over the last three days. Dead tired from another long day of combat against increasingly desperate odds, I had been trying to get an hour of rest. As I glanced around the vaulted cellar, illuminated only by a few

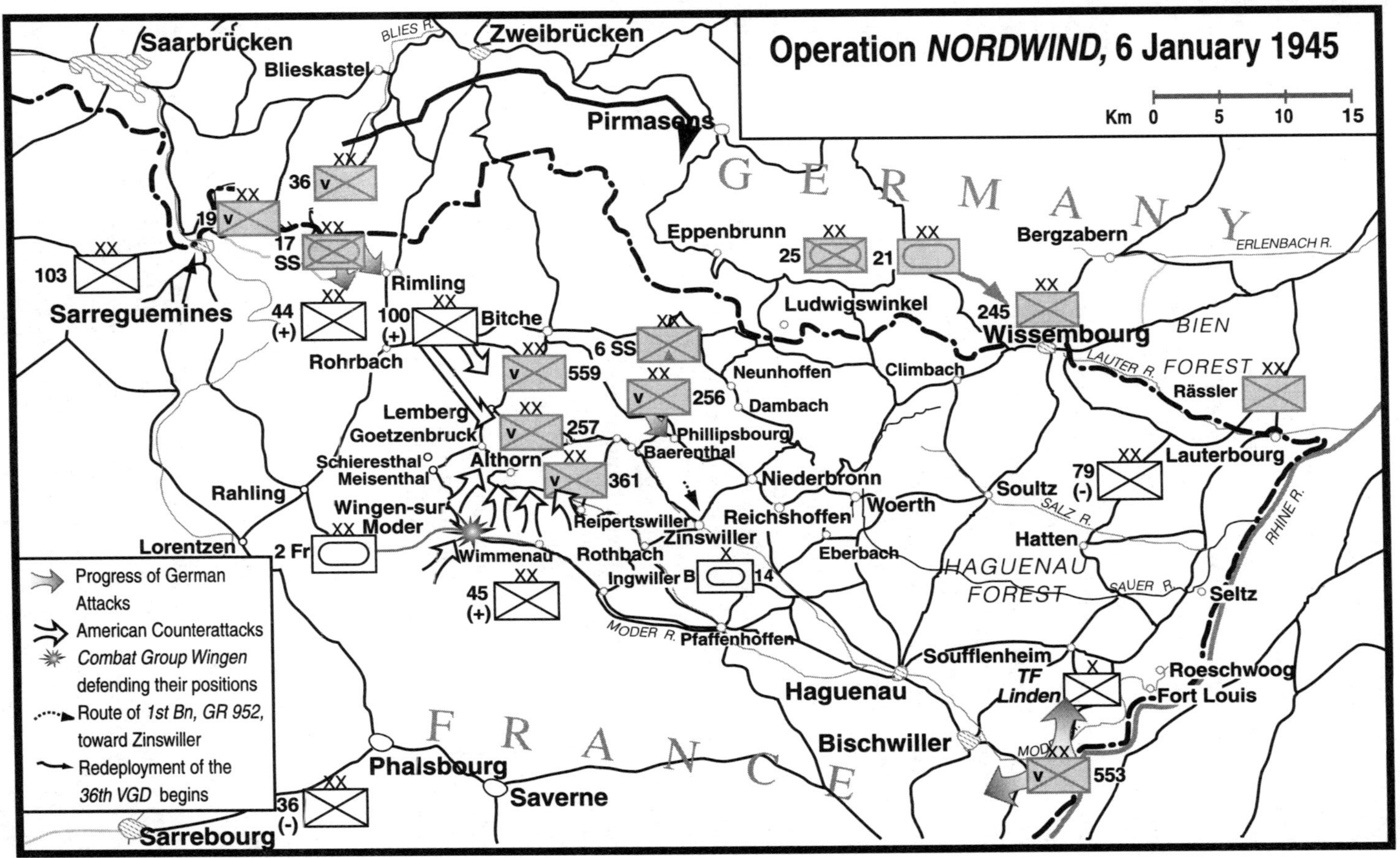
Operation NORDWIND, 6 January 1945
Km 0 5 10 15
GERMANY
FRANCE
BLIES R.
ERLENBACH R.
BIEN FOREST
LAUTER R.
RHINE R.
SALZ R.
SAUER R.
MODER R.
HAGUENAU FOREST
Saarbrücken
Blieskastel
Zweibrücken
Pirmasens
Eppenbrunn
Ludwigswinkel
Bergzabern
Wissembourg
Rässler
Lauterbourg
Seltz
Roeschwoog
Fort Louis
Sarreguemines
Rimling
Rohrbach
Bitche
Lemberg
Goetzenbruck
Schieresthal
Meisenthal
Althorn
Wingen-sur-Moder
Wimmenau
Reipertswiller
Rothbach
Ingwiller
Zinswiller
Baerenthal
Phillipsbourg
Neunhoffen
Dambach
Climbach
Niederbronn
Reichshoffen
Woerth
Eberbach
Soultz
Hatten
Soufflenheim
TF Linden
Haguenau
Bischwiller
Pfaffenhoffen
Rahling
Lorentzen
Phalsbourg
Saverne
Sarrebourg
103
19
17 SS
36
44 (+)
100 (+)
6 SS
559
256
257
361
2 Fr
45 (+)
B 14
25
21
245
79 (-)
553
36 (-)
Progress of German Attacks
American Counterattacks
Combat Group Wingen defending their positions
Route of 1st Bn, GR 952, toward Zinswiller
Redeployment of the 36th VGD begins

candles, I could dimly discern the outlines of my sleeping battalion commander, *Hauptsturmführer* Kreuzinger, a few messenger-runners, and two radio operators from our *Signal Platoon*; they, too, now slept the sleep of the forlorn, as they had worn out their radios' last batteries in attempts to establish contact with any German station. There were also three old folks of the local Alsatian population with us in the cellar since last night—a man and two elderly ladies, whose house nearby had been burned down by American artillery fire, joined us in our deep refuge.

A commotion on the street level entrance to the cellar must have awakened me. I could hear a short conversation with our guard on duty at the entrance. *Untersturmführer* Oldenburg, the regimental *Signal Platoon* leader, entered with *Hauptsturmführer* Burgstaller (the *1st Battalion* CO) and his adjutant Carlau. My watch showed 0600.

We then heard the tale of Oldenburg's adventure through the American lines. Accompanied by four NCOs of the regimental bicycle platoon, Oldenburg had left the regimental command post west of Melch last night around 2300. They used forest trails or walked directly through the woods, crossing the Fuchsthal Valley and Kohlhutte, orienting themselves mostly by the shelling of the American artillery on Wingen, where they arrived in the northeastern-most corner of town, at the Lalique glass factory at about 0530. Several times they passed so close to enemy positions that they could hear the Americans talking.[227]

This was the very first contact we had with our regiment in three days. Oldenburg was the officer who brought us our attack order on the Kaesberg on the afternoon of 3 January. Already, it seemed like our time on the Kaesberg had been in another life. What tidings did he bring? Would there be concrete news about our impending relief, about reinforcements on their way? Would he have information on the rumored breakthrough by our regiment's *2d Battalion*? What about the assault gun battalion that we were promised before we went into this bloody adventure? When would this welcome relief arrive?

In only a moment we became all too aware that there was *nothing* of the so urgently expected reinforcements heading our way. In fact, his news was plainly to the contrary. Oldenburg brought higher headquarters' orders for both of our battalions to *withdraw* from Wingen, and to subsequently occupy defensive positions in the Rothbach Valley region.

We were dumbfounded, virtually speechless for the next few minutes. "This can't be true," everyone said. It simply couldn't be that the enormous sacrifices of two full *Jäger* battalions in the accomplishment of a dangerous and risky mission were to be purely in vain.

Seeing and fully understanding our anguish, Oldenburg tried to explain. He had witnessed the developments in Schreiber's command post since his return from the Kaesberg on the night of 3 January. They had waited in increasing desperation for *any* message from us in Wingen; almost the entire radio section of the regimental Signal Platoon had done nothing else but listen to all potential frequencies, only to receive nothing but static. No messenger had turned up. The first patrol, dispatched by the *1st Battalion* late on 4 January must have been caught by the Americans; the Keefer-patrol, dispatched by us only seven hours ago, if not also caught, must have passed Oldenburg somewhere south of Kohlhutte. All that was known at Schreiber's regimental command post was a rather cryptic and short intercept from enemy radio traffic, namely "German troops in Wingen!" passed to Schreiber from *LXXXIX Corps* late on 4 January.

Although there never were telephone lines to the Wingen battalions, the line to *Generalmajor* Philippi's *361st VGD* command post in the forester's office at Bannstein functioned. Schreiber had pressed Philippi repeatedly for relief forces to make a break to Wingen. (His own *2d Battalion* had not arrived yet from Denmark.) But neither Philippi nor the *LXXXIX Corps* seemed to have any reserves that could be committed, much less an entire assault gun battalion.

During all this patient explanation by Oldenburg, it slowly dawned on us that we had been ordered to seize Wingen by a headquarters which obviously had no assurance that suitable reinforcements would be available when we succeeded in our mission. While we only knew that the order had finally come from the *361st VGD*, to which our *Combat Group Schreiber* was attached, we doubted that Philippi was its real originator; we suspected the latter to be in a much higher headquarters.

Oldenburg continued to explain that when Schreiber finally realized that *no* headquarters, at any level of the *NORDWIND* operation, had *any* forces on hand to exploit the situation at Wingen, he started urging a quick withdrawal order. He was not willing to sacrifice his *Jägers* for nothing. Finally, in the evening of 5 January, the order to withdraw from Wingen arrived at Schreiber's command post, and he promptly dispatched Oldenburg on his mission.[228]

We had listened to Oldenburg's explanations without many interruptions or questions. Perhaps we still were too stunned by this turn of events. Now that Oldenburg has finished, though, we tried to turn our minds to the obvious consequences of this unexpected change of our situation. It was already too late to organize an immediate withdrawal; the new day would be dawning in only a short while. We would have to wait for the mercy of the coming night's darkness to even have a shred of a chance to effect a withdrawal unrecognized by the enemy.

While we reached universal consent that we would have to remain in Wingen for another day, we also knew that we would have to use all means to minimize our casualties, sparing the lives and limbs of our men to the best of our capabilities. On the other hand, we would have to watch that none of our elements got cut off during the delaying actions we planned for the rest of the day. These became our two maxims governing our tactics during the coming hours.

We used the last of this night's darkness to inform our company COs of the changed situation, urging them to conduct a delay in their sectors, trading space for time to spare their men. We also warned them to carefully maintain contact with the elements on their flanks, to avoid getting cut off. As it later ironically turned out, this day would become the bloodiest one for both sides in the fighting at Wingen . . . after we had *already received the order to withdraw*.

There were many problems we had to solve during the day, not the least was the disposition of our wounded. As pressing as this concern was, we nevertheless had to set priorities, which meant that we had to make preparations for surviving this day first.

Burgstaller and Carlau informed us what changes they had made within their *1st Battalion* during the night. They had pulled back *3d Company* from its untenable positions to the south of the western underpass and had ordered its CO, Hans Jacobs, to build a makeshift stronghold in the house at the street intersection next to the center underpass ("the Blue House"). Improvised physical roadblocks on both streets to the right and the left also included antitank mines. Positions were established in and around the house for men armed with *panzerfausts*. Hans Jacobs used a captured American jeep to move his company command post into what had been the *lst Battalion* command post. Burgstaller and Carlau were moving out and looking for a new CP in the vicinity of the Roman Catholic church.

The *1st Battalion*'s *6th (headquarters) Company*, under Paul Kürten, consisting of the *Signal Platoon* and *Pioneer Platoon*, had now only a combat strength of fifteen men. They had been deployed in the vicinity of the Catholic church. In return, our *3d Battalion* had attached its headquarters company (the *15th*, under *Obersturmführer* Bullenda) with its two similar platoons to the *1st Battalion*, which had employed most of it in the vicinity of the railroad station and its freight yard to the west of the station building.

All such activities of the *1st Battalion* elements were designed to consolidate positions for combat on the new day, and they had been concluded by about 0500.[229] There had been no substantial changes within our *3d Battalion* sector during the night.

We had not finished our exchange of vital information when American artillery fire began, already long expected by us. It increased in intensity and seemed to be concentrated on two sectors, namely the wooded heights north of the railroad, and the immediate vicinity of the Catholic church, right where we were staying. After half an hour, when there was a pause in the shelling, Burgstaller and Carlau made a dash for their new command post, a partly damaged house with a storage cellar for firewood, not far away. Oldenburg stayed with us.

*****

On the other side, Brigade General Herren arrived at Cheves' 2d Battalion, 274th Infantry command post at Puberg punctually at 0600, and they immediately drove out together to the forward command (or observation) post on the easternmost rim of Puberg Forest. This position provided a perfect vista of all of Wingen, the town's portion south of the railroad embankment—and that was what counted today. Cheves left General Herren and his entourage in foxholes situated in the relative safety of a cluster of bushes, and with his officers moved to "Villa Frantz," the building he had earmarked last night as his observation post. Cheves had used most of last night to make detailed plans for today. Not trusting the intelligence he had received about the Germans' strength of "not more than fifty," he had decided to attack with his companies in depth, echeloned to the right, leading with Company F, followed by Company E on the right in support, and Company G in reserve following Company F. He split up Company H, his heavy weapons company, with its 1st Heavy Machine-gun Platoon under Captain Davenport's immediate control, in direct support of the Fox Company attack. The rest of How Company—namely the other four-gun .30-caliber water-cooled machine-gun platoon and the Heavy Mortar Platoon's six 81mm mortars—would be at his own (Cheves') disposal. The 2d Battalion's Anti-Tank Platoon (from the battalion headquarters company) would go into position at the forest edge, and support the attack with the direct fire of its three 57mm antitank guns.

Lieutenant Colonel Iverson, with elements of his 3d Battalion, 276th Infantry, would make an assault abreast with and to the left of Cheves' battalion, advancing through the forest north of the railroad embankment, the "commanding ground which loomed like a tower" over Wingen.[230] The well-placed German positions there had posed permanent threats with strong enfilading fire into all American attempts to move east of the underpass.

At 0745, the artillery began its preparatory fires, as requested. Cheves could be satisfied to this point as everything seemed to go by his plan, but for the tanks of the 781st Tank Battalion. They had still not reported to him, and were overdue.

Shortly before the scheduled completion of the artillery preparation at 0800, Captain Davenport moved out with his Fox Company, first within the safety of the forest and parallel to its edge in a southerly direction, but then

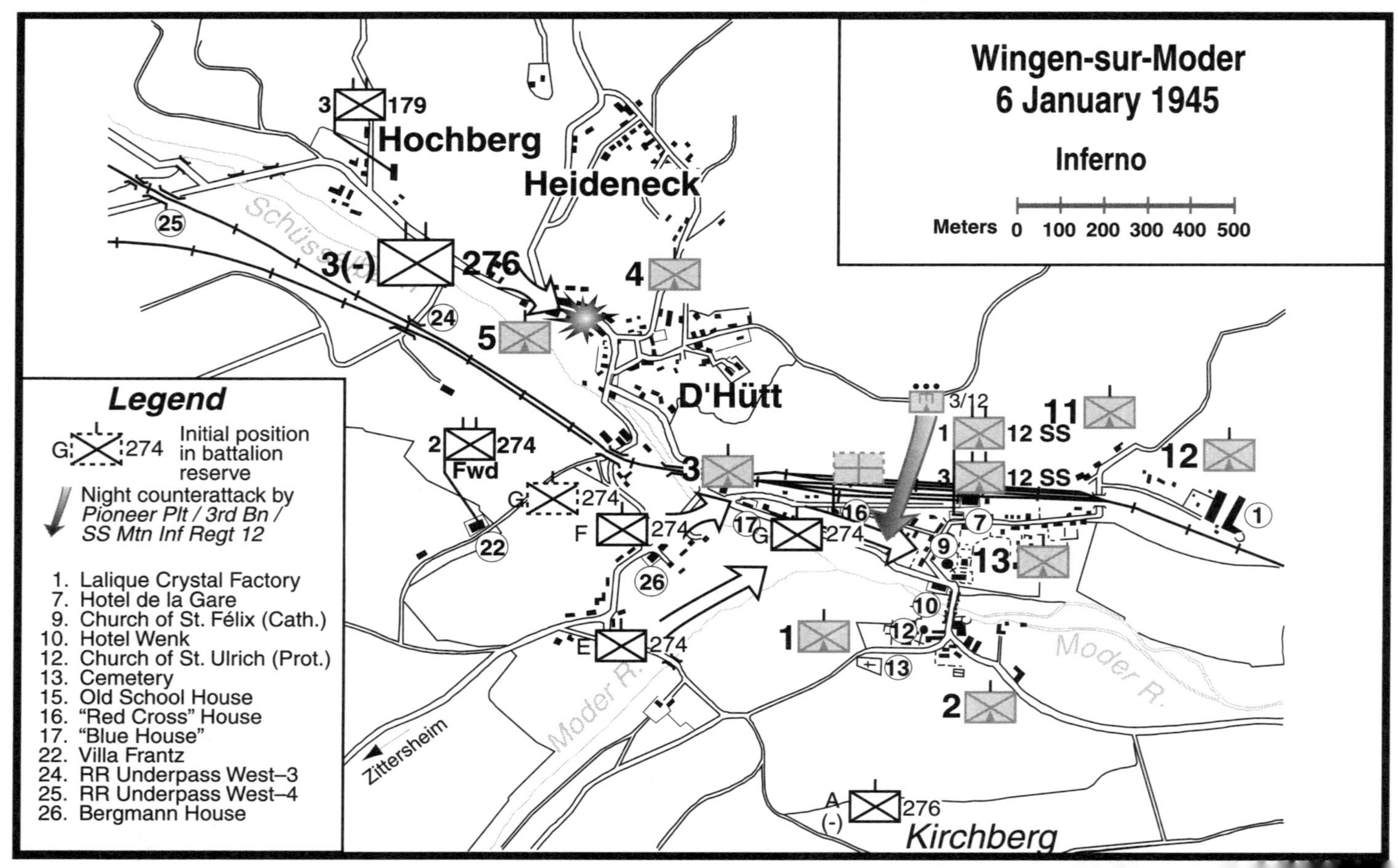

Wingen-sur-Moder
6 January 1945
Inferno
Meters 0 100 200 300 400 500
Hochberg
Heideneck
D'Hütt
Kirchberg
Moder R.
Zittersheim
179
276
274
3/12
12 SS
Fwd
Legend
Initial position in battalion reserve
Night counterattack by *Pioneer Plt / 3rd Bn / SS Mtn Inf Regt 12*
1. Lalique Crystal Factory
7. Hotel de la Gare
9. Church of St. Félix (Cath.)
10. Hotel Wenk
12. Church of St. Ulrich (Prot.)
13. Cemetery
15. Old School House
16. "Red Cross" House
17. "Blue House"
22. Villa Frantz
24. RR Underpass West–3
25. RR Underpass West–4
26. Bergmann House

at 0800 sharply onto the Zittersheim Road, toward Wingen. He was forced to advance without the support of the promised tanks, as they were still nowhere to be seen.

It was not even 0800 when General Herren summoned Lieutenant Colonel Cheves for the first time this morning. Herren wanted Cheves to order his 2d Battalion company commanders to "rush through to the far end of the town," justifying this by saying, "There are only a few Germans in there; in fact, I wouldn't be surprised if all [had] pulled out."

Not prepared to alter his initial orders, Cheves—on further prompting by the General—selected to change this to a short "Proceed through town as rapidly as possible!" to Davenport, ordering nothing but the obvious.

This early incident gave Cheves qualms about the coming hours. In retrospect he wrote, "[The General's] standing behind me was like having a huge, dark cloud hanging over my head."[231]

From his vantage point on the upper floor of Villa Frantz, Cheves had a clear view of Wingen, including the Zittersheim Road and the "deadly underpass." The artillery fire had now already shifted to plaster the forested hill north of the railroad. Included in the barrage were smoke rounds to keep the German machine gunners from observing his companies' advance. [232]

Fox Company had advanced without opposition through the entire length of the Zittersheim Road, had reached the road junction on the south side of the underpass, and was now turning east. The company had split up. The 1st Platoon (Lieutenant Chester Davis) and Captain Davenport were planning to take the right fork (*rue Principale*), followed by 3d Platoon (Lieutenant James Haines) in reserve. The 2d Platoon (Lieutenant Lino Della-Bianca) took the left fork (*rue de la Gare*, along the railroad freight yard). Ahead of them, standing in the apex of the fork, was a blue-painted, two-story house.

There was still no German small arms fire. Cheves must have wondered if General Herren had been right with his assumption that the Germans had already pulled out.

As they cautiously advanced further, the Fox men had seen a couple of corpses in the road ditch, and suddenly heard an anonymous warning, "Watch out for the Blue House!" just as small arms fire scythed into them. The Germans occupying the building had waited until the Fox men had been in full sight, only *fifteen meters* away before opening up with their deadly machine-gun fire.

This sudden burst of automatic fire from such short range killed one sergeant and wounded six other men, including the company commander, Captain Davenport, as well as his loyal radio operator PFC Wayne Morningstar. Despite their wounds, Davenport and his radio man carried on. Cheves, waiting for reports from Fox Company, finally had Davenport on the radio. "I've been wounded, but I'm not stopping. We will drive them out!" Cheves detected a deadly determination in Davenport's last sentence.

The shouted warning had come from one of the "corpses" in the roadside ditch, namely Lieutenant Edwin D. Cooke (Company B, 276th Infantry) who together with Lieutenant Glenn Peebles (1st Battalion, 276th Infantry) had participated in yesterday's attack by the composite company of 3d Battalion, 276th Infantry through the underpass. They had been unable to return with the retreating forces due to the heavy German automatic fire, which pinned them down. They had stayed in the ditch all afternoon and throughout the night, playing "possum" so effectively that the German soldiers who took their wristwatches and knives had taken them for dead. Entirely exhausted and weakened by eighteen hours' exposure, both were eventually evacuated after the fight in this immediate sector was over.

The combat for the Blue House lasted one hour, until 0930. Bazooka rockets, added to the hail of small arms fire, subdued its stubborn occupants, whereupon German resistance from the next houses on the street increased even more as the men of Fox Company tried to push on.

With his leading elements, Captain Davenport crawled along the ditch on the *rue Principale,* when this group was hit again by the enemy who had patiently waited before cutting loose with angry blasts. This time, one more sergeant was killed on the spot, as well as the radioman, Morningstar, and Davenport was wounded *twice* more, including a heavily-bleeding facial wound above the right eye. This took place immediately after Davenport had a radio conversation with his 2d Platoon leader, Lieutenant Della-Bianca, on the northern branch of the fork, along the railroad embankment. Responding to his CO's question, namely whether he could go on, Della-Bianca had answered, "I'll try, although I think it's not possible at all."

Bleeding so heavily that his vision was impaired, Davenport finally had to relinquish his command. He ordered Sergeant Charles R. Pettey, who was the ranking NCO of the small group, to carry on. After Morningstar had been killed, there had been no one to operate the radio, and Pettey ordered the radio to be destroyed.

Lieutenant Lee Mahon, the company's executive officer, had been reconnoitering for a more favorable position for his machine-gun crews. Moving up front to take command, Mahon got hit by a German sniper, who requested that he surrender. When Mahon refused and tried to scramble into a covered position, the German marksman put a round through his chest, killing the executive officer almost instantly.

Enemy automatic weapons fire came not only from the houses to Fox Company's front but also from the left flank, from the well-placed German positions on the rim of the forested heights directly beyond and above the railroad embankment. Exposed squads of Fox Company also received crossfire from their right flank, from the cemetery and houses in its vicinity. The only cover available to the harassed Fox men were shallow road ditches on both streets of the "Fork."

The 2d Platoon squads on Fox's left flank, trying to move along the railroad embankment, were using a shallow ditch. Here their German foes waited in upper-floor windows looking directly down into that ditch and, when seeing the ditch filled with an entire squad, opened fire. As one of the survivors later described the dire situation, "All we could do was lay low and pray, and hope that the Germans would think we were all dead." All but two quickly became casualties, most of them killed.

On the right side of the fork, on *rue Principale,* a squad of Lieutenant Davis' 1st Platoon was ordered to protect the right flank. In executing that order, they had to cross an open snow-covered field in plain sight of the enemy. Spotting the squad, enemy machine guns immediately cut loose at them, not only from the houses on their left, but also from the cemetery. The Fox men tried for cover on the bank of the nearby Moder River. Unable to find protection on the dry banks, they looked for refuge in the icy waters of the creek. "One by one, [they] splashed in."

The light-machine-gun section in support behind that 1st Platoon squad was also ordered to move across that open field. Taken under the same crossfire, the machine-gun section soon had one man killed and six others wounded, without being able to find a suitable position.

Being out of radio contact, the platoons tried to make up the loss of communication by firing flares to mark their positions for the supporting elements. This, however, simply drew more intense fire from the Germans.

The progress of the Fox Company attack slowed down considerably, because the Germans seemed to be everywhere. "Progress was limited to a house-by-house, room-by-room, painstaking, and costly battle for this important French town," Colonel Samuel Conley, the 274th regimental commander, wrote only weeks after the events, when the memory of the fight was still fresh. Only then "it was disclosed that the [enemy] consisted of two battalions of elite *SS* troops. . . . The fanatical determination of this enemy was demonstrated by the fact that they would not surrender until completely out of ammunition and any further resistance would have been suicide."

Cheves wrote, "The unyielding enemy was everywhere: on the hills overlooking (Fox); on the second floors, attics, first floors, and basements. The well-constructed masonry buildings provided them with an ideal fortress from which to defend."

In the house-to-house fight, Fox men resorted to hand grenades in trying to blast their way in. "The Krauts battled desperately and refused to give up.

We were fighting at a mad frenzy and had no time for prisoners," Cheves chronicled.

From his command/observation post, Cheves noticed that Davenport had so far not requested supporting fire on obstacles blocking his path. He could not know that Davenport had already been forced to relinquish command due to his heavy wounds, and that the Fox radio had been destroyed. Even if he had received such requests, there was not much Cheves could have done. At that time he still waited for the tankers to report, and he did not have an artillery forward observer with him, much less with his attacking company to direct the fire effectively. His How Company 81mm mortars had no forward observer either, and his 57mm antitank guns—even if in favorable positions—were of no use as long as friend and foe were intermingled in a close house-to-house fight. This was one of the many disadvantages of the organization of Task Force Herren, whose supporting artillery was still in the United States, completing their training.

Cheves and his small crew at Villa Frantz had been without a direct contact with Captain Davenport for an extended period already and eventually suspected that the SCR 300 radio of Fox Company had gone dead. Cheves dispatched one of his messengers with a spare radio set, who had to make a long detour to safely reach his destination. After quite a while, Captain Boyea (S-3 of the 2d Battalion, 274th Infantry) at the observation post actually received signals from Fox again.

It was Lieutenant Della-Bianca of the 2d Platoon who was on the radio, and in the conversation with his battalion commander reported being in the "Blue House," and urgently needing help, namely mortar fire on German nests of resistance to the left of the cemetery from whence Fox men received flanking fire. He added that from his vantage point, he could observe and adjust the strike of the rounds. After another ten minutes, Della-Bianca was satisfied that his targets had been obliterated by the How Company 81mm mortars.[233]

It was only then that Cheves received the report that Davenport had been evacuated, and that his replacement in command, First Lieutenant Mahon, had been killed. Appreciating that his Fox Company was close to being leaderless, he told Della-Bianca to hold fast, and that he could expect after a while that another company would pass through his remaining men to continue the attack.

Thus Fox Company's mission had come to an end. Its men had valorously done their job. They had crashed through the outer defenses of a superior enemy, which fought desperately to hold on, until being either reinforced or receiving order to withdraw. Cheves acknowledged, "These men, new to combat, had an enthusiasm and daring that no longer existed in the more experienced veteran outfits."

Fox had paid a heavy toll during the four hours of its first exposure to combat. Of the 120 men that had started at 080O, nineteen had been killed, and another forty wounded. In addition, there were many hypothermia casualties, who had also to be evacuated. Further, not all casualties had been due to enemy action; two rounds of friendly mortar fire had fatally wounded two men, and wounded another four as well.

*****

Only 300 meters to the east of the intertwined front, in our own command post in the vaulted cellar of the *Hotel de la Gare*, we were desperately waiting for direct reports from our companies.

Burgstaller and Carlau of the 1st Battalion had joined us with their little staff around 1100. Their makeshift command post in the cellar of a badly damaged house had proved too insecure and they had correctly assumed that during the crucial next hours it would be much wiser to combine our two battalion command posts.

Lacking direct communication, all we could go by was the combat noise, which slowly came our way. We knew by that single source of intelligence that the focal point of this morning's American attack seemed to be the positions occupied by our *3d Company*, specifically against its "bulwark," the "Blue House" at the fork in the road. Having no reserves, there was little we could do but trust in the leadership of Hans Jacobs, the *3d Company* commander, and wait for the developments.

*****

General Herren had already appeared twice during the morning hours at Cheves' observation post, requesting briefings on the details of the situation. His manner showed signs of impatience. Cheves offered "to take the remainder of [the] troops and personally lead a charge into town." His suggestion did not appeal to General Herren at all, though, who said he did not want to lose him as a casualty. Cheves was satisfied with this "vote of confidence," and was looking forward to work without being too-often disturbed by the general. Much later, in retrospect, Cheves sympathized with General Herren, saying that he felt Herren had been in a "delicate position;" after all, on the previous evening, Herren had promised the VI Corps commanding general, Major General Brooks, that his men would clear Wingen of the enemy on this day. Now, he was there to make certain that the job was done.

For Cheves, there was also work to be done. He had to coordinate his forces and support for the afternoon continuation of the attack. In the meantime, the tank commander had finally reported to Cheves at his command post in Villa Frantz. Captain John E. Simkins, commander of Company B, 781st Tank Battalion, arrived with his armor several hours too late to still be of assistance to the desperately fighting riflemen of Fox Company. Cheves blamed the late arrival of the tank company and the subsequent lack of direct fire support for a portion of the high losses sustained by Fox Company during its assault that morning.[234]

Cheves would have problems with his armor support most of the day, a nagging problem which was not much attenuated in its effect by the fact that its commander, Captain Simkins, had been a classmate of Cheves' at Clemson Military Academy, graduating in 1939.[235] All tanks of Company B, 781st Tank Battalion were still one kilometer from the first houses in Wingen, namely on the Zittersheim Road in the southwest. Simkins was hesitant in the employment of his tanks. During the last two days of combat he had supported 2d Battalion, 276th Infantry and had lost two of them in the previous day's action, in full sight from the upper floor of Villa Frantz. He, therefore, did not want to take new chances, and wanted to make sure that he was getting ample infantry support to protect his tanks from *panzerfaust* teams hiding in the buildings. Being a separate tank battalion, the 781st did not have any armored infantry elements in support.

After getting Cheves' assurance that there would be sufficient infantry support, Simkins went off to bring up his tanks. Cheves hoped that at least his renewed afternoon assault would be supported by tanks.

Instead, Captain Simkins eventually returned to Cheves' command post with his 1st Platoon leader, Lieutenant Gus Sitton. They were hesitant to move their tanks to the underpass as Cheves wanted, unless they were "surrounded by [friendly] infantry." Being told that there were men of Company G waiting for them at the railroad underpass, Lieutenant Sitton finally departed to get his tanks moving.

But after quite some while, the tanks (clearly seen by Cheves from his vantage point in Villa Frantz) had stopped again on the Zittersheim Road instead of making contact with Cheves' assault elements at the underpass. Listening to the radio conversation between the platoon leader in one of the tanks below, and his company commander next to Cheves in the command post, it seemed this time there was a "minefield on the road" that was keeping the tanks from proceeding further. Cheves ordered his Ammunition and Pioneer (A&P) Platoon to clear the "minefield." The A&P men arrived and simply tossed the mines aside; only then did the tanks very slowly and cautiously proceed.

Cheves had decided to hold Fox Company at the line it had reached shortly before noon, and direct his other two rifle companies to pass through Fox to continue the attack during the afternoon. George Company, under First

Lieutenant Fred ("Casey") Cassidy, was still on the left, generally on the *rue de la Gare* along the railroad embankment. Easy Company, under Captain Eugene Sisson, was on the right, along the *rue Principale.* These streets paralleled each other, some fifty to sixty meters apart, and ran basically east-west.

The second attack of Cheves' battalion was to start at 1300, and was to be proceeded by an artillery barrage, to concentrate on the wooded heights north of the railroad embankment. General Herren was dismayed by this "late" start of the renewed attack. He had not taken into account that it had taken Cheves an hour to relay the firing orders to the artillery observer of the 160th Field Artillery Battalion, who was not at Villa Frantz, but with the 1st Battalion, 276th Infantry at the Kirchberg, almost two kilometers away.

*****

Both battalion staffs of *Combat Group Wingen* bunched together in the vaulted cellar of the *Hotel de la Gare,* with no direct report from any of our companies. All we could go by was the battle noise that now seemed only 200 meters away to the west.

Around 1300 we experienced another artillery barrage of at least fifteen minutes' duration, directed against the suspected entrenchments of our companies in the woods north of the railway station. We could only hope that our men had dug their foxholes deeply enough to overcome this terrific fire.

*****

Cheves hoped that his renewed attack—that punctually started at 1300—would proceed at a faster pace, now that the enemy should have "softened." By now he knew that there must be a lot more than "only fifty" Germans in the town. His men had captured at least fifty prisoners during the morning attack.

His hopes, however, would not be realized. After the war, he recalled, "Our progress, however, continued painfully slow [*sic*]. It was a slugging match against an experienced, determined enemy, the best in the German Army. My foot soldiers battled for every house, crawling in ditches, jumping through windows, blasting through doors, and fighting hand-to-hand combat in its most primitive, savage form."

In addition to the determined enemy in the houses to their front, both George and Easy Companies experienced continuous crossfire from the vicinity of the cemetery on their right and from the dominating terrain north of the railroad embankment on their left. Of these threats, the latter was the more formidable. Cheves remarked, "From well-concealed fortifications in the thick forest, an unseen enemy poured murderous enfilade fire into our flanks." Cheves had planned the support of Company C, 276th Infantry in such a way that this company should attack parallel to his own forces through the adjacent northern wooded high ground to eliminate exactly this enemy enfilade fire.

Captain Greenwalt's Company C, 276th Infantry had launched its attack at 1100 and had reported to its regiment at 1434, "still moving slowly; 4 to 5 enemy in each dugout with automatic weapons."[236] At 1620, the 276th Infantry CP at Zittersheim received the report from Lieutenant Colonel Iverson, its 3d Battalion commander, that one platoon from Company I and one from Company B had now been attached to the attacking Charlie Company, but still the progress made was "very slow."[237] In his chronicle, Cheves just states that the task for Company C, 276th Infantry had turned out to be "insurmountable" for them.

Cheves' Heavy Weapons Company had displaced its heavy machine guns forward to give both attacking rifle companies closer support. One of their water-cooled .30 caliber heavy machine-gun crews had taken position in a second story window of the Bergmann house on the southeast side of the Zittersheim Road. This position offered a good field of observation and fire not only to the east of Wingen—the direction in which the rifle companies were advancing—but also to the forested high ground north of the railroad embankment.

George Company had started its attack in a column of platoons—1st, 2d, and 3d—along the railroad embankment. Lieutenant Cassidy employed a simple but effective technique of fire and movement; he concentrated the fires of his company's three 60mm mortars, two .30-caliber air-cooled machine guns, and nine BARs on singular points of enemy resistance, while his men dashed from house to house for cover. This technique of consolidated, overwhelming fire, enabled him and his men to reach their assault position beyond the first four houses which had already been cleared by Fox Company, but there they were stopped by the deadly fire from the high ground on the left. Opening up with all firepower on hand, alternately to the high ground, and to the machine-gun nests in the vicinity of the cemetery on the right, Cassidy's men momentarily suppressed the enemy crossfire, and enabled a further advance of George Company's lead platoon.

To the right of Company G, Easy Company was trying to advance also. After it had reached the last houses cleared by Fox Company before noon, Easy also attacked in a column of platoons, with the its 1st Platoon (Lieutenant Wayne Meshier) leading. The attack bogged down immediately when this platoon met its first resistance. Lieutenant Meshier was searching for a more favorable route of advance, but was wounded when jumping through a window. He dove under a disabled jeep, and was killed when he was hit again, this time by fire from the cemetery. "The constant enemy fire made it suicide to stick your neck out," reported Sergeant Ernest Swain, who at that time was accompanying Meshier. Only when the tanks finally arrived—again, belatedly—did the advance of both companies gain momentum.

Cheves and General Herren, who was constantly inquiring after the latest developments in the situation, could have been nearly satisfied with the much better progress being made by the afternoon attack, especially in comparison with the morning's effort by Fox Company. Nevertheless, the enfilading fires from the high ground to the left were holding up further progress. It did not take Cassidy, whose George Company was most exposed to this constant threat, long to explode during a radio message to Lieutenant Colonel Cheves, "For God's sake, can't somebody do something about that hill to our left? Where is the 276th that is supposed to be up there?"

During a renewed conversation with Lieutenant Colonel Iverson on this matter, Cheves found out—to his horror—that the 276th elements had not advanced very far at all. They had gained only little of the enemy-occupied high ground, and were now more than 500 meters *behind* the leading elements of the attacking forces in the town. This left a huge gap to the left rear of George Company. Having at least now a more clearly defined location of the 276th troop positions, Cheves could provide Cassidy some help. Before getting the exact location of the 276th troops in the northern wooded heights, however, it was impossible to neutralize that area for fear of hitting friendly elements, whose foremost location was indiscernible. Now, he called for additional artillery and mortar fire onto the high ground to the north. This seemed to satisfy Cassidy, for the moment.

Around 1645, about an hour before dark, Captain Simkins, the tank company commander, approached Cheves and requested permission to withdraw his tanks to Zittersheim for the night. He said his tanks were out of ammunition and fuel, and needed servicing. Cheves replied with an emphatic "No!" He could not *imagine* that any combat troops attached to his unit would move back to rear areas to stay in comfortable quarters for the night, while his men were freezing and fighting for their lives.

Dusk settled slowly, and both George and Easy Companies seemed to be in the home stretch, finally making good progress, with apparently only a few houses left to be cleared. This pleased General Herren, who departed with the impression that he had kept his word, given last night to General Brooks. Cheves could be satisfied too, but if he was, it was too early.

Just then, the tank company commanding officer again appeared to nonchalantly announce that Herren had just given him permission to withdraw his tanks for the night, pointing through the window to the tanks that were moving back toward Zittersheim. There was nothing more that Cheves could do.

When pulling out and leaving the riflemen alone with their job, just shortly before it was actually finished, one of the tankers' parting shot was a shout that, "We don't fight at night!" Not surprisingly, his remark drew vicious curses from the soldiers of George Company, as they girded for a freezing night to be spent within a few meters of hundreds of *Waffen-SS* mountain infantrymen.

*****

In our joint command post, both battalions' staffs were trying to concentrate on planning tonight's breakout, but had to postpone the planning for a more essential task—first, we had to survive.

Shortly after the afternoon's artillery barrage lifted, between the steadily rising, terrific noise caused by the small arms of both sides, we heard the dry, "cracking" sounds of tank cannon fire, occasionally coupled with the din caused by tank tracks grinding through the snow and across cobblestones as the tankers shifted their positions. All of the combat noise that only hours ago had originated in the vicinity of the Blue House at the street fork, slowly and menacingly approached our cellar refuge.[238]

Lacking any direct communication with our fighting companies and not receiving reports from them, Carlau, accompanied by one of his NCOs, went up into the attic of a nearby damaged house to survey the situation. In the gathering darkness, he could not discern anything definite.

It was high time for us to act. From our underground fastness, we could imagine without much fantasy that it would not take more than a few minutes until the Americans would be knocking on our door. We had to get out and immediately organize a counterattack, otherwise we would get smoked out—or worse.*

Both Carlau and I took all able-bodied men in our immediate vicinity, armed with whatever we had—mostly submachine guns and rifles—and ran out into the dark of the street, lit eerily by the flickering fire of burning

*Another reason for our immediate counterattack was that we feared a breakthrough of the American forces to the Catholic church, which would liberate the 256 American prisoners there. In sober retrospect, this fear seems to have been unfounded: any liberation of the (already unguarded) American POWs would have caused the American side more problems by the chaos it would have created in evacuating them to their rear.

houses. Jointly, our small force of some eight to ten men quickly rounded the corner of the hotel building to the right of our cellar exit, and ran up the short street to the railroad station, which still seemed to be in our hands.

Crossing the multi-track railroad yard, we were met by our *3d Battalion pioneer platoon* under *Oberscharführer* Horst Stiehl. We had reached him by messenger in his position on the wooded high ground with the order to reinforce our counterattack with his platoon of some forty men. It seemed like his platoon was dispensable, at least for the moment, for with the onset of night, the Americans had already quit their attack on our high ground positions for the day. Our force had now a strength of close to fifty men.

After shortly assembling at the far end of the freight yard near the steep embankment, we split up in two groups of about equal strength. The one further in the west was led by Burgstaller, the *1st Battalion* CO, the more easterly one by Carlau and me.

The pure darkness was broken only in a few places lit up by the flames of buildings set afire by the American artillery. Thanks to the limited observation, our little force reached the railroad freight yard without being detected by the Americans. But for the same reason we could not make out any specific target down below between the houses of Wingen, where the American spearhead must be. Only occasional muzzle flashes in the dark gave them away. Going also by the battle noise, they must have been on this side of our aid station by now, and there did not seem to be any further nests of German resistance in the houses between the aid station and the Catholic church-. For all we knew, or rather assumed, the aid station must have already fallen into American hands during the last daylight hours.

Mustering the courage of the desperate, we stormed across the railroad tracks, crossed the *rue de la Gare* and charged over the fences, yelling and firing with all we could still muster—mindless of the ammo shortage, blind to the response of an occasional American machine gun. We soon recognized that we must have hit the unsuspecting American spearhead perpendicularly in its left flank. It seemed like we caught the enemy by surprise, and eventually we felt that we must have stopped his previous advance; his responses became progressively weaker, and at least part of his forces might have even withdrawn some distance to the west. Leaving Stiehl with his platoon in selected positions commanding the scene, Burgstaller, Carlau, and I returned to the CP with our messengers.

We felt utterly exhausted, and the same seemed to be true for the enemy. The noise almost abruptly quieted down except for some occasional small arms fire.

As the fires in the burning houses flickered and died to embers, the deep mountain darkness enveloped us. The battle of the day seemed to be over.[239]

*****

From his vantage point in Villa Frantz, Lieutenant Colonel Cheves had just witnessed on the street below the withdrawal of the tanks of 1st Platoon, Company B, 781st Tank Battalion. They were heading back to Zittersheim and he knew that he would not see them again this day.

Cheves felt left alone with his problems, the most important of them being that he perceived his forces to be overextended. This perception stemmed from his realization that the reinforced Company C of his sister regiment, the 276th Infantry, was far behind the spearheads of his Companies E and G in town. Without control of the high ground paralleling his force in the village, his left flank was exposed. Now that the tanks had left for good with the General's permission, and the light fading rapidly, Cheves did not see how he could still clear the town before dark. He therefore issued orders to halt the attack and organize a defense for the night.[240]

Cheves' orders were barely out on the radio to his still struggling rifle companies when we started our counterattack. It was already quite dark, and the tanks had left the rifle companies they were supposed to support. Morale among leaders and led in the rifle companies was approaching a low point for the day, as the men of 2d Battalion, 274th Infantry began to feel abandoned and alone in the quickening gloom. The German counterattack came at precisely this psychologically vulnerable moment. For Cheves in his elevated command post, our counterattack started with a "series of loud explosions," followed by a bright glow over the rooftops to the silhouetted buildings. He could see the Germans charging across the railroad tracks, swooping down the embankment into the flank of his George Company. The attack had driven through the center of the company, isolating his most advanced elements from the forces further in the rear.

Cheves' first thought was that the enemy finally had been reinforced. For him it was a "known fact that the Germans were striving desperately to exploit [their] breakthrough, the deepest into the Seventh Army lines by several miles."

The German counterattack had hit both companies, Easy and George, but it hit George the hardest because it was the nearest to the German defenses and was the most exposed. George Company's Sergeant George Krumme had cut loose with a machine gun in rapid fire and thus had succeeded in stopping the attack for a short while, long enough for his CO, First Lieutenant Cassidy, to move back those of his men who had been caught out in the open. He moved them to some houses at the edge of the town. The night that now followed was "to this day the longest" in his life; he had left the majority of his men in eastern Wingen and was unaware of their fate.[241] On the radio,

Cassidy reported to Cheves that he had only "five or six men left with him, and that he had been cut off from the rest." Sisson's Easy Company was also hit.

Rounding up the remaining men of Fox Company, Cheves couldn't find Lieutenant Chester Davis, who was now Fox's senior surviving lieutenant. Nevertheless, he tried to organize the rest of his battalion's men into a perimeter defense against German forces, possibly already reinforced by new infiltration.

Cheves was worried, and had "visions of losing [his] entire battalion in [the] first fight." He feared "two or three enemy battalions bearing down on [his battalion] from all directions."[242]

He ordered his Heavy Weapons Company and the supporting 160th Field Artillery Battalion to concentrate their fires around the railroad station.

In his After Action Report to General Patch, commanding general of the Seventh Army, Colonel Conley (CO, 274th Infantry) wrote,

> [The] ferocious charge [by the enemy] succeeded in splitting and isolating the attacking companies. Everything was utter confusion. . . . The fires from the many burning buildings to the rear of E and G [companies] proved more of an advantage to the enemy as it afforded them silhouetted targets whenever the men attempted to move. Scenes of death were everywhere as the two forces intermingled in a battle for life amidst exploding hand grenades, bazooka rounds crashing through buildings, and detonating artillery shells.
>
> The enemy counterattack was successful insofar as delaying the attack was concerned, and the main forces of L and G [companies] were required to establish a defensive position for the night some 200 yards to the rear of the furthest point of advance where a reorganization could be effected. [On the other hand] numerous gallant groups of both companies held out all night in isolated buildings surrounded by the enemy.[243]

Although 2d Battalion, 274th Infantry's intentions of "hunkering down" for the night were interrupted by our counterattack, the other American units in Wingen did not suffer the same interference with their plans. At 1900, Lieutenant Colonel Iverson also ordered Company C (attached to his 3d Battalion, 276th Infantry) to dig in for the night in its current location. This order corresponded with the intentions of the TF Herren G-3, who at 2100—after having been briefed on the situation at Wingen—ordered, "Dig in, hold, patrol!"[244]

Over in the zone of 1st Battalion, 276th Infantry, a more aggressive plan took shape. There, the battalion commander requested intermittent artillery harassing fire for the coming night on the high ground north of Wingen, and at 2335 acknowledged that artillery fire is “falling nicely.”[245]

After the German counterattack, the opinion among participants on the American side about further German action was a matter of controversy. In a special report on “Activity in Wingen,” the S-2 of the 179th Infantry wrote on the evening of 6 January that the German forces, “aware of their being cut off from their main forces, seem determined in their efforts to keep control of the town. Possibly believing and waiting for reinforcements and heavy weapons support from the north-northeast.”[246]

The intelligence assessment of the 274th Infantry in its Unit Report 9 for 5/6 January was more ambivalent. The regimental S-2 wrote, “Enemy in Wingen is capable of withdrawing or of staying and fighting to the last man. Either capability may be put into effect immediately.” The author then added this somewhat declamatory rejoinder, “Neither plan will have any material effect on our mission.”[247]

At about the same time, Colonel Morgan and his staff of the 276th Infantry Regiment arrived at the most accurate and factual conclusions, probably based on their more extensive contact with prisoners taken from *Combat Group Wingen*, “Enemy intends to defend Wingen . . . awaiting artillery support and reinforcements. Enemy contemplates making a breakthrough from Wingen if no contact is made with [other] troops in this area.”[248]

*****

After returning from the successful counterattack to our joint command post in the cellar, we tried to start our deliberations again at the point at which we had been interrupted. We were now really pressed for time, as the darkness for which we had waited was already upon us. What did we have to consider and plan in detail if we wanted to successfully disengage our elements from the enemy tonight, as the first stage of our exfiltration from Wingen?

There were a number of issues that required immediate resolution. What were we to do with our American prisoners of war? We decided to leave them in the church, because we would not have enough men to guard them—there were 256 by latest count. Besides, they would only impede our withdrawal, and perhaps even give us away. Evacuating them with us was simply impractical. We did, however, decide to take the eight US officer POWs with us to the German lines, something like a bounty or a trophy, as a testimony of our success in Wingen.

We were fully aware of the fact that our withdrawal would be on a demanding cross-country course, and that we had many of our own soldiers who, although only slightly wounded, would be unable to walk and climb the mountains on our clandestine exfiltration routes. We would have to leave them here in Wingen to be soon captured, but then hopefully evacuated and treated in US Army hospitals. We had to leave it to our company leaders to decide whom to take with us on the march, and whom to leave behind due to unfitness for the upcoming stress.

Since early afternoon we had had no communication with our aid station; it must already have been captured by American troops. The only comfort we had was that our many wounded would be cared for by Dr. Lautenschlager, whom we knew would remain in charge. We trusted him implicitly to do his best to have our wounded evacuated to American hospitals as soon as possible.

What actually happened at the aid station during the afternoon of this day, we learned only decades later.

## - III -
## Good Faith and Betrayal

The first American unit approaching the "Red Cross House" on that day was the 2d Platoon of Fox Company, 274th Infantry during their attack.[249] According to their company history, men of the 2d Platoon located *Hauptsturmführer* Dr. Hans Lautenschlager and the American medical lieutenant, who informed the Fox men that all German and American wounded had been transferred last night from the schoolhouse to another building nearby.* Until then, orders had been issued and obeyed not to shoot at the school since that hosted an aid station. Now, after this had been cleared, orders were given for the Americans to fire at the schoolhouse with everything available.

*Hauptsturmführer* Dr. Lautenschlager had been out of contact with his battalion commander and staff since the *1st Battalion* had relinquished its original command post next to the aid station during the night. Now he was definitely on his own, because there was no hope that the situation would change. He had to decide for himself what was in his wounded charges' best interests.

Lautenschlager subsequently had a long discussion with his American medical colleague from 1st Battalion, 179th Infantry, during which he made the following proposal: he would release from custody the medical captain,

*The information in Fajardo's book that the wounded had been taken to the church is incorrect.

his assistant, and his ten American medics, together with the twenty American soldier sick-cases and wounded in the aid station, under the condition that all German wounded were to be evacuated to American hospitals for treatment without delay. For himself, Lautenschlager wanted the assurance that, being the only medical officer of *Combat Group Wingen,* after successfully turning over the aid station, he would be returned to his unit to further care for his men who might subsequently become casualties.[250]

The American medical captain was satisfied with this arrangement, and went with him to the command post of 2d Battalion, 274th Infantry in Villa Frantz, escorted by American soldiers, presumably from Company G, 274th Infantry, since it was this company that attacked along the *rue de la Gare,* on which the "Red Cross House" was situated. On the way, they were called into the Bergmann House on the Zittersheim road. There was a heavy machine-gun squad of Company H, 274th Infantry in position there and also more American and German wounded, who were promptly attended to by Dr. Lautenschlager as well.[251]

When the party arrived at Villa Frantz, they were met not only by Lieutenant Colonel Cheves and his S-3, Captain Boyea, but also by Major Paul Durbin, at that time regimental S-2 of the 274th Infantry. Later, this group was joined by Brigadier General Herren.[252]

Major Durbin later recalled that Dr. Lautenschlager's "concern was that his aid station was in danger of fire from American troops. His exact words were, 'You will be killing your own men!' indicating that there were a number of wounded Americans as well as Germans."[253]

Dr. Lautenschlager further related the terms of his agreement with the 1st Battalion, 179th Infantry's surgeon, "The American medical officer assured me that the American commanding officer had accepted our mutual agreement. Thereupon the *3d Company* (in positions directly in front of the aid station) ceased its resistance, and the aid station was turned over to the American troops." Dr. Lautenschlager wrote, "The bitter house-to-house fight had approached our aid station. In the interest of the more than 100 German wounded and 20 American wounded, I contacted the commanding officer of the *3d Company* and requested that he cease his resistance." That last house in front of the aid station at the time of Lautenschlager's request was occupied by the *3d Company*'s commander, the wounded *Obersturmführer* Jacobs and the last seven of his men, fighting out of the cellar.[254]

Lautenschlager continued, "I was then brought to the American aid station, where I could talk once again with the American medical officer and his assistant. The captain as well as his commanding officer, a major, both thanked me for the good treatment of their wounded and medical personnel."[255]

So far, so good, but when Dr. Lautenschlager was ready to return to German lines, the Americans reneged on the agreement made by their doctor. Instead, Lautenschlager was taken prisoner. The reason given was that the riflemen bringing him to the command post had failed to blindfold him. As a result, he had seen the disposition of American troops in the area, and that knowledge would "jeopardize Trailblazer men." The decision must have come from General Herren, who also gave the same reason for his decision, when Major Durbin protested that the German was "under protection of a flag of truce." Durbin was requested to bring Dr. Lautenschlager to the 274th's CP for questioning, together with four other German POWs. Durbin wrote later, "The very angry German medical officer (he had his Red Cross prominently displayed) . . . rode in front with me, hands on his head. I don't like to think of myself in that situation." Immediately thereafter, Major Durbin asked to be transferred from his S-2 job, and went to the 3d Battalion, 274th Infantry to serve as Lieutenant Colonel Karl Landstrom's battalion executive officer.[256]

As will be seen, the ongoing combat forestalled a quick evacuation of the aid station, which was ultimately only evacuated on the afternoon of 7 January.

## - IV -
## The Continuing Ordeal for the Citizens of Wingen

The plight of those members of the civilian population who had chosen to stay in Wingen—or who had been trapped in their homes by the sudden events before they could get away—was worsening with the approach of close combat, and with each artillery barrage. Sometime during the afternoon, black billows of smoke started to curl skywards: the Hotel Wenk had received an artillery hit, causing a fire in its cellar.

Paula Felden, the owner of Hotel Wenk, later wrote about the suffering she and twenty-five other civilians endured on this day. They had looked for safety in the hotel's cellar and found that,

> Time crept by. Starting at daylight, the fighting increased and was unending. Around 1 PM there began an incredible concentration of gunfire. Until then, we had been praying continuously, but now we fell into silence. We were panic stricken and paralyzed by fear and horror. We huddled together in small, silent groups, desperation in our souls.
>
> After about an hour, we began to smell smoke. One of the women opened the door leading up to the hall. *The coke was on fire!* An entire

box car of coke, which we had received about six weeks before. The smoke and gas filled our cellar all at once. Only instant flight could save our lives! No time was lost. Women grabbed their children, all only barely dressed, and some with only slippers. The men carried my gravely ill mother. It was an instant, desperate flight into the uncertain.

We ran into the open daylight as fast as we could. Stepping over dead bodies, tumbling over weapons and debris, to reach the adjacent garage. The chickens and pigs could not be saved, and burned to death. A few courageous men and women jumped back into the cellar to get whatever they could to protect us from the freezing weather. Burning trucks loaded with ammunition blocked our way.

After about two hours, we fled from the garage to a neighbor's house across the street, but the Germans had withdrawn into it. We wanted to leave, but they permitted us to stay there, and they left instead. An hour later, they came back, under orders of their commanding officer; so we went back out on the road into the midst of a terrifying shower of bullets and debris.*

Somehow, we managed to reach the glass factory [north of the railroad tracks, at the east end of town]. We looked for a cellar, but could not find one. Tortured by hunger, pain, and fear, that night did not seem to end.[257]

With her relatives and friends, Madame Annie Mathié had reached one of the houses in the northeasternmost corner of Wingen, beyond the eastern railroad underpass, on the previous night. They had spent the day in the cellar of that house together with German soldiers and their wounded comrades. Annie Mathié chronicles that,

The last day was the worst. The squad of German soldiers occupying this house kept running in and out of the cellar. Orders were given and the soldiers took turns, relieving each other. Down below the house was a wall, where they had several machine guns positioned which fired constantly. Each shot drew answers from the other side. Every time when the house or they received an artillery hit, we drew still closer together. American artillery in positions at Zittersheim drummed on Wingen more and more.

The fear and terror we suffered during this day defies all description. We had nothing to eat. In the haste of leaving our house we had brought the laundry instead of the grocery bag. The hunger was not as bad as the thirst. The German soldiers who stayed with us shared whatever they had with us, so we survived.

*This was in the sector of our *2d Company.*

The number of soldiers continued to diminish. We now knew their names, and when we asked, "Where is Franz, where is Peter?" they answered, "They've had it!" Wounded kept being brought into the cellar continuously, and a medic took care of them, but there was a shortage of medication and medical supplies. The last night in the cellar, or better, the inferno, still lay ahead of us.[258]

## - V -
## The Door Closes

During this period, the line of contact of the opposing forces ran from approximately Meisenthal in the west to Reipertswiller in the east. In the west, it was occupied on the American side by the 179th Infantry Regiment, which faced elements of the *257th VGD* (namely, *GR 457*) in the *XC Corps* sector. In the east, the American side was occupied by the 180th Infantry Regiment, generally facing the *361st VGD* (here with *Combat Group Schreiber* of the *NORD Division*) in the sector of the *LXXXIX Corps*.

This was the first day on which the 180th Infantry Regiment was to be joined in its attack to the north by its sister regiment, the 179th Infantry. The men of the 179th had spent the last few days holding entrenched positions, generally between "The Columns" crossroads south of Meisenthal and the D-12 district road leading from Kohlhutte to Wimmenau.

The objective for the 180th was to be the Zintsel Valley on both sides of Mouterhouse, six kilometers to the north of their present line. The objectives of the 179th were to be first Althorn and then the Breitenbach Valley between Marteau Neuf and Lemberg. The 1st Battalion, 314th Infantry Regiment (presently at Wildenguth) was also to join in, on the right of the 180th. The total effect would be to close the last few remaining kilometers of the original ten-kilometer hole torn in the American lines in the wake of the retreat of Task Force Hudelson. It would also completely isolate *Combat Group Wingen*.

In his regimental Field Order no. 80, the commander of the 180th originally planned to attack with two battalions abreast, and the 1st Battalion on the left was to be supported by the following:

One platoon of the regimental Cannon Company with two M3 105mm infantry howitzers;
One platoon of the regimental Antitank Company with three 57mm AT guns; and
One platoon of Company B, Chemical Mortar Battalion with four 4.2" [107mm] heavy mortars.[259]

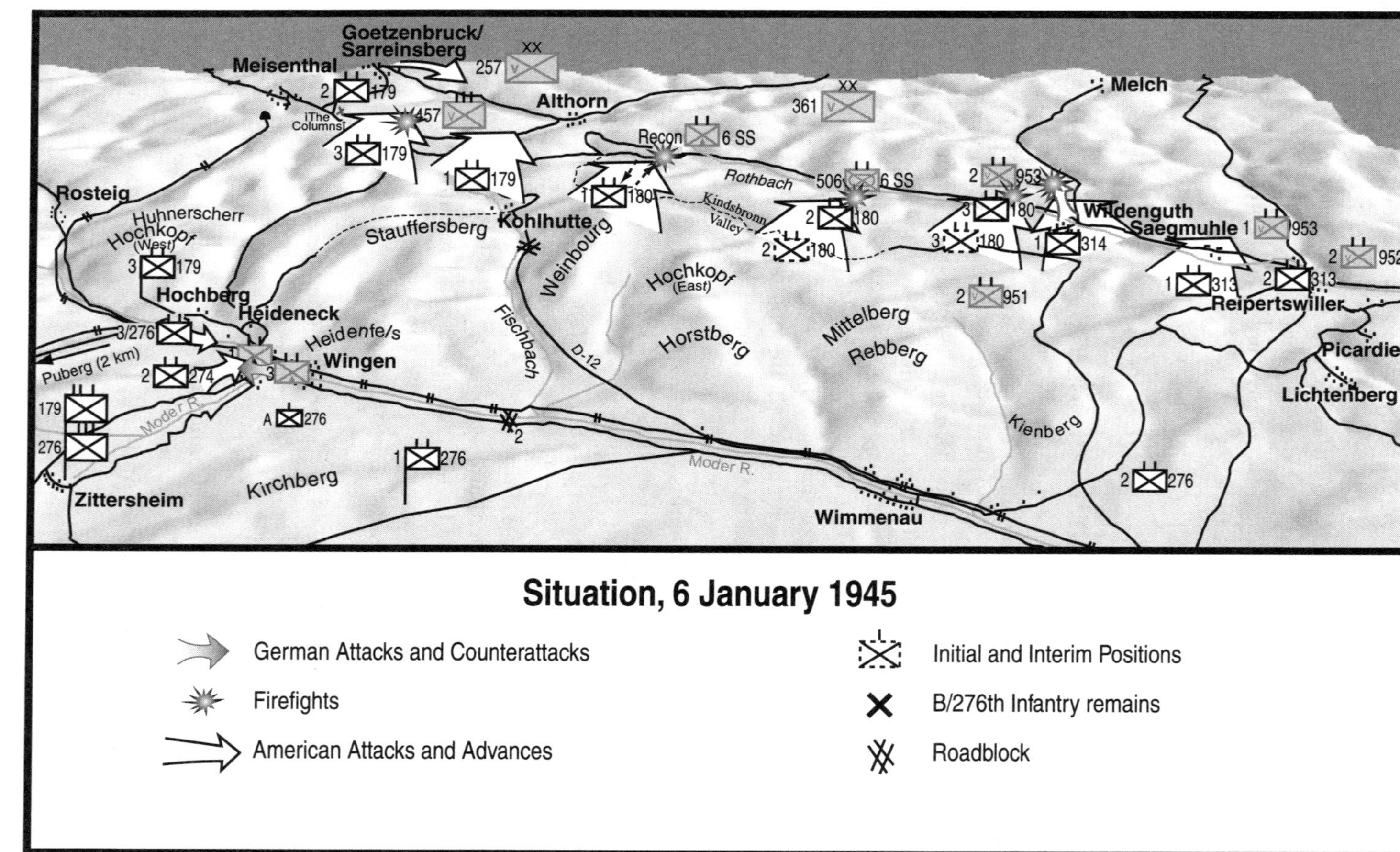
Goetzenbruck/
Sarreinsberg
Meisenthal
The Columns
Althorn
Melch
Recon
6 SS
Rothbach
Rosteig
Huhnerscherr
Hochkopf (West)
Stauffersberg
Kohlhutte
Weinbourg
Kindsbronn Valley
Wildenguth
Saegmuhle
Hochkopf (East)
Hochberg
Heideneck
Heidenfe/s
Wingen
Puberg (2 km)
Fischbach
D-12
Horstberg
Mittelberg
Rebberg
Reipertswiller
Picardie
Lichtenberg
Moder R.
Kienberg
Kirchberg
Zittersheim
Wimmenau
Situation, 6 January 1945
German Attacks and Counterattacks
Firefights
American Attacks and Advances
Initial and Interim Positions
B/276th Infantry remains
Roadblock

The support for its 3d Battalion on the right was identical. This battalion had been in regimental reserve in the vicinity of Wimmenau for the last two days. The 2d Battalion was to act as regimental reserve and assemble in the south of the Kindsbronn Valley, southwest of Wildenguth, ready to counterattack in either zone of the attacking battalions.

That was the original plan, which would have spared the hard-hit and suffering 2d Battalion from attacking further this morning, and grant its men a deserved day of rest instead. But late on the evening of 5 January, Colonel Dulaney and his S-3, Major Schroeder, had decided that the 3d Battalion should not have to worry about the "debits" left by the 2d Battalion, but should instead pass through the easternmost company of the 2d Battalion (Company E), while leaving the 2d Battalion to its task, namely that of "cleaning out" the German forces in front of it, as far as the forest road down in the Rothbach Valley.

So it happened that the 180th Infantry on this morning attacked with all three battalions abreast, 1st Battalion on the left (west), 2d Battalion in the center, and 3d Battalion on the right. Soon after the regiment crossed the line of departure (LD), the men of the 180th Infantry realized that they had stuck their heads into a hornet's nest. The German MLR along that part of the Rothbach Valley was occupied by the *Reconnaissance Battalion NORD*, one of the units that had arrived during the last few days from its temporary march quarters in Denmark, and had reinforced *Combat Group Schreiber*, the advance forces of the *6th SS-Mountain Division NORD*.

The first combat occurred in the 2d Battalion zone. At 0943, Company G hit the German MLR and encountered small arms fire as they attacked Hill 330. At 1006, the unit to its right reported, "quite a bit of machine-gun fire" in the George Company zone. After about an hour and fifteen minutes of fighting, the commander of Company G estimated that there were "about one hundred Germans" taking part in the firefight with his unit; only about twenty minutes later, at 1125, George Company sustained a German counterattack into its left flank, which it beat back.

At 1413, the 2d Battalion reported that, "All hell has broken loose with Company G. They jumped off ten minutes ago, going to try to take the hill (Hill 330), but now they are digging in and organizing."

Supported by one platoon from Company E, the men of George Company were finally able to drive off the enemy by 1524 hours, after about 5fi hours of savage fighting.

At 1730, the 2d Battalion reported that Hill 330 had been secured, and that during consolidation on the objective, it discovered that the defenders had dug a total of some ninety fighting positions for two to three men, formed in a complete circle. Eight dead soldiers from *3d Company, SS-Panzer-Grenadier Battalion 506* and three knocked-out machine guns were found.

American combat patrols down to the forest road in the Rothbach Valley made no contact with the enemy.[260]

The withdrawal of the *SS-Panzer-Grenadier Battalion 506* is chronicled in the German literature as follows, "*Battalion 506* detached itself around 1400 on 6 January from the enemy which attacked with armored support and followed up, arrived in the MLR at Fuchsthal. Here, presently only its *3d Company* was incorporated into the defense."[261]

On the left flank of the 180th's attack, after advancing 200 yards by 1008 hours, Able Company also encountered German resistance, including not only very heavy small arms fire, but 75mm artillery and 20mm automatic cannon fire as well. By 1100 hours, the company was counterattacked by an estimated 100 to 150 Germans. The Thunderbird forward observers adjusted artillery fires very close to the Company A positions, while Baker Company assembled to go to the aid of its sister company. Nevertheless, by 1128 hours, Able Company was compelled to withdraw to its original position along the LD for the morning's attack.[262]

At the same time that Able was making contact with what was probably the German MLR in the center of the 1st Battalion's zone, Charlie ran into what was probably a German outpost. After it advanced down the forest road to the Rothbach Valley, supported by tanks and tank destroyers, in an attempt to outflank the German line from the west, Charlie received intense artillery fire. Just during its brief tenure in the vicinity of Fuchsthal around 1400, this single company was blasted by an estimated 300 rounds coming from "at least a battalion of German artillery." With Able rebuffed in the center and Charlie being slammed by German artillery, the commander of the 1st Battalion decided to withdraw Charlie to its previous positions as well.[263]

The Charlie Company action around Fuchsthal also appears in the *Kriegstagebuch* of the *257th VGD*. "A patrol from *GR 457* at 1030 reports an (enemy) company with 4 tanks in support marching through Fuchsthal in a northeasterly direction."[264]

While the 1st Battalion was running into heavy resistance on the left, and Company G was slugging it out on Hill 330 at the western end of the 2d Battalion's zone, Company E was taking fire from the forested heights northwest of the road junction north of Wildengüth.[265]

Company I, to the right of Company E, reported contact at 1204 with the enemy east of the Melch Valley Road, 800 meters north of the road junction. Forty minutes later, they reported, "We have Germans on both flanks now." This company maintained contact with the advancing Company A, 314th Infantry on its right, and remained in contact with the Germans all day.[266]

At 1058, Company F arrived at Wildenguth to relieve 1st Battalion, 314th Infantry. It was later joined there by most of Company L. Wildenguth was the target of heavy interdictory artillery fire during the day.[267]

Late in the evening, the 180th's regimental executive officer gathered the current casualty figures from the 1st Battalion's commanding officer. Company C had suffered most, namely five killed and fifteen wounded, with another seven men that "went to pieces," obviously suffering nervous breakdowns from battle shock. Company C's remaining strength in the field was sixty-four men. Company A had only eighty-one men on the line, and received an officer from Company B to bolster its leadership strength. Company B was the most robust of the 1st Battalion's rifle companies, with ninety-three men in foxholes in the snow by the end of the day.*

*****

It was during the Charlie Company withdrawal to the LD that *Unterscharführer* Keefer's patrol came to an end. Keefer had gotten his orders in the cellar of our *3d Battalion* CP to exfiltrate through enemy lines and contact the first German officer he could find, and make his report. His report was to be a summary of the current situation of *Combat Group Wingen*, including that our ammunition and food were running out, there were numerous wounded, and we were anxiously awaiting required reinforcements. After he had chosen his two men to accompany him, Keefer left shortly before midnight on 5 January. What happened to his patrol we heard only thirty-five years later.

One hour after leaving Wingen, essentially following the same route by which we had entered town during the night 3/4 January, Keefer and his men heard American soldiers on guard talking with each other, and carefully bypassed them. (Coincidentally, at about the same time, *Untersturmführer* Oldenburg with his officer's patrol was sneaking through the American lines in reverse, namely *into* Wingen, to deliver the order to withdraw.)

Crossing the D-12 district road around dawn on 6 January, Keefer and his comrades saw three American tanks or tank destroyers to their left, with some soldiers in between, manning a roadblock. The new snow obviously gave the vicinity of their crossing point enough light to be recognized from the roadblock, from whence a jeep with a three-man crew was dispatched to

*180th Infantry Regiment S-3 Journal, 6/7 January, message no. 86 at 2037. When considering these strength figures, it should be remembered that at full strength, an American rifle company was authorized 193 men. Interestingly, these companies' morning reports tell a little more about the story. Evidently, the Americans were quite active in returning casualties to action, or scraping up replacements. According to official morning reports for the days of 6 and 7 January 1945, the strengths were as follows:

Company A: 121 before the attack on 6 January, and 115 by the morning of 7 January.
Company B: 138 before the attack on 6 January, and 137 by the morning of 7 January.
Company C: 111 before the attack on 6 January, and 105 by the morning of 7 January.
Morning Report figures: Reel 20.2088, Item 17436, NARA Annex in St. Louis, MO.

investigate the place where they had just crossed. The Americans called after our men who had already disappeared into the woods, but did not follow them.

Keefer's patrol made cautious and slow progress to the northeast. After crossing the Kindsbronn Valley at noon, and after climbing the opposite heights again, they suddenly found themselves in the rear of American positions (it was Company C, 180th Infantry). At first, the small German element was not recognized as strangers; they succeeded in concealing themselves by crouching very low. Eventually, however, while moving to the rear to reoccupy their position at the LD, the American riflemen stumbled over our three men and took them prisoner.[268]

*****

While the 180th Infantry achieved mixed results in its attack toward the Zintsel Valley, the attack of the 179th Infantry developed as follows. The 1st and 3d Battalions, 179th Infantry on this morning jumped off at the same time as the 180th on the right. (2d Battalion, 179th Infantry was still occupying defensive positions in the vicinity of Goetzenbruck-Sarreinsberg.)

Attacking to seize the German-held Kaesberg Heights north of the district road between Goetzenbruck and Wimmenau, the rifle companies of both attacking battalions met with heavy German small arms, mortar, artillery, and self-propelled gun fire throughout the day.

Their opponents were from *GR 457*. Its companies were well dug in on the northern side of the Goetzenbruck-Wimmenau road, and had outposts south of it, notably so to the southwest of the road junction near a shrine, "St. Peter of the Twelve Apostles."

On the left, the 179th's 3d Battalion attacked with Companies I and K leading, and Company L in reserve. Company I experienced stiff German resistance around 1045 hours, when it was between 500 and 600 meters short of the district road where the enemy MLR was expected. Only after the supporting tanks had found a usable access road and could join in the combat was Item Company able to advance across the district road. By the end of the day, it was in position halfway between the prominent cross roads at "The Columns" and the Apostles' Monument, occupying the foxholes abandoned by their German builders.

With armored support from the start, Company K advanced north along the Wingen-Huhnerscharr road to its junction with the district road. It ultimately overwhelmed German resistance north of the district road and, at day's end, occupied positions on the Kaesberg, some 400 meters north of the road junction. Sub-elements established two roadblocks on the district road, 300 meters west and the east of the road junction.

On the right of the regimental zone, the 1st Battalion, 179th Infantry attacked with Companies B and C abreast, leaving Company A in its reserve position. Supported by tanks, both leading companies advanced along the district road in a northerly direction. At 1235 hours, Company C, 179th Infantry had already arrived at its day's objective, namely the eastern slope of the Kaesberg. It did not meet enemy resistance.

At the same time that Charlie Company reached its objective, Baker Company, following to the left of Charlie, ran into a German roadblock at the junction of the district road with the forest road that led east into the Fuchsthal and Rothbach Valley. By the day's end, however, Company B reported that it had overwhelmed the German roadblock with the support of three tanks, capturing the roadblock's six defenders. After that, the men of Baker Company also advanced to the eastern slope of the Kaesberg, extending Charlie Company's position on its left in southwesterly direction.

As an anti-infiltration measure, Able Company was ordered to conduct contact patrols between the 1st and 3d Battalions, but also—following a request from the S-3, 180th Infantry Regiment—between the rightmost-company of the 179th (Company C) and the left-most company of the 180th (Company C).

The S-3 of 180th Infantry informed his counterpart in the 179th that his regiment would establish a roadblock on the east-west stretch of the district road north of Kohlhutte, with one platoon of its Company L.[269]

The combat which involved the two battalions of the 179th Infantry Regiment on this sixth day is described from the German perspective in the *Kriegstagebuch* of the *257th VGD* as follows:

> Around 1330, strong enemy forces attacked almost simultaneously against the crossroads southeast of Meisenthal ("The Columns") and against the road junction one kilometer north of Kohlhutte. While the attack southeast of Meisenthal broke down in our artillery and rocket fire, the enemy succeeded in enveloping our easternmost strongpoint, which was without contact with its neighbor, and to occupy the Kaesberg subsequently. This necessitated our left company to withdraw two hundred meters in a northerly direction to avoid being enveloped in its flank. Enemy attacks against the new position were repulsed.
>
> The enemy attacks on different places between Sarreinsberg and the Kaesberg lead to the presumption that the enemy is striving to clear the entire road between Sarreinsberg via Wingen to Wimmenau.
>
> The Commanding Officer of *GR 457* applies for shortening his MLR, which is situated far to the west. . . . [New line of resistance] to be: Klosterberg-East–Plackenberg-West-Langenberg-West. Division commander applies for Corps' consent, with the argument that . . . there is

> no absolute necessity to hold the present line, after our own forces have been withdrawn from Wingen, Wimmenau, and Reipertswiller.*

During this day, *GR 457* defended itself on the southern slopes of the Kaesberg, north of the district road from positions that first had been established during 3 January by *Combat Group Wingen*, who then evacuated these defense lines during the night 3/4 January when making its roundabout march on Wingen.

At the end of the day's fighting north of Wingen, even though the two regiments of the 45th Infantry Division (and the attached battalion, 79th) had not reached all assigned attack objectives, the gap in the American lines that had existed since the morning of 1 January had been closed. Unbeknownst to us in Wingen, during our upcoming exfiltration we would be trying to find our way not through a tear in the fabric of the American lines, but between the very threads of newly-repaired cloth.

## - VI -
## The Beginning of the End of the Battle of Wingen

Back in our joint command post in the cellar, after we had come to the decisions concerning the fate of our wounded and of the American prisoners of war, we had to quickly inform the company commanders of both battalions. During the darkness of the evening, we could again freely walk the streets and communicate with our companies.

There was consensus among all officers at the end of this meeting in the cellar that clandestinely breaking contact with the enemy would be the most difficult and critical phase of this evening's operations. Here again, this was more difficult for the *1st Battalion*, since its elements were in direct contact with the enemy. Carlau decided to inform the commanders of the *1st* and *2d Companies* himself, accompanied by a messenger. While on his way to their respective positions, he stumbled while jumping over a hole in the Moder Bridge, fell on his head and, besides serious bruises, suffered a concussion.

The NCO in command of *2d Company* (its CO, *Untersturmführer* Luginbühl, had been wounded) had to withdraw his unit first. This delicate operation—during which the Americans facing him must not detect his men's

*It is interesting and intriguing to note that this entry in the *KTB* of the *257th VGD*, which mentions the withdrawal of *Combat Group Wingen*, was written on the evening of 6 January 1945—when we were still in Wingen. This is a clear indication of not only good communications—across a corps boundary, no less—between the command posts of the *257th* and *361st VGDs*, but also of confidence in our ability to withdraw from our tenuous position behind enemy lines.

movement—would occur under the protection of the *1st Company* (commanded by *Obersturmführer* Strauch). Then, after briefly securing the entire bridgehead over the Moder by itself, *1st Company* would follow the *2d Company*'s withdrawal route as well. Both companies were to take the route passing the Catholic church, then creep along the eastbound street south of the railroad embankment to the eastern underpass. The assembly area for all elements was the wooded heights north of the easternmost houses in Wingen, north of the Lalique glass factory.

Since the two remaining men from the *3d Company* had appeared at the joint command post, and reported that all their defended houses had been taken by the Americans, it was decided that reconnaissance in that direction would be senseless, because there were no longer any of our elements there anyway.

During the day, the *4th (heavy machine gun) Company* (commanded by *Untersturmführer* Rutschmann), positioned on the wooden northern heights, had been forced to partly yield to the attacks of elements of the 276th Infantry. Not many men had returned from that company.

Together with Kürten, (CO of *6th Company*), Carlau organized a timely break in contact of the remaining *1st Battalion* units from the enemy.[270]

The commanders of our *3d Battalion* companies were summoned to the command post, briefed, and instructed. The *11th Company* was to break contact slowly. Fortunately, the *12th Company* was, in principle, already in the assembly area. The *13th Company*, south of the railroad embankment, was to hold until the *1st Battalion* elements withdrew, and was then to follow them to the eastern underpass.

Of our units that were charged with safeguarding the railroad station area with its switching yard, only our *Pioneer Platoon* was still available, and was scheduled to leave the scene last. The rest of our *15th (headquarters) Company*, commanded by *Obersturmführer* Bullenda, with parts of our *Signal Platoon*, employed as infantry, had become lost even before our late afternoon counterattack.

Our *13th Company*, commanded by *Obersturmführer* Schütze, was—*inter alia*—charged with guarding the prisoners of war. Its *3d Platoon* had guards outside the church. They had to be withdrawn, but not before informing the 256 American enlisted POWs that "Wingen after our counterattack was again entirely under German control," a declaration that drew laughter from the American side, whose soldiers apparently could not be convinced. The church doors were locked and our guards withdrawn without the POWs in the church being aware of it.

*Obersturmführer* Schütze tasked a few especially reliable men to escort the eight American officer prisoners, seven of whom were from 1st Battalion, 179th Infantry, and one from the 3d Battalion, 276th Infantry. These

American officers, who had been separately quartered in the Catholic church's rectory, were to accompany us on our hike back to German lines.

After all this had been taken care of, we left our joint command post. We had said good-bye to the twelve to fifteen seriously wounded men who we had bedded down in the cellar before leaving. They would stay together in the care of the three elderly Alsatian civilian occupants, awaiting the new day, and the coming of their American captors.

*****

I went slowly down the street leading east to the eastern underpass. Almost all houses to the right and the left of this street, which runs parallel to the railroad embankment, were burning, giving the scenery an eerie illumination. I remained under the quasi-shelter of the underpass by myself, directing the passing groups of both our battalions *en route* to the assembly area. (To this day, I still see myself standing in the underpass.)

It started to snow heavily. As the flakes whirled and settled in the scarred and battered valley, they helped us conceal our withdrawal by further obscuring the enemy's vision and smothering what little sound the equipment-laden *Jägers* made as we faded away from the town. Every so often, perhaps three times per minute, an American artillery round roared across the underpass and exploded somewhere not far from me in the woods of the northern heights.

Another small group passed me in the underpass. "Are you the last ones?" I asked. "We don't know, *Untersturmführer,*" was their honest and frustrating answer. It was hard for me to believe that our withdrawal could continue peacefully, undetected by the Americans. Who will come next? Another squad of ours, or an American patrol already in pursuit?

In between such existential questions, I was consumed with thoughts about our entire Wingen operation, entirely disillusioned with our initial success that seemingly came so easily. What had we gained with all our sacrifices, our many casualties, dead and wounded? Hadn't we actually been sent into this bloody adventure by the German high command, which from the start *must* have been unsure of its capability to exploit an eventual success on our side, a success by our *Combat Group Wingen*? It was utterly frustrating to follow up this line of thinking, though, because we couldn't change anything anyway . . . nor would we have been able to change anything from the start.

All we could do now was to concentrate fully on our present task, here and now. We had to exfiltrate through American lines without being detected, following back and returning on the route Oldenburg had found safe and unobstructed by US forces, just twenty hours before.

It must have been around midnight when a platoon sergeant entering the underpass with his men told me he believed that they are the very last coming out of Wingen, and was quite certain that there were no Germans left behind. That was the moment when I, too, left Wingen, joining his small group on our way to the assembly area.

*****

During the evening, all intelligence gathered in the various American command posts pointed to the probability that the German battalions would withdraw from Wingen during the coming night. The American forces surrounding the town were getting orders to be prepared for just this event.

The 1st Battalion, 180th Infantry had organized a provisional platoon supported by one tank to establish blocking positions at the eastern exits of Wingen on the railroad line, as well as on the district road D-12, both about halfway between Wingen and Wimmenau. The 180th's I&R Platoon, accompanied by one tank, was to coordinate fires with this provisional platoon. Another measure of preparation against contingencies that could result from an outbreak of the two *SS* battalions presently in Wingen was the transfer of Company F, 180th Infantry from Wildenguth—where it just this morning had relieved the 1st Battalion, 314th Infantry—to the western outskirts of Wimmenau.[271]

Asked by the 180th Infantry regimental executive officer whether and how the 1st Battalion, 180th Infantry would be prepared "if those Krauts get out tonight from Wingen," the battalion commander reassured him, "We have an all around defense!"[272]

# - VII -
# Battle Analysis

## *The Price of Incomplete Preparation*

The inexcusably late appearance of the tank platoon which had been ordered to support 2d Battalion, 274th Infantry attack during the morning hours of this day was one of the causes for the high casualties sustained by Fox Company. The tanks came so late that they could not be employed during this company's attack, but only during the afternoon action, supporting George and Easy Companies' attacks. This ruined the rhythm and momentum of the entire plan.

As it soon turned out, applying combined arms units and their concomitant weapons was by far the most effective way to operate. The unchallenged American artillery and mortars could pin us in our positions, inflicting casualties whenever we tried to move about within Wingen, while their tanks blasted our strongpoints in the buildings, facilitating the American infantry's close assaults. This was not only the most effective way, it was the only *sensible* way to attack an objective on which German mountain infantrymen had turned the houses into a fortification immune to small arms fire.

As Cheves pointed out, the lack of infantry-tank coordination dated way back into the history of the 70th Infantry Division's truncated training experience. "It was my first experience working with [tanks] . . . in our extensive training and field maneuvers back in the States, we had never worked with them."[273]

While Fox Company had no opportunity to take advantage of any such "tank-infantry coordination" simply for the reason that there *were no tanks* with which to coordinate, there had been other heavy weapons available, but the record bears only occasional testament to the use of the 81mm mortars (from Company H, 274th Infantry) being used. During his battalion's attack, Cheves had resorted to employing one platoon of 4.2-inch heavy mortars from a supporting chemical mortar battalion; four AT guns of the 276th Infantry, and the Cannon Company of his own regiment. Being weapons that had to be towed into position by a truck and carefully emplaced, it can be seen that even these antitank guns lacked the maneuverability (not to mention the armored protection and firepower) of a Sherman tank, however.

In addition to the experience problem, another of the disadvantages accruing to the hasty and austere circumstances of Task Force Herren's commitment to combat became obvious during this battle. Since the 70th Infantry Division's artillery brigade was still in the United States, General Herren placed the 160th Field Artillery Battalion in "direct support" of the 2d Battalion, 274th Infantry. (He must have been authorized by the CG 45th Infantry Division to do so, because the 160th Field Artillery Battalion belonged to that division.) Normally, such a close support arrangement meant that the forward observers from the artillery would accompany the attacking riflemen of Fox, and later George and Easy Companies. This did not happen, for reasons still unexplained. The next best situation to facilitate responsive fires would have been to place an artillery liaison party with Lieutenant Colonel Cheves and his S-3 in their command post, to coordinate the fires of the field artillery battalion. Even a single forward observer placed here would have been very useful, as Cheves' CP had the singular advantage of a perfect view down into that part of Wingen being assaulted by the 2d Battalion, 274th Infantry's rifle companies.

Astoundingly, even this was not arranged. The liaison element of the 160th Field Artillery Battalion was located with the 1st Battalion, 276th Infantry "about a mile or so off to our [Cheves'] right somewhere." As a result, it took the commander of the infantry battalion conducting the main attack into Wingen on 6 January a *full hour* to relay fire commands to his supporting artillery. Perhaps the 160th's liaison teams and forward observers were off supporting their usual elements of the 45th Infantry Division's organic infantry regiments, but the price to the men of the infantry battalions attacking Wingen was nevertheless high indeed.

The regrettable losses (especially among Fox Company riflemen) due to friendly fire may have also resulted from the fact that the attacking riflemen obviously had not been accompanied by an observer responsible for the fire control of the mortar platoon.

## The Experience Differential

Night withdrawals are one of the most delicate, difficult operations imaginable. Not only must the soldiers find their way through their own lines in the middle of the night, but they must do it silently, depriving the enemy of any recognition of what is going on before them. Finally, all of these exact, clandestine actions must be carried in meticulous coordination with the other withdrawing units, so that the departure of any one unit does not leave a gaping hole in the evaporating lines. Successfully breaking contact with the Americans in Wingen required exquisite timing; superb noise and light discipline; and perfect night land navigation—all of which had been honed during three years of combat against the Red Army in north Karelia. Fortunately, our men also had a rather clear and correct notion about the exact locations of the Americans, which houses had been occupied by the opposing forces, and so forth. The decision not to reconnoiter in the direction of the *3d Company* must be seen in the same context: we had heard from two of its men who were sure that buildings in their sector had been occupied by the Americans, so going there would be both pointless and dangerous.

We also hoped that—as a side effect of our counterattack—the Americans would not be too eager to send patrols out during the hours of darkness. This certainly was the main prerequisite for our withdrawal of some 210 men to succeed; even the best withdrawal can be suddenly and disastrously converted into a rout if the enemy catches wind of what is happening, and decides to pursue vigorously to exploit the situation.

As will be shown, the Americans were not aware of our departure before 0700 the next morning, when unexpected events developed in the last minutes of mountain darkness in the snow-decked ridges of the Low Vosges.

## Morale

Although they suffered appalling losses to hypothermia, friendly artillery, and mortars, as well as German small arms fire, the American infantrymen of the 2d Battalion, 274th Infantry and certain elements of the 276th Infantry continued the attack, despite only sporadic support from other units. It was a grueling baptism of fire for these men, and their persistence in their mission speaks well for their individual and small-unit cohesion and discipline.

Among the veterans of *Combat Group Wingen*, the sentiments of our men when leaving Wingen on that late evening may be described as threefold:

* Utter frustration that, by order of higher headquarters, we had to leave the place for which we had fought so hard, and lost so many of our comrades—the feeling that all our efforts had been "for nothing."
* Sweet relief that we—the men quietly marching out of Wingen that night—were surviving largely unscathed.
* Acute awareness of the absolute necessity of summoning all of our remaining psychological and physical resources, to be fully awake during our stealthy exfiltration through only vaguely recognized enemy lines, despite utmost exhaustion.

Whatever the mistakes made or gambles lost by certain of our higher headquarters, our heads were out of the noose that had been slowly tightening around our collective head in Wingen. Now, in the night winter air, we were marching toward our assembly area, and from thence back to our own lines. Had we avoided the gallows altogether, or were we only stumbling up the icy stairs of another scaffold?

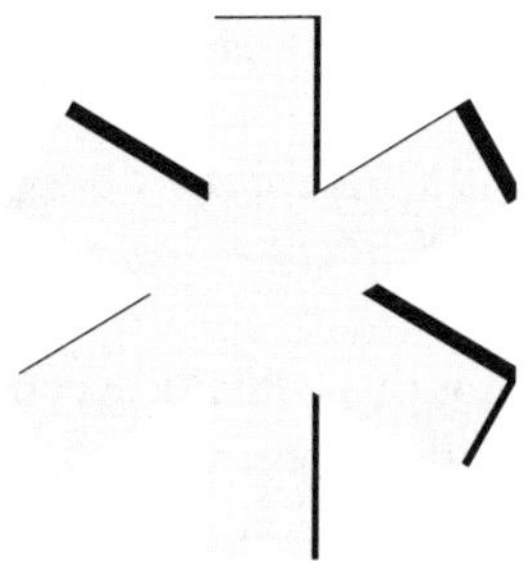

# The Seventh Day: Withdrawal

## - I -
## A Worsening Situation

By 7 January, the situation for *1st Army* and the *NORDWIND* offensive had changed drastically. The objective of the first five days' efforts and suffering had been directed toward the seizure of the passes in the Low Vosges; this was the precondition set by Hitler for the employment of the operational reserve, namely the *21st Panzer Division* and the *25th Panzer-Grenadier Division*. By the early hours of the seventh day of 1945, however, the focus had shifted to the Wissembourg Corridor on the northern end of the Plain of Alsace. Both divisions had been moved from their assembly areas on the Low Vosges front on the sixth and before the day was out, would attack from north of Wissembourg toward the south.

On 6 and 7 January, the Deputy Chief of the Armed Forces (*Stellvertreter, Wehrmachts-Führungsstab*) visited *Generaloberst* Blaskowitz and his staff of *Army Group G*. He summarized his findings there as follows:

> Morale and the conduct of the soldiers are still irreproachable, despite the utmost physical exertion and evident materiel superiority of the enemy. After overcoming his first shock, the methodicalness of the enemy and his persistence in defense has grown. The enemy is able to place fresh troops into combat time and again by relief, whereas our own troops, on the other hand, have to stay in combat without recess. The evident waning fighting strength of our own troops is explicable not only by the brevity and insufficiency of training time together within the Reserve Army, but also by the absence of the old reliable NCOs and competent battalion and company commanders. . . . A prerequisite for any new assault would be personnel replacements. Also the artillery has proven to be insufficient, which goes likewise for its forward observation and radio equipment.[274]

It thus being evident that there was no possibility of further progress in the Low Vosges without reinforcements or at least massive replacements, all eyes became focused on the forthcoming attack by the *XXXIX Panzer Corps*, consisting initially of the *21st Panzer Division* and *25th Panzer-Grenadier Division*, under the direction of *Army Group G*.

The recall of *Combat Group Wingen* must be seen within this context. Even though we had seized and occupied such an outstanding position on 4 January—one fully capable of facilitating the decisive penetration along the Moder Valley that could have allowed the armored reserves to break out onto the Plain of Alsace—there were no forces available to consolidate, much less exploit, the gain. Essentially, all forces of *XC* and *LXXXIX Corps* were committed to holding their positions to the north, while *XIII SS Corps* was unable to break through from the northwest. No forces, other than the armored reserves themselves, were available to punch through to us in Wingen and create a corridor through which the exploitation force could flow. It was this late insight on the part of higher headquarters that finally motivated them to order the withdrawal of the remnants of *Combat Group Wingen*.

## - II -
## Out of the Frying Pan . . .

It was shortly after midnight that, together with the last small group of soldiers who had left Wingen, I arrived in the assembly area in the northeasternmost corner of the town, on the forested heights beyond the last houses. Most of our *Combat Group*, or rather its remnants, were already there, standing around in small groups. I soon found the group of officers from both battalions, and reported to *Hauptsturmführer* Kreuzinger, my commander.

Without much discussion, we agreed that *Untersturmführer* Oldenburg, who had led the officers' patrol into Wingen not twenty hours before with the withdrawal order from *Standartenführer* Schreiber, should lead our exfiltration. He had, after all, discovered a safe route from the German lines into Wingen; he would be the one most likely to be able to retrace his steps back to the main line of resistance, avoiding contact with hostile elements.

We were waiting for the last of the men from the *1st Battalion*, elements of the *4th Company*, who had to disengage themselves from active contact with the enemy. As we waited, we were subjected to intermittent American artillery fire, falling a little too nearby for comfort. This fire indicated to us that the Americans had already detected our withdrawal.

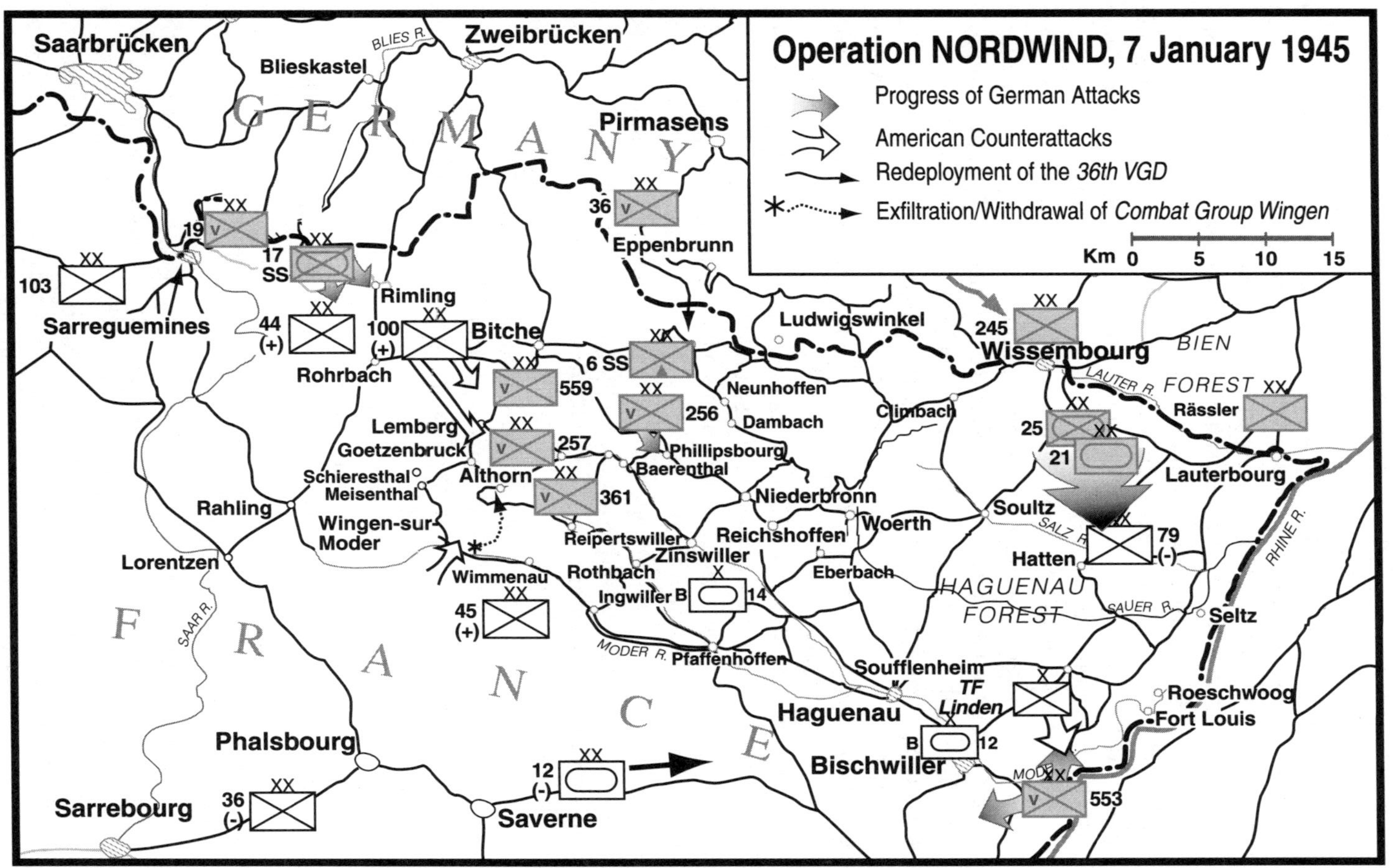
Operation NORDWIND, 7 January 1945
Progress of German Attacks
American Counterattacks
Redeployment of the 36th VGD
Exfiltration/Withdrawal of Combat Group Wingen
Km 0 5 10 15
Saarbrücken
BLIES R.
Blieskastel
Zweibrücken
GERMANY
Pirmasens
Eppenbrunn
Sarreguemines
Rimling
Rohrbach
Bitche
Ludwigswinkel
Wissembourg
BIEN FOREST
LAUTER R.
Rässler
Lauterbourg
RHINE R.
Neunhoffen
Dambach
Climbach
Lemberg
Goetzenbruck
Schiresthal
Meisenthal
Althorn
Phillipsbourg
Baerenthal
Niederbronn
Reichshoffen
Woerth
Soultz
SALZ R.
Hatten
Rahling
Wingen-sur-Moder
Reipertswiller
Zinswiller
Rothbach
Ingwiller
Wimmenau
Eberbach
HAGUENAU FOREST
SAUER R.
Seltz
Lorentzen
SAAR R.
FRANCE
MODER R.
Pfaffenhoffen
Soufflenheim
Haguenau
TF Linden
Bischwiller
Roeschwoog
Fort Louis
MODER
Phalsbourg
Sarrebourg
Saverne
103
19
17 SS
44 (+)
100 (+)
36
6 SS
559
256
257
361
245
25
21
79 (-)
45 (+)
14
12
12 (-)
36 (-)
553

Finally, we decided that all of the men who were going to get out of Wingen had linked up with our group, and we slowly began the cross-country march through the dark mountains. Exactly what lay to the north, we had no way of knowing. The Americans might have tried to surround us with positions facing south, that is, toward Wingen itself; at a minimum, we expected that they had established some sort of positions facing north, to prevent further German advances toward the town in which we had been fighting for three days. In any case, there were bound to be patrols; listening and observation posts; and all manner of other enemy activity in the area through which we were about to travel on this bleak and black night.

At about 0200, with Oldenburg leading, we set off in a long, single file. No attempt was made to organize the men into companies, or even battlalions; we did not even take a head count prior to our departure from the assembly area. We did, however, take measures against breaks in contact, much as we had during the infiltration four long days ago. We knew that only by sticking together did we, with our ammunition and strength running low, have any chance of making it out alive. At best, we figured we had a fifty/fifty chance of withdrawing successfully.

A thick and steady snow fell, masking the sound and sight of our progress. For all the help it gave us, it also caused a problem. In their physically weakened state, Oldenburg and the men of his lead element had a great deal of difficulty breaking a trail for the rest of us. Time and again, I passed up and down the long line to make sure that no one became misoriented or broke contact. More than once I passed the group of eight sullen American officers who accompanied us against their will, guarded by two men of our *13th Company*. I mustered something like a bit of personal sympathy for them. They must have felt themselves victims of their own naiveté at best, or professional failure at worst. At least some of them had to have been responsible for the lax security conditions that had allowed us to overrun them three days before.

Eventually, we crossed the district road and climbed the path up to the Weinbourg Heights. The snow muffled all sound. We had encountered no enemy outposts, patrols, or positions of any kind to this point. Actually, most of us were too exhausted to care very much. There was a certain dangerous degree of carelessness overtaking us, which could easily lead to disaster in case of emergency or confrontation with the enemy.

After traversing the Weinbourg ridge, we descended cross-country to the district road, which we reached south of the wayside inn called the *"Kaminthaler Hof."* (It belongs to the hamlet of Kohlhutte, and was locked, its inhabitants probably evacuated.) It must have been around 0530 when we reached the road in front of the inn. Oldenburg was of the opinion that by now, we must have passed all of the American defensive positions, and were

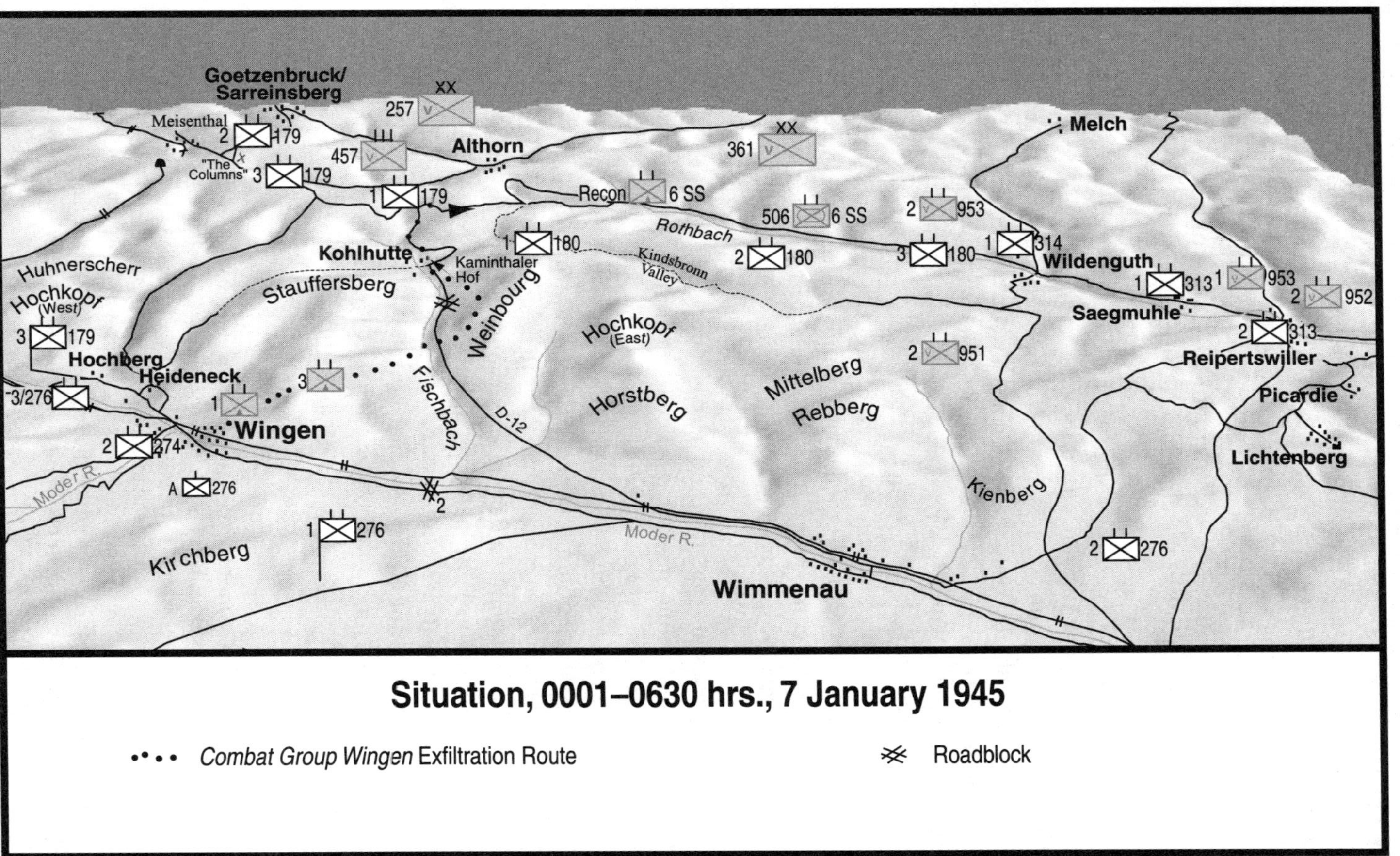


Situation, 0001–0630 hrs., 7 January 1945

• • • *Combat Group Wingen* Exfiltration Route

Roadblock

in the middle of the no-man's-land between our respective defensive lines. We now had to make a decision regarding the need for dispatch (the beginning of morning nautical twilight was less than ninety minutes away) versus the requirements for security. Given the state of our men, we decided that the former was now more important. Thus, we assembled the troops on the road in front of the *Kaminthaler Hof.* Four MG-42s, facing the cardinal directions relative to our line of march, had to suffice for security as we organized along the roadside.

In this relatively secure position, we took our first headcount. Our *3d Battalion* came out of Wingen with three officers and 107 enlisted men. The *1st Battalion* could count six officers and 110 enlisted men. Thus, of the 725 men who had embarked on this mission just a week before, fewer than a third made it out of Wingen *en route* to their own lines on the morning of the last day of the battle. Worse, even some of these would not make it back to German lines on this day.

I ordered all companies to take stock of the remaining machine-gun ammunition, and found we had a total of 360 rounds between them. After cross-leveling this paltry sum, there was barely enough for five seconds' worth of fire per gun, given the 1200-round/minute cyclic rate of the new MG-42s. The effects of fatigue, coupled with anxiousness to get back to our lines and the natural effects of combat in the dark could easily combine to cause the guns to use up all of our precious machine-gun ammo in the first two bursts. We warned all gunners to be especially parsimonious with their fire.

The officers and non-commissioned commanders held a short conference. *Untersturmführer* Oldenburg reiterated his opinion that we had passed the American main line of resistance, and that the road before us must be clear.* By the dim illumination of a flashlight, we conducted a map reconnaissance under the protection of the inn's partially enclosed entrance. I copied the graphics from his map onto my own, showing the German line of resistance along the Fuchsthal and Rothbach-Thal, as well as the location of *Standartenführer* Schreiber's command post in the western part of Melch. Before Oldenburg had departed on his mission to find us (on the evening of 5

*In assembling this estimate of the situation, Oldenburg had access only to the intelligence posted at the headquarters of *Combat Group Schreiber* on the evening of 5 January, after which he had departed for his most recent journey through American lines. On that day, the line of contact between German and American forces in this sector was indeed still about halfway between the Moder and Rothbach Valleys. With a bit of luck, Oldenburg and his small party during the night of 5/6 January had slipped past all American positions. The status of his information early on 7 January was therefore at least twenty-six hours old, and no longer valid.

January), Schreiber had already designated part of the Rothbach Valley line to be occupied by our *3d Battalion* upon our return from Wingen. The *1st Battalion* was designated to initally go into reserve. Of course, he had no idea that our strength would have been so diminished.

To facilitate this arrangement, both battalion commanders agreed that from this point, the *3d Battalion* should lead what remained of our exfiltration. No difficulties were to be expected, and we knew that when we reached the Fuchsthal after descending from the pass down to the Rothbach Valley, we would encounter our own troops, most probably the division reconnaissance battalion, the *SS-Reconnaissance Battalion 6 NORD.*

I volunteered to take charge of the advance guard of our battalion, and to lead it back to our lines. I not only had marked the map, but had fairly memorized the route we were going to take. According to Oldenburg, we should be making contact with friendly units barely five kilometers down the road. The remainder of the advance guard consisted of the remnant of our *11th Company*. With only two NCOs and five junior enlisted men, it was by far the weakest company, with effectively no combat value. Under the command of *Oberscharführer* Heuer, it was, however, perfectly suitable for the task of scouting ahead of the main body of the combat group.

Around 0600, I left the Kaminthaler Hof with this small remnant of a once proud company, marching single file down the district road. The remainder of the battalion followed some 300 to 400 meters behind, with the *1st Battalion* following in column. After a completely uneventful move of less than two kilometers, we came to the junction with the forest road. No enemy were seen or heard (not that we expected any!), and the only indication of the enemy's presence at this point were a few antitank mines placed in the middle of the road. We left them where they were.

It had taken us about thirty minutes to march to the road junction, where we turned off on the forest road that would lead us to the pass dividing the Fischbach Valley from the Rothbach Valley further to the east. The pass appeared as "Elevation 364" on the map, so we had to ascend about thirty meters (vertical distance) along the forest road. With the deep tracks we were leaving in the snow, there was no need to leave guides behind to ensure the rest of the battalion would follow. The time was 0630.

*****

Even as we were slipping out of Wingen during the previous night, Lieutenant Colonel Cheves, commanding officer of 2d Battalion, 274th Infantry, had been mulling over how to accomplish the mission of seizing Wingen on the next day.

His attacking companies (Easy and George) had been split by our counterattack late on 6 January, thus depriving him of the goal of "clearing" Wingen that day. "Complete victory had been within our grasp," Cheves later wrote, but the victory that was the focus of so much pressure, from the VI Corps commander on down, had eluded him and his men that night.[275]

Worse, the counterattack had cut off the foremost elements of these two companies, while the remainder had withdrawn to the houses in the western end of town. The remnants of Fox Company had been deployed to protect the battalion's flanks in the event of another German attack. Overall, then, his depleted battalion was in no posture for an immediate resumption of the attack first thing in the morning, although that was exactly what he would be expected to do by Generals Herren, Frederick, and Brooks.

To confuse the situation more, there had been reports through the night that "small groups of Germans were seen withdrawing toward the eastern end of town," but Cheves did not trust that this meant his problems were over or even simplified.[276] In making preparations, he was willing to assume only the worst, namely that the late counterattack was evidence that the German presence in Wingen had been *reinforced,* not diminished. Perhaps the withdrawals noted by forward elements were only the exchanging of tired troops for fresh ones. Cheves had to anticipate another difficult day ahead.

He concentrated on solving three problems that had hampered his unit's mission accomplishment to that point. First, he had to secure the cooperation of the tanks. Next, he had to coordinate the action of the battalion of the 276th Infantry on his left. Finally, he absolutely required a resolution of the awkward and unresponsive system of calling for and adjusting fires in support of his battalion's attack; relaying his requests and spotting reports through the 1st Battalion, 276th Infantry back on the Kirchberg was totally unsatisfactory.

Late on the evening of 6 January, Lieutenant Colonel Cheves visited the 276th's regimental command post in Zittersheim to coordinate everything "to the minutest detail." He found a simple solution to his second problem: the lead elements of the mixed forces of the 276th Infantry would fire a white star cluster every fifteen minutes. This would mark their position as they attacked over the forested heights north of the railroad in the morning, whether they were making progress or not. In this way, Cheves and his subordinate commanders would know exactly where they were, and would tailor their maneuver accordingly, rather than assume that they were keeping pace.

The third problem was solved even more directly. Cheves left his S-3, Captain Boyea, at the command post in the Villa Frantz, and collocated himself in a kind of "forward" command post with the CP of the 1st Battalion, 276th Infantry, on the northern slope of the Kirchberg. Here, he had a direct view of the battlefield and immediate access to the forward observer from the 45th Division's artillery that was supporting Task Force Herren. Any radio traffic from his forward companies that could not be received at this location would be relayed by Captain Boyea and his team at Villa Frantz.

The remaining problem, that is, that of securing effective cooperation from the supporting tank company, could only be resolved in a less than fully satisfactory fashion. Cheves had to provide a mine-clearing detail from his own battalion to *precede* the tanks and clear a way for them.

Cheves set the time of his battalion's attack for 0900 on 7 January, an hour after sunrise. This late start had both advantages and risks. It would give the commanders of Companies E, F, and G time to posture their fractured and dispersed units for the coordinated effort that *must* on this day secure the remainder of the Wingen. It would also allow for the additional time inevitably taken by the tanks to make their appearance. On the other hand, it would fall a full two hours after the German defenders would stand-to, in anticipation of an American attack shortly after first light.

Before daybreak on 7 January, Lieutenant Colonel Cheves joined Captain Curtis Brooks at his command post on the Kirchberg. Brooks, who until three days before had been the S-3 of 1st Battalion, 276th Infantry, was now the acting battalion commander, in the wake of the breakdown suffered from the shock of combat by his predecessor on the morning of 4 January. Cheves was more than satisfied by the location of his new forward CP, because it afforded him an even better view of exactly that part of Wingen in which his battalion's attack was about to take place. A mere 600 meters distant, the vista was now available to him and to the forward observer, as well as to Brooks, who occupied the dugout with them.

Predictably, the tanks were late, so Cheves had once again to postpone the attack by several minutes. Nevertheless, his mine-clearing party was already at work, making the battlefield safe for the Shermans' crews.

When the attack finally started, Lieutenant "Casey" Cassidy's George Company surged toward their first objective, namely the house in which Sergeant Krumme's platoon had been cut off during our counterattack on the previous night. The house contained about twenty able-bodied men, who immediately rejoined their company in the attack; the fifteen wounded who had sought shelter there during the night were evacuated to the rear. Cheves followed their "liberation" on the radio.[277]

After this point, the attack proceeded systematically. "The tanks would sit back and blast at a house, and then we would charge in, throwing hand grenades. Kraut POWs were coming in as we raced toward the far end of the town. . . . House after house fell," Cheves later chronicled.

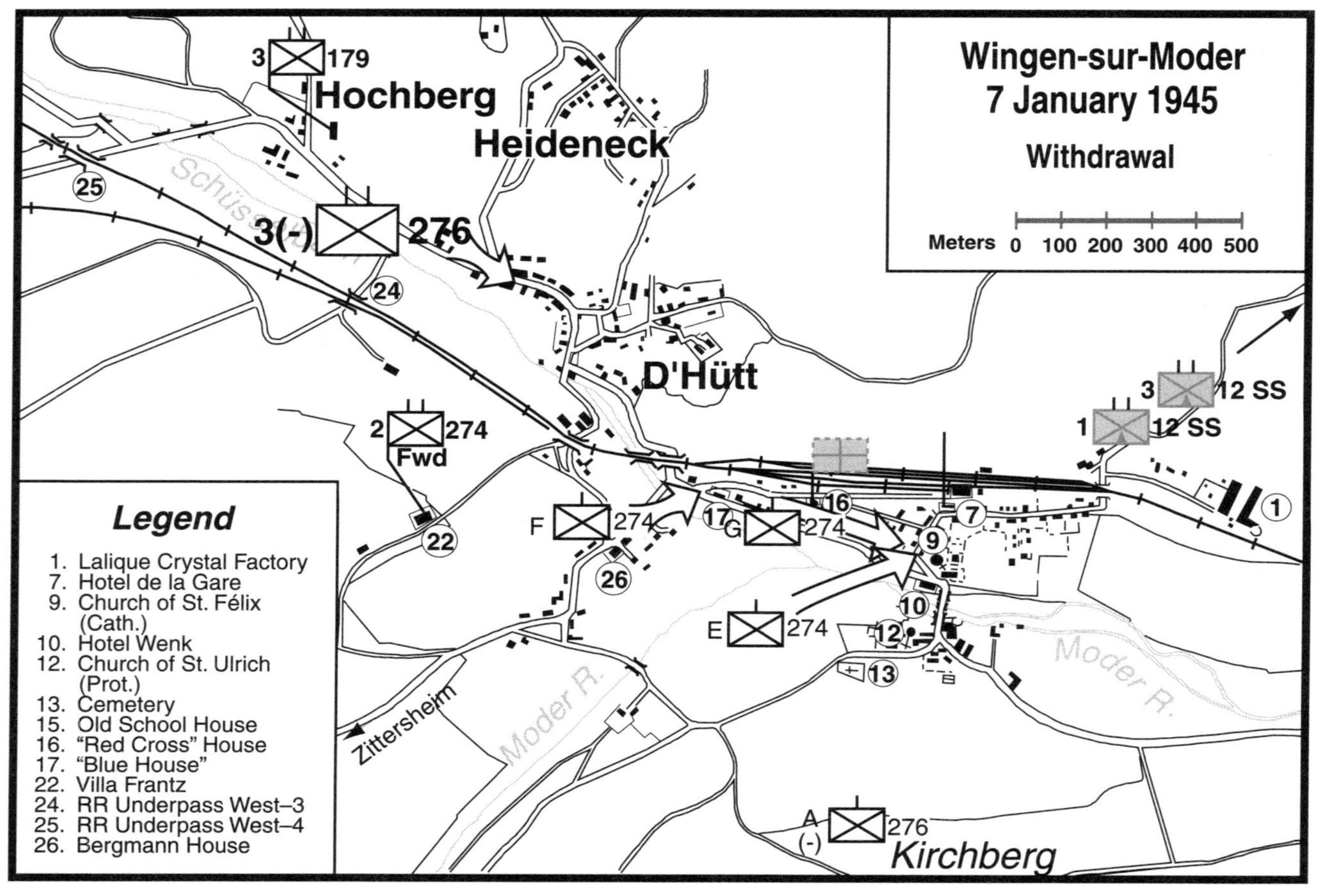

Wingen-sur-Moder
7 January 1945
Withdrawal
Meters 0 100 200 300 400 500
3 179
Hochberg
Heideneck
3(-) 276
D'Hütt
2 274 Fwd
3 12 SS
1 12 SS
F 274
G 274
E 274
Moder R.
Moder R.
Zittersheim
A (-) 276
Kirchberg
Legend
1. Lalique Crystal Factory
7. Hotel de la Gare
9. Church of St. Félix (Cath.)
10. Hotel Wenk
12. Church of St. Ulrich (Prot.)
13. Cemetery
15. Old School House
16. "Red Cross" House
17. "Blue House"
22. Villa Frantz
24. RR Underpass West–3
25. RR Underpass West–4
26. Bergmann House

# - III -
# . . . Into the Fire

Before the final attack on Wingen—now "defended" only by those members of *Combat Group Wingen* who were too badly wounded to accompany us on the exfiltration—even began, *Oberscharführer* Heuer and I were climbing the forest road, just behind the lead element consisting of the six other men of *11th Company* who were still on their feet. Following the winding course, which led in a generally northeasterly direction, Heuer and I followed at about thirty-meters' distance. To our right, the ridge dropped off precipitously to the floor of the valley and the district road, on which the rest of the combat group was now following. In the dim illumination of moonlight reflecting off the freshly-fallen snow, we could perceive that on the left was a sparsely-vegetated forest, with almost no undergrowth.

Just ahead of the next bend in the road, we knew we would be reaching the positions at the top of the pass, where we had encountered our first Americans during the night of 2/3 January. Although it was only four days since, it seemed to me that it had been about a decade since that first firefight with our new foe. Such was the effect of almost constant wakefulness and combat in the interim.

As we rounded the bend, we perceived a dark, bulky object in the middle of the road; our lead element was just passing it, squeezing by on either side between the snowy boughs of the trees and the sides of the shape. Coming nearer, we discerned that it was a tank, and an American one at that. Its crew seemed to have been alerted by the passage of our men. We could hear the crew talking inside. Just then, Heuer and I noticed that the bow machine gun was taking aim on the men ahead of us, clearly lining up for a burst that could kill them all. We heaved our last hand grenade through the easily-opened hatch on the turret. Just as the last of the six scouts disappeared around the bend, Heuer and I jumped from the tank into the woods on either side of the vehicle, fearful that the detonation of our grenade would cause the tank's ammunition to go up any second.

Although the ammunition did not explode, an unanticipated kind of hell soon broke loose over our advance guard party. The positions we had overrun several nights before were still occupied, and the American defenders assumed that the German attack was coming from the direction on which their defensive positions were oriented, namely to the northeast. Alerted by the muffled explosion of our hand grenades in the tank just behind their lines, they now started firing blindly into the woods to their front.

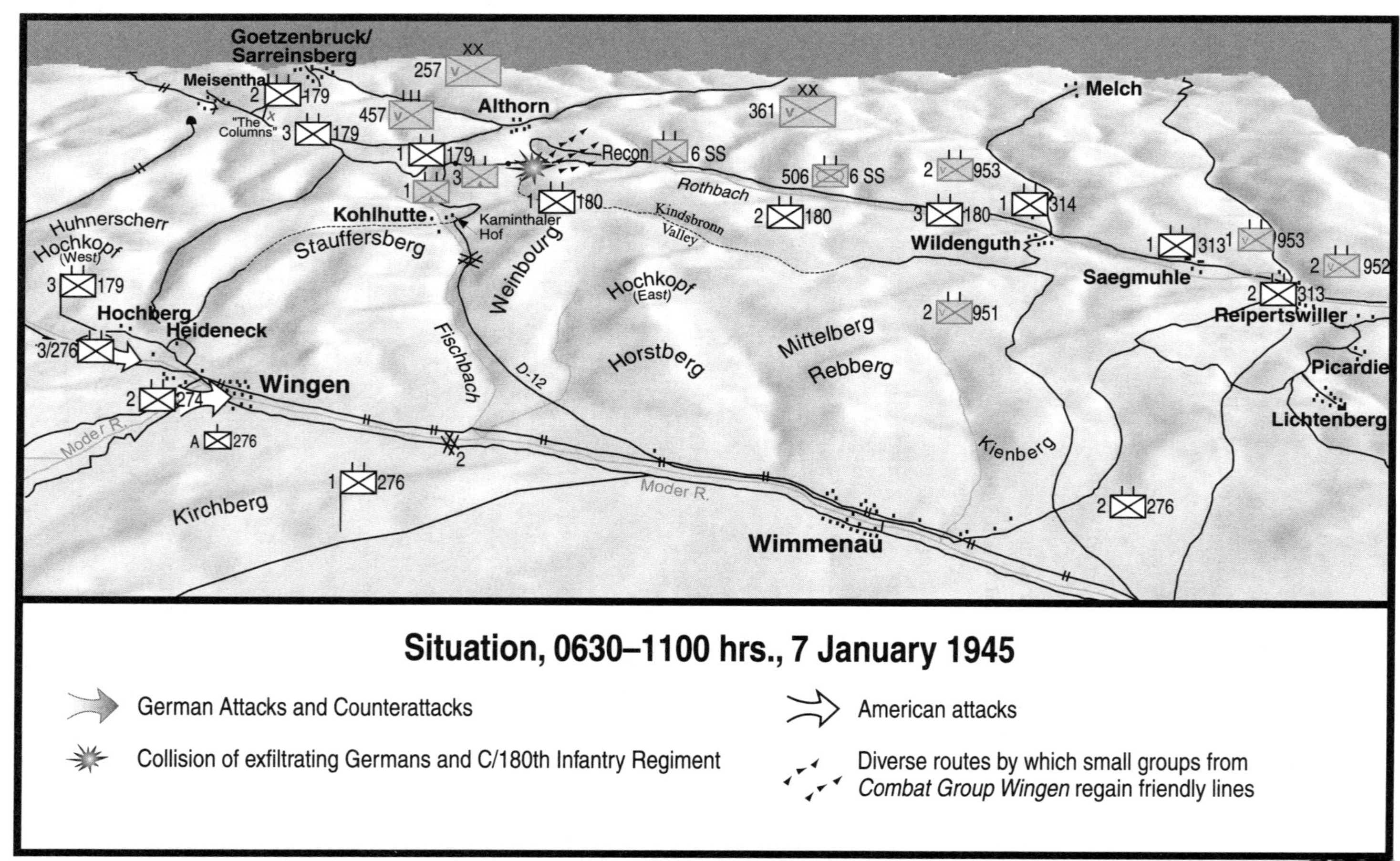


Situation, 0630–1100 hrs., 7 January 1945

These were the positions of Company C, 180th Infantry Regiment, now postured to plug part of the gap originally left by the disintegration of Task Force Hudelson. Although the 180th's executive officer had warned the 1st Battalion commander as recently as a few hours before about the possibility of a German break out from Wingen during the night, and had been told that the battalion was already postured for "all around defense," this was simply not the case in Charlie. They were oriented exclusively toward the north.

The American fire rapidly changed direction, however, when the unmistakable sound of German machine pistols and MG-42s joined the cacophony from the rear of their positions, as the *3d Battalion* moved up the forest road and made contact with the defenders.

The *13th Company* and *Pioneer Platoon* were the first to join the fray. Reaching the burning American tank, two of their number saw one of the Sherman's crew attempting to escape through a hatch on the turret, his head and torso already outside the vehicle. Wounded in the legs and calling for help, the American tanker was rescued by Horst Stiehl, the commander of the *Pioneer Platoon,* and Otto Löwenbruck, a section leader in *13th Company,* who laid him in the road alongside one of the other wounded crewmen.[278]

When the firefight broke out, the eight American officer POWs took cover in a shallow ditch on the left side of the forest road. Suddenly, taking advantage of the situation, all eight men scrambled to their feet as one and ran down the long slope to the right, clearly expecting that to lead them back to their own lines. *Oberscharführer* Hans Kast, one of the men detailed to guard them, called out, "Let them run!" as they disappeared into the gloom. Their return to American control was acknowledged by an entry in the S-3 Journal of the 179th Infantry Regiment, which logged four of them by name:

> 1325 . . . Lt. Wilcox, Lt. Shields, Lt. O'Brien, Capt. Bernhardt, and a major from 276th Inf. All recovered from enemy.[279]

As the battlefield became illuminated with the coming dawn, two other *13th Company* soldiers stumbled upon a foxhole manned by two members of Company D, 180th Infantry. Kicking over the unattended .30-caliber water-cooled heavy machine gun perched on the rim of the hole, the younger trooper, Fritz Spohn, called to the crew to come out. One came right out, but the other had difficulties. He was too nervous and unable to open the zipper of the sleeping bag in which he was still warmly encased. To his initial horror, Spohn immediately sought to help him by drawing his Finnish *puuko* (dagger) and slicing the bag open. Both American soldiers were taken prisoner and employed as litter bearers for the wounded of *13th Company.*[280]

The leading elements of *3d Battalion, SS-Mountain Infantry Regiment 12* had borne the brunt of the combat with the American forces, which blocked the exfiltration route. Our sister battalion had provided cover of the rear and left (west) flank, but had avoided decisive engagement with the American defenders. After over an hour of shooting, *Hauptsturmführer* Burgstaller, commanding officer of the *1st Battalion,* urged his brother battalion commander, Kreuzinger, to disengage and maneuver left toward the Rothbach Valley. From there, he and his men would try to break through and reach the German lines.

Kreuzinger apparently thought that the Americans had been dislodged from their positions in the vicinity of the pass road. Entirely misinterpreting the situation, he assembled his exhausted *Gebirgsjäger* on the road in tactical road march formation in preparation for leading them down the narrow defile in the Rothbach Valley. No sooner had the men assembled, however, than the Americans zeroed in on them with artillery and mortars. Although the American small arms fire encountered in the woods had inflicted relatively few casualties, the indirect fires they now so accurately and swiftly adjusted cut huge swaths in the ranks of the German survivors, particularly Stiehl's *Pioneer Platoon.* The bursts, which exploded in the treetops and showered fragments of hot steel and jagged wood over the exposed exfiltrators were especially lethal.

All men now tried frantically to escape the hail of shrapnel and splinters. Most of them disintegrated into small groups and tried to evade the fire by running directly downhill, away from the road in the direction of the Fuchsthal and the Rothbach Valley. At the same time, the *1st Battalion*—along with our *13th Company*—was also receiving mortar and artillery fire. As they tried to run through the snowy woods, they ran into automatic weapons fire from the positions of Company C, 179th Infantry, the righmost (easternmost) unit of the very battalion whose headquarters personnel were so near liberation in the village of Wingen to the south.

Initially, the American command echelons were confused regarding just what was really happening in the dark hills above Wingen. At the headquarters of the 180th Infantry Regiment, the staff believed that the attack had originated from the north or northwest, and that it had been initiated by fresh German troops attempting to break through to Wingen. This impression was reinforced by a report from one of the liaison officers from the 171st Field Artillery Battalion, who conveyed a message received from one of his forward observers with Company C that the German effort was coming from the northwest.[281]

Only after 0900 did it become clear to Colonel Dulaney and his staff that the action above Wingen was the result of an exfiltration from the village and not an attack to relieve or reinforce the German forces there. Upon interrogation, two POWs taken by 1st Battalion, 180th Infantry—both forward observers of the *7th Battery, SS-Artillery Regiment 6 NORD*—provided this information, which was promptly passed to the regimental CP.[282] Thus, although the situation remained far from clear for the Americans, by this point key leaders in the 45th Infantry Division were aware that at least *some* German forces were attempting to break out from Wingen.

Nevertheless, the concern of additional German troops attempting to break through to Wingen prompted the commanding general of the 45th Infantry Division to release the 3d Platoon of the division's cavalry reconnaissance troop to the control of the 179th Infantry Regiment. The CO of the 179th Infantry used the platoon's M8 armored cars to patrol the road between Wimmenau and Kohlhutte in an effort to detect and halt further southward progress of arriving German forces.

*****

Even as his men were moving forward into Wingen, Lieutenant Colonel Bob Cheves, CO of the 2d Battalion, 274th Infantry, received a message in his observation post on the northern slope of the Kirchberg, "PASSPORT hit hard. Direction of attack: Wingen."

Recognizing that PASSPORT was the code name for the 180th Infantry, and remembering from his briefing at the 276th Infantry command post that all three battalions of the 180th Infantry would be in positions in the Rothbach Valley, poised to continue their attack this morning, Cheves could only assume that additional elements of *SS-NORD* had finally arrived and entered the fray north of Wingen. He, therefore, had every reason to believe that enemy forces were on their way to reinforce the two isolated battalions opposing his battalion there.

The CO of 1st Battalion, 276th Infantry, Captain Brooks (whose CP Cheves co-occupied) seemed perturbed by the contents of the message about the 180th's situation. "What will we do?" he asked his fellow battalion commander.

Bolstered by the success achieved by his men so far that morning, Cheves' response was laconic. "Why, we will defend right here," he pronounced.

Writing after the war, Cheves admitted, "We were not called upon to test the defensive measures which we quickly incorporated," concluding inaccurately that it was because "the 180th held." Actually, the false warning of the impending arrival of German reinforcements did not in any way affect the offensive operations of his units in Wingen. The commanders of the advancing companies knew nothing about it.

In Wingen, elements of the 1st and 3d Battalions, 276th Infantry, and 2d Battalion, 274th Infantry—supported by Company B, 781st Tank Battalion and the 160th Field Artillery Battalion—surged into Wingen against no resistance. Once well into the town, Cheves remarked, "It [was] now apparent that the bulk of the remaining German troops had withdrawn, leaving only a small covering force of scattered men, most of them surrendering on first opportunity."

Only later did the Americans realize that the "covering force" in fact consisted solely of wounded men who remained behind only because they were not fit to accompany the withdrawing German forces. These men surrendered promptly in the sure knowledge that after being taken into American custody, contrary to the rough customs of the Red Army during our war at the Arctic Circle, they would be evacuated by their captors and afforded quality medical treatment. Having done their duty and been unable to continue resistance, what more could they do?

Easy Company of the 274th Infantry Regiment was the first to reach the church of St. Félix. In their attempts to reach their buddies the night before, the men of Company E had encountered fierce resistance, so it was with the utmost caution that they approached the place on this morning. When the main doors were opened, "a horde of GI-clad Americans rushed out," Cheves later wrote. "It was a heart-warming scene to watch as fellow Americans continue[d] to stream out of the church, asking but one question, 'Where's the rear?' and then moving out in that direction." Cheves, witnessing this scene from his OP only 500 meters away, ordered a sergeant from his headquarters to lead the liberated soldiers from Wingen all the way to Zittersheim, and to turn them over to their respective regiments, the 179th and 276th. In his instructions to the NCO, he added, "be sure that no Germans are hiding out in that group."

Along with the liberation of about 300 of their comrades, the Americans also captured the 420 *SS-Gebirgsjäger* who were too seriously wounded to accompany us on our withdrawal. According to their official US records, since the early morning hours of 4 January, when we first came upon Company B, 276th Infantry in the woods northwest of Wingen, the attackers had sustained the following casualty totals:

| | |
|---|---|
| 1st Battalion/276th Infantry | 125 |
| 2d Battalion/274th Infantry | 65 |
| 3d Battalion/276th Infantry | 52 |

These casualties were sustained in addition to the 306 prisoners from Headquarters Company, 1st Battalion, 179th Infantry and Service Company, 179th Infantry we had taken on the morning of 4 January.

For the proud veterans of the 179th Infantry Regiment, it had been a disaster that was narrowly retrieved. Despite the best efforts of its 1st Battalion, a battalion headquarters had been overrun and captured almost intact, as had a major portion of the regimental supply infrastructure. Perhaps out of more than a little embarrassment over this loss, the 179th apparently reported that it, not the combat rookies of Task Force Herren, had retaken Wingen and redeemed the loss of four days before. The records of its sister regiment, the 180th Infantry, clearly reflect this with the report at 1332 hours on 7 January that, "Pagan [the radio call sign for the 179th Infantry Regiment] got about 125-150 Americans out of Wingen."[283] In fact, the 179th Infantry had nothing to do with this; the infantry combat at Wingen had been a purely Task Force Herren affair. The desire of the 179th to conceal their barely-recovered disaster may have even been heightened by the disdain that many of the regiment's combat veterans felt for the units of Task Force Herren, which the official chronicler of the 179th Infantry Regiment's called "American *Volksturm Grenadiers.*"[284] In any case, while the soldiers who reoccupied Wingen on 7 January may have been incompletely trained, they certainly did not lack valor or soldierly virtue.

For these men, the soldiers of the 1st and 3d Battalions, 276th Infantry and the 2d Battalion, 274th Infantry, the battle of Wingen-sur-Moder had been a hellish baptism of fire. Not only had they lost many good men to our bullets, but—unbeknownst to them—they had lost dozens of casualties to their own artillery and mortar fire, for not one fragment of the flying steel that cut down so many of their men as they attacked again and again for four days had originated from the muzzle of a German weapon. Such fire support was impossible, because as mentioned before, none of the man-portable radios carried by our forward observers could transmit beyond the Wingen valley, and we had lost our radio truck long before reaching our objective. Among the many disadvantages to being committed piecemeal—that is, attached to another division while their own artillery and division headquarters were still in the United States—was the difficulty inherent to the always tedious and potentially dangerous coordination of artillery fire. Among the many challenges faced by the elements of Task Force Herren in their first combat, this one was perhaps the most deadly.

In addition to the problematic American artillery fire adjustment, their armor support had been spotty. Further, confidence in the chain of command must have suffered as a result of the severe pressure from higher echelons The frequent interventions by Generals Frederick and Herren can only have added to, not relieved, the already tremendous stress faced by every man in the Task Force elements attacking Wingen.

Tactically, the Americans had retaken Wingen and erased an "abcess" in their lines. As the US Seventh Army *Report of Operations* put it, "On 6 January [*sic*] the tenacious defense offered by the enemy was overcome; the town was cleared. This action marked the elimination of the enemy's deepest penetration in the Low Vosges." Of the actions of the other elements of US VI Corps fighting in the Vosges, the *Report* records, "All advances were painfully slow on 7 January, and the line was pushed forward only a mile north of the Wildenguth-Reipertswiller road. At last, however, it was apparent that enemy troops were on the defensive and that the force of their attack had spent itself."[285]

This retrospective conclusion was clearly accurate. All chances of securing routes for the passage of armor through the Low Vosges had disappeared, and in any case, the operational reserves had been reallocated to their new mission on the Plain of Alsace. The exceptional flexibility demonstrated by the US VI Corps in general and the 45th Infantry Division in particular in their rapid disposition of troops to close the gap created by the disintegration of Task Force Hudelson effectively ended any chance that *XC* or *LXXXIX Corps* had to accomplish their missions in *NORDWIND*.

In the *Army Group G* record, the account of the day's action was even more prosaic. "On the front between Sarreinsberg and the Zintselbach Valley, the enemy launched more attacks in up to battalion strength, which remained unsuccessful," its author noted. Regarding the fate of *Combat Group Wingen,* although the entry's estimate of its' survivors' strength is overstated, it is also basically accurate:

> Approximately half of the combat group which had been employed in Wingen (Moder) and had defended the town for three days against attacks by superior forces, and in so doing had inflicted high enemy casualties, has been able to fight its way back to the main line of resistance, after destroying captured enemy tanks, weapons, and vehicles.[286]

But for the 205 survivors of the original 725 members of *Combat Group Wingen* who made it back to German lines on 7 January, there was much more to the last few days' action than a simple recounting of casualties, inflicted and sustained. Exhausted and confused, they were more than a little disappointed in their situation. The *Gebirgsjäger* of *1st* and *3d Battalions, SS-Mountain Infantry Regiment 12* had successfully infiltrated American lines over difficult terrain in severe weather; they completely surprised, attacked, and seized an objective from an enemy disposed in depth; and, without the benefit of artillery support or the assistance of the *Luftwaffe*—much less the promised armored reinforcement—subsequent tenaciously defended their objective in the face of more than three times their own number of attackers accompanied by tanks and lavishly supported by artillery and mortars.

The last engagement of this, the second battle for Wingen in about thirty days, ended on the snowy hills a few kilometers north of the town later that morning. After the last of the Germans had faded out of sight of their positions, the men of Company C, 180th Infantry surveyed the ground on both sides of its positions and counted the casualties. Charlie Company had lost ten men killed in action; an unknown number were wounded (some had already been evacuated to the battalion aid station); and two men were missing, probably captured by the attacking *Gebirgsjäger.* The company commander reported that his men had found the bodies of thirty Germans, and had captured three more who, being wounded, would be evacuated through medical channels. Two of the captives were enlisted men, he continued, and one was an officer.

He was right. I was the officer.

After proceeding about 100 meters, one of them remembered that I had not been searched. My captors turned me about, had me place my hands up against a tree, and spread my legs, as per regulations. They searched the pockets of my greatcoat, and found half a pack of American cigarettes and about twenty loose rounds of 9mm Parabellum ammunition for my pistol. Somebody picked up my map case, and carried it from then on.

In a few more minutes, we reached a depression with an outcrop of sandstone, covered by fresh snow; it appeared to be the command post of the company whose uninvited guest I had been for the last few hours. The sergeant rendered his report to the captain, who was obviously the commanding officer. There were a few other junior officers standing about, as well as a few NCOs. Someone tried to interrogate me, but I feigned ignorance of the English language. Over the protestations by my escort, who insisted that I did indeed understand English, my interrogator summarily ended his questioning having gotten only name and rank.

The captain initiated a series of reports to higher headquarters over the field telephone, after which I was taken away in a jeep down a snow-crusted forest road. The driver kept his carbine across his lap, even while driving, and the guard behind me in the rear seat kept the muzzle of his submachine gun in my back. For me, the war was over.

# Editor's Epilogue

The S-2 (Intelligence Officer) Journal of the 180th Infantry Regiment—the outfit which captured *Untersturmführer* Zoepf—duly recorded the 1st Battalion's accomplishment. Of their officer captive, the log reads, "He will not talk."

Wolf Zoepf finished the final chapter of this book on 22 December 1998, and promptly departed with his wife to spend the Christmas holiday with one of his sons, his daughter-in-law, and his granddaughter in Karlsruhe. On Christmas night, he collapsed from internal bleeding caused by an aneurism that had never been even suspected. In a coma for the next two weeks, he left this mortal plain on 8 January 1999, exactly fifty-four years and one day after leading his men out of the tightening noose around Wingen.

With the publication of this book, after more than fifty-five years, Wolf Zoepf has finally talked.

PAGE NO. 3 FROM: 070001 Jan 45 (Date & Hour) TO: 072400A Jan 45 (Date & Hour) PLACE: 777346

| TIME IN | TIME OUT | SERIAL NO. | INCIDENTS, MESSAGES, ORDERS, ETC. | ACTION TAKEN |
|---|---|---|---|---|
| 1045 | | 19 | From Blue to Regt: "K" Co. captured 2 PWs from the 1st Co. of the 506th Bn. in the vic. of (775385). Entire Bn. is dug-in on the southern slope of Le Hochbourg to (769389). The third Bn can observe enemy digging in around hill from (775385) to (775388). The PW reports that there is only one mortar left and that it is in position on the top of Le Hochbourg. Capt Gloesmer is C.O. The CP of the Bn. is on top of Le Hochbourg. Meals and ammo is brought in at night from town to north about 6 kilometers distant. They have 8 MGs. The 3rd. Bn received 60 rounds of 105mm in Wildenguth from the northeast. "K" Co fought 15 Germans at 0800A and drove them off. | |
| 1155 | | 20 | From Red to Regt: 3 PWs, 2 EM and 1 Officer, all wounded (going through medical channels). They broke out of Wingen. They are from the 1st and 3rd. Bns. of the 12th. Regt. They took our Prisoners along with them and them sent the Americans back into Wingen again. They kept the Officers but the PWs do not know where they are (4 American Officers). When they pulled out of Wingen they left every thing behind except their S/A weapons. They left all the German wounded that could not walk in Wingen, they took their own wounded with them that could walk. They say the 4th. Co. is 50 men strong. The 13th. Co. is 80 men strong. The Officer is a Staff Officer from Bn. and He will not talk, He said that they did not insist that our Officer PWs talk and he expected the same treatment from us. | |

# Rank Equivalences

## Officer

| ***US Army*** | ***German Army*** | ***Waffen SS*** |
|---|---|---|
| General of the Army | *Generalfeldmarschall* | *Reichsführer SS** |
| General | *Generaloberst* | *Oberstgruppenführer* |
| Lieutenant General | *General der Infanterie, General der Panzertruppen*, etc. | *Obergruppenführer* |
| Major General | *Generalleutnant* | *Gruppenführer* |
| Brigadier General | *Generalmajor* | *Brigadeführer* |
| No equivalent | No equivalent | *Oberführer* |
| Colonel | *Oberst* | *Standartenführer* |
| Lieutenant Coloonel | *Oberstleutnant* | *Obersturmbannführer* |
| Major | *Major* | *Sturmbannführer* |
| Captain | *Hauptmann* | *Hauptsturmführer* |
| First Lieutenant | *Oberleutnant* | *Obersturmführer* |
| Second Lieutenant | *Leutnant* | *Untersturmführer* |

## Enlisted

| ***US Army*** | ***German Army*** | ***Waffen SS*** |
|---|---|---|
| Master Sergeant First Sergeant | *Stabsfeldwebel* | *Sturmscharführer* |
| Technical Sergeant | *Oberfeldwebel* | *Hauptscharführer* |
| Staff Sergeant/ Technician 3d Grade | *Feldwebel* | *Oberscharführer* |
| Sergeant/ Technician 4th Grade | *Unterfeldwebel* | *Scharführer* |
| Corporal/ Technician 5th Grade | *Unteroffizier* | *Unterscharführer* |
| Private First Class | *Gefreiter/Obergefreiter* | *Rottenführer* |
| Private | *Soldat* (*Grenadier* in the Infantry, *Kanonier* in the field artillery, etc.) | *SS Mann* |

*Although some Allied charts indicate that the *SS* equivalent rank of *Generalfeldmarschall* is *Reichsführer-SS*, this was really a political honorific bestowed only on Heinrich Himmler himself. As a result, the highest *Waffen-SS* rank is really *Oberstgruppenführer.*

# Notes

1. *Führungshauptamt geheime Kommandosache* no. 47/41.

2. Earl F. Ziemke, *The German Northern Theater of Operations, 1940–45* (US Department of the Army: Pamphlet 20–271, 1959), 320. Ziemke lists the following German-Finnish military conferences: 25–28 May 1941 at Salzburg and Berlin; and 3 June 1941 at Helsinki. The Finnish president and his Foreign Affairs committee approved the results of the military conferences on 3 June 1941.

3. *Oberkommando der Wehrmacht (OKW), Kriegstagebuch (KTB)* 7, 913.

4. *Task Force NORD Ia* (G-3) order 64/41, 5 June 1941. Subject: March Instructions *(Kgr "N"–Ia 64/41 gKdos 5.6.41: Marschbefehl)*.

5. *Task Force NORD Ia* secret order 331/41, 17 June 1941. Subject: Warning Order (for march into assembly areas). (*Kgr NORD Ia–331/41 geh. 17.6.1941: Vorbefehl*).

6. *SS-Division NORD Ia* secret order 2/41, 17 June 1941. Subject: Change of Designation and Structure (*SS-Division NORD / Ia–2/41 geh. 17.6.1941: Umbenennung und Gliederung*).

7. Memorandum, Commanding General, *SS-Division NORD*, 23 June 1941, to the Commanding General, *XXXVI Corps (SS-Division NORD–Kommandeur–23.6.1941, Schrbn an den Herrn Kommandierenden General des XXXVI A.K.)*.

8. Memorandum, Commanding General, *XXXVI Corps*, 24 June 1941, to the Commanding General of *SS-Division NORD (Höheres Kommando XXXVI–Befehlshaber–24. Juni, Schrbn an den Herrn Kommandeur der SS Division NORD)*.

9. Most Secret Status Report, *SS-Division NORD Ia*, 30 June 1941. Subject: Report on the Status of the Division *NORD (SS-Division NORD Ia 9 /41 gKdos 30. Juni 1941, Zustandsmeldung der SS-Division NORD)*.

10. George H. Stein, *Geschichte der Waffen-SS* (Düsseldorf: Droste, 1967), 117; and Bernd Wegner, *Hitlers politische Soldaten–Die Waffen-SS, 1933–45* (Paderborn, West Germany: Ferdinand Schöningh, 1988/3d Ed.), 177, 180.

11. John H. Wuorinen, ed., *Finland and World War II, 1939–1944.* (NY: Ronald, 1948), 105.

12. Ibid., 106.

13. Ibid., 109.

14. Ibid., 113.

15. Manfred Menger, *Deutschland und Finland im zweiten Weltkrieg—Genesis und Scheitern einer Militärallianz, Mil.Hist Studien Nr. 26* (Berlin: Militärgeschichtliches Institut der DDR, 1988), 116. Also Ziemke, 157.

16. The causes of the disaster at Salla have been well-documented. Probably the best-researched English-language source is Ziemke, 157, although at the time of writing in 1959, he did not have access to all the German sources. Another excellent work is Eero Kuussaari and Vilho Niitemaa, *Finlands Krig 1941–1945,*

*Landstridskrafternas Operationer* (Stockholm: Helsingfors, 1949), 89 and 95. Also see Menger, 119, which identifies Soviet sources; Joachim Ruoff, "*Salla und die SS-Division NORD*" in the April 1984 issue of *Der Freiwillige* (Munin); and Alfred Steurich's response to Ruoff's article, a letter appearing in the June 1984 *Der Freiwillige.*

17. Jukka L. Mäkelä, *Im Rücken des Feindes—Der finnische Nachrichtendienst im Krieg* (Stuttgart: Frauenfeld, 1967), 99–100.

18. Franz Schreiber, *Kampf unter dem Nordlicht—Deutsch-finnische Waffenbruderschaft am Polarkreis—Geschichte der 6. SS-Gebirgs-Division NORD* (Osnabrück: Munin, 1969), 58.

19. Comments about this initial failure in many books on *Waffen-SS* combat history haunts the veterans of *SS-NORD* to this day.

20. Keith E. Bonn, *When the Odds Were Even* (Novato, CA: Presidio, 1994), 192.

21. Ziemke, 169.

22. Schreiber, *Kampf unter dem Nordlicht,* 107.

23. Ibid., 109.

24. Schreiber, *Kampf unter dem Nordlicht,* 133, 139, and 148.

25. Waldemar Erfurth, *Der Finnische Krieg 1941–1944* (Munich: Limes, Wiesbaden-München, 1950), 71.

26. Schreiber, *Kampf unter dem Nordlicht,* 165.

27. Schreiber, *Kampf unter dem Nordlicht,* 165ff, and Erfurth, 81.

28. *OKW KTB* 7, 1942, 2:1346; Erfurth, 82.

29. Schreiber, *Kampf unter dem Nordlicht,* 174–193.

30. Ibid., 197; Lothar Meininghaus Personal Diary. After the war, Ruoff suggested that *NORD* was the only German division with specialized training and such extensive experience in forest warfare.

31. Ibid., 254.

32. Ibid, 259ff.

33. Schreiber, *Kampf unter dem Nordlicht,* 264; and Erfurth, 230.

34. Schreiber, *Kampf unter dem Nordlicht,* 267–281; K. W. Lapp, "Ssenosero" in *Die Kameradschaft–Unabhängiges Mitteilungsblatt für Soldaten* (Innsbruck: Die Kameradschaft), no. 5/1994, 4–5, and no. 6/1994, 4–5.

35. The best-researched English-language version of this is, again, in Ziemke. Specifically, see Chapter 14, "The Undefeated Army," 292–310. The most comprehensive German-language treatise on Operation *BIRKE* is contained in *OKW KTB 1944–1945,* 1:868–913. This version also includes the political and military developments, which ultimately led to the separate peace.

36. Meimi Mäntyniemi and Vesa Rinne, "*Kun Puna-armeija miehitti Kuusamon syksylla 1944*" ("How the Red Army Occupied Kuusamo in the Autumn of 1944"), *Koillisanomat (Northeastern News)* (Kuusamo: Undated), 1–8.

37. Ahto, 252.

38. Ibid., 280f.

39. Ibid., 80.

40. *OKW KTB* 7, 917; also Jochen Brennecke, *Schlachtschiff Tirpitz* (München: Heyne, 1959), 76–158.

41. This appraisal of the planning of *NORDWIND* is based primarily on primary source documents, including the eight-volume series of the *Kriegstagebuch des Oberkommandos der Wehrmacht* (War Diary of the Wehrmacht Supreme Command) compiled by Dr. Percy E. Schramm; original orders signed by *Generalfeldmarschall* Gerd von Rundstedt and *Generaloberst* Johannes Blaskowitz; the original German language manuscripts written by German officers during their post-war US custody [the US Army Europe (USAREUR) Historical Series]; *Kriegstagebücher* of *Army Group G* and some of the German divisions participating in *NORDWIND*; and the personal memoirs of some German generals.

The most recent and exhaustive study in English of the planning and preparations for *NORDWIND*—as well as its implementation—has been accomplished by Keith E. Bonn in his book, *When the Odds Were Even*. The quasi-official presentation by the US Army Center of Military History, written by Jeffrey J. Clarke and Robert Ross Smith in *From the Riviera to the Rhine* (US Government Printing Office, 1993, 492–532), concentrates primarily on the reactions of US forces.

42. Seventh Army Staff, *Seventh Army in the German Offensive*, a sixteen-page narrative prepared at the request of the Army and Navy Journal, 1945, 1 and 3.

43. Ibid., 2.

44. Percy E. Schramm, ed., *Kriegstagebuch des Oberkommandos der Wehrmacht 1944–1945*, 2:1347ff.

45. Horst Wilutzky, "The Offensive of Army Group G in Northern Alsace in January 1945." MS B-095, USAREUR Series, 1947, 16.

46. Ibid., 18.

47. Ibid., 19–20.

48. The following USAREUR manuscripts were used for documentation:

Bernhard Kögel, "Offensive Operations of the 256th Volks-Grenadier Division in Northern Alsace during January 1945 (Operation NORDWIND)." MS B-537, 1947, 13.

Ernst Linke, "Participation by the 257th Volks-Grenadier Division in the Offensive Operation NORDWIND." MS B-520, 1947, 10–11.

Erich Petersen, "IV Luftwaffe Field Corps/XC Infantry Corps, 18 September 1944–23 March 1945." MS B-071, 1946, 1–2.

Alfred Philippi, "Attack by the 361st Volks-Grenadier Division in Northern Alsace." MS B-428, 1947, 16.

Kurt Reschke, "LXXXIX Infantry Corps in Operation NORDWIND, from 31 December 1944–13 January 1945." MS B-765, 1948, 7.

Clarke and Smith claim that this event took place on 28 December, but all German participants place it on 27 December.

49. Hermann Jung, *Die Ardennen-Offensive 1944/45* (Göttingen: Musterschmidt, 1971), 179–180.

50. Reschke, MS B-765, 9–10.

51. Ibid., 12.

52. Kurt Hold, "The Winter Battles in the Vosges." MS B-767, USAREUR Series, 1948, 9.

53. Philippi, 18.

54. Linke, 12–13.

55. Philippi, 28.

56. Seventh Army, "Estimate of the Enemy Situation No. 6," 29 December 1944 (College Park, MD: US National Archives II), Record Group 407, Entry 427, Box 4761, 6.

57. Ibid., 6.

58. Seventh Army, *Report of Operations* (Heidelberg: Aloys Graef, 1946), 560.

59. Ibid., 561.

60. Donald C. Pence and Eugene J. Petersen, *Ordeal in the Vosges* (Sanford, NC: Transition, 1981), 18–19.

61. 117th Cavalry Reconnaissance Squadron (Mecz), *After Action Report for January 1945*, 4.

62. Ibid., 2.

63. Michael A. Bass, *The Story of the Century* (New York: Criterion, 1946), 100.

64. Philippi, 25.

65. Philippi, 32–33.

66. Kögel, 6–9.

67. Philippi, 27–28.

68. Ibid., 29.

69. Bonn, 198.

70. Events from the S-3 Journal of the 179th Infantry Regiment for 1–2 January 1945, NARA Record Group 407, Entry 427, Box 11091.

71. Philippi, 30.

72. Ibid., 30.

73. Karl Emmerich, *First Army's Battles in Lothringen and North-Elsass from 15 September 1944–10 February 1945, Part III, 20 December 1944–10 February 1945.* MS B-786, USAREUR, 1947, 40–41.

74. Ibid., 39.

75. Linke, 22–23.

76. This total based on figures in morning reports for these units as follows: 19th Armored Infantry Battalion, Reel 16.340, Item 10792; 179th Infantry Regiment, Reel 20.208, Item 17435; 141st Infantry Regiment, Reel 20.207, Item 17410, NARA, St. Louis, MO.

77. Hugo Lange, correspondence with the author, 1997. Lange was a member of *Unterscharführer* Budt's patrol on the night of 2 January.

78. Kögel, 19.

79. *Army Group G (Oberkommando der Heeresgruppe G) KTB 3b, 1.12.–131. 12.1944*, 3.

80. Philippi, 28; Linke, 22; Kögel, 31.

81. Philippi, 29.

82. Letter of Commendation quoted in *Operations Summary of the 45th Infantry Division* / Germany and Alsace, 1–31 January 1945, dated 23 Feb 1945, 1.

83. Kurt Freiherr von der Mühlen, "Report Concerning the Participation of the 559 Volks-Grenadier Division in Operation Nordwind." MS B-429, USAREUR Series, 1947, 7.

84. Zoepf, *Marsch,* 10–20.
85. 179th Regiment History, 104.
86. Zoepf, *Marsch,* 11–12; Meininghaus, Personal Correspondence, 7.
87. Carlau, 4.
88. 45th Infantry Division G-2 Journal, 3 January 1945, 0730 and 1115 hours.
89. Interview with BG Mataxis, 8 March 1998.
90. 179th Infantry S-3 Journal, 3 January 45, 1030 and 1115 hours.
91. 45th Infantry Division G-2 Journal, 3 January 45, 1410 hours.
92. Ibid., 1445 hours.
93. Philippi, 39 and 41; Reschke, MS B-765, 43.
94. 45th Infantry Division G-2 Journal, 3 January, 1630, 1822, 1830, and 1920 hours.
95. Ibid., 2010 and 2115 hours.
96. Carlau, 4–6; Zoepf, *Marsch,* 27–35; Meininghaus, Personal Correspondence, 22ff.
97. Philippi, 40.
98. Philippi, 41; Reschke, MS B-765, 44.
99. 45th Infantry Division G-2 Journal, 3 January, 7, 2115 hours.
100. Ibid., 8, 2255 hrs.
101. Lowry, 32–33, 37.
102. Message passed from Blaskowitz to von Obstfelder, recorded in *Army Group G KTB, / Ia Nr.141/44 g.Kdos/chefs. 27.12.44 / 2000 hours.*
103. Philippi, 6; von der Mühlen, 4.
104. von der Mühlen, 10; Linke, 24; Reschke, MS B-765, 51.
105. Philippi, 12; von der Mühlen, 6.
106. *Army Group G KTB*, 22. This refines Wilutzky's account in which he recalls this decision having been made a day earlier. Wilutzky, 25–26.
107. Petersen, 26; Linke, 24–25.
108. Carlau, 7; Meininghaus, Personal Diary, 18; Zoepf, Personal Diary, 26.
109. The US side is pictured here from: Cheves et al., *Snow Ridges,* 25–27; Lowry, 37–40; 3d Battalion, 276th Infantry Unit Report 7, 3 January.

Further information was gained from individual veteran stories as printed in the 70th Division Association quarterly *Trailblazer*: Joseph L. Aceves (Co. B, 276th): Spring/Summer 1989; William Greenwalt (CO, Co. C, 276th): Fall 1988; Howard Sylvester (Co. C, 276th): Winter 1990; Jack J. Herman (Co C., 276th): Spring 1996.

110. 179th Infantry S-3 Journal, 4 January, entries at 0450 and 0500.
111. Lowry, 39, 40.
112. Ibid., 40; Cheves et al., *Snow Ridges,* 27.
113. Lowry, 40.
114. Ibid., 41–43.
115. 45th Infantry Division Operations Journal, 1–31 January, 6.
116. 180th Infantry. Field Order no. 79/3 January.
117. 276th Infantry S-3 Journal 3–4 January no. 40. Order BG Herren to CO 276th Inf–1000/4 January.

118. Schreiber, *Kampf unter dem Nordlicht,* 320–345; also Consolidated IPW Report to G-2 Periodic Report no. 131, 5 January.

119. Wallace Robert Cheves, *L'Operation NORDWIND et Wingen-sur-Moder, 2éme* (Miami, FL: n.p., 1979), 37–41.

120. Paul Kürten, "*Kämpfe der 6. SS-Geb.Div. NORD um den Ort Wingen-sur-Moder*" (*Der Freiwillige,* February 1986).

121. Ibid.; Carlau, 6–9.

122. Carlau, 9; Dr. Lautenschlager's private diary and letter to Eric Frank, Zittersheim (undated, ca. 1977).

123. Zoepf, Personal Diary, 7.

124. Zoepf, in an unpublished manuscript, *Marsch auf Wingen* (1987), 74–76.

125. 3d Battalion, 276th Infantry, Unit Report no. 7, 2–3 January.

126. Cheves et al., *Snow Ridges,* 30.

127. 3d Battalion, 276th Infantry, Unit Report no. 8, 3–5 January; and *Trailblazer,* Fall 1989, 12.

128. 3d Battalion, 276th Infantry, Unit Report no. 7, 2–3 January.

129. Ibid., no. 8, 3–5 January; *Trailblazer Quarterly,* Fall 1989.

130. 276th Infantry S-3 Journal, 4 January, nos. 41–48.

131. Unit History of the 781st Tank Battalion, "Battle of Wingen 4–7 January 1945," Annex 1, 1.

132. Ibid.

133. Cheves et al., *Snow Ridges,* 33.

134. *Trailblazer,* Winter 1996, 10.

135. 781st Tank Battalion, 1.

136. Cheves et al., *Snow Ridges,* 44–45.

137. Cheves et al., *Snow Ridges,* 40–46; 274th Infantry Unit Report no. 7, 2–4 January, 2.

138. 180th Infantry S-3 Journal, 4 January, entry no. 83 at 1818.

139. Ibid., entry no. 84 at 1822.

140. Ibid., entries no. 45 at 1140 and no. 51 at 1235.

141. 45th Infantry Division Operations Narrative, 1–31 January, 6–7.

142. 180th Infantry S-3 Journal, 4 January, entry no. 88 at 1912.

143. Ibid., entries no. 66 at 1528 and no. 85 at 1840.

144. 45th Infantry Division Operations Narrative, 6.

145. 180th Infantry S-3 Journal, 4 January, entry no. 65 at 1526.

146. Ibid., entry no. 63 at 1450.

147. Carlau, 10.

148. Original text: "*4.1.45–Major Schuster–Oberst Emmerich. . . Seit 9.00 Uhr 300 deutsche Soldaten in Wingen (H-Meldung)*"

149. Zoepf, *Marsch,* 87–88.

150. Bass, 73–74.

151. Louise Rauscher, "*Wingen-sur-Moder/Dans la tourmente de L'Operation NORDWIND 3–7 Janvier 1945.*" 1989, 12; and Bonn, 151. As will be shown, the fatal losses to the civilian population during this "First Battle of Wingen" were three times higher than during the "Second Battle," 4–7 January 1945.

152. Paula Felden, "*Wingen sur Moder*" (Société d'Histoire et d'Archéologie de Saverne et Environs, 1977) 65.

153. 45th Infantry Division G-2 Periodic Report. no. 131 for 4 January. It is interesting to note that all three counterattacks were wrongly credited to the *2d Battalion, GR 952,* even though prisoners from *SS-Panzer-Grenadier Battalion 506* had already been captured during this day, and identified as such.

154. Lowry, 40.

155. 45th Infantry Division G-2 Journal, no. 817: 041130.

156. For the US Army of 1944–45, the procedure for selecting defensive positions was governed by Field Manual 100-5, *Operations*, ch. 11, "The Defensive."

157. 276th Infantry S-3 Journal, 65a.

158. Videotaped lecture by BG Theodore Mataxis, USA (Ret.) on the occasion of the dedication of a monument to the 70th Infantry Division at Fort Benning, GA, October 1997. During its training in the Zone of the Interior, then-Captain Mataxis had served as the 70th Infantry Division's Assistant G-3 in charge of training; during *NORDWIND*, then-Major Mataxis served consecutively as XO, then (after 6 January), CO, 2d Battalion, 276th Infantry. See also Bonn, 178–179; and Robert R. Palmer, Bell I. Wiley, and William R. Keast, "The Building and Training of Infantry Divisions" in *The Procurement and Training of Ground Combat Troops* (Washington, DC: Historical Division, Department of the Army, 1948), 463–488.

159. 276th Infantry S-3 Journal, 3–4 January, entry no. 77 at 1720

160. 180th Infantry S-3 Journal, 4 January. The verbatim quotation is from entry no. 95 at 2135 (CO 3d Battalion, 180th Infantry). This action is reported in six entries between no. 71 (at 1602) and no. 96 (at 2143). During all these days, we never experienced any American tank operation during the hours of darkness—when evening came, the tanks pulled out.

161. *Army Group G KTB*, 22–25.

162. *257th VGD KTB*, 5 January 1945.

163. Philippi, 47–49.

164. Philippi, 46.

165. Carlau, 9–10, 12.

166. Cheves et al., *Snow Ridges*, 46–48.

167. 276th Infantry Unit Report no. 9, 04 1800 January–05 1800 January 1945.

168. Richard Armstrong, quoted in Lowry, 45.

169. Lowry, 47.

170. Ibid.

171. Ibid., 49.

172. Cheves et al., *Snow Ridges*, 49–50.

173. 276th Infantry S-3 Journal, 4–5 January.

174. Jack J. Herman, "Recollections of Charlie Company," in *The Trailblazer*, Spring 1996, 6–8.

175. 276th Infantry S-3 Journal, 4–5 January.

176. Herman, 6–8.

177. 3d Battalion, 276th Infantry, Unit Report no. 8, 4–5 January.

178. 276th Infantry S-3 Journal, 4–5 January.
179. Cheves et al., *Snow Ridges*, 60.
180. Lowry, 47.
181. Ibid.
182. 276th Infantry S-3 Journal, 4–5 January; order from TF Herren dated 1200, and entered in journal at 1245.
183. Paul Kürten, in *Der Freiwillige*, February 1986, 26–27.
184. Carlau, 12.
185. Ibid., 13.
186. In American literature about the battle for Wingen, this was subsequently referred to as "the Red Cross building."
187. Arthur Stelzer, in letters to the author, May 1996 through January 1997.
188. Howard Sylvester, in *The Trailblazer*, Winter 1990, 18.
189. Lowry, 47.
190. Ibid., 51.
191. Ibid., 50.
192. Cheves et al., *Snow Ridges*, 57.
193. Carlau, 12–13.
194. Cheves et al., *Snow Ridges*, 51.
195. Ibid., 58.
196. Lowry, 58.
197. Cheves et al., *Snow Ridges*, 60.
198. Ibid., 67.
199. Ibid., 70.
200. Ibid., 70–71. This is substantially identical with 276th Field Order no. 4, dated 05 2300 January 1945.
201. Ibid., 51, 69–71.
202. Ibid., 71.
203. Carlau, 12–13; Kürten, 27.
204. 179th Infantry S-3 Journal, 5 January 1945, from 0415 to 1510; also 179th Infantry S-2 Periodic Report for 5 January 1945, paragraph 2a.
205. 180th Infantry S-3 Journal, 4–5 January 1945, message nos. 21, 24, and 26.
206. 180th Infantry S-2 Journal, 4–5 January 1945, message nos. 14 and 16; 45th Infantry Division G-2 Journal, 4–5 January 1945, message no. 10 at 2135.
207. 180th Infantry S-2 Journal, 4–5 January 1945, message no. 26.
208. 180th Infantry S-3 Journal, 4–5 January 1945, message nos. 32, 38, and 55; 180th S-2 Journal, 4–5 January 1945, message nos. 19, 20, and 26.
209. 180th Infantry S-3 Journal, 4–5 January 1945, message nos. 71 and 73; 180th Infantry S-2 Journal, 4–5 January 1945, message nos. 22, 23, and 27.
210. 180th Infantry S-3 Journal, 4–5 January 1945, message nos. 81 and 87.
211. 180th Infantry S-3 Journal, 4–5 January 1945, message no. 55; 180th Infantry S-2 Journal, 4–5 January 1945, message no. 19, 1.
212. 180th Infantry S-3 Journal, 4–5 January 1945, message no. 76ff.

213. 180th Infantry Field Order no. 80, dated 5 January 1945.

214. 180th Infantry S-2 Journal, 4–5 January 1945, message no. 27; 180th Infantry S-2 Journal, 5–6 January 1945, message no. 1. No other patrol activity from that night was mentioned in the reports.

215. 180th Infantry S-3 Journal, 4–5 January 1945, message nos. 88–90.

216. 180th Infantry S-2 Journal, 4–5 January 1945, message no. 24.

217. Two women of Wingen have left their testimony about their experiences during these days in the town. They lived only a few hundred meters apart: Paula Felden, whose parents owned the Hotel Wenk on the Moder River between the two churches, and Annie Mathié, who lived not far from the railroad station. These descriptions were printed (in German) in the booklet *Wingen-sur-Moder* (*Société d'Histoire et d'Archéologie de Saverne et Environs,* 1977). Excerpts of this were translated into English and included by Wallace Robert Cheves, *L'Operation NORDWIND.*

218. Mathié, 65, and Cheves et al., *Snow Ridges,* 65–66.

219. Ibid.

220. Felden, 63, and Cheves et al., *Snow Ridges,* 66.

221. 180th Infantry S-3 Journal, 4–5 January, message no. 89.

222. Ibid., 91.

223. 276th Infantry Narrative Report, 19 November 1944 to 31 January 1945, 6.

224. *OKW KTB*, 997 and 1349; *Army Group G KTB*, 6 January 1945, 33–34.

225. *Army Group G KTB*, 6 January 1945, 30–31.

226. Ibid., 29; *OKW KTB*, 99.

227. 45th Infantry Division G-2 Consolidated IPW Report, as Annex to G-2 Periodic Report no. 133, 5.

228. Ibid., 5; also Schreiber, "*Die letzten Wochen des Geb.-Jäger-Regt. 12 Michael Gaissmair*" (*Der Freiwillige*, issue and date unknown),322; Carlau, 14; Philippi, 58; *Army Group G KTB*, 35; Höhne, 2; and Reschke, MS B-765, 61.

It is interesting to note that in MS B-428, Philippi places the withdrawal of "two *SS* battalions" three days later than it actually took place, that is, on 9–10 January, instead of the actual dates of 6–7 January. Similarly, even Schreiber wrote (322) that ". . . Wingen is relinquished in the evening hours of 8 January." Reschke made the same mistake, writing, "1st Army . . . finally gave permission to withdraw both *SS* battalions from Wingen . . . behind the MLR." Höhne, commanding *LXXXIX Corps,* admits, "But then we lacked the troops to exploit this success [Wingen]. Corps was thus forced to order the withdrawal of these battalions after a few days." On the other hand, the *Army Group G KTB*—the most reliable, truly primary source document—correctly recorded on 7 January that, "Approximately half of the *Combat Group* had been tasked to take Wingen (Moder) and had occupied the town against superior enemy attacks, thereby inflicting heavy, bloody casualties on the enemy (*hohe blutige Verluste*), had forced its way out (of Wingen) back to the MLR, after destroying the captured tanks, weapons and vehicles."

229. Carlau, 14.

230. Cheves et al., *Snow Ridges*, 71.

231. Ibid., 73.

232. Events of the attack by Company F, 274th Infantry have been chronicled on the basis of the following:

Cheves, *L'Operation NORDWIND*, 72–93; Cheves et al., *Snow Ridges*, 65–75; Fajardo, Ramon, *"Fox" 274th* (June 1945), 19–32; Samuel Conley, "After-Action Report Wingen-sur-Moder (February 1945)," *The Trailblazer*, Summer 1992, 6–8; Edmund C. Arnold, *The Trailblazers: The Story of the 70th Infantry Division* (Richmond, VA: 70th Infantry Division Association, 1989), 126–129.

233. Events during the attack of Companies E and G of the 274th Infantry Regiment have been chronicled on the basis of the following: Cheves, *L'Operation NORDWIND*, 80–94; Cheves et al., *Snow Ridges*, 74–79; Charles Blackmar, *Trailblazer Quarterly* (Spring 1990 and Winter 1991); Frederick J. Cassidy, in an unpublished manuscript, "Memories of Wingen," 5ff, and in the *Trailblazer Quarterly* (Winter 1995); Conley, 6–8; James McCullough, *Trailblazer Quarterly* (Winter 1997); and Arnold, *The Trailblazers*, 128–131.

234. Cheves, in a letter to the author, October 1977.

235. Clemson Military Academy became Clemson University, a coeducational civilian school, in 1955.

236. 276th Infantry S-3 Journal, 6 January, entry nos. 26 and 40.

237. Ibid., entry no. 49.

238. Carlau, 14–15.

239. Although its existence is well documented in all relevant American reminiscences and primary sources, the exact time of the counterattack is not listed anywhere. The most likely time seems deducible from the 276th Infantry S-3 Journal, 5–6 January and 6–7 January 1945:

Entry no. 50, 5–6 January, 1700: "1st Bn CO 276th: estimate town cleared, but not hill to west. (Obviously, this should read "north.")

Entry no. 1, 6–7 January, 1830: "CO 1st Bn 276 reports enemy counterattack in progress in Wingen from east to west."

Entry no. 2, 6–7 January, 1842: "CO 1st Bn 276 reports that 2d Bn 274 has been pushed back to north-south road in Wingen."

According to Annex C of G-2 Periodic Report no. 132 of H, 45th Infantry Division, 6 January, the sunset at Wingen-sur-Moder on this date was at 1653, with darkness (end of evening nautical twilight) at approximately 1750. Thus, in the opinion of many German participants, including the author, our counterattack did not last more than thirty minutes. Thus, it can be estimated that the German counterattack started around 1810 and lasted until no later than 1840.

240. Cheves et al., *Snow Ridges*, 90.

241. Cassidy, 6.

242. Cheves et al., *Snow Ridges*, 92.

243. Conley, 4–5.

244. 276th Infantry S-3 Journal, 6–7 January 1945, message nos. 3 and 6.

245. Ibid., message nos. 4 and 10.

246. 179th Infantry Regiment S-2 Special Report, "Activity in Wingen," 6 January.

247. 274th Infantry Unit Report no. 9, 5–6 January 1945.

248. 276th Infantry Unit Report no. 10, 5–6 January 1945.

249. Fajardo, 22.

250. Dr. Hans Lautenschlager, MD, Personal Diary—here quoted from a copy of his letter to the American Red Cross, written while in French military custody as a prisoner, 15 December 1945.

251. William Frankel, (Company H, 274th Infantry) in the *Trailblazer* (Summer 1990), 9.

252. Paul Durbin, in the *Trailblazer* (Summer 1990), 8.

253. Ibid.

254. Dr. Lautenschlager in a letter to Erik Franck, Zittersheim, undated, but circa 1977.

255. Ibid.

256. Durbin, 8.

257. Felden, 64 (German language). Also Cheves et al, *Snow Ridges*, 94 (English language).

258. Annie Mathié, 65 (German language); and in Cheves et al, *Snow Ridges*, 95 (English language).

259. 180th Infantry Field Order no. 80.

260. 180th Infantry S-2 Journal, 5–6 January, message nos. 6, 8, 11, 14, 23, 33; also 45th Infantry Division, Operations Summary, 1–31 January, 10.

261. Schreiber, *Die letzten Wochen des Geb.-Jäger-Regt. 12 Michael Gaissmair*, 321.

262. 180th Infantry S-2 Journal, 5–6 January, message nos. 9, 10, and 12; 45th Infantry Division Operations Summary, 1–31 January, 10.

263. 180th Infantry S-2 Journal, 5–6 January, message nos. 9, 18, and 24; 45th Infantry Division Operations Summary for 1–31 January 1945, 10.

264. *257th VGD KTB*, 6 January 1945.

265. 180th Infantry S-2 Journal, 5–6 January, message no. 14.

266. Ibid., message nos. 15 and 16; 45th Infantry Division Operations Summary, 1–31 January, 10.

267. 45th Infantry Division Operations Summary, 1–31 January, 10.

268. Karl Keefer, in Zoepf, *Marsch*, 77–86. Also 180th Infantry S-3 Journal, 5–6 January, message nos. 19 and 32; Annex to 45th Infantry Division G-2 Report no. 133, "Consolidated IPW Report," 7 January.

269. 179th Infantry S-3 Journal, 5–6 January; 179th Infantry S-2 Periodic Report, 5–6 January; 45th Infantry Division Operations Summary, 1–31 January, 9–10.

270. Carlau, personal diary, 15–16.

271. 45th Infantry Division Operations Summary, 1–31 January, 10.

272. 180th Infantry S-3 Journal, 6–7 January, message no. 86 at 2037 hours.

273. Part of the training of which the men of the US Army's Task Forces Linden, Harris, and Herren had been deprived was the "combined arms phase,"

during which deploying divisions were to receive several months of experience of tactical operations with armor units. Palmer et al., 448–449; Arnold, *The Trailblazers*, 37–38; and Keith E. Bonn, quoting BG Theodore C. Mataxis (Commander, 2d Battalion, 276th Infantry in WWII) in *With Fire and Zeal: The 276th Infantry Regiment in World War II* (Hampton, VA: Aegis, 1998), 11.

274. *OKW KTB*, vol. 8, 1000.

275. Cheves et al., *Snow Ridges*, 97.

276. Ibid.

277. Ibid., 100–101.

278. Stiehl and Löwenbruck as told to the author in *Marsch*, 95–100.

279. 179th Infantry S-3 Journal, 7 January, as reported by Major Crouse, 1st Battalion, 179th Infantry. The unnamed officer from the 276th Infantry must have been Major Bob Natzel, executive officer of the 3d Battalion, 276th, captured on the afternoon of 4 January.

280. Lorenz Haberbusch as told to the author in *Marsch*, 101. Loss of the machine gun and capture of the crew confirmed in the 1st Battalion, 180th Infantry S-3 Journal by entries at 0910 and 0918.

281. S-2 Journal, 180th Infantry, 7 January, 0730.

282. Ibid., 0915.

283. 180th Infantry Regiment S-2 Journal, 7 January, 3.

284. Warren P. Munsell, Jr., *The Story of the Regiment: A History of the 179th Infantry Regimental Combat Team*. (San Angelo, TX: Newsfoto, 1946), 103.

285. Seventh Army, *Report of Operations*, 575.

286. *Army Group G KTB*, January 1945, 35.

# Bibliography


Arnold, Edmund. *The Trailblazers: The Story of the 70th Infantry Division.* Richmond, VA: 70th Infantry Division Association, 1989.

Bishop, Leo V., et al, eds. *The Fighting Forty-Fifth.* Baton Rouge, LA: Army and Navy, 1946.

Bonn, Keith E. *When the Odds Were Even: The Vosges Mountains Campaign, October 1944–January 1945.* Novato, CA: Presidio, 1994.

Brenner, Karl. "*Die 6.SS-Gebirgs-Division "Nord" und ihr Anteil an der Operation 'Nordwind'* " (The 6th SS-Mountain Division and its participation in Operation NORDWIND). MS B-476, USAREUR Series, March 1947.

Carlau, Hans-Hermann. Personal Diary, January 1945 (unpublished).

Cheves, Wallace R. *L'Operation NORDWIND et Wingen-sur-Moder, 2ème* (Operation *NORDWIND* and Wingen-sur-Moder). (Miami, FL: private, 1979).

Cheves, Wallace, G. W. Krumme, and E. W. Brook, eds. *Snow, Ridges, and Pillboxes: A True History of the 274th Infantry Regiment of the 70th Division in World War II.* (Privately published, 1946).

Clarke, Jeffrey J., and Robert Ross Smith. *Riviera to the Rhine.* Washington, DC: US Army Center of Military History, 1993.

Docken, Don. *Combat History: Company C, 1st Battalion, 275th Regiment, 70th Division.* Privately published monograph, 1990.

Emmerich, Karl. "*Die Kämpfe der 1. Armee in Lothringen und Nordelsass, Teil III: 20.12.1944 - 10.2.1945*" (The Battles of the 1st Army in Lorraine and Northern Alsace, Part III: 20 December 1944–10 February 1945). MS B-786, USAREUR Series, December 1947.

Fisher, George. *The Story of the 180th Infantry Regiment.* San Angelo, TX: Newsfoto, 1947.

Foster, Hugh F. "Battle in the Lower Vosges–Summary of Earlier Operations." Unpublished monograph, 1995.

Guderian, Heinz. *Erinnerungen eines Soldaten* (Recollections of a Soldier). Neckargemünd: Kurt Vowinkel, 1976.

Haupt, Werner. *Rückzug im Westen, 1944* (Withdrawal in the West, 1944). Stuttgart: Motorbuch, 1978.

*Heeresgruppe G* (Army Group). *Kriegstagebuch* (KTB) (*Army Group G* unit journal) December 1944–January 1945.

Heiber, Helmut (Editor). *Hitlers Lagebesprechungen—Protokollfragmente seiner militärischen Konferenzen, 1942-1945.* (Hitler's Situation Discussions—Fragments of the minutes of his military conferences). Stuttgart: Deutsche Verlags-Anstalt, 1962.

Hodge, Charles. "Memoirs." Unpublished manuscript, 1980.

Höhne, Gustav. "*Der Angriff in den Vogesen, 1.1.45 bis 1.13.45*" (The Attack in the Vosges, 1 January 1945–13 January 1945). MS B-077, USAREUR, June 1946.

Hold, Kurt. "*Die Winterschlacht in den Vogesen*" (Winter Battles in the Vosges). MS-B-767, USAREUR, March 1948.

Jung, Hennann. *Die Ardennen-Offensive, 1944/45* (The Ardennes Offensive, 1944–45). Göttingen: Musterschmidt, 1971.

Kögel, Bernhard. "*Angriff der 256.Volks-Grenadier-Division im Nordelsass im Januar 1945 (Unternehmen 'Nordwind')*" [Attack of the 256th Volks-Grenadier Division in January 1945 (Operation *NORDWIND*)]. MS B-537, USAREUR, May 1947.

Kühner, Otto-Heinrich. *Wahn u7 nd Untergang, 1939-1945.* (Illusion and destruction, 1939–1945) Stuttgart: Deutsche Verlags-Anstalt, 1957.

Kürten, Paul. "*Kämpfe der 6.SS-Geb.Div.'Nord' in den Ort Wingen-sur-Moder*" (Combat of the 6th SS-Mountain Division NORD in the vicinity of Wingen-sur-Moder). *Der Freiwillige*, Feb 1986, 26–28.

——. Personal Correspondence, 1979–1984 (unpublished).

Lautenschlager, Hans. Personal Diary, January 1945 (unpublished).

Linke, Ernst. "*Die Teilnahme der 257.Volks-Grenadier-Division an der Angriffs-operation 'Nordwind'.*" (The Participation of the 257th Volks-Grenadier Division in the Offensive Operation NORDWIND). MS B-520, USAREUR Series, May 1947.

Lowry, Frank, et al. *Company A, 276th Infantry in World War II.* Privately published collection of recollections by members of the unit in WWII, 1991.

Meininghaus, Lothar. Personal Diary, 1943–January 1945.

——. Personal Correspondence, 1985.

Mennel, Rainer. "*Die Schlussphase des Zweiten Weltkrieges im Westen (1944/45) - Eine Studie zur politischen Geographie*" (The Closing Phase of the Second World War in the West (1944–45): A Study Through Political Geography). Osnabrück: Biblio, 1981.

Munsell, Warren P., Jr. *The Story of a Regiment: A History of the 179th Regimental Combat Team.* San Angelo, TX: Newsfoto, 1946.

*Oberkommando der Wehrmacht* (*OKW*), *Kriegstagebuch* (*KTB*) (High Command of the German Armed Forces journal). Edited by Percy E. Schramm. Bonn: Bernhard & Graefe, 1964.

Parker, Danny S. "War's Last Eruption." *Military History*, September 1992, 42–49.

Pence, Donald C., and Eugene J. Peterson. *Ordeal in the Vosges.* Sanford, NC: Transition, 1981.

Petersen, Erich. "*Kampfraum südlich Zweibrücken-Bitsch, 6.12.44–25.1.45*" (Combat Zone South of Zweibrücken-Bitche, 6 December 1944–25 January 1945). MS B-071, USAREUR Series, June 1946.

Philippi, Alfred. "*Angriff der 361.Volks-Grenadier-Division im Nord-Elsass im January 1945*" (Attack of the 361st Volks-Grenadier Division in Northern Alsace in January 1945). MS B-428, USAREUR Series, February 1947.

Pommois, Lise M. *Winter Storm: War in Northern Alsace, Novermber 1944–March 1945.* Paducah, KY: Turner, 1991.

Reschke, Kurt. "*Abwehrkampfe des LXXXIX. Armee-Korps im Unterelsass und im Westwall vom 6. bis 31.Dezember 1944*" (Defensive Combat of LXXXIX Corps in Lower Alsace and in the Westwall from 6 to 31 December 1944). MS C-003, USAREUR Series, June 1948.

——. *"Das LXXXIX. Armeekorps in der Operation "Nordwind" vom 31.12.1944-13.1.1945"* (LXXXIX Corps in Operation NORDWIND from 31 December 1944–13 January 1945). MS B-765, USAREUR Series, January 1948.

Rittgen, Francis. *Operation NORDWIND: 21 déc 44–25 janv. 45.* Sarreguemines, France: Pierron, 1984.

Samsel, Harold. "History of the 117th Cavalry Recon Squadron." Unpublished monograph, collection of supporting, related documents, n.d..

Schreiber, Franz. *Kampf unter dem Nordlicht* (Combat under the northern lights). Osnabrück: Munin, 1969.

——. *"Die letzten Wochen des Geb.-Jäger-Regt. 12 Michael Gaissmair"* (The last weeks of Mountain Infantry Regiment 12 "Michael Gaissmair"). *Der Freiwillige*, issue and date unknown.

Spiwoks, Erich, and Hans Stöber. *Endkampf zwischen Mosel und Inn–XIII. SS-Armeekorps* (Final combat between the Mosel and Inn Rivers–XIII SS-Corps). Osnabrück: Munin, 1976.

Volksbund Deutsche Kriegsgräberfürsorge e.V. (Association of German War Graves Caretakers) *Elsass-Lothringen, Vogesen* (Alsace-Lorraine, Vosges). Report, 1994, and correspondence, 1997.

Zoepf, Wolf T. Personal Diary, September 1944–February 1946, unpublished.

——. *"Die 6. Gebirgsdivision NORD während der Operation "Nordwind," Dargestellt aus zeitgeschichtlichen Dokumenten"* (The 6th Mountain Division NORD during Operation NORDWIND, Presented from Contemporary Historical Ddocuments). Unpublished monograph, 1987.

——. "The Battles for Phillippsbourg, Dambach, and Baerenthal." Unpublished monograph, 1987.

——. "German Opponent Recalls Wingen Battle." *The Trailblazer* (Journal of the US 70th Infantry Division Association), Fall 1990.

——. *"Marsch auf Wingen"* (March on Wingen). Unpublished monograph, 1987.

——. Recollections regarding leadership, the law of land warfare, and the American opposition at Wingen. Responses to questionnaire by Keith E. Bonn, as part of research for a forthcoming book, 1996.

United States Army Unit Records.

The author procured the following records primarily from the US National Archives, then located at the Suitland Archives branch, Suitland, MD (today, these records would be available from the Archives II in College Park, MD). Some 45th Infantry Division records were obtained from the 45th Infantry Division Museum, Oklahoma City, OK, with the assistance of the museum's director, Captain Michael Gonzales, US Army (Retired). Company Morning Reports were procured from the National Archives and Records Administration (NARA) Annex, St. Louis, MO.

Seventh Army. *Report of Operations*, vol. II. Heidelberg: Aloys Graef, 1946.
VI Corps. Historical Record, January–23 April, 1945.
45th Infantry Division
G-2 Periodic Reports 128–150 (31 December 1944–23 January 1945).
G-2 Journal, 3–7 January 1945.
G-2 Report. "Consolidated IPW (Interrogation of Prisoners of War) Report, 1–20 January 1945."
G-3 Report. "Operations of the 45th Infantry Division, Germany and Alsace, 1–31 January 1945."
179th Infantry Regiment Operations Journal, Periodic Reports, and Intelligence Journal, 1–31 January 1945.
179th Infantry Regimental Commander's Report. "Unit History for the Period 1–31 January 1945." 12 February 1945.
179th Infantry Regiment Company Morning Reports, January 1945. Item 17435, Reel 20.208.
180th Infantry Regiment Operations Journal, Periodic Reports, and Intelligence Journal, 1–31 January 1945.
180th Infantry Regimental Commander's Report. "Unit History for the Period 1–31 January 1945." 15 February 1945.
180th Infantry Regiment Company Morning Reports, January 1945. Item 17436, Reel 20.208.
141st Infantry Regiment. Company Morning Reports, 1–31 January 1945. Item 17410, Reel 20.207.
274th Infantry Regiment. Company Morning Reports, 1–31 January 1945. Item 11786, Reel 16.372.
276th Infantry Regiment. Company Morning Reports, 1–31 January 1945. Item 26046, Reel 20.245.
117th Cavalry Reconnaissance Squadron (Mechanized)
S-3 Journal, January 1945.
After Action Report: Bitche Action, 1–3 January 1945.
19th Armored Infantry Battalion. Company Morning Reports, 1–31 January 1945. Item 10792, Reel 16.340.

# Index

Units and their abbreviations as used in the index are: Armored Infantry Battalion (AIB); Field Artillery Battalion (FA Bn); Cavalry (Cav); Grenadier Regiment (GR); Infantry Division (Inf Div); SS-Infantry Regiment (SS-Inf Regt); SS-Mountain Infantry Regiment (SS-Mtn Inf Regt); Task Force (TF); Volks-Grenadier Division (VGD).